CONIECTANEA BIBLICA • NEW TESTAMENT SERIES 28

JONAS HOLMSTRAND

Markers and Meaning in Paul

An analysis of
1 Thessalonians, Philippians
and Galatians

ALMQVIST & WIKSELL INTERNATIONAL
STOCKHOLM

Revised edition of the author's doctoral dissertation, presented at Uppsala University on 18 May 1996.

Abstract

Holmstrand, Jonas, 1997. *Markers and Meaning in Paul. An Analysis of 1 Thessalonians, Philippians and Galatians* (Coniectanea Biblica. New Testament Series 28), 244 pp., Uppsala. ISBN 91-22-01761-5

The purpose of this thesis is (1) to study the use of transition markers in 1 Thessalonians, Philippians and Galatians; (2) to examine what arrangements of the texts these markers result in; and (3) to explore the implications of these arrangements for our understanding of the line of thought in each of the letters.

   The thesis consists of five chapters. The first discusses the object and method of the study and earlier research. The three letters are then analysed in separate chapters, the same methodology being used for each of them. First, existing suggestions as to the arrangement of the letter in question are presented and the problem of its integrity is discussed. Then a basic analysis is carried out, in which the structure of the text is determined in the light of the transition markers recorded and general observations concerning the line of thought. The results are summarized in a tabular overview, which is followed by a commentary on the transition markers observed and the implications for the line of thought in the letter. The fifth chapter summarizes and discusses the results of these analyses.

   The analyses result in a description of the transition markers occurring in the three letters, suggestions as to how the texts should be structured and arranged, and a partly new understanding of them. In the latter respect, the letters are found to be more uniform than they are commonly perceived to be. Each of them ultimately seems to serve a single, practical purpose, and to consist of larger coherent textual entities than are usually assumed to be present. The text arrangements arrived at also reveal the importance of *imitatio* thinking in all three letters, with a focus on the crucified Christ and the persecuted Paul. It therefore seems all the more important to relate the statements made in the letters to their historical circumstances and purposes.

Key words: Bible, New Testament, Paul, 1 Thessalonians, Philippians, Galatians, transition markers, text structure, *imitatio*.

Translated by Martin Naylor

ISBN 91-22-01761-5

Distributed by Almqvist & Wiksell International, Stockholm
Printed in Sweden by Gotab, Stockholm, 1997

*To Pernilla,
Hanna and Karin*

Preface

This book is a revised and translated version of my thesis *'Jag vill att ni skall veta, bröder...' Övergångsmarkörer, textstruktur och innehåll i Första Thessalonikerbrevet, Filipperbrevet och Galaterbrevet*, which was written as part of a doctoral programme in New Testament exegesis at Uppsala University between 1990 and 1996. Many people, in a variety of ways, have been involved in and contributed to its preparation. Here I would in particular like to mention and thank my supervisor, Professor René Kieffer, for all his encouragement and support in the course of my work, and Professor Lars Hartman, for his dedicated involvement, constructive criticism and invaluable help. In addition, I want to thank Professor Edvin Larsson, Professor Jan Bergman, Dr Per Block, Dr Anders Ekenberg, Dr Tord Fornberg and all the other members of Uppsala University's New Testament seminar for their many valuable suggestions and for the inspiring discussions and agreeable companionship we have shared during these six years.

Furthermore, I am indebted to Professor Jerker Blomqvist, Lund, and Professor Troels Engberg-Pedersen, Copenhagen, both of whom have critically reviewed my thesis and made valuable comments on it prior to the publication of this English version. In this context I would also like to thank Martin Naylor, who not only recast the text into readable English, but whose competent translation also inspired several improvements in the text.

Finally, I wish to express my heartfelt gratitude to my wife Pernilla and to my parents, who have supported, aided and inspired me in every way in the writing of this book.

Uppsala, June 1997
Jonas Holmstrand

Contents

1. Introduction   13
   A. The critical question   13
   B. Object   15
      Provisional formulation of the object of the study   15
      What is a text?   16
      How is a text organized?   17
      How do we perceive text structures?   19
      The term 'transition markers'   21
      Focus and delimitation of the study   22
      What phenomena could conceivably serve as transition markers?   24
      Instructive and thematic opening markers   24
      Instructive and thematic closing markers   28
      Contrastive opening markers   29
      Attention-attracting and intensity-heightening transition markers   31
      Final formulation of the object of the study   32
   C. Method   32
      Methodological reflections   32
      Procedure   33
   D. Related research   34
2. The First Letter to the Thessalonians   38
   A. Introduction   38
      Arguments in support of 1 Thessalonians being a compilation   40
      Arguments for regarding 1 Thess 2:13(15)–16 as an interpolation   42
      Arguments for regarding 1 Thess 5:1–11 as an interpolation   46
   B. Basic analysis   48
      1:1   48
      1:2–3:13   48
      1:2–2:16   48
      1:2–10   48
      2:1–12   52
      2:13–16   54
      2:17–3:10   56
      3:11–13   60
      4:1–5:25   61
      4:1–12   61

		4:13–5:11	63
		4:13–18	63
		5:1–11	64
		5:12–22	66
		5:23–24	68
		5:25	68
		5:26–28	69
	C.	Arrangement of the text	70
	D.	Transition markers	74
		Interaction	75
		Instructive and thematic opening markers	76
		Instructive and thematic closing markers	77
		Contrastive opening markers	80
		Attention-attracting and intensity-heightening transition markers	80
	E.	Implications for the line of thought in the letter	81
		Overall structure of the letter	82
		Key motifs	84
3.	The Letter to the Philippians		88
	A.	Introduction	88
		Arguments for an interpolation within Phil 3:1–4:9	90
		Arguments for regarding Phil 4:10–20 as an interpolation	93
	B.	Basic analysis	96
		1:1–2	96
		1:3–2:30	96
		1:3–11	96
		1:12–2:18	98
		1:12–18c	98
		1:18d–26	99
		1:27–2:1	100
		1:27–30	100
		2:1–11	102
		Excursus: Difficulties in the interpretation of 2:5–11	103
		2:12–18	106
		Excursus: The punctuation of 2:14–18	108
		2:19–30	113
		2:19–24	113
		2:25–30	114
		3:1–4:9	115
		3:1	115
		3:2–16	117
		3:17–21	121
		4:1–9	122

	4:10–18	124
	4:19–20	126
	4:21–23	126
C.	Arrangement of the text	127
D.	Transition markers	132
	Interaction	132
	Instructive and thematic opening markers	133
	Instructive and thematic closing markers	134
	Contrastive opening markers	137
	Attention-attracting and intensity-heightening transition markers	137
E.	Implications for the line of thought in the letter	139
	Overall structure of the letter	139
	Key motifs	141
4.	The Letter to the Galatians	145
A.	Introduction	145
B.	Basic analysis	148
	1:1–5	148
	1:6–10	148
	1:11–2:21	153
	1:11–12	153
	1:13–2:21	154
	1:13–24	154
	2:1–10	156
	2:11–21	157
	3:1–4:11	165
	3:1–5	165
	3:6–4:7	166
	3:6–14	166
	3:15–4:7	169
	4:8–11	172
	4:12–5:10	173
	4:12–20	173
	4:21–5:1	176
	5:2–10	178
	5:11–6:13	181
	5:11–13a	181
	Excursus: The interpretation of verse 5:11	182
	5:13b–6:10	187
	6:11–13	191
	6:14–16	194
	6:17	195
	6:18	195
C.	Arrangement of the text	196

    D. Transition markers   202
        Interaction   202
        Instructive and thematic opening markers   203
        Instructive and thematic closing markers   205
        Contrastive opening markers   208
        Attention-attracting and intensity-heightening transition markers   208
    E. Implications for the line of thought in the letter   209
        Overall structure of the letter   210
        Key motifs   213
5. Summary and conclusions   217
Abbreviations   220
Bibliography   221
Index of authors   236
Index of Greek words (selected)   239
Index of passages (selected)   240

1. Introduction

A. The critical question

Editors and interpreters of Paul's letters have had difficulty dividing the texts into their constituent parts. It is apparent from a comparison of different editions, translations and commentaries that, while there are certain traditions in this respect, in many cases there is no consensus. Clearly, this is at least partly because of the difficulties that have been experienced in discerning the internal coherence of the texts. Some find these difficulties insuperable and seek refuge in compilation theories of one kind or another, while others attempt, with the help of refined analytical methods, either to explain traditional arrangements of the texts or to find new, alternative ones. How the study presented in this thesis relates to those attempts is a question to which I shall return once I have defined my own purpose and methods.

As regards the problems just referred to, I suspect that some of them at least can be traced to a lack of understanding of or due attention to Paul's use of language, combined with powerful and rigid theological expectations regarding the texts. The following are a few examples of the observations that have aroused this suspicion.

The second chapter of Galatians is commonly divided into the following sections: 2:1–10, 11–14, 15–21.[1] The account of the episode at Antioch thus appears to end at 2:14, with 2:15–21 regarded as a new section in which Paul discusses how a person is justified. Many exegetes keep 2:11–21 together as one section, but end the quotation at 2:14.[2] If this is correct, 2:15–21 must be regarded as a kind of comment by Paul to the Galatians about the Antioch episode he has just related. Either way, it is assumed that in 2:15 Paul moves on to a new type of presentation, at a different level and of a different character to the preceding text.

But was Paul really in the habit of beginning new accounts in this way? With an undefined ἡμεῖς? With an asyndetically added clause which either lacks a verb or in which the verb does not occur until late on in the clause?[3] Is there in fact anything in the text that would have persuaded a contemporary

---

[1] E.g. GNT, NJB, NT-81, Betz 1979, Bruce 1982 and Fung 1988.
[2] E.g. NEB, TOB, Guthrie 1973, Borse 1984, Vielhauer 1978 and Rodhe 1989.
[3] For alternative interpretations of the opening construction, see pp. 159, note 41.

reader — approaching this text from the beginning for the first time, without the prior understanding of the modern reader and not guided by the typographical paragraph marks of modern editions[4] — *not* to construe 2:15 as a continuation of Paul's words to Peter in Antioch? I do not believe that there is, and would ask whether this modern arrangement of the text is not in fact determined by the theological expectations placed upon it. The motif in Galatians with which theologians have long been most preoccupied is justification by faith, a topic which is first expressly addressed in 2:15–21, before receiving further attention in the following chapters. It is not unreasonable to assume that this fact has made interpreters particularly inclined to insert a break before 2:15, thus obtaining a coherent treatise on this subject.

A similar conclusion can I believe be drawn as regards the first chapter of Romans. A common arrangement of the text is as follows: 1:1–7, 8–15, 16–17.[5] Quite a number of interpreters see 1:8–17 as a unity, but give it labels such as 'introduction and theme' and then subdivide it between vv. 15 and 16, making this analysis little different in practice from the first alternative.[6] In both cases, 1:8–15 is regarded as a kind of introduction, in which Paul does what convention requires, before moving on to the actual theme of his letter.

But are major new departures or statements of themes in Paul's letters not usually put in rather different terms from 'For I am not ashamed of the gospel'? Do they not tend to be worded more like 1:13: 'I want you to know, brothers, ...'? Is it not in fact rather odd to treat three sentences beginning with γάρ as a separate paragraph with a distinct function of its own, namely that of setting out the theme of the entire epistle? Here too, then, we have reason to ask whether this subdivision of the text has not primarily been guided by theological expectations. The central theme of Romans has for a long time been regarded as justification by faith,[7] and this motif does not appear until 1:16 f. This has presumably resulted in a greater tendency to regard the preceding verses as part of the formalities and 1:16 f. as the beginning of the treatment of the real theme of the letter.

These two examples concern passages in which I suspect that inadequate understanding of or insufficient attention to the authors' linguistic habits, combined with compelling theological expectations, has resulted in dubious delimitations of textual entities. In certain other cases, difficulties in finding links between different units of the text are responsible. In 1 Thessalonians, for

---

[4] GNT even inserts the heading 'Jews, like Gentiles, are Saved by Faith' here.

[5] E.g. GNT, NJB, TOB, Nygren 1944, Black 1981, Cranfield 1977, Maly 1979, Käsemann 1980 and Morris 1988.

[6] E.g. Vielhauer 1978.

[7] This view is now contested, however. Among those who have questioned it are Albert Schweitzer (1930, p. 220) and Krister Stendahl (1976, p. 3).

example, exegetes have had problems with 2:1–12. Many have read this passage as an *apologia*,[8] which gives it a more or less independent function in relation to what precedes and follows it. But the passage begins with γάρ and is followed by διὰ τοῦτο. In normal Pauline and Koine Greek usage in general, this is a strong indication that it stands in a causal relationship to the surrounding sections of the text, which, moreover, are similar.[9] We have to ask ourselves whether the problem here springs from an expectation that Paul would never talk about himself and his conduct in favourable terms unless compelled to do so by aggressive and malicious slanderers. Somewhere in the background one can sense the anguished conscience of Martin Luther.[10]

Many more examples could be given, but these must suffice to illustrate the type of observation that has led me to pose the critical question whether inadequate understanding of or attention to Paul's use of language, combined with powerful theological expectations regarding his letters, has not sometimes resulted in the texts being divided in ways which fail to do justice to the linguistic evidence and which have sometimes prevented interpreters from seeing important links within the texts.

B. Object

Provisional formulation of the object of the study

The critical question posed above centred on two factors which may have resulted in arrangements of Paul's letters which disregard the linguistic features of the texts and obscure important links within them. The first was an inadequate understanding of or insufficient attention to Paul's linguistic habits. It is consequently important to study linguistic phenomena which

---

[8] E.g. Marshall 1983, Vielhauer 1978 and Holtz 1986. H. Hübner (1993, p. 42) regards it as an apology with protreptic and paraenetic elements, thus covering every eventuality.

[9] It is remarkable how ready commentators are to accept a discrepancy between the linguistic structure of the text and its alleged semantic structure. In Holtz 1986, for example, we read: 'Die VV 1–12 sind eine Einlage, die zwar nach beiden Seiten mit dem Kontext verbunden ist, die aber doch in deutlicher Selbstständigkeit ihr Thema entfaltet' (p. 65). On the same page we can also read, regarding the relationship between vv. 1–12 and vv. 13–16: 'Die beiden Themen stehen trotz ihrer sprachlichen Verknüpfung gleichrangig nebeneinander.' Cranfield (1977) writes regarding Rom 1:16b–17: 'While it is no doubt formally tidier to treat them as a part of the division which began with 1.8, the logical structure of the epistle stands out more boldly when they are presented as a separate main division.' Many more examples could be quoted.

[10] Cf. Barclay 1988, pp. 226 f.

affect the way a reader or listener perceives the textual structures of the Pauline epistles and to see what subdivisions of the texts such phenomena result in. The second factor was powerful theological expectations. If these expectations have resulted in the texts being divided in ways that are incompatible with their linguistic features, it is of interest to ask what would be the theological implications of the arrangements that follow from the linguistic phenomena just referred to. The object of this thesis is thus threefold, and can for the time being be formulated as follows: *(1) To study linguistic phenomena which affect the way a reader or listener perceives the text structure of Paul's letters; (2) to examine what arrangements of the texts these phenomena result in; and (3) to explore the implications of these arrangements for our understanding of the line of thought in each of the letters.*

This general outline of my object needs to be developed upon and defined more precisely, particularly as regards the phrase 'linguistic phenomena which affect the way a reader or listener perceives the text structure of Paul's letters'. To be able to do this, it is necessary to touch briefly on the questions of what a text is, and how it is organized. These questions are wide-ranging and difficult, and the subject of ongoing reflection and discussion in the field of text theory. Here, I shall briefly examine just a few general aspects which are of particular relevance to my analysis.

What is a text?

A text can be described as a communicative act.[11] As such, it can be considered from three points of view: (1) that of *pragmatics*, which studies the relationships between signs and sign users; (2) that of *semantics*, which is concerned with the relationships between signs and the phenomena to which they refer; and (3) that of *syntax*, which deals with the formal relationships of signs to one another.[12] These three vantage points are not completely distinct, but rather mutually dependent. That is to say, it is not possible to study one of these dimensions of the text without also paying some attention to the others.[13]

As a communicative act, a text is in addition characterized by *extension*, *delimitation* and *coherence*.[14] Of these characteristics, the last can be

---

[11] E.g. Grosse 1976, p. 13, and Gülich & Raible 1977, pp. 26 ff.

[12] These semiotic distinctions can be traced back to Morris (1938, pp. 6 ff., 13–42), and have been criticized as being difficult to maintain (e.g. Allwood 1976, pp. 234 f.). They will suffice for my limited purposes here, however.

[13] Plett 1975, p. 52.

[14] Plett 1975, pp. 52–119.

regarded as primary.[15] It is often, but need not be, found in all three of the text dimensions referred to above. In a letter, for instance, several matters may be raised which have no more in common than the fact that the sender happens to want to communicate them to the recipient on the occasion in question.

The critical question posed earlier was whether the texts of Paul's letters have not been divided in ways that have been guided to too great an extent by the prior theological understanding of the modern reader — i.e. by a factor external to the texts, located mainly within the pragmatic dimension — without proper account being taken of internal factors, to be found primarily within the syntactic and semantic dimensions. Since the primary task of this study is to examine phenomena of the latter type, it will quite naturally have something of a syntactic and semantic slant. However, the pragmatic dimension will also be involved in a number of ways. Some of the linguistic phenomena which I shall be looking at, e.g. certain constructions which instruct the recipients or indicate the theme, are clearly pragmatic in character. In addition, I am convinced that these phenomena have to be studied in context and in relation to the train of thought running through the text in question, which means that my study of them will constantly take into account observations concerning the development of thought in Paul's letters. This will mean paying further attention to pragmatic factors, although, in line with the critical question set out at the beginning of this thesis, I shall attempt to remain close to the text and to confine myself to observations that are as straightforward and uncontroversial as possible, an approach which will in general give less prominence to the pragmatic dimension.

How is a text organized?

To define more precisely what 'linguistic phenomena... affect the way a reader or listener perceives the text structure of Paul's letters', it is also necessary to look briefly at how texts are organized and what is meant by 'text structure'. The latter concept relies on the fact that every text consists of different units of meaning, which are related to one another in specific ways. I use the word 'meaning' here in a broad sense, encompassing not only lexical, but also grammatical and pragmatic meaning. The smallest units, phonemes, do not carry meaning in themselves; they merely distinguish larger units with different meanings. Grouped in particular constellations, they form morphemes, which are the smallest meaningful units of a text. In specific combinations, morphemes form larger units of meaning, lexemes, which can in turn be combined into phrases and clauses. The latter can then be grouped into

---

[15] See Hirsch 1967, pp. 236 ff., and Wiklander 1984, p. 47.

sentences, paragraphs and chapters. Finally, as can be deduced from the earlier discussion, an entire text can be regarded as a unit of meaning (in this wider sense).[16] The combining of units of meaning to form new, larger units of meaning thus appears to be a characteristic of language and probably has something to do with the cognitive abilities of human beings: the human mind appears to have a very limited capacity — in both a temporal and a quantitative sense — to store the details of the surface level of a text, and therefore has to rapidly impose some form of organization on them.[17]

It is the whole of this organization of units of meaning at different levels which constitutes the structure of a text. The expression 'text structure', however, is normally only used to refer to higher-level units of meaning than the clause. There is no obvious dividing line, however. It is not even clear in every case where a clause begins and ends. It is for example open to discussion whether, in an early Greek manuscript with few punctuation marks, ΑΝΕΒΗΝΔΕΚΑΤΑΑΠΟΚΑΛΥΨΙΝΚΑΙΑΝΕΘΕΜΗΝΑΥΤΟΙΣ (Gal 2:2) is to be seen as a clause with two predicates, as two clauses but one sentence, or as two sentences. In this thesis, I use the expression 'text structure' as referring, by definition, to units of meaning at various levels above the clause, but in practice confine myself to dividing the text down to the level at which linguistic phenomena of the kind which interest me here still clearly operate. In this connection, a certain degree of arbitrariness will be unavoidable.

Even with these constraints on my use of the expression 'text structure', it will refer to units of meaning at, in principle, an unlimited number of levels (in any given case, however, the number must always be limited, since every text is by definition a finite entity). Text structures will therefore often be fairly complex. Earlier I mentioned 'paragraphs' and 'chapters' as examples of larger units of meaning of this kind. Such concepts are related to the conventional devices used in our system of writing to mark units of meaning in texts. Those devices are fairly unsophisticated, and do only very limited justice to the often complex structures of texts. I shall therefore avoid this terminology, except where its use is specifically called for, for example in discussions of the paragraph and chapter divisions of modern editions. Instead, I shall use the term 'section' to refer to units of meaning at all these levels. Where appropriate, distinctions such as section/subsection will be introduced.

A factor which further complicates the structure of a text is that elements which logically correspond to one another in a text may have entirely different formal properties. In a syllogism, for example, certain premisses may

---

[16] See the earlier reference to extension, delimitation and, above all, coherence as characteristics of a text.

[17] Beaugrande & Dressler 1983, pp. 48, 88.

be presented with such brevity that they are perceived as a single unit of presentation, whereas another premiss may require more space and be presented in several similar units.[18] Consequently, what might be called the logical structure and the communicative structure of a text do not always entirely coincide, even if they are interrelated. In this study, the latter type of structure will be our primary concern.

How do we perceive text structures?

What factors, then, are decisive to our perception of text structures? We are probably concerned here with a variety of factors at different levels in the text, interacting in complex ways. Without making any claim to give an exhaustive account, I shall attempt here to identify some of the more important factors involved.

As the discussion above has suggested, perceiving text structures involves discerning units of meaning in the text which are larger than clauses and understanding the mutual relationships among them. To be regarded as a unit of meaning, a text sequence must have a certain coherence as regards its content — in principle, it should be possible to give it a heading — and it must be delimited by certain breaks in terms of content. In other words, it ought to be possible to distinguish such units of meaning by observing links and breaks in the content of the text.

The problem is, however, that a text is usually full of such links and breaks at different levels. Every new sentence entails something of a discontinuity in content, a change of topic, but at the same time it is usually linked semantically to the previous sentence. Clearly, though, sentences are grouped into larger units of meaning, which must mean that the changes of topic between certain sentences will be more 'significant' than those occurring between others. The fact that such changes of topic are more significant may, but need not, mean that they are appreciably more obvious or clear-cut *per se*; many tangible links exist even between larger units of meaning. It means, rather, that they involve a leading or text-organizing motif.

It is not always apparent which of the motifs in a text are leading or text-organizing. In modern writing systems, therefore, as was noted earlier, formal devices have been developed solely to signal significant changes of topic,

---

[18] See the earlier discussion concerning the link between text structure and human cognitive abilities.

namely the use of paragraphs and chapters (leading motifs are sometimes also defined by the use of headings). In spoken texts, such changes can be marked with the help of tone, tempo, pausing or emphasis.[19]

Although in antiquity texts were often read aloud,[20] it was of course the reader rather than the writer who inserted such signals of the spoken medium into the text. All the indications are that, in written texts, there were originally no or very few formal marks of significant changes of topic.[21] The ancient reader must therefore have relied primarily on other phenomena in the text to discern these changes of topic. A reader of a modern text, incidentally, has to do just the same, since paragraph and chapter marks — as was observed earlier — are inadequate as means of signalling and defining often complex structures at different levels in a text. In the following, I shall refer to the linguistic phenomena which can guide the reader in this respect as *transition markers*.

[19] Concerning the differences between spoken and written texts, see e.g. Traugott & Pratt 1980, p. 260, and Nida & Faber 1974, p. 126.

[20] Opinions differ as to how widespread reading aloud really was in ancient times. See e.g. Balogh 1927; Knox 1968; and Starr 1991.

[21] In the oldest preserved manuscripts, we find rudimentary attempts to mark text divisions, but there do not appear to be any very firm traditions as regards the marks to be used or where they are to be placed. In $\mathfrak{P}^{46}$ (*c.* 200) there are only a very few original punctuation marks. In addition, there are small spaces scattered over an otherwise unbroken string of text. Some of these spaces follow abbreviations, but in some cases they appear to reflect a change of topic. The number of definite instances of this is quite small, however, and it is often unclear why these particular transitions were marked, but not others. B (4th century) makes use of a system of small spaces in the text, mainly associated with new units of meaning, such as sentences or paragraphs, and occasionally with natural pauses. These spaces are only found within lines; if a new unit of meaning begins on a new line, it is not specifically marked. Quite a number of semicolons also occur in the text, but some of them at least are clearly later additions. In ℵ (4th century), new 'paragraphs' (of widely varying extent) are marked by the use of a new line extending into the left-hand margin. A (5th century) makes similar use of a first line extending into the margin, combined with an enlarged initial letter. On the other hand, this scribe does not always begin a new 'paragraph' on a new line: if the previous 'paragraph' ends at the beginning of a line, he continues (for reasons of economy or taste?) on the same line after leaving a small space, but then begins the following line in the left-hand margin and with an enlarged initial letter. Sentences are separated by either small spaces or semicolons. In B, ℵ and A there are in addition different systems of κεφάλαια for the gospels.

Clearly, then, the earliest manuscripts contain the seeds of formal systems of text division marks, but none of them has yet gained general acceptance. Eusebius's division of the gospels into κεφάλαια (4th century) and the subdivisions of Paul's letters which are normally ascribed to Euthalius (presumably later than those of Eusebius) eventually gained some currency, but only the chapter divisions introduced by Stephen Langton in the 13th century, which deviate quite significantly from these earlier arrangements, can be said to have come into more general use.

The term 'transition markers'

The term 'transition markers' could perhaps give the impression that we are dealing here with a uniform group of phenomena with a clear function. However, it should be regarded rather as an umbrella term for a diverse collection of phenomena, whose only common denominator is the fact that, in specific cases, they more or less clearly signal significant changes or transitions in the text to the reader or listener. Often, moreover, it is only the combined effect of several such signals that causes us to perceive a change as a significant one.

I divide transition markers into two groups. The first of these I call *closing markers*, which are linguistic phenomena signalling the ending of a text unit and thus preparing the receiver (i.e. the reader or listener) for a significant change of topic. The second group I refer to as *opening markers* — linguistic phenomena which signal the beginning of a new unit in the text and thus confirm the change of topic. These two types of transition marker interact to lead the receiver past or through the transition. However, we must expect the nature of their interaction to vary, depending for example on the importance and character of the transition and on the rhetorical effect which the sender wishes to achieve (a section may for example be brought to a very abrupt close to give the impression of indignation, shame etc.[22]).

Transition markers can be considered from the following three angles:

1. *Conventionality:* Unlike the paragraph and chapter marks of modern written texts, these linguistic expressions usually have other primary functions. Their role as transition markers is connected with conventional strategies of expression within the language concerned, which are probably logically determined to only a limited extent.[23] At all events, it is clear that, at this level, the linguistic system is highly flexible, providing considerable scope for the development of a personal style, or idiolect.[24] To be serviceable, this idiolect naturally has to remain within the confines of a larger dialect, but the

---

[22] See e.g. BDF §482 concerning ἀποσιώπησις.

[23] It has at any rate proved considerably more difficult to describe linguistic behaviour in logic-based grammatical terms at the text level than at the level of the clause (see Beaugrande & Dressler 1983, pp. 24 f., concerning *inter alia* the Konstanz group's attempts to formulate a generative text grammar). Beaugrande and Dressler therefore choose rather to talk of 'regulative principles... that control textual communication rather than define it'. Three such principles, they suggest, are 'efficiency', 'effectiveness' and 'appropriateness' (1983, p. 11). Behind the patterns and tendencies of textual communication, moreover, they see the cognitive capacities of the human individual, which result in people organizing their experience and knowledge with the help of patterns and typologies (1983, pp. 210 ff.).

[24] For a discussion of system and variation in language, see Traugott & Pratt 1980, p. 7, and Beaugrande & Dressler 1983, p. 54.

fact that a person only selects and exploits some of the modes of expression available in the language gives his or her speech or writing a personal character, and among other things this reinforces the signalling function of the transition markers that are linked to these modes of expression.

2. *Contextuality:* If the role of these linguistic expressions as transition markers is connected with conventional strategies of expression, it is clear that it is also context-dependent: the expressions concerned take on this role when they occur in particular contexts. In this regard, significant factors include the individual concerned (since there is scope to develop personal strategies of expression[25]), the genre (a narrative for example is often chronological and spatial in organization, while an argument usually builds on cause–effect relationships[26]), and the immediate context (an οὖν following a completed close, for instance, has a different function from an οὖν that occurs before the close has been completed).[27]

3. *Relativity:* Certain linguistic expressions mainly serve to structure the text (e.g. 'In the following, I intend to discuss three questions: first..., secondly... and thirdly...'). But most of the expressions we are concerned with here are only secondarily signals of transition and, as we have seen, this function is dependent on the context and on a convention which is not particularly rigid or unambiguous. It thus follows that they do not always have the same transition-marking function (δέ may for example be an important marker of a transition at a high level in the text in one context, whereas in another context it can indicate a contrast which is far less critical to the structure of the text).

Focus and delimitation of the study

In view of the conventionality of transition markers, a more empirical study of these phenomena in the Pauline epistles is to be recommended.[28] Only by such means can we gain a familiarity with Paul's idiolect and linguistic habits in this respect. Ideally, the study should take in all the letters of Paul that have been preserved. Given the contextuality and relativity of transition markers, however, the line of thought in any given letter must constantly be taken into account. Such a study of all the extant Pauline letters would be too far-reaching a task for the present thesis. I have therefore chosen to confine my

[25] Cf. Nida & Faber 1974, p. 132, and Beaugrande & Dressler 1983, p. 54.

[26] Nida & Faber 1974, p. 132.

[27] Cf. Thiselton 1979, p. 79, concerning conventionality and contextuality in semantics.

[28] Such an approach is in line with Gülich and Raible's critique of one-sidedly axiomatic-deductive text models (1977, pp. 17–21). Cf. also Beaugrande & Dressler 1983, p. 211.

study to the First Letter to the Thessalonians, the Letter to the Philippians and the Letter to the Galatians. My reasons for choosing these particular epistles are as follows:

1. They are all usually — and quite rightly — regarded as authentically Pauline, enabling conclusions to be drawn from them regarding Paul's use of language.

2. They are of a length that is suited to the purposes of this study. They are long enough to contain more complex text structures, but not so long as to prevent several letters being examined. This provides a comparatively varied range of evidence on which to base any conclusions about Paul's linguistic habits.

3. They also enable me to introduce a certain degree of progression into my discussion, since, of these letters, 1 Thessalonians appears to have the clearest and Galatians the most obscure structure. We can thus gradually venture into more difficult territory as we become more familiar with Paul's use of language. It is this aspect, rather than the chronology of the epistles, that has determined the order in which the analyses are carried out. The temporal dimension seems to me to be of less interest in this context, since other factors — such as topic and text type — probably have a greater impact in terms of variations in the occurrence of transition markers than a time difference of a few years.

In the following, I assume — like the majority of exegetes — that these letters have one and the same author (whether he held the pen or dictated them), and that that author is Paul. If these assumptions are questioned, that will of course have a bearing on my broader conclusions about Paul's idiolect. However, it will only affect my analyses of the individual epistles to a limited degree. I have therefore chosen not to enter into the question of authenticity here, but rather to leave it to the reader to apply the results of this study in the light of his or her own position on that issue. The strikingly similar results that emerge from the individual analyses may at any rate be considered to confirm the first of my two assumptions.

The question of authorship is further complicated by various theories about compilations, additions and the use of traditional material in the letters. The most important compilation theories will be touched on in the introductions to the individual analyses. As regards the borrowing of traditional material, I would suggest that it is unlikely to have had any significant impact on the occurrence of transition markers.

What phenomena could conceivably serve as transition markers?

On the basis of the earlier discussion about textual organization, we can deduce that the following properties will be exhibited by transition markers:

1. Since they delimit and mark units of meaning, expressions which *indicate the theme* of the text or provide *other instructions to the receiver* about it should be able to act as transition markers. The sender may after all be expected to indicate to the receiver in some way, at the beginning of a new unit of meaning, what its meaning is and, at the end of it, what its meaning was.[29] Such expressions will include guidance not only on the actual subject-matter of the exposition, but also concerning other aspects of the communicative act, such as mode of presentation and text type. They will be referred to as *instructive* and *thematic* transition markers.

2. Since transition markers draw attention to changes of topic and contrasts of meaning, linguistic phenomena which *indicate contrast* should be able to function as transition markers. These will be termed *contrastive* transition markers.

3. Since it is a matter of giving prominence to *significant* changes of topic, linguistic phenomena which *attract attention* or *heighten the intensity of the text* can probably also serve this function. These will be referred to as *attention-attracting* and *intensity-heightening* transition markers.

These properties are by no means mutually exclusive. On the contrary, they are related and may be expected to co-occur. To some extent they may even be said to be different sides of the same coin. A thematic opening marker, for example, may be said to draw the attention of the receiver to a change of topic which entails a contrast with what has gone before. Often, however, one or other of these aspects is most clearly to the fore.

Instructive and thematic opening markers

We can now go on to ask what phenomena have these properties and could thus conceivably act as transition markers. Beginning with instructive and thematic markers, we can note that the receiver can be informed about key motifs or features of the text in a wide variety of ways. The sender may for example make a direct statement about what he or she intends to do in the communicative act that is to follow: e.g. 'I shall now tell you about my brother.' Since such a statement thematizes the actual communicative act, it is

---

[29] Concerning the use of the word 'meaning' here, see above, p. 17.

often called a *metacommunicative clause*.[30] The characteristic feature of such a clause is the fact that it contains a metacommunicative verb, i.e. a verb referring either to the coding of the text, such as 'say' or 'promise', or to its decoding, such as 'hear' or 'listen'.[31] A metacommunicative clause can provide a number of instructions about the communicative act, e.g. concerning the sender, the receiver, the topic and the mode of presentation. It should be noted that such clauses can occur at different levels in the text. They may for example thematize the communicative act constituted by the text itself, but they can also thematize communicative acts that are reported in the text.[32]

Instructions to the receiver may in addition assume the form of express attitudes to or assessments of what is stated in the text: e.g. 'I rejoice that...', 'I wish that...', 'I consider it necessary that...' or 'I presume that...' Attitudes and assessments of this type are summed up in E. U. Grosse's term *metapropositional base*.[33] This term designates instructions to the receiver about how a proposition is to be understood,[34] whether it is to be perceived as real, realizable, perhaps possible, necessary, wanted, or good or bad.[35] It is thus clear that a metacommunicative clause normally either is itself or contains a metapropositional base. A metapropositional base need not consist of an entire clause, but may in certain cases be expressed, for instance, by an adverb (e.g. 'presumably', which corresponds to the clause 'I presume that...') or the use of mood (e.g. 'Come!', corresponding to 'I want you to come/insist that you come'). Like metacommunicative clauses, metapropositional bases can occur at different levels in the text. They can for example express an attitude or assessment on the part of the sender in the present situation (e.g. 'I want

[30] See e.g. Gülich & Raible 1979, p. 87, Hellholm 1980, pp. 80–84, and Johanson 1987, p. 26.

[31] Gülich & Raible 1979, p. 27.

[32] See e.g. Hempfer 1973, pp. 173 ff.; and Hellholm 1980, pp. 83 f.

[33] Grosse 1976, pp. 15 f.

[34] To Grosse, 'metapropositional base' and 'proposition' are *semantic* terms (Grosse 1976, p. 16), which means that they do not denote the linguistic expression itself, but the idea or meaning which it expresses. He can therefore claim, for example, that metapropositional bases form a closed set, although the number of possible ways of expressing each base is unlimited (Grosse 1976, p. 45). Propositions, too, can be expressed in different ways (Grosse 1976, pp. 95 ff.): for example, by means of full clauses (e.g. 'I insist *that you come*'), infinitive or participial constructions (e.g. 'I urge you *to come*'), pronouns (e.g. 'I want *this*') or noun constructions (e.g. 'I want *your agreement*'). They may also occur in an elliptical form (e.g. '*Just a minute!*', corresponding to 'I ask you *to wait a minute*'). I am aware that this terminology, distinguishing as it does between linguistic expressions and their meanings, is not entirely unproblematic from the viewpoint of the philosophy of language (see e.g. Larsson 1978, pp. 88 f.). For the limited purposes of this study, however, I consider it acceptable and serviceable.

[35] Grosse 1976, pp. 45–50.

you to come'), but they can also express the attitude of an addressee or a third party (e.g. 'He wants you to come') or of the sender in a different situation (e.g. 'I wanted you to come'). In these last-mentioned cases, it is possible to understand a further metapropositional base, which expresses how the sender sees the metapropositional base that is set forth and its proposition (e.g. 'I assert that he wants you to come'). A metapropositional base dominated by another base in this way is referred to by Grosse as a secondary metapropositional base.[36]

The actual subject-matter, the proposition, can be expressed in different ways, e.g. in the form of a prepositional phrase ('I shall now tell you about my brother's life'), a *that*-clause ('I shall now tell you that my brother...'), an infinitive construction ('I promise to come') or a cataphoric (forward-looking) text-summarizing noun, pronoun, pronominal adjective or pronominal adverb ('I shall now tell you a funny story (the following, this)').[37] Of these means of stating the topic, *prepositional phrases* and *cataphoric text-summarizing nouns, pronouns, pronominal adjectives and pronominal adverbs* act as headings or as pointers giving prominence to something in the text, and can be said to function as opening markers in their own right. They can be combined with one another and/or a *that*-clause, thus reinforcing the statement of the topic ('I shall now tell you this funny story about my brother...'). These ways of indicating the topic can also occur more independently, unconnected with a superordinate metacommunicative or metapropositional verb, e.g. 'Regarding my brother, he was...'. Similar independent topic statements can be made with the help of a *nominativus pendens* or a *similar proleptic construction*, such as 'The woman who works at the bank, I saw her arrive...' or 'My brother, if he doesn't get any recognition soon, he'll resign'. They can also be made using *rhetorical questions:* 'What happened when my brother arrived? Well, he...'

However, the topic can also be indicated entirely within the framework of an ordinary sentence, by means of special emphasis on a new key motif. This can for example be achieved by *fronting* the motif or placing it in some other

[36] Grosse 1976, p. 47. In the sentence 'I want you to come', too, the metapropositional base 'I assert' (i.e. 'I assert that I want you to come') could of course be understood, but in this case Grosse does not refer to the metapropositional base 'I want' as secondary. This is because its properties differ from those of metapropositional bases such as 'he wants' or 'I wanted'. For instance, the sentence 'I want you to come' can be turned into a command — 'Come!' — which is not the case with the sentences 'he wants you to come' and 'I wanted you to come'. The declarative value of the indicative form can thus be 'neutralized' in the first sentence, but not in the last two. See Grosse 1976, pp. 47–50, for further discussion.

[37] Gülich and Raible (1979, pp. 87–90) — like Hellholm (1980, pp. 84–87) and Johanson (1987, pp. 27 f.) after them — distinguish between substitution at the abstraction level and substitution at the meta level. This distinction is unnecessary in the present context, however, since I do not rank the different transition markers.

stressed position ('Yesterday I saw...'), or by means of a *cleft or pseudo-cleft sentence* ('What happened yesterday was that...'). In addition, extra emphasis can be achieved by the use of various *emphatic pronouns and adverbs*, such as demonstrative and reflexive pronouns ('He himself said that...') and words like 'precisely', by *repeating the co-referent of a pronoun (renominaliza-tion[38])* or in Greek by *'unnecessary' use of a personal pronoun* (ἐγὼ δὲ λέγω...).

The head words of the subject and predicate can be said to be the main pillars of a clause, and therefore carry strong emphasis in their own right. Often they are also in initial or some other stressed position. Their central, emphasized role means that noticeable changes regarding them suggest *per se* that the text is taking a new turn. Consequently, a *striking change of grammatical subject* or a *conspicuous change of tense*, for instance, can be seen as a kind of statement of topic.

In this connection, the genre-dependent nature of markers should also be observed. Since certain types of text are normally organized around certain types of motif, the receiver is particularly likely to perceive accentuated statements of these particular motifs as key topic statements. A narrative, for instance, is normally organized around the time, place and participants involved in the sequence of events related. In such texts we therefore have a tendency to regard *references to time, place and persons* as key topic statements.[39]

Within a text, moreover, what I shall term *recurrences* — expressions reiterating, referring back to or re-echoing earlier passages — can act as a kind of thematic opening marker. If, for instance, there has been a long digression in a text, the resumption of a key motif or feature of the section that preceded the digression can signal that the digression has come to an end and that a new section continuing the earlier discussion has begun. Such recurrences of key motifs may be visible in the surface text in the form of direct repetitions, but they may also be of a more purely semantic nature and assume the form of free allusions. Apart from motifs, recurrences may involve phenomena such as the use of a certain person, number, tense or mood.

In some discussions of transition markers — or what I term opening markers — they are ranked in a hierarchy, the aim being to use them to identify different levels in the text.[40] However, markers placed on the higher rungs of such a hierarchy have also been found to occur in transitions at relatively low

[38] Gülich & Raible 1979, pp. 94–97, and Hellholm 1980, pp. 94 f.

[39] See, for example, what a vital part these 'universals of discourse' play in B. Olsson's analysis of Jn 2:1–11 and 4:1–42 (1974, pp. 79 f., 82–88 and 138–159.

[40] Gülich & Raible 1977, pp. 75 f., Hellholm 1980, pp. 78-95, and Johanson 1987, pp. 24 f.

levels in the text, and vice versa.[41] While I believe that there is something to be said for hierarchies of this kind — if properly understood[42] — I shall refrain from establishing one at this initial stage and see what hierarchy, if any, emerges from my empirical investigation. I am able to do this because my analytical model offers other means of distinguishing the different levels of a text, the most important of them being an examination of the interaction between different opening and closing markers and, in particular, the role of recurrences in that connection. What is more, my study of transition markers is constantly linked to the overall progression of thought in each letter, which will provide a purely thematic confirmation of any hierarchies that emerge from it.

Instructive and thematic closing markers

We have already noted that the sender may be expected to indicate in some way at the end of a unit of meaning what its key meaning was. This can presumably be done in the form of a summary or a conclusion or some other indication of the consequences of what has been said. This concluding statement of the principal meaning of a section will probably also correspond in some way to the statement of the theme or the instructions to the receiver given at the beginning of the section. Any expression containing a suggestion of a summary, conclusion or consequence and entailing some kind of a recurrence of the opening or starting-point of the section can thus serve as a closing marker.

The occurrence of a summary or conclusion can be explicitly signalled with the help of a *metacommunicative clause*, such as 'I sum up:...', 'To sum up, it may be said that...', or 'From this I draw the conclusion that...'. A conclusion or consequence can also be indicated by a *rhetorical question:* 'What then does this mean?' Another, and probably commoner, device is the use of *inferential particles*, such as 'then', 'therefore' or 'thus'. The same result can be achieved using a *conditional complex sentence:* 'If this is the case, then...'. Statements of consequences, perhaps at lower levels especially, can also assume the form of *consecutive or final subordinate clauses*. They can occur in other syntactic forms, too, e.g. as a *main clause beginning with 'and'* ('and they lived happily ever after'), but in such cases the function of indicating consequences cannot be deduced from the syntactic construction, but solely from the content of the clause.

---

[41] Wienold 1983, pp. 218 ff.

[42] Johanson observes that hierarchies of markers have to be understood heuristically, rather than axiomatically (1987, p. 25).

A section can in addition end with an *assessment or reaction* on the part of the sender, which can also be said to be a kind of statement of consequences. It may begin with a *metapropositional verb* (e.g. 'I am convinced that...', 'I hope that...' or 'I am afraid that...') or assume the form, for example, of a *wish* ('May that be the case!') or a *command* ('Do so!'). In the New Testament and other Jewish and Christian texts, a closing wish or other indication of consequences can be further underscored by an emphatic and confirmatory ἀμήν.

Another indication of a summary, conclusion or consequence is the occurrence of *anaphoric (retrospective) text-summarizing pronouns, pronominal adjectives, pronominal adverbs or nouns.* Such phenomena often occur in metacommunicative or metapropositional clauses (e.g. 'From this I draw the conclusion that...' or 'This state of affairs alarms me').

Recurrences looking back to the opening or starting-point of the current section can be of different kinds, ranging from *direct repetitions* of key clauses or words to vaguer *allusions*. They may also assume the form of *direct answers to opening questions*, for instance. In addition, recurrences may involve phenomena of a more formal nature, such as the use of a particular tense or mood.

A reference back to the opening of a section is not the only means of signalling that the section is drawing to a close. At the end of a subsection of a longer text sequence, recurrences of key motifs from earlier subsections of the same larger section can serve the same function.

Recurrences of phenomena occurring at the beginning of a section are a sign that the aim of that section has been achieved and that it is now time to define a new aim. However, an account may also have more natural end-points. The story ending quoted above — 'and they lived happily ever after' — is one example of this. In Paul's letters, references to consequences with an *eschatological perspective* probably function in this way.

Contrastive opening markers

For natural reasons, only opening markers can indicate contrast. Of the linguistic phenomena listed above as thematic and instructive opening markers, the majority can also be said to be contrastive (e.g. emphatic changes of motif or changes of grammatical subject). However, we still have to consider a number of phenomena which cannot be said to state a theme, but which do indicate a contrast. Primarily, we are concerned here with *adversative particles.*

We cannot expect every adversative particle to serve as an opening marker, though. First of all, it should be observed that the role of such particles as contrastive opening markers varies from one language and one text to another. In a text in which the sentences largely follow on from each other asyndetically, such as a text in modern English, they are probably less important in this regard. In such a text, they perhaps express coherence rather than discontinuity. On the other hand, in a text in which sentences are regularly coordinated with the help of connective particles, such as in Koine and Classical Greek, they may be expected to be more important as indicators of breaks or contrasts.

Secondly, it should be noted that — according to J. Blomqvist — Greek has three different types of adversative coordination: (1) the balancing adversative particle δέ (German 'aber') coordinates two elements which can be true at the same time, but between which some sort of opposition is considered to exist (e.g. οὐ καλός ἐστιν, σοφὸς δέ); (2) the eliminative adversative particle ἀλλά (German 'sondern') coordinates elements which are semantically incompatible (e.g. οὐ καλός ἐστιν ἀλλὰ αἰσχρός); (3) modifying adversative particles, such as μέντοι, πλήν and μόνον, connect elements which entail only a partial opposition to what has gone before (e.g. καλοί εἰσι πάντες, πλὴν οὐ πάντες ὁμοίως).[43] Of these, the balancing adversative particle δέ is best suited to marking the type of significant change of motif that occurs at transitions between sections, since the other two types presuppose a closer relationship between the two coordinated clauses than is normally present when such a change of topic occurs. This does not mean, though, that ἀλλά or a modifying adversative particle could not occur at certain transition points in a text. Nor does it mean that δέ always marks a significant — in the sense of text-organizing — change of motif.

Apart from adversative particles, certain other types can also be used to mark a transition to a new element in an account. In New Testament Greek, the normally inferential οὖν is probably the particle most commonly used in this way.[44]

A completely different, but semantically related way of indicating a transition to a new element in a text is to use a *conditional complex sentence*, in which the conditional clause encompasses the key findings of the preceding section and the main clause states the theme of the new one ('If this is the case, what then shall we think of this?'). In Greek prose style, a μέν... δέ construction is also used as a transitional phrase; here, the first clause sums up what was said in the previous section and the second announces what is to be treated in the following one (ταῦτα μὲν οὖν Πέρσαι τε καὶ Φοίνικες λέγουσι· ἐγὼ δὲ περὶ μὲν τούτων οὐκ ἐρῶ, ἀλλά...).[45]

[43] Denniston 1954, pp. xlix f.; Blomqvist 1969, p. 21; and Blomqvist 1981, pp. 57–70.
[44] Cf. English 'then'.
[45] Blomqvist & Jastrup 1991, pp. 266 f.

Finally, mention should be made here of *asyndeton*. Since in Greek — as opposed to modern written English, for example — sentences are regularly coordinated using connectives, asyndeton stands out as a break in the presentation. Such breaks may occur for different reasons or serve different purposes, but they may be a sign of a significant change of motif.[46]

Attention-attracting and intensity-heightening transition markers

Here there is no reason to consider opening and closing markers separately, since on the whole we are concerned with the same phenomena, with the same functions, namely attracting attention or heightening the intensity of the text. Several of the phenomena that have been considered as thematic or contrastive markers can also be said to be more or less attention-attracting or intensity-heightening (e.g. cleft sentences and emphatic pronouns and adverbs). What we still need to deal with here, then, are phenomena which are characterized more exclusively by the latter properties.

A type of attention-attracting phenomenon which can be mentioned first of all is of course a *direct exhortation to the addressee to be attentive*, e.g. 'Note...!', 'Pay attention to...!', 'Look...!', 'Listen...!' Closely related to such direct commands are *attention-attracting interjections*, such as 'hey' in English or the frozen forms ἴδε or ἰδού in Greek. Often, the use of a form of *address* probably also has the function of attracting attention. However, it can also serve to define and provide information about the addressee.

Phenomena of this kind which directly attract attention can be used to heighten the intensity of the text, but the latter can also be achieved in many other ways. Here I shall confine myself to mentioning a few common characteristics of an intense text: *short sentences, asyndeta, elliptical and brachylogical constructions, anacolutha, repetition, expressions of close personal involvement (e.g. verbs such 'appeal', 'assure'), interjections and rhetorical questions.*

I would like to conclude this discussion of what phenomena could conceivably function as transition markers with a general observation: it should be borne in mind that, in antiquity, a letter was often read aloud and, what is more, that to some extent at least Paul's letters appear to have been dictated.[47] This may influence the way we assess certain phenomena. It is for

---

[46] See e.g. Schwyzer & Debrunner 1950, pp. 632 f.; Denniston 1952, pp. 99–123; and Denniston 1954, pp. xliii–xlvi. In Paul's letters, asyndeton appears to occur quite regularly after rhetorical questions and in conjunction with exhortations, for example. It can also be used to achieve a certain rhetorical effect.

[47] See e.g. 1 Cor 16:21.

example possible to heighten the intensity of a text or perhaps enhance the impression of recurrence of an earlier motif by means of special use of rhythm and sound.

Final formulation of the object of the study

The object of this study may now be considered to be sufficiently clearly defined. It is: *(1) to study the use of transition markers of the kinds specified above in 1 Thessalonians, Philippians and Galatians; (2) to examine what arrangements of the texts these markers result in; and (3) to explore the implications of these arrangements for our understanding of the line of thought in each of the letters.*

C. Method

Methodological reflections

The definition of the object of this study given above appears to suggest a linear or 'one-way' process, moving from transition markers to lines of thought. In practice, however, the task cannot be undertaken in this way. As was observed earlier, because of their contextuality and relativity transition markers have to be studied in the light of the progression of thought in the text concerned.[48] At the same time, though, our perception of the latter phenomenon is dependent on how the text is divided up. In other words, we have to reckon with a certain circular movement, in which transition markers and lines of thought shed light on each other. This is not a closed circle, however, since the two factors are not only determined by each other. Transition markers are not just contextual, but also conventional and, to some extent, logical or natural, and our perception of the train of thought is also determined, for example, by relationships existing at the semantic level. Nevertheless, in my opinion these two factors are so interdependent that neither of them can be properly understood without reference to the other.

---

[48] F. Siegert (1985, p. 112) and M. Bachmann (1992, p. 103) believe that, to a large extent, structure analysis is a matter of argumentation analysis. Such a view, however, may very well result in inattention to the formal properties of a text.

An awareness of this circular or spiral movement has influenced the structure of my analyses, in that the actual groundwork consists of a 'basic analysis', in which I subdivide the text with reference both to the occurrence of transition markers *and* to the train of thought. In this basic analysis, all the individual aspects of the study are in other words considered at the same time. In line with the critical question which the study addresses, however, I attempt to place the emphasis on the transition markers and, as regards the line of thought, confine myself to observations that are as straightforward and uncontroversial as possible, based on the instructive and thematic transition markers identified.

Procedure

1 Thessalonians, Philippians and Galatians are each analysed in turn. The same procedure is used for each letter. I begin with an introduction, in which I present the various arrangements of the text concerned that have been proposed in the modern exegetical literature and address the question of its unity. My aim in examining modern proposals concerning textual organization is to place the present analysis in its scholarly context, to further underline the need to carry it out, and to underpin the assertions I make at various points in the thesis concerning earlier research and the difficulties experienced in discerning the structure of these texts. My reason for addressing the question of unity is of course that the position reached on this question does to some extent influence the analysis, above all as regards our understanding of the progress of thought in the texts.

I then go through the entire text of the letter concerned, noting transition markers and, in the light of the instructive and thematic ones, making general observations about the line of thought and dividing up the text on this basis. This is the actual groundwork of each analysis; the remaining sections consist of summaries of or comments on the results of this basic analysis.

The basic analysis is followed by a tabular overview of the arrangement of the text that has emerged from it. In this overview, each section is provided with a heading and a listing of its most important transition markers. It thus summarizes the development of thought and the occurrence of transition markers in the letter concerned.

The next step is a commentary on the transition markers observed, in which I attempt to discern patterns and tendencies in their occurrence in the letter. Here I pay particular attention to different levels in the structure of the text. The arrangement of this section follows that of the presentation of different transition markers given in the present chapter. Following a few introductory reflections on the interaction of the different markers, I thus examine, in turn, instructive and thematic opening markers, the corresponding closing markers, contrastive opening markers and finally attention-attracting and intensity-heightening transition markers.

Subsequently, I go on to comment on what implications the text arrangement identified has for our understanding of the line of thought in the text. Here I begin by examining how this arrangement affects our understanding of the overall structure of the letter. Attention then turns to individual motifs which are given greater prominence by the particular way the text has been divided.

It should perhaps be pointed out that my comments on the transition markers and the line of thought in each letter represent an analytical step going beyond the basic analysis. The results of the basic analysis thus do not automatically stand or fall with the reader's assessment of these comments. On the other hand, that assessment will of course depend entirely on the reader's assessment of the basic analyses.

This, then, is how the individual analyses are structured. The thesis ends with a few general reflections on the results of the analyses.

D. Related research

At the very beginning of this introductory chapter, I promised to return to the question of how the present study relates to other attempts to determine the text structures of Paul's letters, once I had defined my object and methods more precisely. I shall now keep that promise.

Basically any exegetical work on the Pauline epistles involves drawing conclusions about the structure of the text concerned. Strikingly often, however, even in commentaries, texts are broken down into sections without further comment. This underscores the suspicion which I expressed under the heading 'The critical question' above, namely that text divisions are often strongly influenced by the exegete's ideas about the progression of thought, without due account being taken of the linguistic structures of the text. At all events, interpreters appear to assume that their exposition of the sequence of thought in the letter in question will be so convincing in itself that further comment on the way the text is divided would be superfluous. Given the many competing expositions and arrangements that have been put forward, this is quite remarkable.[49]

---

[49] See for example the introductions to each of the analyses below.

As has been mentioned, though, a good many attempts have been made, using various methods of analysis, to arrive at better and more reliable delimitations of the text sequences making up Paul's letters. One method that has been used to this end is *epistolary analysis*,[50] that is, a form-critical study of the epistles of Paul in the light of what we know about letter-writing in antiquity in general. For comparison, such studies make use in particular of the large number of papyri that have been found in Egypt since the end of the last century. Comparisons of this kind naturally have their place, but their value in determining the main divisions of Paul's letters is significantly limited by the method's strongly genre-oriented approach, since many of the factors of significance to the subdivision of the texts are likely to be of a general linguistic nature, rather than genre-related.[51] What is more, the link in terms of genre between the Pauline epistles and the Hellenistic letters they are compared with is far from clear, since they exhibit appreciable differences, for example in both length and content.[52] At all events, this method of analysis needs to be supplemented with methods which also take account of the more general linguistic elements of the texts.

Another tool that has been used to determine the text structures of Paul's letters is *rhetorical analysis*, which involves applying rhetorical theory and terminology, generally deriving from classical rhetoric, to an analysis of the letters. Rhetorical analysis can be undertaken for different purposes and in different ways. Up to now, its main significance as regards establishing the subdivisions of Paul's letters has lain in its endeavour — above all using the *dispositio* of classical rhetoric — to discern and identify the different elements in the texts.[53] The principal weakness of most such attempts has been the lack of a proper analysis of the syntactic and semantic relationships within the text.[54] Without such an analysis, there is a considerable risk of subordinate motifs being overemphasized and misconstrued to make the text fit an expected pattern. If the wrong motifs are perceived to be text-organizing, this in turn will result in incorrect arrangements of the text. Symptomatically, some rhetorical analyses have resulted in text divisions which are in conspicuous

---

[50] Works dealing more specifically with the structuring of Paul's letters include Schubert 1939, Sanders 1962, White 1972, Doty 1973, Boers 1975/76 and Alexander 1989. Works of some relevance to the question include Wiles 1974, White 1986 and Weima 1994.

[51] Many of the features which White (1972), for example, discusses as 'transitional formulae' in the epistolary literature are probably in fact of a more general linguistic character. Cf. Schnider & Stenger 1987, p. 168.

[52] Köster 1979, pp. 33 ff.; Johanson 1987, pp. 5 and 173. Cf. also Reed 1993, pp. 292 f.

[53] E.g. Kennedy 1984, Jewett 1986, Watson 1988 and Smit 1993.

[54] B. Johanson (1987) is aware of this weakness (pp. 5 f.) and therefore combines a rhetorical with a text linguistic analysis.

conflict with the linguistic structures of the text.[55] Using classical rhetoric as an analytical language is of course in itself perfectly legitimate, although it should perhaps be observed that *dispositio* in particular was a somewhat neglected area of it.[56] It should be pointed out, however, that it is hardly reasonable to treat classical rhetoric as a kind of essential key to a proper understanding of Paul's letters, since the aim of classical rhetoric was not to produce speech that was accessible only to rhetors. What is more, such a treatment of classical rhetoric involves assumptions concerning the access of both Paul and his addressees to this rhetoric which are highly questionable and not easy to prove.[57] At any rate, to determine the text structures of the Pauline letters, most of the rhetorical analyses performed up to now need to be supplemented with proper analyses of the syntactic and semantic relationships within the text.

A third type of analytical method that has been used to determine the text structures of Paul's letters is *discourse analysis*, or *text linguistic analysis*. The analytical models and languages used here derive from modern text theorists, such as T. A. van Dijk, E. Gülich, W. Raible, W. U. Dressler and R.-A. de Beaugrande.[58] Usually, these theorists apply an axiomatic-deductive approach, which means that their text models are to a large extent based in logic. The examples they give are as a rule drawn from modern French, German or English, and herein lies the weakness of analyses based exclusively on such text models.[59] As was observed earlier, language is not exclusively logical, but is also characterized by conventionality and relativity. These analyses therefore need to be supplemented with more empirically oriented studies of the text structures of Paul's letters.[60]

The method of analysis used in this thesis is above all inspired by the last-mentioned method, but to a certain extent also by those referred to earlier. However, it attempts to be more empirical in approach than text linguistic analyses usually are, to take greater account of the syntactic and semantic

---

[55] H. D. Betz (1979), for example, argues that there is an opening at the first level of text structure in Gal 1:12, even though there is nothing in the text to suggest a major new departure at that point, whereas there are opening markers in both Gal 1:11 and 1:13 (see analysis below). Similarly, he finds openings at the same level in Gal 2:15 and 5:1, where once again there is little that could be regarded as an opening marker (see analysis below). R. Jewett (1986) finds an opening at the first level of text structure in 1 Thess 1:6, which I also consider remarkable.

[56] Plett 1989, p. 16; Hellholm 1993, p. 126.

[57] Cf. Reed 1993, pp. 322 ff.

[58] E.g. van Dijk 1977, Gülich & Raible 1977, Gülich & Raible 1979, de Beaugrande & Dressler 1983, and van Dijk 1985.

[59] More extensive text linguistic analyses of Paul's letters include Schenk 1984, Johanson 1987, Pelser *et al.* 1992 and Guthrie 1995.

[60] Concerning the rationalistic tendencies of text linguistics, see Gülich & Raible 1977, pp. 18–21, and de Beaugrande & Dressler 1983, p. xiv and 2:11.

relationships within the text than rhetorical analyses generally do, and to have a more general linguistic emphasis than is found in epistolary analysis. As a result, it can hopefully offer a meaningful complement to these methods of analysis.

2. The First Letter to the Thessalonians

A. Introduction

Before turning to the actual analysis of 1 Thessalonians, I shall begin by presenting a number of modern suggestions as to the arrangement of this epistle and touching briefly on the discussion about its unity.[1]

For the purposes of this review of relevant scholarship, I have compared the arrangements proposed in eight commentaries, which I believe to be reasonably representative of the modern literature. In addition, I have studied the divisions of the text put forward in five monographs.[2]

I pointed out earlier that 1 Thessalonians appears to me to have a somewhat clearer text structure than Philippians or Galatians. This does not mean, though, that there is any consensus in the exegetical literature about how this letter should be divided; on the contrary, many different subdivisions of the text have been proposed. However, the disagreement does not seem as far-reaching here as it is in the case of Philippians or Galatians. Most scholars appear to be agreed on *where* the more important transitions occur. What they primarily differ over is the level to which some of these transitions should be assigned.

As regards the higher levels of division of the epistle, the sources consulted are in relative agreement. The majority (eleven) identify 1:1 as the opening of the letter. Diverging proposals are 1:1–5 and 1:1–10.[3] Most (nine) regard 5:23–28 as the closing section of the epistle. An alternative proposal is 5:25–28.[4] The remainder, the actual body of the letter, is then usually considered to fall into two parts, with the transition at 3:13/4:1.[5] However, some (four) also assign other transitions, e.g. 1:10/2:1, 2:12/13 or 2:16/17, to this level of text division.[6]

---

[1] For my reasons for doing so, see p. 33.

[2] *Commentaries:* Best 1972, Ellingworth & Nida 1976, Friedrich 1976b, Marshall 1983, Morris 1984, Juel 1985, Holtz 1986 and Wanamaker 1990. *Monographs:* Doty 1973, Vielhauer 1978, Kennedy 1984, Jewett 1986 and Johanson 1987.

[3] Jewett 1986 and Kennedy 1984, respectively. Both base their conclusions on rhetorical analyses.

[4] Friedrich 1976b, Marshall 1983, Holtz 1986 and Johanson 1987.

[5] Doty 1973, Ellingworth & Nida 1976, Friedrich 1976b, Vielhauer 1978, Juel 1985, Holtz 1986, Jewett 1986, Johanson 1987 and Wanamaker 1990.

[6] E.g. Best 1972 (1:2–10, 2:1–12, 2:13–16, 2:17–3:13, 4:1–5:22) and Kennedy 1984 (1:2–10, 2:1–8, 2:9–3:13, 4:1–5:22).

As regards the lower-level subdivisions of the letter, we can note that views differ most widely with regard to the first half of the letter (chapters 1–3). There is admittedly a certain amount of agreement that 1:2–10, 2:1–12, 2:13–16 and 2:17–3:13 constitute distinct units,[7] but views then differ as to what level they belong to. Some (five) consider them all to be at the same level.[8] Others (four) first divide the passage 1:2–3:13 into two and assign some of the sections mentioned to the next level down.[9] Yet others advocate an initial tripartite division of this section.[10]

Concerning the second half of the letter, there is somewhat greater agreement. Here, the basic arrangement can be said to be 4:1–12, 4:13–5:11 and 5:12–22(24). The principal variations are that some commentaries and monographs (five) divide 4:1–12 into smaller units from the outset,[11] while others (three) suggest an initial division of 4:13–5:11 into 4:13–18 and 5:1–11.[12]

Certainly, then, there are differences between the arrangements that have been proposed, but as a rule they do not appear to be very fundamental. The greatest and most important variations are to be found regarding the first half of the letter (chapters 1–3).

Turning next to the question of unity, it may be observed that the unity of 1 Thessalonians has repeatedly been called into question. In the following, I shall present the key arguments for the most important compilation and interpolation theories and explain why I am not prepared to use any one of them as a starting-point for my analysis, but choose rather to treat the letter as a unity. First I shall present and assess the arguments in favour of regarding 1 Thessalonians as compounded from several Pauline epistles. Although several different theories of this kind have been presented,[13] they are based on

---

[7] These sections are distinguished by Best 1972, Doty 1973, Ellingworth & Nida 1976, Friedrich 1976b, Marshall 1983, Juel 1985, Holtz 1986 and Johanson 1987. Vielhauer 1978 and Wanamaker 1990 accept 1:2–10, 2:1–12 and 2:13–16 as distinct entities, but divide 2:17–3:13 into several shorter sections (Vielhauer 1978: 2:17–3:5, 3:6–10, 3:11–13; Wanamaker 1990: 2:17–3:10, 3:11–13).

[8] Best 1972, Ellingworth & Nida 1976, Vielhauer 1978, Marshall 1983 and Juel 1985.

[9] Friedrich 1976b, Holtz 1986 and Johanson 1987 first divide the section into 1:2–2:16 and 2:17–3:13, whereas Doty 1973 splits it into 1:2–10 and 2:1–3:13.

[10] Wanamaker 1990 suggests 1:2–10, 2:1–3:10 and 3:11–13; Kennedy 1984, 1:2–10, 2:1–8 and 2:9–3:13; and Morris 1984, 1:2–3, 1:4–2:16 and 2:17–3:13.

[11] Best 1972 (4:1–2, 3–8, 9–12), Ellingworth & Nida 1976 (4:1–2, 3–8, 9–12), Friedrich 1976b (4:1–8, 9–10a, 10b–12), Juel 1985 (4:1–8, 9–12) and Jewett 1986 (4:1–8, 9–12).

[12] Doty 1973, Vielhauer 1978 and Wanamaker 1990.

[13] Three different compilation theories may be mentioned: Eckart 1961, pp. 30–44 (*Letter 1:* 1:1–2:12; 2:17–3:4; 3:11–13. *Letter 2:* 3:6–10; 4:9–10a; 4:13–5:11; 5:23–26, 28. *Non-Pauline:* 2:13–16; 3:5; 4:1–8, 10b–12, 18(?); 5:19–22, 27); Schmithals 1964, pp. 295–315 (*Letter 1:* 1:1–2:12; 4:2(3)–5:28. *Letter 2:* 2:13–4:1(2)); Schenke & Fischer 1978, pp. 65–71 (*Letter 1:* 2:13; 2:1–12; 2:17–3:4; 2:14; 4:1–8; 3:11–13. *Letter 2:* 1:1–

similar lines of reasoning.[14] I shall then go on to consider the two principal interpolation theories,[15] the first concerning 1 Thess 2:13(15)–16 and the second relating to 1 Thess 5:1–11.[16]

Arguments in support of 1 Thessalonians being a compilation

1. The letter contains two typical letter openings, one in 1:2 and the other in 2:13.[17]

2. The 'thanksgiving' that begins in 1:2 is concluded in 1:10. Cf. 1 Cor 1:9, Phil 1:11.[18]

3. The epistle contains two typical letter endings, one (incomplete) in 3:11–4:1 and another in 5:23–28.[19]

4. In Paul's letters, practical matters are always dealt with at the beginning or the end, and not in the middle of the letter, as would be the case in 1 Thessalonians if it were regarded as a unity (2:17–3:10).[20]

5. The section beginning at 2:13 has no logical connection with what has gone before. The lack of a clear link is underlined by the linguistically clumsy introduction: καὶ διὰ τοῦτο καί...[21]

6. The favourable attitude in 2:17–3:10 to the situation among the Thessalonians is in contrast to the *apologia* in 1:5–2:12 and to the attempts in 4:3–5:22 to remedy the significant deficiencies in their faith.[22]

7. The two sections 2:17–3:4 and 3:6–10 presuppose different situations.[23]

The first four of these arguments are of a form-critical nature and rest on specific perceptions of the structure of Pauline letters; the last three relate to content. A number of objections can be raised to all of these arguments. As

10: 3:6–10; 4:13–17; 5:1–11; 4:9–12; 5:12–22, 23–26, 28. *Red.*: 2:15 f.; 3:5; 4:18; 5:27).

[14] For more detailed answers to the arguments put forward in support of these compilation theories, see e.g. Kümmel 1962, pp. 213–27, and Best 1972, pp. 29–35.

[15] More complex, but less widely supported interpolation theories have been presented by Demke (1973, pp. 103–24) and Murro (1983, pp. 86–94).

[16] *1 Thess 2:13(15)–16:* e.g. Pearson 1971, pp. 79–94, Boers 1975/76, pp. 140–58, and Schmidt 1983, pp. 269–79. *1 Thess 5:1–11:* Friedrich 1973, pp. 288–315. For *more detailed refutations*, see Rigaux 1974/75, pp. 318–40, Collins 1979, pp. 67–106, Plevnik 1979, pp. 71–90, Okeke 1980/81, pp. 127–36, Donfried 1984, pp. 242–53, and Weatherly 1991, pp. 79–98.

[17] Schmithals 1964, pp. 301 f.; Pearson 1971, pp. 88 f.; and Schenke & Fischer 1978, p. 67.

[18] Sanders 1962, pp. 355 f., and Schmithals 1964, p. 301.

[19] Schmithals 1964, pp. 301 f., and Schenke & Fischer 1978, p. 67.

[20] Schmithals 1964, p. 303.

[21] Eckart 1961, pp. 33 f., and Schmithals 1964, pp. 304 f.

[22] Schmithals 1964, pp. 303 f.

[23] Eckart 1961, p. 34, and Schenke & Fischer 1978, pp. 67 f.

regards the first, it can be pointed out to begin with that the expression εὐχαριστῶ/οῦμεν τῷ θεῷ is not confined exclusively to the opening sections of Paul's letters (see 1 Cor 1:14; 14:18); the mere presence of such an expression is thus not enough to classify something as the opening of a letter. In this case it may in addition be noted that there are clear indications that 1 Thess 2:13–16 forms part of the 'thanksgiving', beginning at 1:2, which opens the letter.[24] The particle γάρ in 2:1 and the prepositional phrase διὰ τοῦτο in 2:13 suggest that the passage 2:1–12 is subordinate in content terms to the preceding and the following text. Furthermore, it may be noted that it is not unusual for Paul to round off a section by referring back to its opening phrases (see e.g. 3:1–5; 4:1–12). An example of this in the opening section of a letter is Phil 1:3–11, where in 1:9 Paul begins the final sentence of the section with the metacommunicative verb προσεύχομαι, which looks back to εὐχαριστῶ τῷ θεῷ μου... ἐν πάσῃ δεήσει μου... τὴν δέησιν ποιούμενος in 1:3 f.[25]

Regarding the second argument, it is by no means clear that 1:10 brings the opening 'thanksgiving' to an end.[26] There is admittedly an eschatological perspective here which suggests something of a conclusion, but the opening that occurs in 2:1 (γάρ) shows that the new section is subordinate in terms of content to the preceding one. The eschatological perspectives in 1 Cor 1:9 and Phil 1:11 are followed by more obvious fresh starts. As for the third argument, it is, as E. Best points out, possible to cite similar wishes occurring at points other than in letter conclusions, e.g. in Rom 15:5 f., 13.[27] The fourth argument is based on an assumption to which there are in fact one or two exceptions. W. Schmithals claims that 1 Cor 4:14–21 is the *only* exception.[28] This assertion presupposes, though, that we accept his view of the unity of Philippians; otherwise, Phil 2:19–30 must be recorded as a further exception.

Arguments 5 and 6 are based to a large extent on the assumption that 1 Thess 2:1–12 is an *apologia*; however, it is by no means essential to make that assumption,[29] and a simpler solution to the problems raised in these arguments therefore seems to me to be to question it. As regards the final

---

[24] See e.g. Schubert 1939, p. 20, Kümmel 1962, p. 219, and Holtz 1986, pp. 24 f.

[25] Like P. Schubert (1939, p. 18), I find this example fully comparable to the construction in 1 Thess 1:2–2:16, even though the latter text is appreciably longer and the recurrence of earlier material in it involves a greater element of repetition than in Phil 1:3–11. It seems to me that H. Boers (1975/76, p. 142), in his criticism of Schubert, is being overly quantitative in his reasoning.

[26] Schmithals himself indicates that he is aware of the weakness of this argument (Schmithals 1964, p. 301).

[27] Best 1972, p. 32. Cf. also Demke 1973, pp. 105 ff.

[28] Schmithals 1964, p. 303, note 19.

[29] See e.g. Lyons 1985, pp. 191 ff., and Schoon-Jansen 1991, p. 64.

41

argument, it may be asserted, as T. Holtz[30] does, that 2:17–3:4 and 3:6–10 do not presuppose different situations at all, but are linked by 3:5, which there is no valid reason to omit.

Arguments for regarding 1 Thess 2:13(15)–16 as an interpolation

Arguments 1, 2 and 5 above are also used to support the view that 1 Thess 2:13(15)–16 is an interpolation, and they may be evaluated in the same way here as earlier. In addition, however, B. Pearson has put forward a number of content-based arguments (1–4) and D. Schmidt a number of linguistic ones (5–11):

1. The statements made about the Jews in 1 Thess 2:13(15)–16 conflict with what Paul says about them in Rom 11:25 ff. One should also note Paul's pride in his Jewish background, e.g. in Phil 3:5 f., Gal 1:14, 2:15 and Rom 11:1.[31]

2. Nowhere else does Paul blame the Jews for Jesus's death. If 1 Cor 2:8 is a reference to worldly authorities, it presumably alludes first and foremost to the Romans.[32]

3. The phrase πᾶσιν ἀνθρώποις ἐναντίων in 1 Thess 2:15 can be traced to Graeco-Roman anti-Semitism.[33]

4. The closing words of 2:16 probably refer to the destruction of Jerusalem in AD 70 and describe it as a past event.[34]

5. Nowhere else does Paul coordinate two 'matrix sentences' with καί, and nowhere else does καὶ διὰ τοῦτο occur.[35]

6. In 2:14 ff., there are seven levels of 'embedding'. The highest number elsewhere in 1 Thessalonians is five (1:1–11).[36]

7. In 2:15 the nouns κύριον and ᾽Ιησοῦν are separated, which Paul does not do anywhere else.[37]

8. Unlike in 1:6, the genitive attributes of μιμηταί in 2:14 are separated from the word they qualify.[38]

9. The phrase τῶν ἐκκλησιῶν τοῦ θεοῦ τῶν οὐσῶν ἐν τῇ ᾽Ιουδαίᾳ ἐν Χριστῷ ᾽Ιησοῦ is a combination of three different Pauline expressions.[39]

---

[30] Holtz 1986, pp. 24 f.
[31] Pearson 1971, pp. 85 f.
[32] Pearson 1971, pp. 83 ff.
[33] Pearson 1971, p. 83.
[34] Pearson 1971, pp. 81 ff. See also Boers 1975/76, p. 152, and Schmidt 1983, p. 269.
[35] Schmidt 1983, p. 273.
[36] Ibid.
[37] Ibid.
[38] Schmidt 1983, p. 274.
[39] Ibid.

10. In 2:14, the address occurs between an attribute and the word it qualifies. Elsewhere in Paul's letters, it always occurs at a natural break in the clause.[40]

11. The position of τοῦ θεοῦ in 2:13 has an un-Pauline 'harshness' about it. Moreover, elsewhere in 1 Thessalonians, Paul talks about λόγος κυρίου and. not λόγος θεοῦ.[41]

Beginning with Pearson's content-based arguments, we find that the first of them is marred by the lack of a proper analysis of the context.[42] In 1 Thess 2:13(15)–16, Paul is not primarily seeking to give an answer to the question of what the Jews are like or who killed Jesus. His concern is to comfort and encourage the Thessalonians, who have been persecuted by their fellow countrymen (1:6; 2:14), and he does so by showing that this is the fate of the servant of God. In the same way, Jesus, the prophets, Paul and the Judaean churches — all of them Jews — have been persecuted by their fellow Jews. Paul's thinking here is thus clearly typological. His main interest is not in opponents or the Jews, but in the situation faced by the Lord's servants. Quite evidently, therefore, Paul's intention is not to make a statement about the qualities of the Jews as an ethnic group, but merely to underline the fact that Jesus, the prophets and the first Jewish Christians suffered persecution at the hands of their fellow countrymen. All the statements made in 2:14 ff. should be interpreted in the light of this limited purpose. Just as Paul is presumably not claiming that all Thessalonians are cruel persecutors when he uses the words τῶν ἰδίων συμφυλετῶν in 2:14, so he is not describing all the Jews in those terms when he refers to τῶν 'Ιουδαίων in the same verse. The restricted reference of the latter word is indicated by the attributes associated with it in 2:15 f. Paul, then, is not portraying the Jews here as a particularly evil group. Rather, his typological thinking suggests that this pattern of persecution is universal and occurs among both the Jewish and other peoples. It is thus fundamentally wrong to read 2:15 f. as anti-Jewish polemic.[43] Given Paul's typological way of thinking, what is said here about the Jews also applies to every other people. It is consequently clear that these statements about the Jews are not incompatible with Paul's own pride in being a Jew and the hopes which he expresses for Israel, e.g. in Rom 11:25 ff. What he says about the Jews in 1 Thess 2:15 f. is not appreciably different from what he says about them in Rom 9:27 ff. and 10:21, for example.

[40] Schmidt 1983, pp. 274 f.

[41] Schmidt 1983, pp. 275 f.

[42] Both G. E. Okeke (1980/81, pp. 127–36) and K. P. Donfried (1984, pp. 242–53) offer suggestions as to how the tension between 1 Thess 2:13(15)–16 and other statements about the Jews in Paul's letters can be resolved with the help of contextual analysis.

[43] As Schmidt (1983, p. 269) does, for example.

As for Pearson's second argument, it is necessary once again to stress Paul's typological thinking, which means that he is hardly interested in placing the blame for Jesus's death on any particular ethnic group. In 1 Thess 2:15 the typology concerns the persecution which God's servants suffer at the hands of their compatriots, and this makes it natural to underline the specific responsibility of the Jews for the death of Jesus. I consider it highly unlikely that he would not attach any responsibility at all for it to them. After all, he himself played a part in the persecution of the first Christians shortly after Jesus's death (1 Cor 15:9; Gal 1:13 f., 23; Phil 3:6; Acts 7:58; 8:3), and subsequently he has himself suffered persecution at Jewish hands (e.g. 2 Cor 11:24 f.; Acts 9:23; 13:50; 14:2, 5, 19; 17:5).

Concerning the third argument, it should be observed that the expression πᾶσιν ἀνθρώποις ἐναντίων in 1 Thess 2:15 does not describe the Jews in general as enemies of humanity, but rather refers to the particular ones who have persecuted 'us' and hindered 'us' from speaking to the Gentiles so that they may be saved. This expression is very closely linked to the following participial construction, which is subordinate to and explains it. The meaning of the expression is thus not the same here as in Graeco-Roman anti-Semitism.

Turning to the fourth argument, it may be noted that the interpretation of the concluding clause of 2:16 poses a number of difficulties. Does ἔφθασεν refer to a past event, or could it be some sort of 'prophetic' aorist?[44] Does ἡ ὀργή refer here to the eschatological wrath on the day of the Lord? What does εἰς τέλος mean? 'At last', 'completely' or 'until the end'? However we answer these questions, it is far from certain that what is being referred to here is the destruction of Jerusalem. Donfried, for example, suggests that the reference is to the crucifixion.[45]

If we now move on to Schmidt's linguistic arguments (5–11), we find that a weakness in all of them is the inadequacy of the underlying qualitative analysis. To carry out a stylistic analysis of this kind, it is for instance not sufficient merely to observe that 1 Thess 2:15 is the only place in Paul's letters where κύριος and Ἰησοῦς are separated (argument 7). The first thing to do is to ask *why* they are separated *here*. Is it for reasons of emphasis? Or should Ἰησοῦν perhaps be understood as an added explanation? The next thing to do is to study whether similar phenomena or rhetorical devices occur elsewhere in the Pauline epistles. Paul does at any rate separate attribute and head in several places.[46]

---

[44] Concerning the latter view, see e.g. Clark 1940, p. 380, and Caragounis 1989, pp. 21 f.

[45] Donfried 1984, pp. 251 f.

[46] E.g. 1 Cor 7:7, 12; 10:4; 12:24; 2 Cor 7:5; Phil 2:20. Cf. also Weatherly 1991, pp. 94 f.

As for argument 5, we need to ask whether there may be a special reason for beginning 2:13 with καί. Here it seems to me that Phil 1:9 and 1:25, for example, may offer interesting comparisons.[47] As far as the construction καὶ διὰ τοῦτο is concerned, it is true that it does not occur anywhere else in Paul's letters. Usually, διὰ τοῦτο follows on asyndetically from what has gone before: but in a few instances it is combined with γάρ (e.g. Rom 13:6). Are such passages also to be regarded as interpolations? It should be remembered that a fairly limited quantity of Pauline text has been preserved and that we must therefore expect a relatively large number of *hapax legomena* of different kinds. It can also be noted that the construction καὶ διὰ τοῦτο occurs just once in each of the following books of the New Testament: the Gospels according to Matthew, Mark, Luke and John, and the Letter to the Hebrews.[48]

A similar point can be made concerning argument 6. 1 Thessalonians constitutes a very limited body of text, and it is not particularly remarkable that 2:14 ff. should contain a few levels of 'embedding' more than any other part of the letter.[49]

Concerning the eighth argument, too, it has to be asked whether there is any special reason why the genitive attributes of μιμηταί are placed in different positions in 1:6 and 2:14. A conceivable reason for the different positions of ὑμῶν in 1:6 and τῶν ἐκκλησιῶν... ʼΙησοῦ in 2:14 is their differing length. The first of these attributes consists of four letters, the second of over 50. If the latter were placed in the same position as the former, the finite verb would be deferred to an unreasonably late point in the clause. It should be noted in this context that in 1:6 μιμηταί actually has two genitive attributes and that the second one — καὶ τοῦ κυρίου — is in fact separated from the first and placed after ἐγενήθητε (like τῶν ἐκκλησιῶν... ʼΙησοῦ!).

As regards the ninth argument, it would be reasonable to ask whether there may be special reasons for attaching all these attributes to the head τῶν ἐκκλησιῶν in 1 Thess 2:14. The use of the attribute τοῦ θεοῦ contrasts these churches with the Jewish persecutors who displease God (2:15; cf. also 2:2). The geographical details are given in view of the comparison with the Thessalonians' own compatriots. And if one refers to the churches (communities) of God in Judaea. the qualification ἐν Χριστῷ ʼΙησοῦ is more or less essential. Once again. Schmidt's approach proves too quantitative.

Turning to argument 10, one wonders what in fact constitutes a 'natural break' in a clause. In 1 Thess 4:13, the address occurs between the verb ἀγνοεῖν and its necessary complement περὶ τῶν κοιμωμένων, which to me

---

[47] For additional examples and a more in-depth discussion, see Weatherly 1991, p. 92.
[48] Mt 14:2; Mk 6:14; Lk 14:20; Jn 5:16; Heb 9:15.
[49] For a more detailed discussion, see Weatherly 1991, pp. 93 f.

does not seem a 'natural break' in the clause, either — but then, that is from my vantage point. Ancient Greek, with its wealth of forms, offered different possibilities when it came to sentence structure than do modern Swedish or English.[50] To a user of ancient Greek, therefore, these sentence positions may have felt considerably more natural than they do to me.

As for the last argument (11), Paul's constructions sometimes do seem a little 'harsh' to me. Apart from that, it may be noted that the final position of τοῦ θεοῦ in the construction παραλαβόντες... τοῦ θεοῦ is perfectly understandable: the words then correspond to ἀνθρώπων and θεοῦ in the following constructions. The fact that in 2:13 Paul chooses to talk about λόγον θεοῦ probably has to do with the contrast he is seeking to bring out there with human words (cf. also 2:4).

Arguments for regarding 1 Thess 5:1–11 as an interpolation

G. Friedrich has put forward the following arguments in support of the view that 1 Thess 5:1–11 is an interpolation:

1. 1 Thess 4:13–18 and 5:1–11 presuppose different theological situations. The section 4:13–18 is characterized by an eschatological expectation that the Parousia is near, whereas 5:1–11 is addressed to a church which sees it as far distant.[51]

2. There are striking similarities between 1 Thess 5:1–9 and Rom 11–14, but in the latter text, unlike the former, the theology of an imminent Parousia still prevails. In view of the fact that 1 Thessalonians is Paul's first and Romans his last letter, one would expect the converse to be true.[52]

3. In 1 Thess 5:1–11 there are quite a number of non-Pauline words and concepts. The style, too, is un-Pauline. The rest of 1 Thessalonians is written in a living style, whereas 5:1–11 is couched in general terms, formulaic and full of traditional material. The language of 5:1–11 shows similarities to that of Luke's gospel.[53]

4. 5:1–11 has precisely the same structure as 4:13–18, arousing the suspicion that it is modelled on that section.[54]

Concerning the first of these arguments, it should be pointed out that the difficulty does not in fact lie in reconciling the theological ideas of the nearness of the end and the sudden coming of the end. What are incompatible

---

[50] Cf. Kurzova 1985, p. 3.
[51] Friedrich 1973, pp. 291 f., 301–5.
[52] Friedrich 1973, pp. 305 ff.
[53] Friedrich 1973, pp. 292–8, 307 ff.
[54] Friedrich 1973, pp. 298–301.

are Friedrich's reconstructions of the underlying situations and of Paul's intentions in 1 Thess 4:13–18 and 5:1–11. According to Friedrich, the first of these sections was written to calm and comfort its addressees: the Thessalonians should not grieve, as the end is nigh. In the second section, on the other hand, the aim is to warn them not to settle down comfortably in the belief that the Parousia is far off. The question is, though, are these reconstructions correct? I am particularly hesitant about the second of them. The exhortation that rounds off 5:1–11 suggests rather that the aim of the section is not to warn and rebuke, but — as in 4:13–18 — to comfort and encourage. At the beginning of the section, Paul states that the recipients do not need to have anything written to them about the matters in question, since they already know all about them. Such an opening is presumably more in line with the aim of comforting and encouraging than that of warning and rebuking. I shall return to these questions in the section dealing with the implications of the analysis for our understanding of the line of thought in the letter. Here I shall merely observe that there is cause to question the reconstructions of the situations and intentions on which Friedrich's first argument relies.

The second argument is also based on these reconstructions and is thus open to question on the same grounds.

The third argument merely shows that traditional material is present in 1 Thess 5:1–11, and that Luke, too, was evidently familiar with it. We also come across traditional material in 1 Thess 4:14–17 and elsewhere in Paul's letters. Its presence is thus not compelling evidence of an interpolation.[55]

As for the fourth argument, the structural similarities between the sections may of course also be due to the fact that they were written by the same person on the same occasion.

The arguments in favour of the various compilation and interpolation theories are thus in my view generally fairly weak. It should in addition be observed that theories of this kind involve a weakness in themselves, since they require a number of supporting hypotheses about a compiler or interpolator and about that person's intentions and methods. It is therefore my opinion that such theories should only be accepted if there are very powerful reasons for doing so. I do not consider the arguments presented and assessed here to be sufficiently convincing, and therefore proceed in my analysis from the assumption that 1 Thessalonians is a unity. This basic assumption will be supported by the analyses that follow.

The time has now come to move on to the basic analysis of 1 Thessalonians.

[55] Cf. Plevnik 1979, p. 74.

B. Basic analysis

In this section, I intend to go through the whole of the First Letter to the Thessalonians, record the transition markers that occur there and, on the basis of these markers and general observations concerning the line of thought in the letter, determine the structure of the letter. This analysis will then form the basis for a further analysis of the transition markers in 1 Thessalonians and of the content of the epistle. A tabular overview of the arrangement of the text at which I arrive is presented on pp. 71–74., but for the sake of clarity I have also subdivided and added headings to the exposition that now follows on the basis of the major sections which I discern in the text, even though by doing so I am anticipating the results of the analysis.[56]

1:1

Like the other Pauline epistles, 1 Thessalonians begins with particulars of the sender and the recipients and a wish of grace and peace. These elements follow one another asyndetically and are formulaic.[57] In 1 Thessalonians they are unusually brief and contain very few attributes, and their formulaic character thus stands out particularly clearly.

1:2–3:13

1:2–2:16

1:2–10

In 1:2, the actual body of the letter begins. This is an entity which is in principle held together by conjunctions, although a number of asyndeta do occur, above all in the latter part of the epistle. The start of a new section in 1:2 is marked by asyndeton, a lengthy construction which is clearly instructive and thematic, and an attention-attracting address. The long introductory construction is complex and involves a number of points of uncertainty. The main clause is at any rate built around the finite verb of the predicate

[56] For a more detailed discussion of my analytical procedure and the theoretical basis for the analysis, see pp. 32 ff.

[57] What sections are distinguished as the opening and the closing of a letter naturally depends on how we define these concepts. Here, I use them to refer to conventional and formulaic elements at the beginning and end of a letter which are not integrated syntactically or in terms of content with the rest of the text. Even with such a definition, however, uncertainties and borderline cases cannot be avoided. This is particularly true of concluding sections, whose appearance can vary quite considerably among Paul's letters.

εὐχαριστοῦμεν (v. 2) and the conjunctive participles μνείαν ποιούμενοι (v. 2), μνημονεύοντες (v. 3) and εἰδότες (v. 4). This clause is metapropositional and metacommunicative. The finite verb at least clearly describes a communicative act. Formally, it is a different communicative act to the one constituted by the letter, namely one between 'us' and God, but the positive appraisal contained in the verb, thankfulness, is of course also present in the communicative act of the letter, and this is also suggested by the use of the present tense of the verb and the adverbial qualifying it, πάντοτε. The first two participles could possibly also be described as metacommunicative, but they are on the borderline between *verba dicendi* and *verba sentiendi*. The last verb at least clearly belongs to the latter category.

All of these verbs are metapropositional and ultimately provide instructions about one and the same proposition, since what the senders always give thanks for, what they mention in their prayers and what they know in that connection is presumably one and the same thing. An initial hint as to the content of this proposition is already given by the prepositional phrase περὶ πάντων ὑμῶν (v. 2). This is then enlarged on in the noun phrases ὑμῶν τοῦ ἔργου τῆς πίστεως καὶ τοῦ κόπου τῆς ἀγάπης καὶ τῆς ὑπομονῆς τῆς ἐλπίδος τοῦ κυρίου ἡμῶν Ἰησοῦ Χριστοῦ ἔμπροσθεν τοῦ θεοῦ καὶ πατρὸς ἡμῶν (v. 3)[58] and τὴν ἐκλογὴν ἡμῶν (v. 4). The latter noun phrase is subsequently expounded in a ὅτι-clause. There is thus a progression in the presentation of the proposition: first an introductory περί-phrase in v. 2, then heading-type noun phrases in vv. 3 and 4, and finally a descriptive ὅτι-clause in v. 4. The prepositional phrase, which provides a general orientation, and the heading-like noun phrases can be said to function as opening markers in their own right.

The last and most detailed of the statements of the content of the proposition is given prominence by the extended and attention-attracting address ἀδελφοὶ ἠγαπημένοι ὑπὸ [τοῦ] θεοῦ. As εἰδότες is subordinate to εὐχαριστοῦμεν in v. 2 both formally and in terms of content, it is hardly reasonable to view this as the beginning of a new major section.[59] A key issue in assessing this statement of the proposition is then how far the following ὅτι-clause extends. NTG and GNT clearly consider that it continues up to and including v. 5, since they have a full stop after the final ὑμᾶς in that verse. In addition, NTG leaves a space in the text and begins the following sentence with a majuscule. These two editions obviously see 1:6 as a marked opening, although they do not go as far as R. Jewett, who regards 1:6 as the beginning

---

[58] The final prepositional phrase can also be interpreted as an adverbial qualifying μνημονεύοντες.

[59] Morris (1984) sees 1:4 as the opening of a section that continues as far as 2:16.

of a section that extends right through to 3:13.[60] In my opinion, it is misleading even to put a full stop after v. 5, since vv. 6 f. are a direct continuation of the preceding construction. My reasons for taking this view are as follows:

1. The line of thought in the construction that began at 1:2 strongly indicates that 1:6 f. belongs to the same construction. As we have seen, an initial indication of the content of the thanksgiving proposition is provided as early as v. 2 by the words περὶ πάντων ὑμῶν. The thanksgiving thus concerns the *addressees*. In v. 3 the reason for thankfulness is described more specifically as 'your work of faith and labour of love and steadfastness of hope'. in other words, the addressees' *actions*. When, in v. 5, Paul sets about describing in more detail, in a ὅτι-clause, the knowledge underlying the senders' thanksgiving, one expects this to relate in some way to the addressees' actions. If a full stop is placed after v. 5, this is not the case, or at any rate not clearly so: the ὅτι-clause merely states how the senders and their gospel came to the recipients, i.e. describes an action to which the addressees were subjected. If, on the other hand, vv. 6 f. are seen as a continuation of the ὅτι-clause in v. 5, that clause also contains a statement about the addressees' reaction to the senders and the coming of their gospel (v. 6), thus providing the expected link with the addressees' actions. In addition, with this interpretation, there is a reference to a knowledge of the favourable consequences of this reaction (v. 7), further justifying the thanksgiving in 1:2. The main emphasis in the construction, however, is probably on describing the conduct of the addressees.

2. In 1:8 ff., when Paul explains in two γάρ-clauses his assertion in v. 7 that the Thessalonians have become an example to all the believers in Macedonia and Achaia, he does so with reference to the fact that those believers. themselves report about 'our' entrance among 'you' *and* about how 'you' turned to God. In the believers' reports, the two aspects are thus kept together, both 'our' coming to 'you' and 'your' reaction to 'our' coming. It is likely that this is the case in the knowledge of the senders, too, and that it is the whole of this process which they perceive as a sign of the election of the Thessalonians (v. 4). It should be noted that, in 1:9 f. too, the emphasis seems to be on the latter aspect, i.e. the Thessalonians' reaction.

3. In 2:13. when the senders once again speak of their constant thanksgiving to God. they attribute it to the fact that the Thessalonians received the word of God from them, so that it is now at work in them. The cause of their thankfulness is thus the Thessalonians' response to the senders and to the coming of their gospel among them. There is no reason to believe that the constant thanksgiving for the addressees described in 1:2 is distinct from that

---

[60] Jewett 1986. This conclusion is based on a rhetorical analysis.

expressed in 2:13. This suggests that the account of the Thessalonians' reaction to the senders' preaching in 1:6 f. forms part of the statement of the senders' reasons for giving thanks that begins at v. 5.

4. There is no clear linguistic evidence that the ὅτι-clause beginning in 1:5 is completed within that verse. The fact that the copulative particle καί, rather than the balancing adversative δέ, is used here, despite the change of grammatical subject, suggests an immediate continuation of what has gone before, rather than the start of a new section. In addition, we can note a correspondence between the verbs in vv. 5 and 6 f. (v. 5 ... ἐγενήθη... ἐγενήθημεν...; v. 6 ... ἐγενήθητε...; v. 7 ... γενέσθαι...). If the actions of the addressees are the principal reason for the senders' gratitude, it is understandable that the transition to 'you' as the agentive subject in this statement of the grounds for thanksgiving is given prominence by the use of ὑμεῖς.

For these reasons, I regard the ὅτι-clause that begins in v. 5 as continuing in v. 6. 1:2–7 can thus be seen as a single coherent linguistic construction describing the senders' thanksgiving for the addressees. Much of this construction is devoted to setting out the subject-matter of or reason for this thanksgiving, which is done in three steps. First, it is said that thanks are given for 'all of you' (v. 2). The senders then report that they remember 'your work of faith and labour of love and steadfastness of hope' (v. 3). Finally, they say that they know of 'your' election, that 'our' message of the gospel came to 'you' in power and in the Holy Spirit, and that 'you' became imitators of 'us' and of the Lord by receiving the word with joy inspired by the Spirit, amid affliction, and thus becoming an example to all the believers in Macedonia and Achaia (vv. 5 ff.).

The consecutive clause in v. 7 suggests that the long construction is drawing to a close. However, the section that began at 1:2 is still not at an end, since in 1:8–10 the senders add a few explanatory comments (γάρ) to the assertion in the concluding ὥστε-clause in 1:7. In the first of these (1:8), the claim that the Thessalonians have become an example to all the believers in Macedonia and Achaia is explained with reference to the fact that their faith in God has become known everywhere, so that the senders have no need to say anything. This is then illustrated by the second comment (1:9 f.), which describes what all these believers report about the Thessalonians' faith. This description clearly refers back to the account in 1:5 f. of what the senders know about the addressees, knowledge which forms the basis for their thanksgiving to God (1:2). Here, as there, there is first a reference to the nature of (ὁποίαν) the senders' entrance among the Thessalonians, and then to the latter's reaction to their coming. The wording of the two passages admittedly differs, but it is clear that they are referring to the same two-stage sequence of events.

This recurrence of the key content of the thanksgiving that was set out from 1:2 on suggests that the section is being brought to a close. So, too, do the consequence-describing infinitives in 1:9 f., which pursue the line of reasoning to its natural end-point, namely eschatological rescue from wrath.

2:1–12

The occurrence of a close in 1:9 f. is confirmed by a distinct new beginning in 2:1. This is marked by the clearly instructive and thematic construction in 2:1 f. and the attention-attracting address ἀδελφοί. The construction begins with an explicit secondary metapropositional base, which states that the content of the following proposition is something the addressees already know,[61] giving the text here the character of a reminder. The fact that the metapropositional verb is in the second person plural entails a change of grammatical subject at this level of the text (cf. 1:9). This change of subject is given added emphasis by αὐτοί, which reinforces the impression that a new section is beginning. The proposition is then presented in a proleptic and heading-like τὴν εἴσοδον ἡμῶν τὴν πρὸς ὑμᾶς, which is then expanded on in a ὅτι-clause. It thus becomes clear that the focus is now on the senders' successful 'entrance' among the addressees. In the second, positive part of the ὅτι-clause, the metapropositional base is reiterated by the comparative clause καθὼς οἴδατε. Both the proleptic construction and the repetition of the metapropositional base can here be said to serve as opening markers.

It is quite apparent, then, that there is a transition at 1:10/2:1. The question is, at what level? As we have seen,[62] several exegetes regard the new section as relatively independent of the preceding one. In my opinion, however, there are clear signs that the new section is subordinate in terms of content to the one that precedes it. This is suggested to begin with by the conjunction γάρ, which signals an explanation or exposition of something that has gone before. This impression is then reinforced by several recurrences of material found in the first part of the presentation of the reasons for thanksgiving, in 1:5 ff. and 1:9 f. The clearest of these is of course the proleptic τὴν εἴσοδον ἡμῶν τὴν πρὸς ὑμᾶς, which obviously refers back to the wording of 1:9 and indicates that what the new section is taking up and explaining or expounding on (γάρ) is in fact the first part of the statement of the grounds for thanksgiving in the previous section, i.e. the nature of the senders' earlier entrance among the Thessalonians. But we can also observe certain similarities with the wording of 1:5 ff., e.g. the metapropositional οἴδατε (cf. also εἰδότες in 1:4)

---

[61] The primary metapropositional base is λέγω or a similar expression.
[62] See pp. 14 f. and 38 f. above.

and the motif of suffering (compare 1:6 and 2:2). The conjunction γάρ and these recurrences make it clear that the new section beginning at 2:1 is an explanation or exposition of the first part of the presentation of the reasons for the senders' thanksgiving, given in 1:5 ff. and 1:9 f.

That 2:1 really is the beginning of a new section is confirmed by the obvious shift in perspective. The explanatory comments in 1:8 ff. centred on the believers in Macedonia and Achaia and their knowledge of the Thessalonians. From 2:1 on, attention focuses entirely on 'our' coming to 'you' (τὴν εἴσοδον ἡμῶν τὴν πρὸς ὑμᾶς). Formally, this focus is manifested in the fact that the great majority of the finite verbs in 2:1-12 are in the first person plural, a characteristic feature of this section. Another characteristic is the repetition of the metapropositional verb οἴδατε (2:1, 2, 5, 11) and the related expressions μνημονεύετε (2:9) and ὑμεῖς μάρτυρες (2:10). The use of these verbs constantly calls on the Thessalonians to confirm what is being said. On a couple of occasions, even God is invoked as a witness of the truth of what is said (2:5, 10).

The opening assertion about the nature of 'our' entrance among 'you' is followed by two lengthy explanatory comments (2:3 f. and 2:5–8), which both begin with γάρ and which have a similar structure (... οὐ (οὔτε)... οὐδέ (οὔτε)... ἀλλὰ καθώς (... ὡς)... οὕτως...). They expound on 'our' approval by God and how unselfishly and lovingly 'we' behaved. This account culminates in the assertion that, out of love, 'we' were determined to share with 'you' not only the gospel, but also 'our' own selves. This assertion is followed up in 2:9 with a further explanatory comment (γάρ), beginning with an explicitly stated (secondary) metapropositional base (μνημονεύετε) and an address (ἀδελφοί), which is suggestive of a new start. The conjunction γάρ and the fact that the metapropositional base is closely related to the one that has dominated 2:1–8, however, shows that this is only a minor beginning. The proposition is expressed in two nouns — τὸν κόπον ἡμῶν καὶ τὸν μόχθον — which are then expanded on in an asyndetic clause. The new start here proves to be motivated by a slight shift in theme, from the senders' openness despite suffering and opposition to their strenuous efforts not to be a burden to the addressees.

In 2:10 there is another minor new beginning, marked by asyndeton and a further opening statement of the (secondary) metapropositional base: ὑμεῖς μάρτυρες καὶ ὁ θεός. This phrase can be said to refer back to and sum up the metapropositional statements occurring earlier in the section (οἴδατε in 2:1, 2 and 5, μνημονεύετε in 2:9, and θεὸς μάρτυς in 2:5), but at the same time it expresses them with greater force (compare οἴδατε/μνημονεύετε and ὑμεῖς μάρτυρες). This in itself indicates that what is beginning now is the conclusion of this section (i.e. the one that commenced at 2:1). This impression is underlined by the fact that the following proposition (ὡς ὁσίως...) is of a general and summarizing character, that the metapropositional base is highlighted yet again by a comparative clause (καθάπερ οἴδατε), that the latter clause begins with the intensified comparative particle καθάπερ (cf. the more forceful form of the opening metapropositional statement), and that the proposition ends with statements of consequences hinting at eschatological perfection (... εἰς τὸ περιπατεῖν ὑμᾶς ἀξίως τοῦ θεοῦ τοῦ καλοῦντος ὑμᾶς εἰς τὴν ἑαυτοῦ βασιλείαν καὶ δόξαν).

2:13-16

That 2:10 ff. really did constitute a close is confirmed by the fresh start in 2:13, marked by new instructions to the recipients and new indications of the theme. The opening main clause is both metapropositional and meta-communicative,[63] and indicates a clear shift in the metapropositional base. The subject of the metapropositional verb is now 'we' instead of 'you', and the change of grammatical subject is emphasized by the use of ἡμεῖς.[64] The metapropositional verb no longer expresses knowledge, but thankfulness (εὐχαριστοῦμεν). There is thus a significant shift in the metapropositional base in 2:13, but there is also an appreciable change in the content of the proposition: 2:1–12 was about how *'we'* spoke and acted; in 2:13, the proposition focuses on how *'you'* received the word.

In 2:13, then, there are marked changes compared with 2:1–12, at both the metapropositional and the propositional level. These changes, however, entail a clear recurrence of material from 1:2–10. Thus εὐχαριστοῦμεν τῷ θεῷ ἀδιαλείπτως (the metapropositional base) clearly refers back to the opening of the body of the letter in 1:2, and the new formulation of the reasons for thanksgiving in 2:13 (the proposition) — παραλαβόντες λόγον ἀκοῆς παρ' ἡμῶν τοῦ θεοῦ ἐδέξασθε... λόγον θεοῦ — looks back to δεξάμενοι τὸν λόγον... μετὰ χαρᾶς πνεύματος ἁγίου in 1:6.

The content of 2:13 is then explained in 2:14 in the following terms: ὑμεῖς... μιμηταὶ ἐγενήθητε... τῶν ἐκκλησιῶν τοῦ θεοῦ... ἐν τῇ Ἰουδαίᾳ ἐν Χριστῷ Ἰησοῦ, ὅτι τὰ αὐτὰ ἐπάθετε... καθὼς καὶ αὐτοί... This wording echoes ὑμεῖς μιμηταὶ ἡμῶν ἐγενήθητε καὶ τοῦ κυρίου, δεξάμενοι τὸν λόγον ἐν θλίψει πολλῇ... in 1:6. One difference of course is that in 1:6 the addressees

---

[63] Concerning this metapropositional and metacommunicative construction, see above, p. 48 f.

[64] The καί which precedes ἡμεῖς should probably not be linked specifically to that word. Similar constructions involving καί following an expression indicating a consequence or cause occur for example in Lk 1:35, 11:49; Jn 12:18; Acts 10:29; Rom 4:22; and 2 Cor 2:9. In other words, there is cause to suspect that these combinations are idiomatic. Cf. Bauer 1979, under καί.

are said to have become imitators of 'us' and of the Lord; in 2:14, imitators of the churches of God in Christ Jesus that are in Judaea. In 2:15, however, both the Lord and 'we' are mentioned among the victims of persecution. The statement of the reasons for the senders' thanksgiving in 2:13 ff. thus clearly refers back to the second part of the corresponding statement in 1:5 ff.

These recurrences of key motifs occurring prior to 2:1–12 indicate that the latter section is now at an end and a new one is beginning in which these motifs will be dealt with once again. They can thus be described as opening markers. At the same time, they confirm our earlier impression that 2:1–12 was subordinate in content terms to 1:2–10 and that its function was to explain or expound the first part of the statement of reasons for thanksgiving in 1:5 ff. and 1:9 f. Following this explanation or exposition, Paul now once more formulates the matter with which it dealt, i.e. the senders' description of their thanksgiving. This time he focuses on the second part of that description, confirming the suspicion that it was this part which carried the main emphasis.

This relationship between the two sections 2:1–12 and 2:13–16 is also suggested by the words καὶ διὰ τοῦτο in 2:13. Here, the particle καί suggests that the argument is continuing, thus counteracting the impression of a new main section. Like the opening καί in 1:6 and καί in 1:9, it can be said to lead the argument on from the first to the second part of the statement of the reasons for thanksgiving. The prepositional phrase διὰ τοῦτο is presumably anaphoric and indicates that the new statement of the senders' thanksgiving is based on the preceding account: it is because of the nature of their conduct among the Thessalonians that they can feel thankful for the latter having received their word and become imitators. This consequence-indicating διὰ τοῦτο corresponds to the cause-indicating γάρ in 2:1.

The consequence-describing διὰ τοῦτο in 2:13 and the recurrences of material from 1:2, 6 in 2:13 ff. suggest to the listener that the section beginning at 2:13 rounds off the one that began in 1:2. This impression is reinforced by the address in 2:14, which helps to maintain the intensity of the section. The section concludes with a couple of statements of consequences relating to the Jewish persecutors (εἰς τὸ ἀναπληρῶσαι... ἔφθασεν δέ... εἰς τέλος).[65] Whatever these statements refer to,[66] they have an eschatological flavour and express a kind of finality, an end-point.

---

[65] As has already been noted, considerable difficulties are involved in interpreting the last sentence. Whichever interpretation is chosen, however, it presumably refers at any rate to the consequences of the actions of opponents and persecutors — primarily of those to be found among the Jews, but secondarily also of Thessalonian persecutors. Furthermore, I consider that the reference to 'wrath' in immediate conjunction with 'filling up the measure of their sins' has an obviously eschatological ring to it.

[66] See p. 44.

This brings the section 1:2–2:16 to an end. My examination of it has been comparatively detailed, owing to the disagreement that exists concerning the relationships between its various parts. To sum up, my analysis has shown that the section consists of three subsections. In the first (1:2–10), the senders describe, in a lengthy construction, how they thank God for the Thessalonians. The reason for this is said to be that the senders and their gospel came to the Thessalonians in power and in the Holy Spirit and that the Thessalonians became imitators of them and of the Lord by receiving the word with joy inspired by the Spirit, amid affliction, thus becoming an example to all the believers in Macedonia and Achaia. The first section ends with a few explanatory comments on the concluding statement of consequences, giving Paul the opportunity to repeat the essential basis for their thanksgiving: the senders' entrance among the Thessalonians and the latter's favourable reaction to it. In the second subsection (2:1–12), the first of these aspects is then elaborated on in the form of a reminder to the Thessalonians of the bold and self-sacrificial conduct of the persecuted senders among them. In the light of this reminder, there is then (2:13–16) a restatement of the senders' gratitude for the Thessalonians' positive response to this conduct, which involved their becoming imitators of the persecuted churches in Judaea, of the Lord and of 'us'.

2:17–3:10

In 2:17, a new start is made, confirming the presence of a close in 2:13–16. The new beginning is marked by the conjunction δέ, the address ἀδελφοί and new instructions to the recipients and statements of the theme. The new construction begins with a secondary metapropositional base, which consists of the explicit and emphatic subject ἡμεῖς, a participial construction referring to time and circumstances — ἀπορφανισθέντες ἀφ' ὑμῶν πρὸς καιρὸν ὥρας, προσώπῳ οὐ καρδίᾳ — the finite verb ἐσπουδάσαμεν and the intensifying adverbials περισσοτέρως and ἐν πολλῇ ἐπιθυμίᾳ.[67] The proposition consists of the infinitive expression τὸ πρόσωπον ὑμῶν ἰδεῖν. In this way, a new situation and new theme are introduced into the text, namely the senders' strong desire and endeavour to see the Thessalonians again after being separated from them. At the same time, there are clear signs that what begins in 2:17 is not entirely new. There are for example no new instructions here concerning the communicative act of the letter itself, and the text continues to express the senders' favourable views of the Thessalonians.

[67] The primary metapropositional base is γνωρίζω ὑμῖν or some similar expression.

The earnest wish of the senders to see the Thessalonians once more is explained in a διότι-clause, which states that they wanted to come to them, but that Satan blocked their way. In 2:19 f. there are a couple more explanatory comments (γάρ), which are presumably intended to explain the senders' eagerness to see the Thessalonians again. The first of these is in the form of a rhetorical question. In the introductory chapter, we noted that rhetorical questions can function as thematic and instructive opening markers. The role of this rhetorical question is different, however: it is not to raise a question which will subsequently be examined, but to make a statement, namely that the addressees are the senders' hope, joy etc. This is also the reason why it is able to serve as an explanation (γάρ) of what has gone before. In 2:20, the same idea is expressed in declarative form.

Following the two explanatory comments in 2:19 f., the actual narrative account is resumed in 3:1. This is achieved with the help of the conjunction διό, which can be said to correspond to the preceding occurrences of γάρ and, as it were, take us back in the progression of thought to the narrative level. The minor new beginning which this entails is marked by a new construction with an instructive and thematic function. It begins with a secondary metapropositional base with a prominent reference to time and circumstances (μηκέτι στέγοντες) and with the finite verb (εὐδοκήσαμεν) in the aorist, which entails a shift in tense compared with the preceding verses. In the proposition — καταλειφθῆναι ἐν ᾿Αθήναις μόνοι — we can in particular note the place reference, and in the following clause there is also a detailed reference to a person (Τιμόθεον, τόν... συνεργὸν τοῦ θεοῦ). This introduces a new situation and a new phase into the narrative. What is now being related is how the senders dispatched Timothy to the Thessalonians to strengthen and encourage them in their present afflictions (3:1–3a). This occasions a couple of explanatory comments in 3:3b–4, to the effect that this is what the senders are destined for and that they have already prepared the Thessalonians for the possibility of persecution. These comments are introduced by a change of grammatical subject, emphasized by αὐτοί, and a (secondary) meta-propositional οἴδατε, and conclude with a repetition of the latter.[68] This part of the narrative is then rounded off in 3:5 with a clear echoing of the opening words of 3:1,[69] introduced by the consequence-indicating and text-summarizing διὰ τοῦτο.

The close in 3:5 is followed in 3:6 by a new beginning in the narrative. This is marked by the conjunction δέ, the time reference ἄρτι, which is stressed by

---

[68] The primary metapropositional base is λέγω or a similar expression.

[69] One difference is that here Paul expresses himself in the first person singular, rather than the plural. In my opinion, though, we should not make too much of this variation. A tendency to use the singular can also be seen in 2:18.

fronting, the subsequent statement of circumstances ἐλθόντος... καθάπερ καὶ ἡμεῖς ὑμᾶς, and the renewed personal reference to Τιμοθέου which that statement includes. In this way, it is indicated that the narrative is entering a new phase and focusing now on what Timothy's return has entailed.

At the same time, there are certain indications that this new phase is a closing one and that a major conclusion is at hand. The fact that the account of what has been happening, which began in 2:17, has now arrived at the word ἄρτι means in itself that it has reached a natural end-point. In the long presentation of circumstances which follows here, we read how, on his return, Timothy brought good news about the Thessalonians' faith and love and reported that they remembered the senders kindly and longed to see them, just as the senders long to see the Thessalonians. This draws attention once again to the key motif from the beginning of the section in 2:17 — the senders' desire to see the Thessalonians again — which also suggests that this section will shortly be drawing to a close. The impression of a conclusion is then reinforced by the fact that the long statement of circumstances is condensed into a pleonastic text-summarizing διὰ τοῦτο, which gives prominence to the main clause and its consequence-indicating character. Added emphasis is subsequently provided by the attention-attracting address ἀδελφοί. In this accentuated main clause, the consequence of Timothy's good news is said to be that the senders have been encouraged in all their distress and persecution. This statement is supported (γάρ)[70] in 3:9 f. with a rhetorical question which — like the one in 2:19 — corresponds to a statement: the senders cannot thank God enough for the joy they feel because of the Thessalonians and they constantly pray that they may see them again and supply what is lacking in their faith.[71] The section thus closes with yet another recurrence of the key motif of the opening in 2:17.

---

[70] B. Rigaux (1956, p. 482) and B. Johanson (1987, p. 107) claim that γάρ here is inferential rather than causal. To me, this assumption seems doubtful and unnecessary, since it is also quite possible to place a causal interpretation on the word. J. D. Denniston (1954, pp. 56 ff.) is sceptical about interpreting γάρ inferentially under any circumstances. He is, though, prepared to accept that γάρ can have an 'asseverative force', but only in the combinations καὶ γάρ, καὶ γὰρ οὖν, καὶ γάρ τοι, τοιγαροῦν, τοιγάρτοι and sometimes, perhaps, ἀλλὰ γάρ. Cf. pp. 150 f., note 24.

[71] B. Johanson (1987, p. 107; cf. also Wiles 1974 , pp. 177, 184) considers that a new section (3:9–13) begins at 3:9. The arguments for this are that Paul here, in a rhetorical question, reiterates earlier statements of thanksgiving and joy (1:2; 2:13; 2:19–20) and thus indicates a general relationship to all that has been said before, and that there is a shift here to a present-future perspective. As regards the rhetorical question, I have already explained why its function is not to present a new topic (cf. 2:19). The recurrences referred to are obvious, but serve as closing rather than opening markers (cf. e.g. Phil 2:17, in which Paul refers back to Phil 1:18). As regards the shift to a present-future perspective, that shift has already occurred in 3:6 (ἄρτι... ἐπιποθοῦντες ἡμᾶς ἰδεῖν καθάπερ καὶ ἡμεῖς ὑμᾶς). A further argument against seeing 3:8/3:9 as a significant transition is the use of γάρ, which suggests that the rhetorical question has an

In 3:6–10, however, there are not only references back to the opening of the section beginning at 2:17, but also to the one that starts at 1:2. When, in 3:6 ff., Paul says that Timothy has now brought good news of the Thessalonians' faith (τὴν πίστιν) and love (τὴν ἀγάπην) and reported that they remember the senders kindly (μνείαν ἡμῶν ἀγαθήν), and that this has encouraged the senders, he is re-echoing the favourable appraisal of the Thessalonians given in 1:2–7, where the senders said that they gave thanks to God (εὐχαριστοῦμεν τῷ θεῷ) for their work of faith (τοῦ ἔργου τῆς πίστεως), labour of love (τοῦ κόπου τῆς ἀγάπης) and steadfastness of hope, and for the fact that they had become imitators of the senders.[72] The reference back to 1:2–7 then becomes even clearer when, in the explanatory comment in 3:9 f., Paul asks how the senders can thank God enough (τίνα... εὐχαριστίαν δυνάμεθα τῷ θεῷ ἀνταποδοῦναι) for all the joy the Thessalonians have given them, and then talks of the senders praying to God night and day. These recurrences of material from 1:2–7 suggest that not only the section beginning at 2:17, but also the one that began in 1:2, is now being brought to a close.

What follows in 3:11–13 is a section of a clearly concluding character. It can be discussed whether it should be regarded as a component part of the section that began at 2:17 or assigned a more independent function.[73] The difference between the two is not all that great. I have opted for the latter alternative, as the opening in 3:11 is so distinct and 3:11–13 is of such a specific character.

With that interpretation, the account of the senders' thoughts and actions since being separated from the Thessalonians, which began at 2:17, is brought to a close at 3:10. To sum up, it can be said that this account consists of three stages: first, in 2:17 ff., it is explained how the senders have longed to see the Thessalonians again but have hitherto been prevented from doing so. Then, in 3:1–5, they explain how they sent Timothy to strengthen and encourage the recipients in their afflictions. Finally, in 3:6–10, they report how Timothy returned with good news of their faith and love and how this gave the senders renewed courage and life in their distress.

---

explanatory rather than an introductory function. Johanson follows B. Rigaux in interpreting this use of γάρ inferentially, but such an interpretation can be questioned (cf. note 70 above). In 3:11, on the other hand, there seems to me to be a distinct new beginning.

[72] Regarding the last of these points, it may in particular be noted that in both 1:5 and 2:1–12 attention is drawn to the addressees' knowledge of the senders' earlier conduct among them.

[73] Concerning a similar problem relating to Gal 6:14–16, see p. 194 below.

3:11–13

In 3:11, there is a clear new start, marked by the conjunction δέ, the stressed change of subject αὐτός... ὁ θεὸς καὶ πατὴρ ἡμῶν καὶ ὁ κύριος ἡμῶν Ἰησοῦς, and the shift in mood from indicative to optative, which entails a significant change in the metapropositional base. This short section consists of two wishes which both refer back to what has gone before, and it thus clearly has the character of a closing. The first wish (3:11) concerns the senders: that God and the Lord Jesus might direct their way to the Thessalonians. There is thus a clear link here with 2:17–3:10. The second (3:12 f.) relates to the Thessalonians: that the Lord might make them increase and abound in love for one another and for all, so that they may be strengthened in their hearts and be blameless before God at the coming of the Lord. This wish, too, takes up earlier key motifs, although the link with the section 2:17–3:10 is not as direct. The central motif here, the Thessalonians' love, was for example touched on as early as in the opening of the letter body in 1:3 and recurred towards the end of the previous section, in 3:6. The fact that this wish concludes with a description of consequences which looks ahead to the eschatological coming of the Lord is also a sign that there is a close here. If we choose the reading which has ἀμήν at the end of 3:13, that word of course also signals a conclusion.

The very fact that the ending that occurs here is so extensive and well prepared for gives the impression that this is a major close. As we saw in the introduction to this chapter,[74] several exegetes have even been reminded of a letter ending. While it is not necessary to go that far, it is clear that we are concerned here with a closing at one of the highest levels in the letter. The recurrences of material from the opening of the letter body at the end of the previous section and in this section suggest that this close relates to everything written in the letter so far. As we shall see, this is confirmed by the fact that 4:1 begins a section of a different character.

In 3:11, then, the section which began at 1:2 is brought to a close. That section consists of three parts: 1:2–2:16; 2:17–3:10; 3:11–13. The first of these parts describes the senders' thanksgiving to God for the Thessalonians' reaction to their earlier entrance among them. The second reports how the senders have longed to see the Thessalonians again after being separated from them, but have been prevented from doing so and have therefore sent Timothy to strengthen and encourage them, and how the latter has subsequently returned with good news of the Thessalonians' faith and love. In the third part, finally, the senders express wishes regarding themselves and the Thessalonians.

---

[74] See p. 40 above.

4:1–5:25

4:1–12

The occurrence of a close in 3:11–13 is confirmed by the clear new beginning in 4:1, marked by λοιπὸν οὖν, the address ἀδελφοί and a construction that is clearly instructive and thematic. This construction begins with a metapropositional and metacommunicative clause (ἐρωτῶμεν ὑμᾶς καὶ παρακαλοῦμεν ἐν κυρίῳ ᾿Ιησοῦ) which makes it clear that Paul is now moving on to direct exhortations. In 1:2–3:10, favourable views of the Thessalonians and their conduct were expressed, and 3:11–13 included wishes concerning their development, but so far there have been no direct exhortations in the letter. The metapropositional and metacommunicative clause in 4:1 therefore indicates a distinct change in the character of the text.

The proposition, the actual content of the exhortation, is then set out in a ἵνα-clause. It begins with two comparative subordinate clauses, referring to what the Thessalonians have previously received from the senders concerning how they ought to live in order to please God, and to how they are in fact living. These references serve as headings and provide a starting-point and 'benchmarks' for the exhortation. The actual exhortation then follows, after a repetition of the conjunction ἵνα from the beginning of the clause.[75] The fronted subordinate clauses and the repetition of the conjunction lend extra emphasis to the proposition, which is that the Thessalonians should abound even more in the conduct that is indicated by the two benchmarks. These benchmarks correspond exactly to the points that were favourably assessed in 1:2–3:10, namely that the Thessalonians received the senders' message and became imitators of them and of the Lord (1:5 f.; 2:13 ff.), with the result that their lives are now characterized by faith and love (1:3; 2:6). The actual exhortation corresponds to the wish expressed by Paul in 3:12 f. Thus, at the propositional level, the new section beginning in 4:1 is closely linked to the preceding one. What is new is the metapropositional base, the fact that Paul is now directly urging the addressees to act in the manner described. There is therefore reason to ask whether the opening combination of particles λοιπὸν οὖν does not have more of an inferential force than is usually assumed. This does not prevent it also marking a transition to a new phase in the text.[76]

---

[75] Many manuscripts lack the preceding ἵνα.

[76] These alternative meanings of the words are not mutually exclusive; on the contrary, they overlap. They can be regarded as analytically determined subdivisions of a single semantic field. As such, they are partly determined by the 'logic' of the analytical language used, which need not always coincide with the logic of Greek. Cf. Cavallin 1941, pp. 133 f., 137, 144. Concerning the use of λοιπόν to mark a transition to a new phase in a text, see e.g. Cavallin 1941, pp. 136–40, and Blomqvist 1969, p. 102.

The opening exhortation in 4:1 is followed by an explanatory comment (γάρ), beginning in 4:2 with the secondary metapropositional base οἴδατε,[77] which indicates that what now follows is a reminder. The proposition consists of an indirect question, indicating that this reminder concerns the instructions which the addressees previously received from the senders.

The indirect question is then answered in the following verses, as the conjunction γάρ suggests. The beginning of the answer is marked by the secondary metapropositional base τοῦτο... ἐστιν θέλημα τοῦ θεοῦ, ὁ ἁγιασμὸς ὑμῶν. In the latter, the cataphoric text-summarizing τοῦτο can be described as an opening marker in its own right. The proposition then consists of a number of infinitives in 4:3–6, which pose several problems of interpretation. The infinitives in 4:3–5 seem at any rate to refer to sexual morals, but it is unclear whether those in v. 6 relate to sexual morality, legal proceedings or commerce.[78] The long infinitive construction ends in 4:6 with a description of the eschatological consequences of the conduct described and with a comparative clause (καθὼς καὶ προείπαμεν ὑμῖν καὶ διεμαρτυράμεθα) which serves as a reminder of the metapropositional bases in 4:2 f. The concluding character of the statement of consequences is reinforced by the anaphoric text-summarizing πάντων τούτων. Before the whole of the reminder section that began in 4:2 is brought to a close, however, Paul adds in 4:7 f. an explanatory comment (γάρ) on the statement of consequences in 4:6, referring to God's calling and man's responsibility. The strengthened inferential particle τοιγαροῦν marks the fact that the section is being brought to an end.

In 4:9 a distinct new start is made, signalled by the conjunction δέ and a construction which is clearly instructive and thematic. The construction begins with the theme-indicating prepositional phrase περί... τῆς φιλαδελφίας, which is then followed by the secondary metapropositional bases οὐ χρείαν ἔχετε γράφειν ὑμῖν. In the preceding verses (4:2–8), Paul has mainly dwelt on things which the Thessalonians should *not* do, things that the Lord avenges (4:6). With the help of the theme-indicating prepositional phrase, the focus now changes to something positive, something which they should do, i.e. show brotherly love. At the propositional level, there is thus a clear shift in the text here. This is not the case at the metapropositional level, however, since οὐ χρείαν ἔχετε γράφειν ὑμῖν, like οἴδατε in 4:2, gives the text the character of a reminder. This conveys the impression that the new section is at the same level of the text as 4:2–8.

---

[77] The primary metapropositional base is λέγω or a similar expression.
[78] See e.g. the discussion in Holtz 1986, pp. 161 ff.

The reason Paul does not consider it necessary to write to the Thessalonians about brotherly love is then set out in two explanatory comments (γάρ): they have themselves been taught it by God and already practise it in relation to all the brothers in Macedonia.

In 4:10b there is another clear opening, marked by the conjunction δέ, the address ἀδελφοί and a new instructive and thematic construction. This time the metapropositional base, which here is also metacommunicative, comes first: παρακαλοῦμεν... ὑμᾶς. It indicates a resumption of direct exhortation, following the reminders that began at 4:2, and thus looks back to 4:1. The proposition is then set out in the form of infinitives. The first of these is περισσεύειν μᾶλλον, which also echoes 4:1. These clear recurrences at both the metapropositional and the propositional level indicate that the section which opens in 4:10b is bringing to an end what began in 4:1. The recurrence of material from 4:1 also explains why there is no need to elaborate on what is meant in 4:10b by περισσεύειν μᾶλλον: the expression is explained by 4:1 and by the explanatory sections (4:2–8 and 4:9–10a) linked to that verse.

Apart from περισσεύειν μᾶλλον, the proposition includes a further infinitive construction, urging the Thessalonians to aspire to live quietly, to mind their own affairs and to work with their hands (cf. 2:9). The following comparative clause καθὼς ὑμῖν παρηγγείλαμεν relates this exhortation, too, to the benchmarks set out in 4:1, involving yet another recurrence of ideas from that verse. In the closing ἵνα-clause in 4:12 we then find a further echo of 4:1 in the expression περιπατῆτε εὐσχημόνως. The section 4:1–12 is thus brought to a close, and this is confirmed by the fresh start in 4:13.

To sum up, 4:1–12 can be said to be paraenetic in character and to be linked to the exposition set out in 1:2–3:13. It begins with an exhortation to the Thessalonians to abound even more in what they have received from the senders and in the way they are actually living. In 4:2–8 they are then reminded of the senders' instructions, and in 4:9–10a the text touches on how they practise brotherly love at present. Against that background, the exhortation to abound even more is repeated in 4:10b–12, where it is combined with a call to lead quiet, orderly lives.

4:13–5:11

4:13–18

In 4:13 there is then a distinct new beginning, marked by the conjunction δέ, the address ἀδελφοί and a new instructive and thematic construction. The latter begins with the metapropositional bases οὐ θέλομεν... ὑμᾶς ἀγνοεῖν, which indicate that Paul is now moving on from exhortation (4:1–12) to information, although it turns out that this is not the whole story. The ἵνα-clause that follows makes it clear that the information has an edifying purpose, that it is intended to offer comfort and hope, and when the new section eventually concludes with an exhortation, it becomes clear that the information provided also has a paraenetic purpose.

The actual content of this information, the proposition, is at first only hinted at in the prepositional phrase περὶ τῶν κοιμωμένων, which states that it relates to 'those who are sleeping' (i.e. have died). There is thus a shift in 4:13 at the propositional level, too. What Paul wants to say about those who are sleeping is then set out in an explanatory comment (γάρ): God will bring them with Jesus, who died and rose again. This assertion is then supported and expounded in 4:15–17 with the help of a saying of Jesus, which describes how the dead will rise at the coming of the Lord and be taken together with those who are alive to meet the Lord. The beginning of this exposition is marked by the metacommunicative clause τοῦτο... ὑμῖν λέγομεν ἐν λόγῳ κυρίου, in which the cataphoric text-summarizing τοῦτο can be ascribed an opening-marking function of its own. The ending of the exposition is hinted at by the description of the final consequence in 4:17, which begins with καί and the anaphoric text-summarizing οὕτως. One can also note the use of σὺν κυρίῳ, echoing the starting-point in 4:14. There then follows an exhortation regarding what the addressees should do with the information they have been given. It is a kind of statement of consequences, beginning with ὥστε. Its consequence-indicating character is also brought out by the text-summarizing expression ἐν τοῖς λόγοις τούτοις. The addressees are urged to encourage one another with the information they have been given. This closing exhortation thus links up with the statement of purpose at the beginning of the section, which was that the information was being provided so that the addressees would not grieve. This brings 4:13–18 to a close.

5:1–11

The close in 4:17 f. is followed by a new beginning in 5:1, marked by the conjunction δέ, the address ἀδελφοί and a new instructive and thematic construction. This time the topic-indicating prepositional phrase comes first: περί... τῶν χρόνων καὶ τῶν καιρῶν. It states that the new section is about times and dates. In isolation, this topic statement would be fairly empty of meaning, but it becomes comprehensible in the light of the description of the Parousia in the preceding section. The shift at the propositional level that occurs at 5:1 is thus fairly modest, as is the change at the metapropositional level, since the following (secondary) metapropositional bases — οὐ χρείαν ἔχετε ὑμῖν γράφεσθαι — give the ensuing account the character of a reminder.[79] Here too, then, we are concerned with information (cf. 4:13), although it just so happens that the information concerned is already known. It therefore seems justifiable to regard the opening in 5:1 as one of only moderate importance and to keep the new section together with the preceding one (4:13–18). This view is eventually confirmed by the fact that the new section ends with an exhortation that is strongly reminiscent of the one in 4:18 and which clearly refers back to the statement of purpose in 4:13.

The opening assertion in 5:1 about the addressees not needing to have anything written to them about times and dates is followed in 5:2 f. by an explanatory comment (γάρ) stating what the Thessalonians already know about this subject but are being reminded of, namely that the day of the Lord will come like a thief in the night and bring destruction upon those who say there is peace and security. The comment begins with the secondary metapropositional base αὐτοί... ἀκριβῶς οἴδατε, further underscoring that this is a reminder.

In 5:4, the Thessalonians are then contrasted with those who say that there is peace and security and who then suffer destruction. In contrast with such people, it is said that the Thessalonians are not in darkness and that the day of the Lord will therefore not surprise them like a thief. The minor new beginning which this contrast entails is marked by the stressed change of subject (ὑμεῖς), the conjunction δέ and the address ἀδελφοί. At the end of 5:5 there is a change from the second to the first person plural, facilitated and possibly occasioned by the parallels between the circumstances of the Thessalonians and those of the senders (see e.g. 1:6 and 2:14 ff.).

5:6–10 then sets out the paraenetic consequences of the assertions in 5:4 f.[80] The minor transition which this entails is marked by ἄρα οὖν and the shift from the indicative to the subjunctive mood. The paraenetic consequences for 'us' are said to be that 'we' should keep awake and be sober, and put on the breastplate of faith and love and the helmet of hope. This exposition of the paraenetic consequences is rounded off with a ἵνα-clause describing the final consequences and referring back to the key motif of 4:13–18, σὺν κυρίῳ (4:14, 17).

As at the end of 4:13–18, in 5:11 there follows a closing exhortation about what the addressees should do with the teaching they have been given, which is to encourage and build up one another. This exhortation thus ties in very closely in terms of its content, too, with the one in 4:18, indicating that the intention stated in 4:13 is still relevant and reinforcing the impression of a

---

[79] The primary metapropositional base is λέγω or a similar expression.

[80] 5:5b should perhaps be considered to be part of the section 5:6–10. In support of such a view, it may be noted that both the asyndeton and the shift from second to first person may have an opening-marking function. However, it makes little difference to our understanding of the line of thought in the text which of these alternatives is chosen.

65

link between 4:13–18 and 5:1–11. Like the closing exhortation in 4:18, this one begins with an inferential particle, this time διό. It ends with the comparative clause καθὼς καὶ ποιεῖτε, which can be described as a recurrence of the reminder motif of 5:1 f.[81] These recurrences suggest that both the section that began at 5:1 and the one that commenced at 4:13 are being brought to a close here.

To sum up. the section 4:13–5:11 can be said to consist of teaching whose purpose is to encourage and build up the addressees. In the first subsection (4:13–18). this teaching is about God causing the dead to rise and live with the Lord. In the second subsection (5:1–11), the Thessalonians are reminded that the day of the Lord will come like a thief in the night for those who believe themselves to be safe and secure, but that this will not happen to them, since they are children of light, provided that they do not yield to the deeds of darkness. but remain awake and sober. Both subsections close with an appeal to the Thessalonians to encourage one another with the teaching they have received.

5:12–22

The close in 5:10 f. is confirmed by a fresh start in 5:12, marked by the conjunction δέ, the address ἀδελφοί and a new instructive and thematic construction. The latter begins with a metapropositional base which is also metacommunicative: ἐρωτῶμεν... ὑμᾶς. This indicates that the text is once again turning to direct exhortation after 4:13–5:11, which in a sense was a section of a more informative character. At the metapropositional level, therefore. the new section echoes 4:1–12 (see 4:1, 10b), which can be seen as an initial hint that the major section beginning at 4:1 will soon be brought to a close. At the propositional level, on the other hand, there is no clear recurrence of material from 4:1–12, although the exhortations here, too, may well be assumed to be subordinate to the general ethical benchmarks stated in 4:1. The content of the proposition is set out in a couple of infinitives, calling on the addressees to respect and esteem those who have charge of them in the Lord. This is followed by an appeal to the Thessalonians to be at peace among themselves.

Although there is no close in 5:13, there is another new start in 5:14. This is marked by the conjunction δέ, the address ἀδελφοί and a new statement of the metapropositional base: παρακαλοῦμεν... ὑμᾶς. The content of the proposition is then spelt out in a number of short, asyndetically juxtaposed

---

[81] Cf. also the reference in 4:1 to the Thessalonians' actual conduct as an ethical benchmark.

exhortations, urging the addressees to admonish the disorderly, encourage the faint hearted, help the weak and be patient with everyone. While the exhortations in 5:12 f. concerned the Thessalonians' attitudes to their leaders, those set out here relate to their attitudes to the weak. The new beginning and the short asyndetic clauses help to maintain the intensity of the section, which can also be seen as an indication that a major close is approaching. In 5:15 the intensity is then reduced somewhat by a longer, twofold exhortation not to repay evil for evil, but to seek to do good to one another and to all. This is the final exhortation concerning the social sphere.

In 5:16 the intensity is once again heightened by three more brief, asyndetically juxtaposed exhortations, now dealing with spiritual rather than community life. They are positive entreaties to rejoice, to pray without ceasing and to give thanks, corresponding exactly to the senders' conduct as described in 1:2, 2:13 and 3:9 f. This recurrence can be regarded as an indication that the letter is drawing to a close. There then follows an explanatory comment (γάρ) to the effect that this is the will of God. This comment breaks the pattern and lowers the intensity, thus setting off these three exhortations as a unit. Its rounding-off function is also indicated by the anaphoric text-summarizing τοῦτο and the metapropositional base θέλημα θεοῦ ἐν Χριστῷ ᾽Ιησοῦ εἰς ὑμᾶς, which expresses an assessment of what has just been said.

This is followed by a further group of short exhortations, again mainly asyndeta, which also concern the spiritual life. Unlike those that preceded them, they are negative in emphasis. The first two call on the addressees not to quench the Spirit and not to despise the words of prophets. The three remaining ones are linked, and urge the Thessalonians to test everything, hold fast to what is good and abstain from every form of evil. Being connected together, they break the pattern and somewhat lower the intensity of the text, which could be regarded as hinting at a close. In addition, they may possibly begin with the conjunction δέ, in which case the break in the pattern is even clearer, but this reading is somewhat uncertain. The ending here is thus fairly weakly marked, but it is confirmed by the new beginning in 5:23. It can also be deduced from the latter that the conclusion at this point relates to the whole of the directly exhortatory text which began at 5:12.

In summary, it can be said that 5:12–22 is directly exhortatory and thus looks back to 4:1–12, which can be seen as an initial indication that the major section beginning in 4:1 is drawing to a close. The approach of a major ending is also indicated by the great intensity of this section. It begins with an exhortation to respect leaders and to be at peace (5:12 f.). This is followed by three groups of exhortations, the first (5:14–15) concerning community life, chiefly attitudes to the weak, the second (5:16–18) and the third (5:19–22) relating to the spiritual life. The difference between the second and third groups is that the second one is expressed in positive, the third in more negative terms.

5:23–24

As at the end of the account-type section 1:2–3:13, towards the end of the exhortatory section 4:1–5:25 there is a short passage expressing wishes. It is linked both formally and in terms of content to the corresponding section in 3:11 ff. In both cases, the text expresses a wish that God or the Lord will act in such a way that the Thessalonians will be found to be blameless at the coming of the Lord Jesus Christ. The present section differs from 3:11 ff. in that it does not include any wish regarding the senders, which suggests that the letter is ultimately concerned with the situation of the addressees.

The opening of this section is marked by the stressed change of grammatical subject (αὐτός... ὁ θεὸς τῆς εἰρήνης), the conjunction δέ, and the change of mood from imperative to optative, which entails a shift at the metapropositional level. The recurrences in relation to 3:11–13, i.e. the ending of the previous main section, and the expression of wishes give this section as such the character of a close and reinforce the impression that a major conclusion (of the main section that began at 4:1 and of the letter as a whole) is at hand. The section itself ends with a statement of the conviction that God is faithful and will fulfil the wishes that are expressed.

5:25

In 5:25 another new start is made, marked by asyndeton, the address ἀδελφοί in initial position, and a shift from the optative to the imperative. This verse consists of an exhortation to the addressees to pray for the senders (5:25), and is followed by an appeal to them to greet all the brothers with a holy kiss (5:26), a solemn command by the Lord to read the letter to all the brothers (5:27), and a wish of grace. It is debatable which of these elements should be included with the body of the letter and which should be regarded as part of the letter closing. With some hesitation, I have chosen to include the relatively separate exhortation in 5:25 in the letter body and the remaining verses in the conclusion. My reasons for doing so are as follows:

1. When determining the extent of the opening section of the letter, I defined (in note 57) the opening and closing of a letter as 'conventional and formulaic elements at the beginning and end of a letter which are not integrated syntactically or in terms of content with the rest of the text'. I feel

that this definition is applicable to the greeting, solemn charge and wish of grace in 5:26–28. The exhortation in 5:25, on the other hand, seems to me to be at a different level and to be more integrated with the preceding text. Several times in the first half of the letter, the senders mention their troubles, past and present (1:6; 2:2, 9, 16; 3:4, 7). The appeal in 5:25 is made against that background and thus relates in content terms to the main body of the letter. We can also note that another key motif of the first half of the letter is the senders' prayers for the addressees (1:2; 2:13; 3:9 f.; cf. also 3:11 ff.). The exhortation in 5:25 corresponds to this.[82]

2. As regards the question of syntactic integration, it may be noted that, while the exhortation in 5:25 is added asyndetically, the initial position of ἀδελφοί gives the impression that this is a digression or addition, i.e. a section that is subordinate in terms of content, rather than the beginning of something completely new.[83] In addition, it may be observed that, if the word καί is read before περὶ ἡμῶν,[84] the exhortation is linked directly to the wishes that precede it.

For these reasons, I regard the exhortation in 5:25 as a relatively independent appeal which concludes the section 4:1–5:25 and the body of the letter. In content terms, it involves a recurrence of the prayer motif found in 1:2, 2:13 and 3:9 f.

The exhortation of 5:25 thus brings 4:1–5:25 to a close. The latter section contains exhortations to the addressees in the light of the account presented in 1:2–3:13, and consists of five subsections. The first (4:1–12) urges the Thessalonians to abound even more with regard to what they have received and what they are already doing. In the second (4:13–5:11), teaching is given about the coming of the Lord, and the addressees are urged to encourage and build up one another with this teaching. The third (5:12–22) consists of exhortations concerning community and spiritual life. The fourth (5:23–24) and the fifth (5:25) comprise concluding wishes regarding the addressees and a closing exhortation to them to pray for the senders.

5:26–28

The closing section of 1 Thessalonians thus consists of an exhortation to the addressees to greet all the brothers with a holy kiss (5:26), a solemn charge to

---

[82] In Galatians, too, the body of the letter closes with a section containing wishes (6:14–16), followed by a single, relatively independent exhortation (6:17), which clearly relates to what has gone before in the letter. What I propose here as the closing section of the letter body in 1 Thessalonians is thus not without parallel.

[83] Cf. e.g. Rom 10:1; 1 Cor 14:20; Gal 3:15; 6:1; Phil 3:13.

[84] This reading is uncertain.

them by the Lord to read the letter to all the brothers (5:27) and a wish of grace (5:28). The first and last of these elements occur fairly widely in Paul's letters.[85]

With that, the basic analysis of 1 Thessalonians is complete. What remains to be done now is to summarize and analyse the observations that have been made. We shall begin with a tabular overview of the letter.

C. Arrangement of the text

The tabular overview below includes both headings summarizing the line of thought in the letter and details of the most important transition markers. As regards the headings, I have tried as far as possible to base them on the instructive and thematic opening and closing markers found in each section. No attempt is made to present an exhaustive listing of the transition markers in the letter; the aim is to give an idea of the most significant ones. By and large, markers have been categorized in line with the presentation in chapter 1, using the following abbreviations:

Om = Opening marker

Cm = Closing marker

Mc = Metacommunicative clause

Mp = Statement of a metapropositional base

Mp(s) = Statement of a secondary metapropositional base

Q = Rhetorical question

H = Heading- or pointer-type indication of topic

Chr = Chronological statement

Re = Recurrence

Top = Other indication of topic (e.g. stressed change of grammatical subject, reference to place, reference to person)

W = Wish or expressed expectation

Ex = Closing exhortation

Ass = Concluding assessment or evaluation

Tsum = Text-summarizing expression

---

[85] See e.g. 1 Cor 16:19–24, 2 Cor 13:12 f., Phil 4:21 ff., Philem 23 ff.

Esch = Eschatological perspective

Asyn = Asyndeton

Ad = Address

Int = Other intensity-heightening phenomenon (e.g. use of short asyndetic clauses, repetition)

Particles, both contrastive and consequence-indicating, are written out in full. Other connective particles, which are not actual opening markers but which are of significance in understanding the sequence of thought, are given in parentheses. Certain other particles with the function of closing markers, such as ἀμήν and οὕτως, are also quoted. Opening markers are given in the following order: contrastive, instructive and thematic, attention-attracting and intensity-heightening. Closing markers are given in the following order: instructive and thematic, attention-attracting and intensity-heightening. The different types are separated by semicolons.

On the basis of the analysis, the following overview of the letter can be given:

I. 1:1 Opening of the letter:

   1. 1:1a Particulars of senders and recipients

   2. 1:1b Wish of grace and peace

II. 1:2–5:25 Body of the letter: — *Om: Mp/Mc, H; Ad. Cm: W, Re, Esch, Ex; Ad, Int.*

   1. 1:2–3:13 Account of the senders' thankfulness for and joy in the addressees' faith and love — *Om: See above. Cm: W, Re, Esch; Ad, Int, [ἀμήν].*

      A. 1:2–2:16 Account of how the senders thank God for their entrance in power and the Spirit among the addressees and for the latter's *imitatio* of them and the Lord in joyfully receiving the word amid affliction — *Om: See above. Cm: καὶ διὰ τοῦτο καί, Re, Esch; Ad.*

         a. 1:2–10 Statement of the actual thanksgiving — *Om: See above. Cm: Re, Esch.*

         b. 2:1–12 Reminder of the nature of the senders' entrance among them — *Om: (γάρ); Mp(s), H, Top; Ad. Cm: Re, Esch.*

            α. 2:1–8 The boldness and self-sacrifice of the persecuted senders, following suffering and persecution — *Om: See above.*

            β. 2:9 The senders' toil and blamelessness as they proclaimed the gospel — *Om: (γάρ); Mp(s), H; Ad.*

            γ. 2:10–12 Summarizing statement about the senders' blamelessness in conjunction with their preaching — *Om: Asyn; Mp(s), Re. Cm: See above.*

c. 2:13–16 Renewed statement of thanksgiving in the light of the reminder — *Om: (καὶ διὰ τοῦτο καί); Mp/Mc, Re. Cm: See above.*

B. 2:17–3:10 Account of the senders' desire to visit the addressees and their thankfulness and joy on receiving through Timothy the encouraging news of the addressees' faith and love — *Om: δέ; Mp(s), Chr; Ad. Cm: διὰ τοῦτο, Re; Ad, Int.*

a. 2:17–20 Account of how the senders had longed to visit the addressees, but been prevented from doing so — *Om: See above.*

b. 3:1–5 Account of how the senders decided to send Timothy to the addressees to strengthen them in their affliction — *Om: (διό); Mp(s); Chr. Cm: διὰ τοῦτο, Re.*

α. 3:1–3a Account of the sending of Timothy and its purpose — *Om: See above.*

β. 3:3b–4 Reminder that this is what the senders are destined for — *Om: (γάρ); Mp(s). Cm: καθώς, Re.*

γ. 3:5 Repeated account of the sending of Timothy and its purpose — *Om: (διὰ τοῦτο); Re. Cm: See above.*

c. 3:6–10 Account of how the senders have been encouraged in their distress by the good news of the addressees' faith and love brought by Timothy — *Om: δέ; Chr, Top. Cm: See above.*

C. 3:11–13 Concluding wishes concerning the senders and addressees: May God direct 'our' way to 'you' and may the Lord make 'you' abound in love and strengthen 'your' hearts so that 'you' are blameless at his coming — *Om: δέ; Mp, Top. Cm: See above.*

2. 4:1–5:25 Appeals and exhortations to the addressees in the light of the above account — *Om: λοιπὸν οὖν; Mp/Mc, H; Ad. Cm: See above (1:2–5:25).*

A. 4:1–12 Appeal and exhortation to the addressees to abound even more as regards what they have received from the senders and what they are already doing — *Om: See above. Cm: Re.*

a. 4:1 The actual appeal and exhortation — *Om: See above.*

b. 4:2–8 Reminder of the senders' previous instructions — *Om: (γάρ); Mp(s). Cm: διότι... καθώς... τοιγαροῦν, Tsum, Re, Esch.*

α. 4:2 Reference to the earlier instructions — *Om: See above.*

β. 4:3–8 Statement concerning the will of God — *Om: Mp(s); H. Cm: See above.*

c. 4:9–10a Reference to the addressees' existing brotherly love — <u>*Om:*</u> δέ, Mp(s), H.

d. 4:10b–12 Repeated exhortation to abound even more and to lead quiet and orderly lives — <u>*Om:*</u> δέ; Mp/Mc, Re. <u>*Cm:*</u> *See above.*

B. 4:13–5:11 Teaching about the coming of the Lord, as an encouragement and exhortation to the addressees — <u>*Om:*</u> δέ; Mp, H; Ad. <u>*Cm:*</u> διό, Ex, Re.

a. 4:13–18 Teaching about the resurrection of the dead at the coming of the Lord, to comfort the addressees — <u>*Om:*</u> *See above.* <u>*Cm:*</u> ὥστε, Tsum, Re.

α. 4:13 Opening statement of purpose — <u>*Om:*</u> *See above.*

β. 4:14 Statement about the resurrection of the dead with Jesus — <u>*Om:*</u> (γάρ).

γ. 4:15–17 Saying of Jesus to support this statement — <u>*Om:*</u> (γάρ); Mp/Mc; H. <u>*Cm:*</u> οὕτως, Re.

δ. 4:18 Closing exhortation to the addressees to encourage one another with this — <u>*Om:*</u> (ὥστε); Re. <u>*Cm:*</u> *See above.*

b. 5:1–11 Teaching about the sudden coming of the day of the Lord, to encourage and build up the addressees — <u>*Om:*</u> δέ; Mp(s); H; Ad. <u>*Cm:*</u> *See above.*

α. 5:1 Statement concerning what the addressees know about times and dates — <u>*Om:*</u> *See above.*

β. 5:2–3 Reminder that the day of the Lord will come like a thief in the night — <u>*Om:*</u> (γάρ); Mp(s), Top.

γ. 5:4–5 Statement about the addressees being children of light and of the day — <u>*Om:*</u> δέ; Top; Ad.

δ. 5:6–10 Exhortations to 'us' to keep awake and be sober — <u>*Om:*</u> (ἄρα οὖν); Mp. <u>*Cm:*</u> ἵνα, Re.

ε. 5:11 Closing exhortation to the addressees to encourage and build up one another, as indeed they are doing — <u>*Om:*</u> (διό); Re. <u>*Cm:*</u> *See above.*

C. 5:12–22 Appeals and exhortations to the addressees — <u>*Om:*</u> δέ; Mp/Mc, Re; Ad, Int. <u>*Cm:*</u> *See above (1:2–5:25).*

a. 5:12–13 Appeal for respect for their leaders and for mutual peace — <u>*Om:*</u> *See above.*

b. 5:14–22 Exhortations — *Om: δέ; Mp/Mc, Re; Ad. Cm: See above.*

α. 5:14–15 Exhortations to care for one another and for all — *Om: See above.*

β. 5:16–18 Exhortations to rejoice, pray and give thanks — *Om: Int.*

γ. 5:19–22 Warnings concerning the Spirit and prophecies — *Om: Int.*

D. 5:23–24 Concluding wishes concerning the addressees: May God sanctify and preserve 'you', so that 'you' are blameless at the coming of the Lord — *Om: δέ; Mp, Top. Cm: See above (1:2–5:25).*

E. 5:25 Concluding exhortation to the addressees to pray for the senders — *Om: Asyn; Mp; Ad. Cm: See above (1:2–5:25).*

III. 5:26–28 Closing of the letter:

1. 5:26 Exhortation to the addressees to greet all the brothers with a holy kiss

2. 5:27 Solemn charge to the addressees, by the Lord, to read the letter to all the brothers

3. 5:28 Wish of grace

D. Transition markers

The opening chapter included a general discussion of what types of phenomena could *conceivably* serve as transition markers. This discussion was conducted entirely in terms of the logical aspects of language. However, language also has a conventional dimension, and we must also expect transition markers to be contextual and relative. I now wish to comment very briefly therefore on what transition markers do in fact occur in the First Letter to the Thessalonians, and how they operate. I shall not attempt to give an exhaustive account; my aim is simply to identify and describe certain tendencies and recurring patterns, with a view to enhancing our familiarity with this particular facet of the language of 1 Thessalonians and, by extension, the linguistic habits of Paul and of Koine Greek.

This section consists of five parts. First, I comment in general terms on the interaction between different markers, before going on to look in turn at instructive and thematic opening markers, the corresponding closing markers, contrastive opening markers and finally attention-attracting and intensity-heightening transition markers.

Interaction

The basic analysis above made it clear that the various opening and closing markers interact and are interdependent. We can take the transition at 4:18/5:1 as an example. The first sign that a close is approaching is the anaphoric text-summarizing οὕτως in 4:17 and the following clause, which refers back to 4:14 and thus suggests that what is being brought to an end here is the report of the saying of Jesus which began at 4:15. That this is indeed the case is confirmed by the following ὥστε-clause in 4:18, which refers back to the statement of purpose in the instructive and thematic construction that began this section in 4:13. This suggests that the whole of this section is now drawing to a close.

These closing markers are thus related to earlier instructions to the recipients and indications of the theme, and their close-marking function is clearly dependent on that relationship. Nevertheless, the section beginning at 4:13 need not have ended in 4:18. Paul could, for example, have added more exhortations or an explanatory comment of some kind. It is only with the new beginning in 5:1 that it becomes evident that the preceding section has indeed been brought to a close.

The opening in 5:1, however, is in turn dependent on the preceding ending and its instructions and thematic statements. This is indicated by the contrastive particle δέ. The nature of the contrast is made clear by the following instructive and thematic construction, which indicates that the contrast is located primarily at the propositional level, while at the metapropositional level the new section has a clear link with the preceding one (both are intended to provide information). The brevity of the statement of the theme, however, presupposes a knowledge of the subject-matter of the previous section and thus reveals a certain degree of coherence at the propositional level as well. At the same time, the address ἀδελφοί underlines the fresh start to some extent. It is therefore apparent that the precise nature and significance of the opening only becomes clear from the interaction between the different opening markers and the preceding closing markers, which in turn were dependent on earlier opening markers. And so it continues throughout the text. This should be borne in mind when we go on to discuss the individual markers and their characteristics.

Before we do so, however, a few more general comments on the interaction between markers need to be made. First, we can note that transitions are as a rule more strongly marked at higher levels of division of the text than at lower ones. Second, it may be observed that closings in particular are weakly marked at the lower levels. This can be illustrated by the following table of the average number of markers recorded per transition at the different levels of division:

	Transition markers	Opening markers	Closing markers
1st level	14	4	10
2nd level	8.3	3.7	4.6
3rd level	5.9	3.7	2.2
4th level	1.8	1.5	0.3

These two points are really quite natural, but nevertheless worth making. At the higher levels, sections are generally longer and more heterogeneous than at the lower levels, and the listener therefore needs clearer guidance to understand how the text hangs together. The low frequency of *closing* markers at the lower levels is probably due to the fact that endings are perceived as more disruptive of an ongoing exposition than openings.

Instructive and thematic opening markers

As the example above showed, instructive and thematic markers are of fundamental importance in enabling the listener to perceive the precise significance and nature of a transition. Clearly their mutual interaction plays a key role in this respect. We can also note, however, that instructive and thematic markers look somewhat different at different levels. At the highest level of division we find constructions (1:2–7; 4:1) which contain a metapropositional base indicating a wish or assessment on the part of the senders and a proposition concerning the situation or conduct of the addressees. They thus state what the senders want to achieve with respect to the addressees, thereby giving prominence to the pragmatic aspect of the communicative act. This pragmatic emphasis is reflected in the relatively long and detailed statements of the metapropositional bases (1:2 ff.: εὐχαριστοῦμεν τῷ θεῷ πάντοτε... μνείαν ποιούμενοι ἐπὶ τῶν προσευχῶν ἡμῶν ἀδιαλείπτως μνημονεύοντες... εἰδότες; 4:1: ἐρωτῶμεν ὑμᾶς καὶ παρακαλοῦμεν ἐν κυρίῳ Ἰησοῦ). However, the statements of the propositions, too, are quite detailed and include heading-type expressions.[86]

Constructions giving prominence to the pragmatic dimension also occur at the second and third level of division of the text, but here they introduce closing sections which either round off a section at the first level or refer back to one of the openings at that level. We find examples of the second type in 2:13 (εὐχαριστοῦμεν τῷ θεῷ ἀδιαλείπτως, ὅτι... τοῖς πιστεύουσιν), which looks back to 1:2–7, and in 4:12 (παρακαλοῦμεν... ὑμᾶς... περισσεύειν

---

[86] 1:2–7: ... περὶ πάντων ὑμῶν... ὑμῶν τοῦ ἔργου τῆς πίστεως καὶ τοῦ κόπου τῆς ἀγάπης καὶ τῆς ὑπομονῆς τῆς ἐλπίδος τοῦ κυρίου ἡμῶν Ἰησοῦ Χριστοῦ ἔμπροσθεν τοῦ θεοῦ καὶ πατρὸς ἡμῶν... ὅτι τὸ εὐαγγέλιον ἡμῶν... ἐν τῇ Ἀχαΐᾳ.

4:1: ... ἵνα καθὼς παραλάβετε παρ' ἡμῶν τὸ πῶς δεῖ ὑμᾶς περιπατεῖν καὶ ἀρέσκειν θεῷ, καθὼς καὶ περιπατεῖτε, ἵνα περισσεύητε μᾶλλον.

μᾶλλον), 5:12 (ἐρωτῶμεν... ὑμᾶς...) and 5:14 (παρακαλοῦμεν... ὑμᾶς...), which all echo 4:1. A point to be observed here is that these constructions are generally abbreviated compared with the ones they refer back to. Examples of the first type can be found in 5:23 f. and 5:25.[87] In these brief closing sections, the metapropositional base is not expressed in a clause, but merely indicated by the use of mood.

At the lower levels, we find, in addition to the types just referred to, constructions containing metapropositional bases that are neutral with regard to the will of the senders (e.g. τοῦτο... ὑμῖν λέγομεν ἐν λόγῳ κυρίῳ[88]) or secondary (e.g. οἴδατε[89]), and propositions relating to the senders or to persons or concepts expressed in the third person.[90] The metapropositional base is often stated relatively briefly, but propositions are sometimes highlighted by heading-type expressions[91] or by a cataphoric text-summarizing τοῦτο.[92]

At the lower levels, one also finds openings which only include indications of a theme, and lack metapropositional statements. In such cases, the new sections are closely linked to the preceding text and have the same metapropositional base as was relevant there. One example of this is in 5:4, where the stressed subject ὑμεῖς indicates something of a thematic shift, but the metapropositional base expressed in 5:2 presumably still applies. It can also be noted that indications of time, place and circumstances play a key role as opening markers in 2:17–3:10, the only significant section of a narrative character in the letter.[93]

Instructive and thematic closing markers

Since instructive and thematic closing markers usually consist of a summary, a conclusion or some other indication of consequences, which corresponds in some way to the opening or starting-point of the section concerned, they

---

[87] To some extent in 3:11 f., too, although there the first proposition relates to the senders.

[88] 4:15. One exception is οὐ θέλομεν... ὑμᾶς ἀγνοεῖν... ἵνα μὴ λυπῆσθε... in 4:13, which introduces the major section 4:13–5:11 at the second level of division of the text. Here metapropositional bases at two levels are expressed. The first contains an expression of will and involves a proposition relating to the addressees, the second is secondary and is linked to a proposition expressed in the third person.

[89] 2:1; 3:3b; 4:2; 5:2. Other examples are μνημονεύετε (2:9), ὑμεῖς μάρτυρες καὶ ὁ θεός (2:10), ἡμεῖς... ἐσπουδάσαμεν (2:17), εὐδοκήσαμεν (3:1), τοῦτο... ἐστιν θέλημα τοῦ θεοῦ (4:3), and οὐ χρείαν ἔχετε γράφειν ὑμῖν (4:9; 5:1).

[90] *Senders:* 2:1, 9, 10, 17; 3:1, 3b; 4:2. *Third person:* 4:9, 13; 5:1, 2. The construction in 4:3–6 is an exception in this respect.

[91] 2:1, 9; 4:9, 13; 5:1.

[92] 4:3, 15.

[93] See 2:17, 3:1 f. and 3:6.

77

ought to show the same kinds of variation between the different levels of division of the text as instructive and thematic opening markers. This does indeed prove to be the case.

At the two highest levels, we consistently find closings which express what the senders want to achieve with regard to the addressees, i.e. which give prominence to the pragmatic dimension. The two major sections (1:3–2:16 and 2:17–3:10) in the first half of the letter (1:2–3:13) are both brought to a close with statements of consequences (2:13–16 καὶ διὰ τοῦτο καί...; 3:6–10 ... διὰ τοῦτο...), which clearly refer back at both the metapropositional and the propositional level to the introductory assessment of the addressees' conduct in 1:2–7.[94] In the latter case, the statement of consequences is followed by a short section (3:11 ff.) expressing two wishes, one being that the love of the addressees, which has already been favourably assessed, should increase. This brief passage, which reinforces the paraenetic function of the preceding appraisal, marks the end of the first half of the letter.

In the second half of the epistle (4:1–5:25), the first major section (4:1–12) is brought to a close with a construction (4:10b–12) which clearly echoes, at both the metapropositional and the propositional level, the opening exhortation in 4:1. The second major section (4:13–5:11) is rounded off with a closing exhortation (5:11: διό...) which above all looks back to the beginning of the section in 4:13, but also to some extent to the exhortation in 4:1 (see e.g. καθὼς καὶ ποιεῖτε in 5:11). The third major section (5:12–22) opens with a restatement of the metapropositional base expressed in 4:1, which is then kept in focus by the imperatives which follow.[95] After this there is a new short section expressing wishes, this time relating solely to the addressees. It re-echoes the corresponding section in 3:11 ff. and marks the ending of the second half of the letter. The body of the letter concludes with a final exhortation in 5:25. At the two highest levels of division, then, we find

---

[94] 1:2–6: εὐχαριστοῦμεν τῷ θεῷ πάντοτε περὶ πάντων ὑμῶν... ἀδιαλείπτως μνημονεύοντες ὑμῶν... τῆς πίστεως καί... τῆς ἀγάπης καί... τῆς ἐλπίδος... εἰδότες... ὅτι... ὑμεῖς μιμηταὶ ἡμῶν ἐγενήθητε καὶ τοῦ κυρίου, δεξάμενοι τὸν λόγον ἐν θλίψει πολλῇ μετὰ χαρᾶς πνεύματος ἁγίου...

2:13 ff.: καὶ διὰ τοῦτο καὶ εὐχαριστοῦμεν τῷ θεῷ ἀδιαλείπτως, ὅτι... λόγον ἀκοῆς παρ' ἡμῶν τοῦ θεοῦ ἐδέξασθε... ὑμεῖς γὰρ μιμηταὶ ἐγενήθητε... ὅτι τὰ αὐτὰ ἐπάθετε καὶ ὑμεῖς ὑπὸ τῶν ἰδίων συμφυλετῶν καθὼς καὶ αὐτοὶ ὑπὸ τῶν Ἰουδαίων, τῶν καὶ τὸν κύριον ἀποκτεινάντων... καὶ ἡμᾶς ἐκδιωξάντων...

3:6–10: ... Τιμοθέου... εὐαγγελισαμένου ἡμῖν τὴν πίστιν καὶ τὴν ἀγάπην ὑμῶν... διὰ τοῦτο παρεκλήθημεν... ἐφ' ὑμῖν... τίνα γὰρ εὐχαριστίαν δυνάμεθα τῷ θεῷ ἀνταποδοῦναι περὶ ὑμῶν... νυκτὸς καὶ ἡμέρας... δεόμενοι...

[95] 4:1: ἐρωτῶμεν ὑμᾶς καὶ παρακαλοῦμεν ἐν κυρίῳ Ἰησοῦ, ἵνα καθὼς παρελάβετε παρ' ἡμῶν... καθὼς καὶ περιπατεῖτε, ἵνα περισσεύητε μᾶλλον.

4:10: παρακαλοῦμεν δὲ ὑμᾶς... περισσεύειν μᾶλλον... καθὼς ὑμῖν παρηγγείλαμεν, ἵνα περιπατῆτε εὐσχημόνως...

5:11: διὸ παρακαλεῖτε ἀλλήλους... καθὼς καὶ ποιεῖτε.

5:12 ff.: ἐρωτῶμεν δὲ ὑμᾶς... παρακαλοῦμεν δὲ ὑμᾶς...

endings which express what the senders want to achieve with regard to the addressees. The conclusions that occur at the first level are marked in particular by the short sections expressing wishes.

At lower levels, closings contain above all secondary or volitionally neutral metapropositional bases, and propositions which concern the senders or persons or concepts expressed in the third person. At these levels, however, the metapropositional base or the proposition is sometimes not explicitly stated. This is possible because of the limited context. At the third level of text division, we find summarizing or consequence-indicating recurrences containing secondary or neutral metapropositional bases towards the end of 2:1–12 (2:10)[96], 3:1–5 (3:5 διὰ τοῦτο...)[97] and 4:2–8 (4:6 ff. καθώς... γάρ... τοιγαροῦν...)[98], and at the fourth level at the end of 3:3b–4 (3:4 καθώς...)[99], 4:15–17 (4:17 καὶ οὕτως...)[100] and 5:6–10 (5:10 ἵνα...).[101] A recurrence of a special kind is found in 1:9 f., in which Paul uses the third person to draw attention to the propositional content of the opening assessment in 1:2–7.[102] The only conclusion at these levels which expresses what the senders want to achieve with regard to the addressees is the closing exhortation in 4:18 (ὥστε... ἐν τοῖς λόγοις τούτοις), which rounds off the comparatively long section 4:13–18 at the third level of division of the text.[103]

Regarding these indications of consequences, it may also be noted that at the highest level of division they are not introduced by consequence-indicating particles at all; that at the second level they are sometimes introduced by coordinating particles; and that at the lower levels they sometimes assume the form of subordinate constructions (see above).

---

[96] 2:1: αὐτοὶ γὰρ οἴδατε τὴν εἴσοδον ἡμῶν τὴν πρὸς ὑμᾶς, ὅτι οὐ κενὴ γέγονεν,....
2:10: ὑμεῖς μάρτυρες καὶ ὁ θεός, ὡς ὁσίως καί... ἀμέμπτως ὑμῖν τοῖς πιστεύουσιν ἐγενήθημεν, καθάπερ οἴδατε,....
[97] 3:1 f.: ... μηκέτι στέγοντες... ἐπέμψαμεν Τιμόθεον... εἰς τό... παρακαλέσαι ὑπὲρ τῆς πίστεως ὑμῶν...
3:5: διὰ τοῦτο κἀγὼ μηκέτι στέγων ἔπεμψα εἰς τὸ γνῶναι τὴν πίστιν ὑμῶν
[98] 4:2 f.: οἴδατε γὰρ τίνας παραγγελίας ἐδώκαμεν ὑμῖν διὰ τοῦ κυρίου Ἰησοῦ. τοῦτο γάρ ἐστιν θέλημα τοῦ θεοῦ, ὁ ἁγιασμὸς ὑμῶν.
4:6 ff.: ... διότι ἔκδικος κύριος περὶ πάντων τούτων, καθὼς καὶ προείπαμεν ὑμῖν... γὰρ ἐκάλεσεν ἡμᾶς ὁ θεός... ἐν ἁγιασμῷ. τοιγαροῦν ὁ ἀθετῶν... ἀθετεῖ... τὸν θεόν...
[99] 3:3 f.: αὐτοὶ γὰρ οἴδατε... καθὼς καί... οἴδατε.
[100] 4:14: ... καὶ ὁ θεὸς τοὺς κοιμηθέντας διὰ τοῦ Ἰησοῦ ἄξει σὺν αὐτῷ.
4:17: καὶ οὕτως πάντοτε σὺν κυρίῳ ἐσόμεθα.
[101] 5:6: ... μὴ καθεύδωμεν... ἀλλὰ γρηγορῶμεν καὶ νήφωμεν.
5:10: ἵνα εἴτε γρηγορῶμεν εἴτε καθεύδωμεν ἅμα σὺν αὐτῷ ζήσωμεν.
[102] 1:2–6: εὐχαριστοῦμεν τῷ θεῷ... ὅτι τὸ εὐαγγέλιον ἡμῶν οὐκ ἐγενήθη εἰς ὑμᾶς... καθὼς οἴδατε οἷοι ἐγενήθημεν... καὶ ὑμεῖς μιμηταὶ ἡμῶν ἐγενήθητε... δεξάμενοι τὸν λόγον...
1:9: αὐτοὶ γὰρ περὶ ἡμῶν ἀπαγγέλλουσιν ὁποίαν εἴσοδον ἔσχομεν πρὸς ὑμᾶς, καὶ πῶς ἐπεστρέψατε πρὸς τὸν θεόν...
[103] 4:18: ὥστε παρακαλεῖτε ἀλλήλους ἐν τοῖς λόγοις...

Finally, it should in addition be noted that in some of the statements of consequences mentioned above, the argument is pursued to a natural end-point by the application of an eschatological perspective. This is the case in the two sections containing wishes which round off the two halves of the letter at the first level of division (3:11 ff.; 5:23 ff.), at the end of the opening section 1:2–2:16 at the second level, and at the end of subsections 1:2–10 and 2:1–12 of the latter at the third level. The same phenomenon occurs at the third level in 4:6 (4:2–8).

Contrastive opening markers

Contrastive opening markers only indicate *that* a break or transition is occurring in the text. The character and importance of the transition only become clear in the light of the instructive and thematic transition markers that are present and the relationships between them (see the example of how transition markers interact, p. 75 f. above). Certain tendencies in the use of contrastive opening markers themselves can nevertheless be observed. At the two highest levels of text division, all the transitions have markers of this kind. At the lower levels, it is not uncommon for there to be no contrastive markers. As regards the character of these markers, we can note that the only transition at the first level (3:13/4:1) is marked by the relatively emphatic combination of particles λοιπὸν οὖν. At the second level, the balancing adversative particle δέ is used in every case, except in the closing exhortation in 5:25, which follows on asyndetically. At the third and fourth levels of division, we find both δέ and asyndeton.

Attention-attracting and intensity-heightening transition markers

These markers merely attract the attention of the listener or increase the intensity of the text. The reason for attracting the listener's attention or heightening the intensity, however, only emerges from the instructive and thematic markers present and their relationship to one another (see the example of interaction between markers, p. 75 f. above). Certain patterns in the occurrence of attention-attracting and intensity-heightening markers can be observed, however.

These markers occur in particular at higher levels of division of the text and in conjunction with the beginning and ending of major sections. Far and away the commonest type is the use of an address, which occurs as an opening marker at the beginning of most sections at the two highest levels. The only sections at these levels which lack an opening-marking address are the two short wish sections in 3:11 ff. and 5:23 f. At lower levels, address forms functioning as opening markers are found in the opening phrases of the major sections 2:1–12 and 5:1–11, and in 2:9, 4:10b and 5:4. Of these, the one in 4:10b introduces a closing section and should perhaps primarily be regarded as a closing marker at the second level of text division. Examples of the use of an address serving more unambiguously as a closing marker are those in 2:14, 3:7 and 5:14, which occur within the concluding sections 2:13–16, 3:6–10 and 5:12–22 at the first and second levels and which help to maintain the intensity of these sections.

In the great majority of cases, the address used is ἀδελφοί and it occurs inside the clause. In 1:4 this form is extended to include the words ἠγαπημένοι ὑπὸ [τοῦ] θεοῦ and it thus also takes on something of an instructive and thematic function, since it reinforces the favourable assessment of the addressees in this section. In one case, ἀδελφοί occurs in initial position: at the beginning of the asyndetic closing exhortation in 5:25.

Two occurrences of an address serving as a closing marker are associated with other attention-attracting or intensity-heightening phenomena. The cases concerned are those in 3:7 and 5:14, which mark the rounding off of the two halves of the letter. In 3:7 the address follows the pleonastic διὰ τοῦτο, and in the closing section 5:12–22 we can observe the new start in 5:14 and a construction consisting of short, asyndetically linked clauses.

A closing ἀμήν possibly gives extra emphasis to the short wish section which ends the first half of the letter (3:11 ff.), but this reading is uncertain.

E. Implications for the line of thought in the letter

The headings used in the tabular overview of the arrangement of the text have already provided a summary of the progress of thought in the letter, such as it emerges from the arrangement of the text that has been established. What remains to be done here is to comment on these results and draw attention to a number of features which seem to me to be of particular importance to an understanding of the letter as a whole and, by extension, of Paul's thinking and theology. I shall do this in two stages. First, I shall comment on how the text arrangement arrived at affects our understanding of the overall structure and unity of the letter. I shall then examine motifs which this arrangement of the text highlights as being of particular importance.

Overall structure of the letter

One conclusion that can be drawn from the basic analysis undertaken is that 1 Thessalonians appears to be more uniform than is often claimed. The letter can be broken down into two parts, 1:2–3:13 and 4:1–5:25, which are distinct, but nevertheless clearly related to each other. Judging from the instructive and thematic markers present, the first part has the overall purpose of expressing a favourable assessment of the steadfastness in faith and love of the persecuted Thessalonians. This purpose is clearly stated in the opening instructive and thematic construction in 1:2–7, and subsequently restated in the instructive and thematic closing markers in 2:13–16 and 3:6–10, i.e. in the closing portions of the two major subsections of this part of the letter. The section 2:1–12, which is sometimes regarded as an *apologia*, turns out to be subordinate in character and to develop the first element of the statement of the proposition in 1:5 ff. This is indicated by the conjunction γάρ and the following instructive and thematic construction in 2:1, which clearly refers back to the wording of 1:9, the latter in turn echoing the proposition statement in 1:5 ff. This means that 2:1–12 also directly serves the overall purpose set out in 1:2–7, a point that is confirmed by the fact that the renewed statement of the purpose in 2:13–16 is introduced by καὶ διὰ τοῦτο καί. The whole of the first part, 1:2–3:13, thus seems ultimately to serve one and the same object, namely to express approval of the steadfastness in faith and love of the persecuted Thessalonians. The reason for doing so is of course to strengthen and encourage them in their persecution. That this also implies an element of exhortation is made clear by the related wish in 3:12 f., which closes the first part of the letter.

The second part, 4:12–5:25, is more heterogeneous. Fundamentally, it is exhortatory, but it is not as distinctly held together by an overarching statement of purpose. The instructive and thematic markers in its various subsections, however, prove to fit in with the overall object stated in the first part. This is seen most clearly in the first subsection (4:1–12): in its opening instructive and thematic construction in 4:1, the Thessalonians are expressly urged to abound even more in what they have received from the senders and in what they are already doing, i.e. precisely the things that were favourably assessed in the first part (see 1:5 f., 2:13 and 3:6). This exhortation recurs in the ending found in 4:10b–12 and thus appears to be crucial to this section. If this is the case, though, the section as a whole should reflect the persecution faced by the Thessalonians and correspond to the account given in the first half of the letter. And in fact the section can very well be understood in such terms. As was observed in the basic analysis, the more specific exhortations set out in 4:3–6 pose several problems of interpretation, but they do at any rate appear to be chiefly concerned with sexual morals, and the Thessalonians' conflict with their fellow countrymen may well have centred on that issue. This is also hinted at by καθάπερ καὶ τὰ ἔθνη τὰ μὴ εἰδότα τὸν θεόν in 4:5. At all events, the text goes on to hold up, in contrast to the lustful passion of the Gentiles, the divinely taught brotherly love of the Thessalonians, and in that connection there is a specific reference to the brothers in Macedonia, which can be compared with 1:7–10. It may also be observed that the final exhortation in 4:11 is that the recipients should work with their hands, which is a clear echo of 2:9. In other words, the whole of this first subsection can — and in my opinion should — be regarded as directly linked to the first half of the epistle and to the persecution of the Thessalonians.

The second subsection (4:13–5:11) begins with an instructive and thematic construction in 4:13 explaining that the teaching in this section is being given so that the Thessalonians will not grieve. This is reflected in the closing exhortation to the addressees in 5:11 to encourage and build up one another. The purpose of the teaching in this section is thus to provide encouragement and edification, which is the overarching purpose of the first half of the letter. The content of this teaching also proves to be ideally suited to encouraging and building up those who are the victims of persecution: the first part of the section (4:13–18) describes how those who have died will rise to life with Christ, which must of course have been a source of comfort in the face of persecution.[104] The second part (5:1–11) provides instruction about the sudden coming of the day of the Lord. Such teaching must also have offered consolation in the face of the overwhelming might of their persecutors. At the very moment when things are looking bright for their persecutors, just when they believe themselves secure in their superior strength,[105] then, suddenly, the day of the Lord, the liberation, will come. It should be observed that ideas of this kind have already been expressed in 1:9 f.[106] The teaching in 4:13–5:11 thus ties in well with both the first half of the letter and the persecution faced by the Thessalonians.

The third subsection (5:12–22) begins with statements of metapropositional bases in 5:12 (ἐρωτῶμεν... ὑμᾶς) and 5:14 (παρακαλοῦμεν... ὑμᾶς) which echo the corresponding statements at the beginning of the first subsection (4:1). The exhortations that follow are fairly heterogeneous, but overall they are quite relevant to a persecuted community. They talk for instance about the Thessalonians being at peace among themselves (5:13), encouraging the faint hearted, helping the weak, being patient with everyone (5:14), and not repaying evil for evil (5:15). The exhortations in 5:16 ff. correspond to the

---

[104] Cf. 1 Cor 15:30 ff.
[105] I am inclined to construe the subject of λέγωσιν in 5:3 as the persecutors, rather than an undefined 'they' or 'people'. For a similar indefinite reference to opponents, cf. Gal 4:17.
[106] Cf. also 2:16.

conduct of the persecuted senders, as described in the first half of the letter (see 1:2 f., 2:13 and 3:9 f.). There is thus no reason to assume that they do not also ultimately have the purpose of strengthening and exhorting the Thessalonians in their persecution.

That the second half of the letter should be seen as directly linked to the first and that both halves ultimately have the same goal — to strengthen and exhort the addressees — would also seem to be suggested by the fact that the second half closes with a section expressing wishes (5:23 f.) which clearly echoes the wishes at the end of the first half. The concluding exhortation in 5:25 is also appropriate in this context. The senders manifest their concern for the Thessalonians in their persecution by constantly mentioning them in their prayers. This is referred to in 1:2 f., 2:13 and 3:9 f. and actually practised in 3:12 f. and 5:23 f. But the senders, too, are persecuted, and now they are praying for the same support from the Thessalonians.

The instructive and thematic markers that occur at the major transitions and the development of thought in the letter as a whole, then, give us cause to assume that the entire epistle ultimately serves but one purpose, namely to strengthen and exhort the persecuted Thessalonians.[107] This seems to me to be credible in psychological terms, too. If the Thessalonians are faced with the crisis of persecution and the senders are deeply anxious about how they will cope with it (see 2:17, 3:1 ff.), the latter are hardly likely to refer to the addressees' persecution as one item on a long agenda and then move on, say, to shadow-box with imaginary opponents on points of doctrine or to tell the Thessalonians off for not having a correct understanding of the last things.

Key motifs

The arrangement of the text that emerges from the basic analysis gives the idea of *imitatio*[108] a prominent place in this letter. Reading 1:5 and 1:6 f.

---

[107] Concerning the paraenetic purpose of the letter, see also Malherbe 1983, pp. 238 f.

[108] In the Vulgate, μιμηταί in 1:6 and 2:14 is translated *imitatores*. Nevertheless, I use *imitatio* with some hesitation in this context, since the word is sometimes reserved for an outward, superficial type of copying. As far as I can see, there can only be apologetic reasons for such a narrowing of its meaning. My use of the word here presupposes a considerably richer sense. In my opinion, Paul conceives of a process of identifying with and conforming to Christ, which involves the life of the Christian being shaped according to the prototype of Christ, chiefly in an inner sense, but, as a result, to some extent in an outward sense too (see e.g. Gal 4:19; 6:17; Phil 3:10, 21). However, it also involves the actual presence of Christ (see e.g. Gal 4:6). Moreover, we should distinguish between different *imitatio* relationships. The fundamental and primary, indeed ultimately the only object of *imitatio* is Christ. Other *imitatio* relationships are entirely dependent on and subservient to this fundamental relationship.

E. Larsson (1962, p. 17) distinguishes between *Nachfolge*, which he uses to refer to all forms of fellowship with Christ in which Christ or events in the life of Christ serve as a

together gives this concept a key role in the important instructive and thematic construction at the very beginning of the body of the letter (1:2–7). In the last long propositional statement in this construction (1:4–7), which is given extra emphasis by the address ἀδελφοὶ ἠγαπημένοι ὑπὸ [τοῦ] θεοῦ, the idea is expressed in several ways. First, in 1:5, there is a favourable account of the senders' earlier conduct among the Thessalonians, in which one can in particular observe a remarkable oscillation between the senders' gospel and the senders themselves: τὸ εὐαγγέλιον ἡμῶν... ἐγενήθη εἰς ὑμᾶς...[ἐν] πληροφορίᾳ πολλῇ, καθὼς οἴδατε οἶοι ἐγενήθημεν [ἐν] ὑμῖν. Against this background, it is then said in 1:6 that the Thessalonians have become imitators of the senders and of the Lord (καὶ ὑμεῖς μιμηταὶ ἡμῶν ἐγενήθητε καὶ τοῦ κυρίου), the reference to both the senders and the Lord here corresponding to the oscillation between the gospel and the senders in 1:5.[109] This, clearly, is the basis for the senders' favourable assessment of the Thessalonians. What is happening here is that the senders and the Lord are being held up as positive standards and the addressees are then assessed with reference to those standards. But the idea of *imitatio* also finds expression in the following ὥστε-clause in 1:7, in which it said that the Thessalonians, as a result of their conformity to the positive standards set for them, have themselves become an example to all the believers in Macedonia and Achaia (ὥστε γενέσθαι ὑμᾶς τύπον πᾶσιν τοῖς πιστεύουσιν...). This ὥστε-clause is then commented on in a couple of γάρ-clauses. That the hazy distinction between the gospel and the senders in 1:5 was no coincidence is made clear by a corresponding oscillation here between the Thessalonians, the word of the Lord and the Thessalonians' faith: ὥστε γενέσθαι ὑμᾶς τύπον... ἀφ' ὑμῶν γὰρ ἐξήχηται ὁ λόγος τοῦ κυρίου οὐ μόνον ἐν τῇ Μακεδονίᾳ... ἀλλ' ἐν παντὶ τόπῳ ἡ πίστις ὑμῶν ἡ πρὸς τὸν θεὸν ἐξελήλυθεν.

The long, stressed statement of the proposition (1:4–7) in the opening instructive and thematic construction of 1:2–7 is thus permeated by *imitatio* thinking, in which the senders and the Lord are held up as a standard for the persecuted Thessalonians. This provides an entirely adequate explanation for the relatively detailed reminder of the senders' earlier conduct among the addressees that follows in 2:1–12, and tallies with the fact that this reminder focuses in particular on the senders' boldness (2:2 ff.) and self-sacrifice (2:5–

---

model. and *imitatio*, which is reserved for conscious and active imitation. No such distinction is made here, the term *imitatio* being used for all forms of imitation, conscious or unconscious.

[109] A. J. Malherbe (1983, pp. 247 f.) makes a point of the fact that in 1 Thess 1:5 Paul does not write οὐκ... ἐν λόγῳ μόνον ἀλλὰ καὶ ἐν ἔργῳ but οὐκ... ἐν λόγῳ μόνον ἀλλὰ καὶ ἐν δυνάμει καὶ ἐν πνεύματι ἁγίῳ καὶ [ἐν] πληροφορίᾳ πολλῇ, as though he does not want to refer directly to his acts. I think, however, that Malherbe is making too much of this fact, since the following subordinate clauses — καθὼς οἴδατε οἶοι ἐγενήθημεν [ἐν] ὑμῖν — in any case draw attention to the character and former behaviour of the senders.

9), following persecution and suffering (2:2). That this section really is governed by the idea of *imitatio* is confirmed by the renewed expression of a favourable assessment in 2:13–16, the background to which is clearly the reminder given in 2:1–12 (καὶ διὰ τοῦτο καί...). Here, the *imitatio* idea is once more clearly expressed at the propositional level. The first hint of it is probably to be found in 2:13, where it is said that the word of God is at work in the Thessalonian believers (cf. the oscillation between word and person in 1:5 and 1:7 f., referred to earlier), but it is not clearly expressed until 2:14 ff., where it is said once again that the Thessalonians have become imitators. This time, admittedly, the churches of God in Judaea are first mentioned as the standard emulated (2:14), but in the subsequent text both the Lord and the senders are mentioned again (2:15).

The idea of *imitatio* thus permeates not only the statement of the proposition in the opening instructive and thematic construction in 1:2–7, but determines the whole of the opening section 1:2–2:16. The fact that the very opening of the letter looks like this can hardly be without significance for the ensuing text, particularly if the letter as a whole has but one purpose. And numerous traces of this introductory emphasis on *imitatio* can indeed be found in the rest of the epistle. As we saw earlier, the exhortations in the second half of the letter (4:1–5:25) begin with a call to the Thessalonians to abound even more in what they have received from the senders concerning how they should live, and in what they are in fact doing. This is a clear echo of the favourable assessment in 1:2–2:16 (see especially 1:6, 2:12 and 2:13 f.) and hence a reminder of the thinking and standards put forward there. The fact that in 4:3–6 the senders formulate a number of specific commands is no contradiction of this, since the concept of *imitatio* that ran through 1:2–2:16 made no strict distinction between word and person.[110] In 4:9 f., at any rate, mention is made of the Thessalonians' love for all the brothers in Macedonia, which was previously referred to (in 1:7) in connection with their *imitatio*. Nor does the love motif lack areas of overlap with the description of the standards set by the senders in 2:1–12 (see in particular 2:7 f., 11). Another clear reference to this description is found in 4:11, following the repeated exhortation to the addressees to abound even more in what they are already doing. There is thus reason to assume that the standards that were presented in the introduction to the letter also set the tone here, in the opening of the exhortatory section.

As regards the other subsections of the second, exhortatory half of the letter, we can note a clear suggestion of *imitatio* thinking in 4:14. In addition,

---

[110] Cf. the oscillation between word and person in 1:5 and 1:7 f., referred to earlier. See also the wording οὐκ... ἐν λόγῳ μόνον ἀλλὰ καὶ ἐν δυνάμει καὶ ἐν πνεύματι ἁγίῳ καὶ [ἐν] πληροφορίᾳ πολλῇ.

we can observe that there are quite a number of parallels between the exhortations in 5:12–22 and what is said about the standard-setting senders in the first half of the letter. One can for example compare 5:14 f. with 2:10 ff., 3:2 f. and 3:10; and 5:16 ff. with 1:2 f., 2:13 and 3:9 f.

The arrangement of the text that emerges from our basic analysis thus gives a prominent place in the letter to the idea of *imitatio*. It is clearly expressed in the proposition that is stated in the important instructive and thematic construction at the very beginning of the body of the letter, and it then moulds the whole of the opening section in 1:2–2:16. This fact, combined with the observation that the letter appears ultimately to serve a single purpose and that there are reverberations of the same *imitatio* thinking later in the text, means — in my opinion — that it is necessary to assign this concept a fundamental role in the strengthening and exhortation that takes place in 1 Thessalonians.[111] The fact that interpreters have commonly failed to recognize that role is, I believe, one of the main reasons for the difficulties that many have experienced in recognizing the links between the different parts of the epistle, difficulties that have resulted in a fragmentation of the letter and in certain cases in compilation or interpolation theories.

This brings the analysis of 1 Thessalonians to an end, and it is now time to turn our attention to Philippians.

---

[111] Such a use of the *imitatio* motif is in fact in line with other contemporary paraenesis. See e.g. Seneca, *Epp* 6.5 f., 11.9 f., 100.12; Plinius, *Ep* 8.13; Dio Chrysostom, *Disc* 70.6. Concerning the paraenetic purpose of 1 Thessalonians and the role of the *imitatio* motif in that connection, see also Willert 1995, pp. 229–32.

3. The Letter to the Philippians

A. Introduction

Before embarking on the actual analysis of the Letter to the Philippians, I would like to begin here — as in my analysis of 1 Thessalonians — with an overview of a number of modern suggestions regarding the arrangement of the epistle and a brief consideration of the question of its unity.[1]

To this end, I have compared the arrangements proposed in eleven commentaries on Philippians, which I believe to be reasonably representative of the modern commentary literature. In addition, I have studied those put forward in one monograph and three articles.[2] Of the latter, one makes use of a text linguistic method, while the other two are based on rhetorical analyses.[3] This comparison reveals quite a number of similarities, but also appreciable differences between the arrangements proposed.

Beginning with the highest levels of division of the text, we find that the majority of the sources consulted (nine) identify 1:1–2 as the opening of the letter, but that there are also many (six) who consider that 1:1–11 serves this function.[4] Most (ten) of the sources regard 4:21–23 as the closing section of the epistle; other proposals are 4:10–23 and 4:1–23.[5]

Turning next to the main body of the letter, we can first of all note a general tendency, even at the first level of division of the text, to divide it into fairly short sections. All but four of the sources divide the letter body into five or

---

[1] For my reasons for doing so, see p. 33.

[2] *Commentaries:* Lohmeyer 1953, Martin 1959, Johnston 1967, Gnilka 1968, Collange 1973, Friedrich 1976a, Loh & Nida 1977, Schenk 1984, Koenig 1985, Beare 1988 and O'Brien 1991. *Monograph:* Vielhauer 1978. *Articles:* Watson 1988, Alexander 1989 and Rolland 1990.

[3] *Text linguistic method:* Schenk 1984. *Rhetorical analyses:* Watson 1988 and Alexander 1989.

[4] *1:1–11:* Johnston 1967, Friedrich 1976a, Loh & Nida 1977, Koenig 1985, Beare 1988 and Rolland 1990. *1:1–2:* Lohmeyer 1953, Martin 1959, Gnilka 1968, Collange 1973, Vielhauer 1978, Schenk 1984, O'Brien 1991, Watson 1988 and Alexander 1989.

[5] *4:1–23:* Martin 1959. *4:10–23:* Gnilka 1968, Friedrich 1976a, Koenig 1985 and Rolland 1990. *4:21–23:* Lohmeyer 1953, Johnston 1967, Collange 1973, Loh & Nida 1977, Vielhauer 1978, Schenk 1984, Beare 1988, Watson 1988, Alexander 1989 and O'Brien 1990.

more parts.[6] This is presumably a reflection of the difficulties scholars have experienced in discerning the overall semantic coherence of Philippians.

The greatest similarities between the arrangements proposed are to be found with regard to chapters 1–2. Here, all but three of the sources distinguish the following entities: 1:3–11 (if this section is not included with the opening of the letter), 1:12–26, 1:27–2:18 and 2:19–30.[7] Most (eleven) regard these as independent sections at the first level of text division, but in some cases they are combined into larger entities: 1:12–4:9; 1:12–3:1; 1:12–2:18; or 1:27–3:1a.[8]

A relatively large measure of agreement also exists with respect to 4:10–20. All the sources recognize this as a distinct unit, but views differ as to the level to which it should be assigned. Some (four) regard it as part of the letter ending, some (four) consider that it was originally a separate letter, others (three) assign it to the first level of division of the body of the letter, while yet others (three) place it at the second level.[9]

The greatest differences of opinion exist over the arrangement of 3:1–4:9. Almost half (seven) of the proposals compared assume this section to incorporate a compilation or interpolation.[10] Suggestions as to where the interpolated text begins vary between 3:1, 3:1b and 3:2,[11] and, regarding where it ends, between 3:21, 4:1, 4:3 and 4:9.[12] Among those who regard Philippians as a unity, too, there are considerable variations here: some (two) see 3:1–4:9 as a single entity at the first level of division, others (three) view

[6] The four exceptions in this respect are Lohmeyer 1953 (1:3–11; 1:12–4:9; 4:10–20), Johnston 1967 (1:12–26: 1:27–3:1a+4:1–20; 3:1b–21), Friedrich 1976a (1:12–26; 1:27–2:18; 2:19–30; 3:1–4:9) and Rolland 1990 (1:12–2:18; 2:19–30; 3:1–4:9).

[7] Other divisions of the text are proposed by Watson (1988), who regards 1:27–30 as a distinct section; Loh & Nida (1977), who propose a transition between 1:12–30 and 2:1–18; and Lohmeyer (1953), who suggests 1:27–2:16 and 2:17–30. Gnilka (1968) and Collange (1973), who regard the text beginning at 3:1b as an interpolation, include 3:1a in the section beginning at 2:19.

[8] Lohmeyer 1953, Vielhauer 1978, Rolland 1990 and Johnston 1967, respectively.

[9] *Part of letter ending:* Martin 1959 (4:1–23), Gnilka 1968 (4:10–23), Friedrich 1976a (4:10–23) and Rolland 1990 (4:10–23). *Separate letter:* Collange 1973, Vielhauer 1978, Schenk 1984 and Beare 1988. *First level:* Lohmeyer 1953, Alexander 1989 and O'Brien 1991. *Second level:* Johnston 1967 (part of 1:27–3:1a+4:1–20), Loh & Nida 1977 (4:1–20) and Watson 1988 (4:1–20).

[10] Johnston 1967, Gnilka 1968, Collange 1973, Friedrich 1976a, Vielhauer 1978, Schenk 1984 and Beare 1988.

[11] *3:1:* Friedrich 1976a. *3:1b:* Johnston 1967, Gnilka 1968 and Collange 1973. *3:2:* Vielhauer 1978, Schenk 1984 and Beare 1988.

[12] *3:21:* Johnston 1967. *4:1:* Gnilka 1968, Collange 1973 and Beare 1988. *4:3:* Vielhauer 1978 and Schenk 1984. *4:9:* Friedrich 1976a. According to Gnilka 1968 and Collange 1973, the interpolated text continues up to and including 4:1, but also includes 4:8 f.

3:1–21 and 4:1–9 as more independent sections, and yet others (three) divide the text into 3:1–21 and 4:1–20(23).[13]

The proposed arrangements of Philippians which I have compared thus exhibit quite a large degree of variation. This variation *per se* testifies to the difficulties that scholars have experienced in discerning the internal coherence of the letter. Other evidence of these difficulties includes the tendency to fragment the text that was noted earlier and the relatively widespread questioning of the unity of the letter.

The unity question has been discussed for almost two hundred years.[14] In the following I shall begin by outlining the principal arguments for the compilation theories that have been put forward, and then go on to explain why I am not prepared to use any of these theories as the starting-point for my analysis.

The compilation theories generally involve one or two substantial interpolations, one of them within the section 3:1–4:9 (as we have seen, views on its exact extent vary), the other in 4:10–20. The arguments put forward to support them vary somewhat, and it will therefore be appropriate to consider each of the interpolations in turn. We shall begin with the arguments for the first of the proposed interpolations.

Arguments for an interpolation within Phil 3:1–4:9

1. Polycarp's Letter to the Philippians refers explicitly to several letters of Paul to the Philippians (Pol Ph 3:2).[15]
2. The Catalogus Sinaiticus and the writings of George the Syncellus also contain expressions suggesting the existence of several Pauline epistles to the Philippians.[16]

---

[13] *3:1–4:9:* Alexander 1989 and Rolland 1990. *3:1–21, 4:1–9:* Lohmeyer 1953, Koenig 1985 and O'Brien 1991. *3:1–21, 4:1–20(23):* Martin 1959, Loh & Nida 1977 and Watson 1988.

[14] According to D. Cook (1981, pp. 139 f.) and V. Koperski (1993, pp. 599 f.), however, the idea of this epistle being a compilation is not expressed in as early a source as Le Moyne's *Varia Sacra II* from 1685 (p. 343), as present-day advocates of such compilation theories often claim. The earliest evidence of such a theory, according to Koperski, is to be found in J. H. Heinrichs' *Pauli Epistolae ad Philippenses et Colossenses graece* from 1803 (p. 233), where it is suggested that Phil 1:1–3:1 and 4:21–23 were written for the church in general, while 3:2–4:20 was intended only for its leaders (Koperski 1993, p. 602). Heinrichs was then followed, Koperski suggests, by E. G. Paulus (*Censura Dissertationis Krausianae Annall.* 1812, pp. 702 f.) and C. Schrader (*Der Apostel Paulus V*, 1836, p. 233), although these two scholars proposed other delimitations of the text. It is only during the present century, however, that theories of this kind have gained a wider following.

[15] E.g. Bornkamm 1971, p. 202, and Vielhauer 1978, pp. 161 f.

[16] Rahjten 1959/60, pp. 167 f.

3. In Paul's letters, τὸ λοιπόν is used to begin a closing exhortation.[17]

4. The expressed hopes in 4:7 and 4:9 are both typical letter endings.[18]

5. There is a discontinuity of construction and thought at 3:2. After Paul has informed the Philippians about his own situation, exhorted them and recommended his fellow workers, all that remains to be done is to offer a closing exhortation and bring the letter to an end. Instead, Paul suddenly launches into this lengthy polemic against false teachers, disrupting the coherence of the letter.[19]

6. The interpolated text also exhibits the structure of an entire letter (though it lacks an introduction): polemic/biography, general and more specific exhortations, and a closing wish.[20]

7. There is an abrupt change in style and tone at 3:2. Up to this point, the tone of the letter has been one of joy and gentleness. After the exhortation to the Philippians in 3:1 to rejoice, the fierce diatribe and harsh words against false teachers in 3:2 come completely out of the blue.[21]

8. Chapters 1–2 and 3:2 ff. presuppose different situations. Opinions differ, however, as to what those situations must have been. Some scholars argue that chapters 1–2 imply a threat from outside enemies (see 1:27–30), whereas 3:2–9 is concerned with false teachers.[22] Others suggest that both texts relate to the same false teachers, but that they deal with them so differently that different situations must be involved.[23]

The first two of these arguments use evidence from historical sources to lend greater probability in a general sense to the idea of Philippians being a compilation. The other arguments are intended to demonstrate more specifically the presence of an interpolation in 3:1–4:9. Of these, the first four (3–6) are of a more form-critical kind, while the last two (7–8) relate to content. All of them are open to objection.

Regarding the first two arguments, it may be noted that both the Catalogus Sinaiticus and George the Syncellus are late and of relatively little value as sources in this context. The witness of Polycarp thus stands more or less alone in an otherwise unequivocal tradition within the early church. His unique testimony to several letters to the Philippians could be explained in a number of ways. It could for example be an imprecise reference which also includes the two letters to the Thessalonians, or a conclusion drawn from 3:1 and 4:16,

---

[17] E.g. Schmithals 1957, pp. 301 ff., and Vielhauer 1978, p. 160.

[18] E.g. Schmithals 1957, pp. 301 ff., and Bornkamm 1971, pp. 195 f.

[19] E.g. Vielhauer 1978, p. 160.

[20] E.g. Rahjten 1959/60, pp. 171 f., and Bornkamm 1971, p. 197.

[21] E.g. Schmithals 1957, pp. 301 ff., Rahjten 1959/60, p. 168, Bornkamm 1971, p. 196 f., and Vielhauer 1978, p. 160.

[22] E.g. Bornkamm 1971, pp. 199 f., and Vielhauer 1978, p. 160.

[23] Schmithals 1957, p. 305.

or the result of a memory lapse. Even if we accept that Paul did actually send several letters to the Philippians and that Polycarp knew of this, that fact alone does not directly support a compilation theory. The other letters could of course have been lost. Considering that we have two epistles to the Corinthians and two to the Thessalonians, this explanation must surely be considered more plausible.

As regards the four form-critical arguments (3–6), they are all based on conceptions about the structure of Paul's letters, conceptions which prove on closer inspection to be poorly supported or doubtful. It is easy to demonstrate that τὸ λοιπόν does not always introduce a closing exhortation (argument 3). In fact, it only really does so in 2 Cor 13:11. In 1 Thess 4:1 it occurs instead at the beginning of the second half of the letter (cf. also 2 Thess 3:1).[24] It is also clear that expressions of hope of the kind we encounter in 4:7 and 4:9 do not necessarily constitute letter endings (argument 4). This is made clear by 1 Thess 3:11 and 2 Thess 2:16, for example. Arguments 5 and 6 are based on the idea that the epistles of Paul have a uniform basic structure: a narrative section — an exhortatory section — practical matters. But is this really a justifiable assumption to make? If we compare Romans, 1 Corinthians, 2 Corinthians, Galatians and 1 Thessalonians, for instance, we are struck more by their diversity than by their uniformity. Practical matters are by no means always dealt with at the end of Paul's letters: see for example 1 Cor 4:17–20 and 1 Thess 2:17–3:10. Nor are exhortations always confined to the closing sections of his epistles. In 1 Corinthians, for instance, there is a constant alternation of indicatives and imperatives. In other words, there is every reason for caution in making assumptions about a uniform basic structure.

As for arguments 7 and 8, it has to be asked to what extent the alleged tensions in the text are due to uncertain interpretations of details and doubtful reconstructions of the underlying situation. Phil 3:2 is critical to both arguments, but its interpretation poses considerable difficulties: What is the precise meaning here of βλέπετε? What is the background to and meaning of the use of τοὺς κύνας, τοὺς κακοὺς ἐργάτας and τὴν κατατομήν? To whom do these words refer? Arguments 7 and 8 hinge on specific answers to these questions, but those answers cannot be taken as self-evident. For my own part, I believe it is possible to offer other answers which resolve the alleged tensions.

---

[24] See also Alexander 1989, pp. 96 f.

Arguments for regarding Phil 4:10–20 as an interpolation

Arguments 1 and 2 above are naturally also relevant to this interpolation, and warrant the same assessment here. More specific arguments for regarding Phil 4:10–20 as an interpolation are as follows:

1. After the closing exhortations and wish of peace in 4:8–9, 4:10–20 follows abruptly and involves a discontinuity of construction and thought.[25]

2. 4:10–20 is self-contained, a letter in its own right, closing, like the other compiled letters, with an expressed hope in 4:19 f.[26]

3. Chapters 1–2 and 4:10–20 presuppose different situations. Reading 4:10–20, one gets the impression that Epaphroditus has recently arrived with the Philippians' gift. According to 2:25–30, he has had time to arrive, minister to Paul and become so ill that he nearly died. What is more, the news of his illness has reached the Philippians and the news of their hearing of it has in turn reached Paul and Epaphroditus. If such a long interval had elapsed, during which there were clearly several contacts between them, and Paul had not thanked them before, then in Bornkamm's opinion he could at least have been expected to offer an explanation or an apology. Rahjten believes that Paul must have sent a quick letter of thanks to the Philippians, since he was 'always careful to observe the niceties of etiquette'.[27]

4. It is strange that the thanks should come at the end of the letter, especially as Epaphroditus has already been mentioned and more particularly if we assume that Paul's thanks are belated.[28]

The first two arguments are of a form-critical kind, while the last two are more concerned with content. The first and second arguments are based, like argument 4 for an interpolation in 3:1–4:9, on the notion that in 4:8 f. we have a typical letter ending and, like arguments 5 and 6 in the same context, on a specific view of the basic structure of Paul's letters. Both these views have already been questioned. The third and fourth of the arguments here are based on dubious reconstructions of the situation in which the letter originated, and it is in fact possible to arrive at other reconstructions which do not result in the supposed tensions between the different parts of the letter. It is for example conceivable that Epaphroditus fell ill on his journey to Paul, but nevertheless completed his mission — risking his own life in the process — and that this is the service referred to in 2:30. The Philippians could then have heard the news of his illness before he even reached Paul; it is not necessary to assume any further communication between them. Consequently, the Letter

---

[25] E.g. Schmithals 1957, p. 307, and Vielhauer 1978, pp. 160 f.
[26] Bornkamm 1971, pp. 195 f., and Rahjten 1959/60, p. 169.
[27] Rahjten 1959/60, p. 173, Bornkamm 1971, pp. 198 f., and Vielhauer 1978, p. 161.
[28] Bornkamm 1971, pp. 198 f., and Vielhauer 1978, pp. 160 f.

to the Philippians need not have been written very long after Epaphroditus's arrival. And even if the letter of thanks had been delayed somewhat, there would have been nothing very remarkable about that, given that Paul was in prison with the threat of death hanging over him (1:12–26) and perhaps also had a man with a life-threatening illness to look after (2:25–30). Furthermore, it may be noted that Paul's attitude to gifts does not appear to have been altogether uncomplicated. In 1 Thess 2:9, 1 Cor 9:12 and 2 Cor 11:7–11, Paul takes pride in not having been a burden to his addressees, and in Phil 4:11–12 and 4:17 he is careful to emphasize his financial independence and to explain why, despite this, he has accepted support from the Philippians. If Paul found the subject a little sensitive and was keen to tone it down, it is not very strange, either, that he expressed his thanks later on in the letter. What is more, I would argue that the other matters dealt with in this epistle were in fact more crucial and urgent. In my opinion, the letter is imbued with the sense of a life-and-death struggle, and under such circumstances Paul's primary concern is hardly likely to have been 'to observe the niceties of etiquette'.[29] I shall return to the occasion and purpose of the letter in the section dealing with the implications for our understanding of the line of thought in the text.

In my view, then, the arguments adduced in favour of these compilation theories are fairly weak. As I mentioned in the introduction to my analysis of 1 Thessalonians, a weakness inherent to compilation theories in general is that they necessitate a number of supporting hypotheses about a compiler and his intentions and methods. On that count alone, I believe that convincing arguments have to be put forward before such a theory can be accepted. In the case of Philippians, the burden of proof on anyone propounding a compilation theory is even greater, since there are also a number of arguments in favour of regarding the letter as a unity. P. Rolland, for example, has listed some forty lexical and conceptual links between the two halves of the letter.[30] A striking fact is that there is a certain parallelism between the occurrences of the words and concepts concerned in the two halves. In addition, several of the words are relatively uncommon in other letters of Paul, e.g.:

κέρδος κερδαίνειν	Phil 1:21; 3:7,8	κερδαίνειν 5 times in 1 Cor 9:19–22 (κέρδος also in Titus 1:11)
πολιτεύεσθαι πολιτεία	Phil 1:27; 3:20	(πολιτεία in Eph 2:12 and συμπολίτης in Eph 2:19)

[29] Rahjten 1959/60, p. 173.
[30] Rolland 1990, pp. 213 ff.

συναθλεῖν	Phil 1:27; 4:3	(ἀθλεῖν in 2 Tim 2:5)
ἡγεῖσθαι	Phil 2:3, 6, 25; 3:7, 8	2 Cor 9:5; 1 Thess 5:13
ταπεινοφροσύνη ταπεινοῦν ταπείνωσις	Phil 2:3, 8; 3:21; 4:12	ταπεινοῦν in 2 Cor 11:7; 12:21; and ταπεινός in Rom 12:16; 2 Cor 7:6; 10:1.
μορφή σύμμορφος συμμορφίζεσθαι	Phil 2:6, 7; 3:10, 21	σύμμορφος in Rom 8:29, μορφοῦσθαι in Gal 4:19, μόρφωσις in Rom 2:20 (also 2 Tim 3:5)
σχῆμα σχηματίζειν	Phil 2:7; 3:21	σχῆμα in 2 Cor 7:31. μετασχηματίζειν in 1 Cor 4:6; 2 Cor 11:13, 14, 15.
ἐπίγειος	Phil 2:10, 3:19	1 Cor 15:40; 2 Cor 5:1

Moreover, those who have put the case for the unity of the letter have usually endeavoured to show that these conceptual links reflect and are symptomatic of a deeper thematic coherence within the text.[31] I shall not go into this in any more detail here, since to do so would be to anticipate my own analysis. However, the conceptual links mentioned are in themselves, I believe, quite strong evidence of the unity of the letter. I find it hard to imagine different letters, written in different situations and for different purposes, exhibiting such conceptual uniformity. The arguments that have been put forward to support the different compilation theories are not in my opinion sufficiently convincing to outweigh the arguments for the unity of the letter and to justify the acceptance of a compilation theory. In my analysis, therefore, I proceed from the assumption that the Letter to the Philippians is indeed a unity. This initial assumption will be borne out by the analysis I undertake.

With that, the time has come to move on to the basic analysis of Philippians.

---

[31] E.g. Mackay 1960/61, pp. 167 ff.; Pollard 1966/67, pp. 58 ff.; and Garland 1985, pp. 162 ff.

B. Basic analysis

Regarding the structure and method of the following analysis, readers are referred to the opening chapter and to the corresponding section of the analysis of 1 Thessalonians.[32]

1:1-2

Like the other Pauline letters, Philippians begins with particulars of the senders and the recipients (1:1) and a wish of grace and peace (1:2). These elements are formulaic and follow one another asyndetically. In Philippians the first of them is somewhat extended by the inclusion of attributes.

1:3-2:30

1:3-11

In 1:3, the actual body of the letter begins. It is an entity held together in principle by conjunctions, although a number of asyndeta do occur, particularly in the exhortatory sections and in connection with parentheses and digressions. The beginning of a new section in 1:3 is marked by asyndeton and by a long, complex construction which is clearly instructive and thematic. The core of the main clause consists of the finite verb εὐχαριστῶ (v. 3) and the conjunctive participles τὴν δέησιν ποιούμενος and πεποιθώς (v. 6). This main clause is metapropositional and meta-communicative. It in fact describes, not the communicative act constituted by the letter itself, but one between Paul and God; however, the favourable appraisal which it expresses is no doubt also part and parcel of the communicative act of the letter, as is also suggested by the use of the present tense of the finite verb and the adverbial πάντοτε. The three verbs in the main clause may be assumed to describe one and the same communicative act from different points of view, and hence ultimately to give instructions about one and the same proposition. The key instruction to the recipients concerning this proposition is probably the favourable assessment of it expressed by both εὐχαριστῶ and μετὰ χαρᾶς τὴν δέησιν ποιούμενος.

An initial hint as to the content of the proposition is given by the prepositional phrase ὑπὲρ πάντων ὑμῶν in v. 4. This is then elaborated on in the prepositional phrase ἐπὶ τῇ κοινωνίᾳ ὑμῶν εἰς τὸ εὐαγγέλιον... ἄχρι τοῦ νῦν in v. 5 and the ὅτι-clause in v. 6. The content is thus expounded in

[32] See pp. 32 ff. and 48.

96

three stages. First it is merely stated that Paul's thanksgiving concerns the Philippians. Then his joyful prayer is said to be due to their sharing for the benefit of the gospel until now. And finally his gratitude for and joy in this sharing is related to his conviction that the one who began a good work among them will carry it on to completion until the day of Christ. This final step is given strong emphasis by the cataphoric text-summarizing αὐτὸ τοῦτο. In this way, particular prominence is given to the future continuation of their sharing as an essential precondition for Paul's thankfulness and joy.

This is followed in 1:7 by a καθώς-clause, in which Paul justifies the thoughts about the Philippians which he has just expressed. This gives him the opportunity to return to and comment further on the Philippians' sharing up to the present time. This time it is described in terms of their sharing in grace with Paul (συγκοινωνούς μου τῆς χάριτος), who is in prison for the sake of the gospel. The anaphoric text-summarizing τοῦτο at the beginning of this clause helps to draw attention to the ὅτι-clause in v. 6.

This brings to an end the long construction that began at 1:3. It is followed by an explanatory comment (γάρ) in 1:8, in which God is called on as a witness of Paul's longing for the Philippians, and which is presumably intended to support the assertion διὰ τὸ ἔχειν με ἐν τῇ καρδίᾳ ὑμᾶς in v. 7.

In 1:9 there is something of a fresh start, marked by the cataphoric text-summarizing τοῦτο and the metapropositional and metacommunicative προσεύχομαι. It is not a very distinct new beginning, however. This is indicated by the use of καί as the opening particle, which suggests a link rather than a contrast with what has gone before, and by προσεύχομαι, which clearly looks back to the statement of the metapropositional base in 1:3 (εὐχαριστῶ... τὴν δέησιν ποιούμενος).

The proposition follows in the form of a final ἵνα-clause, revealing a futural perspective. Paul's prayer is that the Philippians' love may overflow more and more with knowledge and full insight, so that they are able to determine what is best and be pure and blameless until the day of Christ. Like the forward-looking proposition in 1:6, then, the proposition here is concerned with an increase or intensification of the present praiseworthy conduct of the Philippians and, as in v. 6, the perspective extends up to the day of Christ. The difference is that this favourable conduct is described in v. 6 in terms of sharing, but here in terms of love and knowledge. In addition, it may be noted that both of these future-oriented propositions are given prominence by the use of a cataphoric text-summarizing τοῦτο. In my opinion, there are sufficient similarities between 1:6 and 1:9 to talk about a recurrence at the propositional as well as the metapropositional level. Thus, if in 1:7 Paul returned to and commented on 1:5, in 1:9 he now re-echoes 1:6.

These recurrences of material from the opening of the letter body in 1:3–6, at both the metapropositional and the propositional level, suggest that what has been written in the body of the letter up to this point is about to be brought to a close. A close is also indicated by the following ἵνα-clause in 1:10 f., with its eschatological perspective.

1:12–2:18

1:12–18c

The occurrence of a close in 1:9 ff. is confirmed by a distinct fresh start in 1:12, marked by the conjunction δέ, the address ἀδελφοί and an instructive and thematic construction. The latter begins with the metapropositional bases γινώσκειν... ὑμᾶς βούλομαι, which make it clear that Paul now intends to inform the Philippians about something. This represents a clear shift at the metapropositional level compared with the preceding section, which was dominated by metapropositional bases primarily designed to express a favourable assessment of the content of the proposition. The proposition then follows in the form of a ὅτι-clause stating that Paul's situation (τὰ κατ' ἐμέ) has in fact led to the furtherance of the gospel. There is thus a shift at the propositional level, too, from the Philippians' conduct to Paul's situation. There is common ground between this and the preceding section, however. Here, as before, the proposition is concerned with conduct which benefits the gospel.

How the gospel has been furthered is described in 1:13 f. in a ὥστε-clause: it has become known to everyone that Paul's bonds are in Christ, and this has made the brothers confident to speak the word with greater boldness. The latter point gives rise to a digression in 1:15 ff. about the motives of different groups who proclaim Christ.

In 1:18, this digression is brought to an end by the rhetorical question τί γάρ;, which is answered in a clause beginning with πλὴν ὅτι, a construction which gives it the character of a conclusion or final assessment ('What does this mean? Nothing other than this, that...')[33] and thus indicates a close. The content of this clause — that, in every way, Christ is proclaimed — echoes the opening statement about the furtherance of the gospel in 1:12, suggesting that it is the section beginning there that is being brought to an end. The content of the clause is then summed up in the anaphoric text-summarizing ἐν τούτῳ and is made the subject of a favourable appraisal expressed by the metapropositional χαίρω. This further reinforces the impression of an ending.

[33] See pp. 120, note 75, for further discussion.

1:18d–26

A new beginning follows in 1:18d, although it is not a particularly clearly marked one. This is suggested by the opening particles ἀλλὰ καί, which admittedly indicate a contrast to the preceding text, but at the same time imply a fairly close link with it. The nature of both the link and the contrast is revealed by the following verb χαρήσομαι, which is a clear parallel to the verb χαίρω that has gone before, but differs from it in that it is in the future tense.[34] Thus the same favourable assessment is expressed in the new section as at the end of the preceding one, the difference being that the text is now looking to the future. Like χαίρω, χαρήσομαι can be said to be metapropositional, but having been shifted into the future the favourable appraisal which it expresses has become somewhat removed from the communicative act of the letter and dependent on another metapropositional base ('I assert that...' or some similar phrase), and hence secondary.

The object of the favourable assessment expressed by χαρήσομαι, its proposition, is not stated in the opening sentence. Instead, an explanatory comment (γάρ) follows in 1:19, beginning with a new metapropositional base, οἶδα, which may be regarded as echoing the informative metapropositional base in 1:12. The connection at the metapropositional level with the previous section is thus made even clearer. The proposition is in the form of a lengthy ὅτι-clause (1:19 f.) and concerns Paul's situation turning out for his salvation, in such a way that he will not be put to shame and that Christ will be openly exalted in his body, whether by life or by death. It is these future events which are the object or cause of the future rejoicing mentioned in 1:18d. That these events which will bring Paul joy are the continuation of his present situation is indicated by the anaphoric text-summarizing τοῦτο at the beginning of the ὅτι-clause. The new section is thus clearly linked to the preceding one (1:12–18c) at the propositional level, too. An additional connection is the reference to the future exaltation of Christ in Paul's body, which provides a link with the opening assertion about the furtherance of the gospel in 1:12 (cf. also 1:18). These clear links with 1:12–18c at both the metapropositional and the propositional level confirm the assumption that the new beginning in 1:18d was a relatively minor one. The new section should therefore be kept together with the preceding one.

The concluding words of Paul's statement of the knowledge which causes him to rejoice — εἴτε διὰ ζωῆς εἴτε διὰ θανάτου — give rise to an

---

[34] Before ἀλλά, the words οὐ μόνον δέ (χαίρω) can presumably be supplied. For different uses of ἀλλά, see also the discussion on pp. 108–13.

explanatory digression (γάρ) in 1:21–24 concerning the implications of the two alternatives for him. He feels drawn to both, but for the Philippians' sake it is more necessary for him to remain in the flesh.

In 1:25 f. there follows a construction which has the character of a conclusion and suggests a close. It begins with καί and a text-summarizing τοῦτο, which refers back to the claim in 1:24 that it is important for the Philippians' sake for Paul to remain in the flesh. Instructions concerning this proposition are then given by the metapropositional πεποιθώς, which states that its content is something of which Paul is convinced. This is followed by a further metapropositional verb, οἶδα, which introduces the conclusion Paul draws from the conviction he has just mentioned. This οἶδα is a clear recurrence of one of the opening and dominant metapropositional bases of the section beginning in 1:18d, which suggests that this section is being brought to a close. The proposition is then set out in a ὅτι-clause, and concerns Paul's remaining with the Philippians for the sake of their furtherance and joy in faith, so that their boasting in Christ Jesus will 'overflow'. Here we can in particular note the motif of furtherance (προκοπήν), which looks back to the reference to the furtherance of the gospel at the beginning of the new major section in 1:12 (cf. also 1:18 and 1:20). Also to be noted are the motifs of joy (χαράν) and boasting (καύχημα), corresponding to χαρήσομαι in 1:18 and ἐν οὐδενὶ αἰσχυνθήσομαι in 1:20, even if we are concerned in that context with *Paul's* rejoicing and not being put to shame. These recurrences at both the metapropositional and the propositional level, primarily referring back to the opening of the section that began in 1:18d, suggest that it is that section which is now being brought to a close.

1:27–2:18

1:27–30

The closing of the section 1:18d–26 in 1:25 f. is followed by a fresh start in 1:27, marked by μόνον and a change of mood from the indicative to the imperative. The new beginning at 1:27 is thus relatively weakly marked in purely quantitative terms, and also in qualitative terms, since μόνον is a *modifying* adversative particle[35] and as such links the new section relatively closely to the preceding one.[36] These reasons alone make me sceptical about

---

[35] Concerning this term, see Blomqvist 1969, p. 20, and Blomqvist 1981, pp. 57–70.
[36] Cf. Gal 5:13.

assigning this opening to the first level of division of the letter body, as is proposed in most of the arrangements compared in the introduction to this chapter.[37] My subsequent analysis will bear out this scepticism.

The change of mood from indicative to imperative entails a shift at the metapropositional level from information (1:12 γινώσκειν... ὑμᾶς βούλομαι; 1:19, 25 οἶδα) and favourable assessment (1:18c χαίρω; 1:18d χαρήσομαι). It may be noted, however, that at the beginning of this new section Paul clearly refers back to the metapropositional bases of the preceding text by his use of the words ἵνα... ἀκούω τὰ περὶ ὑμῶν in 1:27 (cf. the knowledge motif in 1:19, 25), and does so again later with the phrase πληρώσατέ μου τὴν χαράν in 2:2 (cf. the joy motif in 1:18). The content of those metapropositional bases is thus kept in focus in this new section as well.

At the propositional level, too, this section is closely connected to the preceding one. The central theme of 1:12–18c and 1:18d–26 was that Paul's situation would result in the furtherance of the gospel (1:12, 18b, 19 f.). At the end of the second of these sections, this idea of furtherance of the gospel was related to the Philippians and described in terms of their *furtherance* and joy *in faith* (1:25 εἰς τὴν ὑμῶν προκοπὴν... τῆς πίστεως). In that context it was also said that the Philippians' boasting would 'overflow' because of Paul's *coming to them again* (1:26 διὰ τῆς παρουσίας πάλιν πρὸς ὑμᾶς). The new section from 1:27 on picks up on this with its opening exhortation to the Philippians that they should only live their lives in a manner *worthy of the gospel of Christ* (1:27 ἀξίως τοῦ εὐαγγελίου τοῦ Χριστοῦ), so that Paul, whether he *comes and sees them or is absent*, will know that they are standing firm in one spirit, striving fearlessly *for the faith of the gospel* (1:27 τῇ πίστει τοῦ εὐαγγελίου). Here too, then, the 'furtherance of the gospel' motif plays a key role. In this context — as in 1:3–11 — it is admittedly linked primarily to the conduct of the Philippians, but the clear reference to 1:25 f. suggests that it also has a secondary link to Paul's situation. The nature of this link is intimated by the similarities of phrasing between the description in 1:27–30 of what Paul wishes to hear about the Philippians and the description in 1:19–20 of the future he expects for himself. We can for example compare μὴ πτυρόμενοι ἐν μηδενὶ ὑπὸ τῶν ἀντικειμένων in 1:28 with ἐν οὐδενὶ αἰσχυνθήσομαι in 1:20, and ἔνδειξις... ὑμῶν... σωτηρίας in 1:28 with τοῦτό μοι ἀποβήσεται εἰς σωτηρίαν in 1:19. The parallelism between Paul's situation and the conduct he hopes for in the Philippians is then made explicit in 1:30, in which the latter are said to be having the same struggle which they saw and *now hear* to be Paul's. This parallelism reveals that the description and the favourable appraisal of Paul's situation set out in the previous

---

[37] Martin 1959, Johnston 1967, Gnilka 1968, Collange 1973, Friedrich 1976a, Schenk 1984, Koenig 1985, Beare 1988, Watson 1988, Alexander 1989 and O'Brien 1991.

sections also had a paraenetic dimension and now provide the starting-point for the new section. It also makes it clear that the basic theme of the preceding sections — that Paul's situation will result in the furtherance of the gospel — is still relevant.

In view of the relatively weakly marked opening in 1:27 and the links that have just been described between the new and the preceding sections, I would argue that the new beginning at 1:27 should not be assigned to a level higher than the third level of division of the letter body, i.e. the same level as the opening in 1:18d.

2:1–11

Following the long exhortation in 1:27–30, a modest new start is made in 2:1. It is marked by the conjunction οὖν and the four opening conditional clauses, joined by asyndeton, which together with the imperative of the main clause, πληρώσατέ μου τὴν χαράν, entail a recurrence of the motif of 'Paul's joy' which occurred at the metapropositional level (1:18) and played a crucial role in the preceding sections. Both the conjunction οὖν and the new recurrence of the dominant metapropositional bases of the earlier sections suggest that the new exhortation is to be seen as elaborating on the preceding one. This also fits in well with the overall progression of thought here. In 1:27–30 the recipients were among other things urged to stand firm ἐν ἑνὶ πνεύματι, μιᾷ ψυχῇ συναθλοῦντες. The exhortation in 2:2–4, the content of which is developed in a ἵνα-clause with a large number of predicative attributes, calls on them to be not only of the same mind (τὸ αὐτὸ φρονῆτε), but also of one mind (τὸ ἕν) (2:2), an attitude characterized by humility (2:3) and looking to the interests of others (2:4).

What is meant by being of *one* mind (2:2 τὸ ἕν φρονοῦντες) is then elaborated on in a further exhortation. Building on the earlier wording, the text now urges the Philippians to be of *this* mind (τοῦτο φρονεῖτε; note the strong emphasis on τοῦτο) which was (or is) also in Christ Jesus (2:5),[38] after which a long relative clause (2:6–9) describes how the latter did not regard equality with God as something to be grasped, but emptied himself and humbled himself to the point of death on a cross (cf. 2:3 f.). The prepositional phrase μέχρι θανάτου, which is given extra emphasis by the repetition in the construction θανάτου δὲ σταυροῦ, brings the account of how Christ humbled himself to a natural end-point. It thus marks the conclusion of this description.

---

[38] The interpretation of this subordinate clause has been much discussed. See the excursus on pp. 103–6.

In 2:9 a new start is made with διό and the stressed change of grammatical subject expressed by ὁ θεός. The particle διό interrupts the long relative construction that began at 2:6 and starts a new sentence. The change of subject marks a clear shift in content, from a description of the attitude of Christ to an account of God's response to that attitude. At the same time, the new construction operates at the same level in terms of content as the preceding verses, in that it also describes Christ's course in life.[39] This construction continues up to and including 2:11 and has the character of an ending. This is suggested by the inferential particle διό with which it begins and by the purpose- and consequence-indicating constructions in 2:10 f. (v. 10 ἵνα...; v. 11 ...εἰς δόξαν θεοῦ πατρός), which describe the eschatological consequences of Christ having humbled himself. What is being brought to a close here is primarily the subsection that began with the exhortation in 2:5, but the comparatively strongly marked opening in 2:12 makes it likely that this is also the conclusion of the section beginning in 2:1.

Excursus (to p. 106): Difficulties in the interpretation of 2:5–11

The meaning of the relative clause in 2:5 — ὃ καὶ ἐν Χριστῷ Ἰησοῦ — has been much discussed. Ultimately, the discussion has centred on whether 2:5–11 is to be understood in a 'paradigmatic' or a 'soteriological' sense. According to the first of these interpretations, the exhortation in 2:5 is to be of that mind that was in Christ Jesus, and his state of mind is then described in the following verses. With this interpretation, it is appropriate to supply a form of εἶναι in the relative clause and to take the prepositional phrase ἐν Χριστῷ Ἰησοῦ to mean 'in (the person of) Christ Jesus'. According to the second interpretation, the recipients are being called on in 2:5 to think in such a manner as is fitting for them in Christ Jesus, after which the text describes the saving work of Christ that has brought salvation to the human race and given people a new starting-point for their actions.

In my opinion, it is somewhat misleading to contrast 'paradigmatic' and 'soteriological' in this way. It is surely apparent that this passage has a soteriological dimension, since it is followed in 2:12 by the exhortation: 'Therefore... work out your own salvation with fear and trembling' (cf. also 1:28). The question is, what kind of soteriology is involved here: does it or does it not incorporate an idea of *imitatio Christi*? As I see it, this should be the focal point of the discussion.

Those who advocate a 'soteriological' interpretation, i.e. deny the presence of *imitatio Christi* thinking here,[40] usually rely on the following arguments:

1. The prepositional phrase ἐν ὑμῖν in 2:5 should be construed as 'among you', since the exhortations in 1:27–2:4 concern relations within the church.

---

[39] Concerning the question whether or not 2:6–11 is to be regarded as an early Christian hymn, see the excursus below, pp. 103–6.

[40] E.g. Gnilka 1968, Friedrich 1976a, Schenk 1984, Koenig 1985, Beare 1988 and Hübner 1993, pp. 327–31.

2. The transitive use of φρονεῖν favours a 'soteriological' interpretation.[41]

3. If ἐν ὑμῖν means 'in the Christian collectivity', the parallel ἐν Χριστῷ 'Ἰησοῦ should also do so.

4. The prepositional phrase ἐν Χριστῷ ('Ἰησοῦ) is normally used by Paul to refer to the risen Christ as the 'place' in which Christians live their lives (e.g. Phil 2:1).

5. The 'soteriological' interpretation accounts for more of the details of the following 'hymn' (2:6–11), particularly vv. 9–11.

6. It also fits in well with Paul's habit of deriving imperatives from indicatives, i.e. Christians should be what they already are through the saving work of Christ.

Regarding the first argument, it could equally well be claimed that the exhortations in 1:27–2:4 in fact refer to such a large extent to attitudes and states of mind that the interpretation 'in you' is to be preferred. Such an interpretation is admittedly slightly tautological, but not intolerably so. (Slight tautologies of this kind are not entirely unusual; the clause τί ἐνθυμεῖσθε πονερὰ ἐν ταῖς καρδίαις ὑμῶν in Mt 9:4, for example, is surely also tautological.) What is more, it should be pointed out that the interpretation 'among you' is also compatible with a 'paradigmatic' understanding of 2:5–11.

On the second argument, it can be observed that τοῦτο could very well be understood as an internal accusative (internal object), rather than an accusative object. In other words, it refers to the actual thinking, rather than what the thinking is directed towards.

Concerning the third argument, it may be noted that, even if the sense 'among you' is accepted for ἐν ὑμῖν, the parallelism does not compel us to interpret ἐν Χριστῷ 'Ἰησοῦ as 'in the Christian context', since the two elements would in any case not be entirely comparable, but rather express such different aspects of the collectivity that they would have to be translated differently ('among' and 'in', respectively). The closest parallelism is achieved if they are translated 'in you' and 'in (the person of) Christ Jesus'.

As for the fourth argument, it has to be said that the precise meaning of the prepositional phrase ἐν Χριστῷ is often unclear; what is more, we must probably expect it to vary according to the context. The meaning of the phrase is not altogether self-evident in 2:5 either; in 1:30, for example, ἐν ἐμοί has been used in a 'paradigmatic' sense.

Turning to the fifth argument, it can be argued that vv. 9–11 serve a purpose even with a 'paradigmatic' interpretation, since they describe the consequences of the road which Jesus trod and the conditions on which the Christian may follow it. This may be compared with what Paul says in 3:10–11 about sharing in the suffering and death of Christ, precisely in the hope of also sharing in his resurrection.

The sixth argument is based on the theological preconception that *imitatio Christi* thinking does not play any essential role in Pauline ethics. The analysis of 1 Thessalonians in the previous chapter gave us cause to question that preconception.

What is more, there is a good deal in the text to suggest that the idea of *imitatio Christi* is indeed present here. We have already noted the parallelism between the description of Paul's situation in 1:12–26 and the exhortations beginning at 1:27, and the explicit mention of this parallelism in 1:30. We can also note how well the finite

---

[41] Gnilka 1968, p. 108.

verbs, i.e. the key elements, of 2:6 ff., which describe the attitude and mind of Jesus (οὐχ ἁρπαγμὸν ἡγήσατο τὸ εἶναι ἴσα θεῷ, ἑαυτὸν ἐκένωσεν, ἐταπείνωσεν ἑαυτόν), correspond to the wording of the preceding exhortation in 2:2 ff. (... τὸ ἓν φρονοῦντες μηδὲν κατ᾽ ἐριθείαν μηδὲ κατὰ κενοδοξίαν ἀλλὰ τῇ ταπεινοφρο-σύνῃ ἀλλήλους ἡγούμενοι ὑπερέχοντας ἑαυτῶν, μὴ τὰ ἑαυτῶν ἕκαστος σκοποῦντες ἀλλὰ [καὶ] τὰ ἑτέρων ἕκαστοι). It is also striking how closely the exhortations which follow in 2:12 f. reflect the description of Jesus's chosen course in life in 2:6–11 (compare e.g. ὑπηκούσατε in 2:12 with γενόμενος ὑπήκοος in 2:8; τὴν ἑαυτῶν σωτηρίαν in 2:12 with 2:19–11; and 2:14 with, in particular, μορφὴν δούλου λαβών in 2:7 and ἐταπείνωσεν ἑαυτὸν γενόμενος ὑπήκοος in 2:8). All these points lend strong support to the view that *imitatio Christi* thinking is in fact present here,[42] and this is not made any less probable by Paul's express exhortation to the Philippians in 3:17 to be his 'fellow imitators' (of Christ, I assume).

Another debate concerning 2:5–11 has centred on whether or not 2:6–11, which in terms of subject-matter stands out from the surrounding text as a result of its focus on Jesus and is in addition somewhat rhythmic in character, is an early Christian hymn. Considerable effort has been put into trying to determine its metre, authorship and original *Sitz im Leben*. Johannes Weiss, for instance, who was the first to assert the poetic character of this section, divided the text into two stanzas, each of four lines.[43] A. Deissman's suggestion was two stanzas of seven lines each,[44] while H. Lietzmann argued that the text was a hymn of 17 lines.[45] Since then, many different ways of dividing up this 'hymn' have been proposed, e.g. six stanzas of three lines each, with a gloss (θανάτου δὲ σταυροῦ);[46] four stanzas of three lines each, without glosses;[47] three stanzas of four lines, with several glosses;[48] two stanzas of nine and seven lines respectively, without glosses;[49] and two stanzas of eight and six lines respectively, with two glosses.[50] Attempts to translate the text into Aramaic have not brought about any decisive breakthrough in the discussion either.[51] Given the significant lack of consensus on the metrical form of this passage, despite a hundred years of scholarship, there is cause not only to doubt the usefulness of that form in clarifying the structure of the passage, but also to join H. Riesenfeld in questioning whether the text really is a hymn or even poetic in the strict sense of the word, particularly since it lacks other typical characteristics of poetry, such as metaphors and other figurative use of language.[52] What is more, one may well ask with Riesenfeld why Paul, who in other

---

[42] Concerning the function of Phil 2:6–11 as an 'exemplar', see Fowl 1990, pp. 92–5.
[43] Weiss 1897, pp. 28 f.
[44] Deissman 1925, pp. 149 f.
[45] Lietzmann 1926, p. 178.
[46] Lohmeyer 1928, pp. 5 f.
[47] Dibelius 1937, pp. 72 f.
[48] Deichgräber 1967, p. 122.
[49] Hofius 1976, p. 8.
[50] Müller 1988, p. 19.
[51] E.g. Fitzmyer 1988, pp. 482 f.
[52] Riesenfeld 1983, pp. 160 ff. Of course one can — as e.g. S. E. Fowl (1990, p. 45) does — give the term 'hymn' such a broad meaning that it covers even Phil 2:6–10, but then it will in my opinion confuse rather than clarify matters.

places sets off quotations from tradition with quotation formulae,[53] does not do so here, but omits the opening of the hymn and begins the quotation with a relative pronoun.[54]

Moreover, the reasons for assuming non-Pauline authorship of this text are not particularly strong, especially if it cannot be demonstrated unequivocally that it is a hymn. The arguments that are usually put forward are the occurrence of (1) words not found elsewhere in Paul's letters, (2) theological motifs differing from those occurring in his other letters and (3) Semitisms. A critical scrutiny of these arguments yields the following results: (1) If we take into account not only individual words, but also words with common roots and compounds, the vocabulary of this passage does not seem particularly un-Pauline. For example, in Paul's letters, μορφή only occurs in Phil 2:6 and 7, but this seems less remarkable when we also find μορφοῦσθαι in Gal 4:19, μόρφωσις in Rom 2:20, σύμμορφος in Rom 8:29 and Phil 3:21, and συμμορφίζεσθαι in Phil 3:10. Similar parallels could be adduced for ἁρπαγμός, ἴσος, σχῆμα, ὑπήκοος, ὑπερυψοῦν and γόνυ κάμπτειν. The only truly original word in Phil 2:6–11 appears to be καταχθόνιος. (2) The theological motifs do not appear to be as un-Pauline as is claimed, either.[55] For example, we also find a contrast between ταπεινοῦν and ὑψοῦν in 2 Cor 11:7 (although that passage is not concerned with the death and exaltation of Jesus); a reference to Jesus's death without the words ὑπέρ ὑμῶν or the like in 1 Thess 4:14; a tripartite division of the cosmos in Rom 10:6 f.; and a reference to the supremacy of Christ, combined with the motif that it is God who gives him everything, in 1 Cor 15:27 f. (3) Semitisms also occur elsewhere in the Pauline epistles, and do not seem to me to be more numerous or more marked here than anywhere else.

With these comments, I am not seeking to deny altogether that this text has a *certain* degree of linguistic originality and that the question of its authorship therefore merits serious consideration, but merely to show that the case normally made against Pauline authorship is not quite as strong as it might perhaps appear at first sight. For the purposes of my study, the authorship question and the possibility of some other original *Sitz im Leben* are not of any great importance, if 2:6–11 fits well into its context in any case, which I consider that it does.

2:12–18

The close that occurs in 2:9–11 is followed by a fairly distinct fresh start in 2:12, marked by the address ἀγαπητοί μου and the return to imperatives in the second person plural after the many indicatives in the third person singular. It can also be noted that here too — as in 2:1 — Paul uses fronted subordinate clauses, this time comparative, as a platform from which to launch into the new section.

At the same time, the use of ὥστε, given emphasis by the address and by the fronted subordinate clauses, makes it clear that what is now beginning is a

[53] Cf. e.g. 1 Cor 1:19; 11:23; 15:3.
[54] Riesenfeld 1983, pp. 157 ff. Cf. also Fowl 1990, pp. 37 f.
[55] See e.g. Schweitzer 1962, p. 93, note 373.

statement of consequences. The consequences concerned are primarily the paraenetic implications of the description of Jesus's course in life given in 2:6–11. At all events, the reference to the Philippians' customary obedience in 2:12 (καθὼς πάντοτε ὑπηκούσατε) has a parallel in 2:7 f. (μορφὴν δούλου λαβών... γενόμενος ὑπήκοος), and the exhortation to them in 2:12 to work out their salvation and the comment in 2:13 about God being at work can be compared with 2:9 ff. The question is, though, whether the statement of consequences that begins at 2:12 does not have a wider reference, going beyond a mere indication of the paraenetic consequences of the verses immediately preceding it. The strong emphasis created by the emotionally charged ἀγαπητοί μου and by the position of the subordinate clauses suggests that this is the case. We can also note that the motif of presence and absence which appeared in 1:27 is taken up again here, and that the salvation motif represents a link with 1:28. The strongly accentuated opening of the statement of consequences and the recurrences of concepts found in the opening exhortation in 1:27–30 give rise to a suspicion that the section beginning in 2:12 is rounding off the paraenetic section that began at 1:27. This suspicion is confirmed as the text unfolds and we find further and more significant recurrences looking back to the beginning of the paraenetic section and to the sections which formed the basis for it (1:12–18c and 1:18d–26).

The exhortation in 2:12 f. is followed in 2:14 by another which develops further on the obedience motif presented in 2:12, calling on the recipients to do all things without murmuring and arguing. The actual exhortation is then followed by a couple of quite protracted statements of purpose and consequences. How far the latter extend depends on how the text is punctuated. NTG has a full stop after ἐκοπίασα in 2:16 and a semicolon after ὑμῖν in 2:17. I myself would suggest a comma in both cases, so that vv. 17 f. are read as a direct continuation of the preceding construction.[56] My reasons for this interpretation are presented in an excursus below. The statements of consequences then continue as far as 2:18 inclusive.[57]

The first statement of consequences — 2:15 f.: ἵνα γένησθε... τέκνα θεοῦ ἄμωμα μέσον γενεᾶς σκολιᾶς... λόγον ζωῆς ἐπέχοντες — relates to the Philippians and refers back to the key motifs of 'living in a manner worthy of the gospel of Christ' and 'standing firm and striving for the gospel, in no way intimidated by one's opponents', which occur in the opening exhortation in

---

[56] For a diagrammatic clarification of the text, and a commentary, see below, pp. 111–13.
[57] It should be noted, however, that most of the points made below are valid even with a more traditional reading of the text.

1:27–30. (Concerning the link between these motifs and the overriding theme of 'Paul's situation resulting in the furtherance of the gospel', see above, pp. 101 f.)

The second statement of consequences — 2:16 ff.: ... εἰς καύχημα ἐμοί... ὅτι... εἰ καὶ σπένδομαι... χαίρω... καὶ συγχαίρετέ μοι — relates primarily to Paul. This reflects the fact that the paraenetic section took as its starting-point the description of Paul's joy-inspiring situation in 1:12–18c and above all 1:18d–26 (see above, p. 100 ff.). That Paul really is referring back to this starting-point here is indicated by several key motifs, chiefly from the account given in 1:18d–26. The motif of boasting (καύχημα) in 2:16 can be compared with ἐν οὐδενὶ αἰσχυνθήσομαι in 1:20 (cf. also 1:26, 28); the motif of 'the possible martyrdom of Paul' (εἰ καὶ σπένδομαι) in 2:17 with εἴτε διὰ ζωῆς εἴτε διὰ θανάτου in 1:20; and the motifs of 'the future rejoicing of Paul and of the Philippians' with χαρήσομαι in 1:18 and εἰς τὴν ὑμῶν... χαρὰν τῆς πίστεως in 1:25 (cf. also 2:2).

These recurrences of material from the opening of the paraenetic section and from the exposition forming the basis for it, in particular 1:18d–26, confirm the suspicion that the paraenetic section is being brought to a close and suggest that this ending also encompasses the preceding descriptions of Paul's situation and the joy to which it gave rise, i.e. the whole of the section beginning at 1:12. This is then confirmed by the new start in 2:19.

To sum up: in the section 1:12–2:18, Paul is informing the Philippians that his situation has resulted and will result in the furtherance of the gospel and in joy for himself. He begins by describing how his situation has indeed had these results (1:12–18c). He then says that he knows that it will continue to do so (1:18d–26). At the end of the latter section, the ideas of furtherance and joy are related specifically to the Philippians. This occasions a paraenetic section (1:27–2:18), in which Paul states what is required of the addressees if the furtherance of the gospel and hence also his own joy are to become realities.

Excursus (to p. 113): The punctuation of 2:14–18

NTG puts a full stop after ἐκοπίασα at the end of 2:16 and a semicolon after ὑμῖν at the end of 2:17. Clearly, its editors consider the syntactic construction that begins at 2:14 to be complete at the end of 2:16 and regard ἀλλά in 2:17 as beginning a new construction, presumably in a similar manner to ἀλλά in Phil 1:18. The new construction is thus seen as a statement saying that Paul rejoices and does so together with the Philippians. The following sentence in 2:18 is then generally understood as an exhortation.

I feel doubtful about this interpretation, for the following reasons:

1. The conjunction ἀλλά is usually an eliminative adversative particle, i.e. it coordinates elements that are semantically incompatible. It is therefore very commonly used after a negation to state the positive alternative. Sometimes — but not at all as often — the preceding clause is positive and the following one is negated. In addition, ἀλλά can occur in special, often elliptical constructions, e.g. after a question or in an apodosis after a conditional or concessive clause. In certain cases it can be weakened and come close to the meaning of a balancing adversative particle. As a rule, however, it retains a good deal of its eliminative adversative force and thus expresses, in one way or another, a tangible, explicit or implicit, opposition.[58]

An examination of all the occurrences of ἀλλά in Paul's letters confirms this. In almost 200 (i.e. approx. 75%) of the total of just over 260 occurrences, the conjunction directly follows a negation and introduces the positive alternative. Of the remaining occurrences, 12 (5%) appear to be cases of ἀλλά reflecting a preceding negation, though less directly, thus indicating a looser connection with what has gone before.[59] In three cases (1%), the conjunction follows a question, with the sense 'No, but rather...' or 'yes, but... not...'.[60] In seven cases (3%) it occurs in an apodosis following a conditional or concessive clause ('if (even though)..., yet...').[61]

Of the remaining 42 occurrences (16%)[62], many seem to involve a construction of the same type as the conditional (concessive) complex sentence with ἀλλά, but consisting of two coordinated clauses rather than a conditional (concessive) subordinate clause followed by an apodosis (see e.g. 1 Cor 6:12: 'All things are lawful for me, but not all things are beneficial', which corresponds to 'Even though all things are lawful for me, nevertheless not all things are beneficial'). Other cases seem to involve elliptical expressions (see e.g. Phil 1:18: χαίρω (οὐ μόνον δέ), ἀλλὰ καὶ χαρήσομαι or Phil 2:27: ἠσθένησεν παραπλήσιον θανάτῳ. (οὐκ ἀπέθανεν δέ), ἀλλὰ ὁ θεὸς ἠλέησεν αὐτόν). What is interesting to note here is that in only two of these 42 cases with a non-standard use of ἀλλά is the word preceded by a negation, and that in both these cases it is immediately followed by a negative expression which prevents us from understanding what follows as the positive alternative to the preceding negative.[63] The

---

[58] See e.g. Denniston 1954, pp. 1–22.

[59] Rom 10:8 (μή in v. 6), 18 and 19 (οὐ in v. 16); 11:4 (οὐκ in v. 2); 12:20 (μή in v. 19); Phil 3:7 and 8 (οὐκ in 3:3); Gal 1:8 (οὐκ in v. 7); 1 Cor 6:11, 11, 11 (μή in v. 9); 12:22 (οὐ in v. 21).

[60] Rom 8:37; 1 Cor 9:12; 10:20.

[61] Rom 6:5; 1 Cor 4:15; 8:6; 9:2; 2 Cor 4:16; 5:16; 11:6.

[62] Rom 4:2; 5:15; 10:2, 16; 1 Cor 3:2, 6; 4:3, 4; 6:12, 12; 7:7; 8:7; 10:5, 23, 23; 14:17, 19; 15:35, 40, 46; 2 Cor 4:8, 8, 9, 9; 7:6, 11, 11, 11, 11, 11, 11; 8:7; 11:1; 13:4, 4; Gal 2:14; 4:8, 23, 29, 30; Phil 1:18; 2:27.

[63] In 1 Cor 4:4 ἀλλά is admittedly preceded by οὐδέν, but the following, strongly emphasized οὐκ ἐν τούτῳ then deviates so clearly from the normal pattern that ἀλλά cannot be seen as a response to the preceding negation, but has to be understood in some other way (here, most appropriately in line with its 'concessive use': 'Even though I am not aware of anything against myself, I am nevertheless not thereby acquitted').

Similarly, in 1 Cor 3:2, ἀλλά is preceded by a negation (οὔπω), but here again we are prevented from seeing this as an instance of the dominant construction type by a heavily stressed negative construction (οὐδὲ ἔτι νῦν) immediately after the conjunction, which breaks the pattern and makes it clear that the contrast here concerns the temporal

reason for this is presumably that the use of ἀλλά in response to a preceding negation is so dominant that any other use of the word is only possible if that use is clearly indicated (e.g. by the inclusion of the word in a special construction, such as in an apodosis following a conditional or concessive clause) or if the construction clearly deviates from the norm (e.g. because ἀλλά does not follow a negation). In Phil 2:16 f., ἀλλά does follows a negation and there is no indication of any other use than the dominant one. I therefore wonder whether a contemporary member of the church, hearing this text 'from the beginning', would not have been inclined to link ἀλλά in v. 17 with the two negations preceding it in v. 16, and thus to understand the words following it as the positive alternative to the preceding negative ones.

2. The verbs in 2:17 are in the present indicative and are usually taken to refer to the present as viewed from Paul's perspective. Such an interpretation, however, implies an abrupt shift in perspective in 2:17. In 2:14 the Philippians were urged to conduct themselves appropriately in the future, after which the consequences of this conduct for the Philippians themselves were set out in 2:15 and its consequences for Paul in 2:16. According to the commonest interpretation, the final part of 2:16 even refers to the Last Day. This reference is then, it is claimed, followed immediately by a statement about Paul's joy at the present time, before the exhortations in 2:18 once again focus attention on the Philippians' future. Quite understandably, commentators have had difficulty discerning a clear link between these verses.

3. The verse 2:17 is usually interpreted as containing an implicit assertion that the Philippians are rejoicing. However, there would be something of a tension between such an assertion and the overall tendency in the Letter to the Philippians, namely that Paul claims to be rejoicing himself (cf. Phil 1:4, 18; 2:2; 4:1, 10), but urges the Philippians also to rejoice (cf. 3:1; 4:4) or expresses a conviction or hope that they will do so (cf. Phil 1:25; 2:28).

---

dimension. In this case the construction is elliptical and οὐδέ indicates that the contrast serves to bring out the additional point being made: οὔπω ἐδύνασθε. (οὐ μόνον δέ), ἀλλ' οὐδὲ ἔτι νῦν δύνασθε.

In 1 Cor 12:24, editors usually insert a full stop before ἀλλά, but this practice is very much open to discussion. The question is whether the new sentence does not in fact run from δέ at the beginning of v. 24, the sense then being: 'Our more respectable members are not in need (of greater honour or respect), but rather God has so arranged the body, giving the greater honour to the inferior member (in terms of honour or respect), in order that...'. The construction is somewhat laboured as a result of contamination between 'not the more respectable members are in need, but the inferior member' and 'not to the more respectable members did God give the greater honour, but to the inferior member', but not so much so that it does not work.

In Gal 2:2 f. there is a construction reminiscent of the one in Phil 2:16 f. Here, too, ἀλλά occurs after the expression εἰς κενὸν τρέχειν. However, certain features are different here, e.g. the change of subject (from 'I' to 'Titus') and the fact that the negation οὐδέ follows immediately, which could indicate that in this case ἀλλά is not following up the preceding negation. It is also possible, though, to regard Gal 2:2 f. as an example of the common usage, with the negative alternative εἰς κενόν... ἔδραμον followed by οὐδὲ Τίτος... ἠναγκάσθη περιτμηθῆναι, which is 'positive' in content terms. As in Phil 2:16 f., the construction is complicated by the fact that the negative alternative consists of a stock phrase, with the result that the positive alternative cannot very well be formulated directly on the basis of it but has to be expressed in completely different terms (cf. the problem of contamination noted above). The construction in Gal 2:2 f., moreover, is complicated by the many negations.

4. As was noted earlier, the sentence in 2:18 is generally understood as an exhortation. One reason for this is probably that it would after all seem a little strange for Paul to tell the Philippians that they are rejoicing, and all the more so if that assertion were made explicitly. However, an argument against interpreting 2:18 as an exhortation is that Paul apparently does not normally begin exhortations with the particle δέ. Usually, they are asyndetic constructions or are linked to the preceding text by an inferential particle (cf. Phil 1:27; 2:1 f., 5, 12, 14, 29; 3:1, 2, 15 f., 17; 4:1–9; 1 Thess 4:18; 5:6, 11, 13–22; Gal 4:12; 5:1, 13, 25 f.; 6:1, 2, 7, 10, 11). Sometimes, admittedly, the particle δέ is used within paraeneses to coordinate exhortations which contrast with one another in some respect or to mark a resumption of exhortation following a parenthetic explanation (cf. e.g. 1 Thess 5:8, 21 (possibly); Gal 5:15; 6:4, 6, 9), but the new start that is assumed to be made with ἀλλά in Phil 2:17 is probably too distinct for some such explanation to apply here. Had Paul wished to move on from statement to exhortation in 2:18, he would — I believe — have had to mark this transition or discontinuity in his text more clearly. In the form which the text has assumed, the first clause can too easily be read as running on into the second.

For these reasons, among others, I question the usual interpretation and would instead suggest that Phil 2:17 f. should be read as a continuation of the construction in 2:14–16, resulting in the following structure:

2:14	πάντα ποιεῖτε χωρὶς γογγυσμῶν...
2:15	ἵνα γένησθε ἄμεμπτοι... μέσον γενεᾶς σκολιᾶς...
	ἐν οἷς φαίνεσθε ὡς φωστῆρες ἐν κόσμῳ...
2:16	εἰς καύχημα ἐμοὶ εἰς ἡμέραν Χριστοῦ,
	ὅτι οὐκ εἰς κενὸν ἔδραμον...,
2:17	ἀλλὰ εἰ καὶ σπένδομαι..., χαίρω
	καὶ συγχαίρω πᾶσιν ὑμῖν,
2:18	τὸ δὲ αὐτὸ καὶ ὑμεῖς χαίρετε
	καὶ συγχαίρετέ μοι.

With this reading of the text, 2:17 f., like 2:15 f., describes the favourable consequences of the Philippians' heeding Paul's exhortation in 2:14. These consequences are thus said to be, among other things, joy for both the Philippians and Paul.

Such a reading avoids the difficulties referred to above (see 1–4). But there are other arguments in its favour, too:

1. It fits well into the wider context. In 1:12–18c, Paul has described his present situation, concluding with the opinion that he rejoices in it. In 1:18d there is then a distinct shift in perspective to Paul's future situation. His description of that situation begins with the assessment ἀλλὰ καὶ χαρήσομαι, and is thus given from that point of view. In 1:25 f., i.e. at the end of Paul's account of the future which he expects, this future joy is related to and described as dependent on the Philippians' furtherance and joy in faith. The text then moves on to the paraenetic section 1:27–2:18. It begins with μόνον and is thus closely linked to what has gone before: the favourable future, bringing joy to both Paul and the Philippians, which was described in 1:18d–26 will become a reality if the Philippians will only follow the exhortations Paul expresses in this paraenetic section. That Paul is still writing from the standpoint of his 'future joy' is confirmed by the second exhortation in 2:1–4, which begins with an inferential

particle: ... οὖν ... πληρώσατέ μου τὴν χαράν. If the whole of the section 1:18d–2:18 is written from the viewpoint of 'Paul's future joy' and that joy has already been related to the future joy of the Philippians (1:25 f.), which has in turn been said to be dependent on the extent to which they heed Paul's exhortations (1:27), it is quite natural for Paul now, at the end of the section, to return to these overarching themes and once again to refer to the joy which will result for himself and the Philippians if they heed his exhortations.

2. With the reading proposed here, then, the paraenetic section 1:27–2:18 closes with an account of the favourable consequences that may be expected if the Philippians heed the exhortations which it contains. This fits the pattern of other Pauline paraeneses, which are usually rounded off with some indication of the expected or desired favourable effects of obedience to their commands (cf. e.g. Rom 15:13, 33; Gal 6:16; Phil 4:7, 9; 1 Thess 5:23 f.).

Naturally, objections can be raised to the proposed reading — otherwise editors would not have chosen to put a full stop before ἀλλά. One might be that this reading is hardly possible if καύχημα and the following ὅτι-clause concern the day of Christ, since 2:17 f. is clearly describing matters of this world (see σπένδομαι). However, that objection is invalid if — as I believe — καύχημα and the ὅτι-clause do not describe conditions *on* the day of Christ, but rather worldly matters which are of significance *for* the day of Christ. This would also explain why Paul here (and in Phil 1:10) writes εἰς ἡμέραν Χριστοῦ and not ἐν ἡμέρᾳ Χριστοῦ, as he does elsewhere.[64] Thus, καύχημα and the ὅτι-clause in 2:16 refer to the same period of time as 2:15–16a, i.e. an undefined, relatively near future within this world. With such an understanding of the temporal dimension, the concessive clause in 2:17 fits the context better, since the hypothetical event which it describes could occur in that selfsame undefined, worldly future.

There is, though, a more serious objection concerning the relationship between 2:17 and καύχημα/the ὅτι-clause in 2:16, focusing on the causal rather than the temporal relationship between the two verses. If the ὅτι-clause in 2:16 expresses the content or the cause of Paul's καύχημα, the proposed construction would seem to be claiming that Paul's καύχημα is due to his own and the Philippians' joy, which seems strange. It is admittedly understandable that these concepts should be closely linked in Paul's thinking, and such a link is confirmed for example by Phil 1:25 f., 2 Cor 7:4 and 1 Thess 2:19. But one would not have expected 'boasting' to be said to be due to 'joy', but rather that the two would be described as parallel reactions to the same situation. However, in Phil 1:25 f., too, Paul talks of the Philippians' furtherance and *joy* in faith *leading to* (ἵνα...) their *boasting* 'overflowing'. Nevertheless, if my understanding of the sequence of thought in 2:16 ff. is correct, there is probably no escaping something of a shift or a looseness in the construction here. It is not unreasonable to reckon with such looseness, however, on the following grounds: (1) the construction in 2:14 ff. is long and complex; (2) the positive alternative cannot very well be formulated directly on the basis of the negative one, since the latter consists of a stock phrase (εἰς κενὸν τρέχειν), but has to be given a new

---

[64] See e.g. Rom 2:5, 16; 1 Cor 1:8; 5:3; 2 Cor 1:14.

formulation, which of course in itself implies a shift in meaning; (3) here, at the end of the section 1:18c–2:18, Paul is naturally drawn towards the overarching theme of 'Paul's future joy'.

For these reasons, I feel that the problem which my reading entails — a certain looseness of construction — counts for relatively little compared with its advantages over the 'traditional' reading: (1) It enables us to affirm the linguistically natural link between οὐ and ἀλλά in 2:16 f. (2) There is no need to assume temporal shifts in 2:16 ff. which are difficult to explain. (3) It is not necessary to assume an implicit assertion about the Philippians' joy in 2:17. (4) The two clauses coordinated with δέ in 2:17b and 2:18 have the same semantic function (that of statements). (5) The conclusion of the section links up naturally with the overall motif, as presented in 1:18c, 25 and 2:2. (6) As in many other places in Paul's letters, the paraenesis concludes with a reference to the favourable effects of obeying its commands.

With the reading of the text which I propose, then, Paul urges the Philippians to do all things without murmuring and arguing, so that they may be blameless in the midst of a perverse generation and shine like stars in the world (note these worldly categories), a condition which will be a cause for boasting by Paul until (or for) the day of Christ and which will mean that he has not run in vain but rather, even if he is killed, rejoices and does so with the Philippians.

2:19–30

2:19–24

The close in 2:12–18 is confirmed by a distinct new beginning in 2:19, marked by the conjunction δέ and an instructive and thematic construction. The latter begins with the metapropositional base ἐλπίζω... ἐν κυρίῳ Ἰησοῦ, showing that Paul is now moving on from exhortation (1:27–2:18) to the expression of a hope. The content of that hope, the proposition, is set out in an infinitive construction and concerns Paul sending Timothy to the Philippians soon. There is thus a shift at the propositional level, too, in 2:19. The personal reference, Τιμόθεον, which is given prominence in the construction, helps to accentuate this shift. However, the new theme is linked to the preceding one by the ἵνα-clause that follows. The section 1:27–2:18 was about the Philippians living their lives in a manner worthy of the gospel of Christ (1:27), so that Paul might hear about this (1:27) and rejoice (2:2, 17). Now the text states that the purpose of sending Timothy is to enable Paul to find out how things are with the Philippians (γνοὺς τὰ περὶ ὑμῶν) and thus to be cheered (κἀγὼ εὐψυχῶ).

There then follow a couple of γάρ-clauses commenting on the excellent qualities of Timothy. These comments are rounded off in 2:22 with a reference to the Philippians' own knowledge of how he has proved himself in the service of the gospel, a reference that renders further comment superfluous.

What should be noted here is that the summary in 2:22 describes Timothy's worth as consisting specifically in his *service of the gospel* (εἰς τὸ εὐαγγέλιον), and thus echoes several earlier, important expressions describing praiseworthy conduct (cf. e.g. 1:5, 12, 27).

This verse is followed in 2:23 f. by a μέν... δέ... construction which clearly brings to a close the section that began at 2:19. This is indicated by the opening τοῦτον, which refers to and sums up the description of Timothy given in 2:20 ff., the inferential particle οὖν, and the very clear recurrence in the first part of the construction of words from the beginning of the section. The second part of the construction consists of an additional concluding assessment, beginning with the metapropositional πέποιθα... ἐν κυρίῳ and expressing the conviction that Paul himself will also come soon (cf. 1:25 f.).

2:25-30

The ending in 2:23 f. is confirmed by the new start in 2:25, which is marked by the conjunction δέ and a construction that is clearly instructive and thematic. The latter begins with what is presumably a secondary metapropositional base ἀναγκαῖον... ἡγησάμην (the primary metapropositional base being γνωρίζω ὅτι or the like), indicating a transition from hope (2:19–24) to a decision that has been taken. The proposition, the content of that decision, then follows in the form of an infinitive construction and refers to Epaphroditus being sent to the Philippians. The accentuated and elaborate personal reference Ἐπαφρόδιτον τὸν... λειτουργὸν τῆς χρείας μου marks something of a shift at the propositional level, too. However, the infinitive itself, πέμψαι, provides a link with the preceding section 2:19–24 and justifies regarding that and the new section as a single entity.

The reason for sending Epaphroditus is set out in a causal subordinate clause in 2:26 and further elaborated on in an explanatory comment (γάρ) in 2:27. In 2:28 Paul then sets forth the conclusion he draws from this explanation. The verse begins with the inferential particle οὖν, and its wording (σπουδαιοτέρως... ἔπεμψα αὐτόν) clearly echoes the opening words of 2:25 (ἀναγκαῖον... ἡγησάμην Ἐπαφρόδιτον... πέμψαι), indicating that the section is being brought to a close. The ἵνα-clause that is added here states that Epaphroditus has been sent so that the Philippians may *rejoice* and Paul be *less anxious*. This statement of purpose is somewhat reminiscent of 2:19, where the purpose of sending Timothy was said to be so that Paul might *be cheered*. However, the joy motif in 2:28 differs from that found in 2:19 and earlier in that it is not clearly linked to the 'furtherance of the gospel' motif.

The conclusion drawn in 2:28, which concerned Paul, is followed by another in 2:29 f. It is linked to the preceding one, but this time it focuses on the consequences for the Philippians. This conclusion also begins with οὖν, and once again the joy motif is taken up (μετὰ πάσης χαρᾶς), now also related to service (λειτουργίας) and the work of Christ (διὰ τὸ ἔργον Χριστοῦ). It thus continues more clearly the thread of thought that has hitherto run through the whole of the letter, namely the furtherance of the gospel and the joy occasioned by it.

The expression of a conclusion in 2:29 f. reinforces the impression that a close is at hand. Primarily, what is being brought to an end is the section 2:25–30. The length of the close and the recurrence in it of the overarching motifs of the text so far, however, can be taken to indicate that it is also bringing a longer section to an end. It is only when we get to the strongly marked opening in 3:1, with its distinct shift in perspective, however, that it becomes clear that what is being drawn to a close here is in fact the whole of the letter so far.

In summary, 1:3–2:30 can be said to consist of three parts: 1:3–11; 1:12–2:18; and 2:19–30. The first of these sections describes Paul's thanksgiving to God for the Philippians' sharing for the benefit of the gospel up to the present time and in the future. In the second, Paul informs the Philippians that his situation has resulted in the furtherance of the gospel and in joy for himself, and that he knows it will continue to do so; this is followed by exhortations which, in the light of Paul's joy-inspiring situation, set out what is required of the Philippians to make his joy complete. In the third part he expresses his hope of sending Timothy to the Philippians soon so that he might be cheered by news of them, and announces his decision to send Epaphroditus to them, to bring joy to them and to himself.

3:1–4:9

3:1

The close in 2:28 ff. is confirmed by a distinct fresh start in 3:1, marked by the particle τὸ λοιπόν, which here primarily indicates a transition to a new element in the text, the attention-attracting address ἀδελφοί μου, the change of mood from indicative to imperative (although the previous section ended with an exhortation, it was predominantly descriptive and expressed in the indicative), and the metacommunicative clause τὰ αὐτὰ γράφειν ὑμῖν ἐμοὶ οὐκ ὀκνηρόν, ὑμῖν δὲ ἀσφαλές, which is a comment on what Paul is now about to do.

The change in mood from the indicative to the imperative entails an appreciable shift at the metapropositional level: in the previous section, 2:25–30, Paul announced a decision; now he moves on to exhortation. At the propositional level, too, there is of course a shift, since the preceding section

115

was primarily concerned with Paul sending Epaphroditus, while the new exhortation appears to concern a more general rejoicing in the Lord.[65] At 3:1 there is thus clearly a shift at both the metapropositional and the propositional level in relation to the section immediately preceding this verse.

However, in my view 3:1 also involves a shift in the actual mode of presentation compared with the preceding text of the letter (1:3–2:30). This earlier text not only proceeded from, but in a sense constantly revolved around Paul's situation and joy. This was also true of the paraenetic section 1:27–2:18, which took as its starting-point the account in 1:18d–26 of Paul's knowledge that his situation would result in the furtherance of the gospel, also among the Philippians, and thus give him cause to rejoice. That this perspective then determined the shape of the paraenetic section was indicated by the recurrences in 1:27 (ἵνα... ἀκούω) and 2:2 (πληρώσατέ μου τὴν χαρὰν ἵνα...) and by the fact that the entire section concluded with a statement about how, by heeding Paul's exhortations, the Philippians would make it possible for him to boast and rejoice. At 3:1 this express focus on Paul is abandoned and the perspective shifts more unequivocally to the situation and joy of the Philippians.

This does not entail any change in substance, however. One purpose of the exhortations in the paraenetic section 1:27–2:18, too, was to bring joy to the Philippians (1:25 f.; 2:17 f.), and in the introduction to my analysis of this letter I drew attention to a number of clear lexical links between the paraenetic section just mentioned and the section beginning at 3:1,[66] which show that there is a connection between the two sections even beyond that first verse. It is I believe against this background that we must understand the meta-communicative clause in 3:1, which comments on the fact that Paul is writing τὰ αὐτά to the Philippians. There has been some discussion about what the words τὰ αὐτά refer to here.[67] Given the recurrences that have been mentioned, a plausible interpretation would seem to be that here, at the beginning of the new section, Paul is commenting on the fact that he is now embarking on a paraenetic passage which is closely related in substance to the

---

[65] The joy motif in 3:1 is not as closely linked to 2:29 f. as one might at first be led to believe. The joy referred to in 2:29 is directly connected with Epaphroditus, his return and his earlier efforts; that referred to in 3:1 is completely divorced from this causal context and appears rather to be linked to the persecution to be endured by the Philippians (see 3:2 f. and 3:17–21).

[66] See the introduction to this chapter, pp. 94 f.

[67] Usually, one of the following views is advocated: (a) the exhortations that follow repeat the contents of an earlier letter, since lost (e.g. Vincent 1897, p. 91; Barth 1947, p. 87); (b) the exhortations that follow repeat what Paul has previously communicated orally (e.g. Gnilka 1968, p. 185; Eriksson 1982, p. 120); (c) the preceding exhortation to rejoice is also found in Phil 2:18 and 4:4 (e.g. Dibelius 1937, p. 86; Lohmeyer 1953, p. 124).

paraenesis of 1:27–2:18, in particular. If this is the case, then τὰ αὐτά refers not merely to the exhortation to rejoice, but to the content or drift of the paraenesis as a whole. That interpretation also does justice to the plural form used. There is thus also cause to ask whether τὸ λοιπόν does not have more of an inferential force here than is usually acknowledged.[68]

3:2–16

After this intervening metacommunicative clause, Paul's exhortations gather fresh momentum in 3:2, with three short, closely related commands joined by asyndeton. This repetitive and intense construction represents a change of style and gives the impression that something of a new start is being made. The interpretation of the exhortations here poses several difficulties, and they have been much discussed. These discussions have centred on the meaning of βλέπετε, the background to and meaning of the terms τοὺς κύνας, τοὺς κακοὺς ἐργάτας and τὴν κατατομήν, and the question of to whom those terms refer. Here I shall confine myself to observing that the recipients are being urged to look at or pay attention to a group of opponents at Philippi,[69] who are described using the three terms. Since it is not specified who these opponents are, and they are not clearly distinguished from those mentioned in 1:28, I consider it most likely that the same opponents are being referred to in both cases.[70]

The last of the terms, τὴν κατατομήν, gives rise to an explanatory comment (γάρ) in 3:3–4a, stating that it is 'we', i.e. not 'they', who are the circumcision,

[68] Cf. the comment on λοιπὸν οὖν in 1 Thess 4:1, pp. 61.

[69] G. D. Kilpatrick (1968, pp. 146 ff.) has rightly expressed scepticism about βλέπετε being translated here as 'beware of', 'watch out for' etc. According to him, that sense is only found in the constructions βλέπετε μή or βλέπετε ἀπό, but in those expressions the 'precautionary element' resides in μή and ἀπό. From this statement, however, it need not be concluded, as J. Schoon-Jansen (1991, p. 155) does, that Paul is referring here to Jews in general as an instance of people who have confidence in the flesh. The function of the phrases τοὺς κύνας, τοὺς κακοὺς ἐργάτας and τὴν κατατομήν seems to me to be, not to identify and introduce a new group in the text, but rather to describe and interpret a group already referred to, namely the opponents mentioned in 1:28 (see Fowl 1990, pp. 98 f.).

[70] What is more, such an assumption does not involve any real difficulties. The opponents in 1:28 appear to be 'outside' persecutors, and those referred to in 3:2 seem to be Jews. Since most instances of persecution of Paul and the early church seem to have been initiated by Jewish groups (see e.g. Acts 4:1–22; 5:17–40; 8:1–3; 12:1–19, 13:50; 14:2, 19; 17:5, 13; 18:12; 20:3, 19; 21:27 f.; 23:12; 1 Thess 2:14 ff.; 2 Cor 11:23 ff.), the two references are compatible. The only difficulty could perhaps be that there appear to have been relatively few Jews at Philippi (Portefaix 1988, p. 73). However, there do seem to have been some Jews there (Acts 16:13), and it would not take very many to instigate persecution. What is more, Jewish groups from elsewhere could very well have been involved (cf. Acts 14:9; 17:13).

'we' who worship the Spirit of God,[71] boast in Christ Jesus and have no confidence in the flesh. The modest new beginning which this entails is marked by the stressed change of grammatical subject (ἡμεῖς). In a closing concessive participial construction, Paul states that he could in fact also have confidence in the flesh.

This concessive construction occasions a lengthy digression about the possibility of Paul having confidence in the flesh and about his boasting in Christ (3:4b–14). The new start which this involves is marked by asyndeton and a conditional clause, in which the key motif 'confidence in the flesh' is taken up from the preceding passage and made the starting-point of the digression. This is followed by a description of Paul's qualifications in the flesh (3:5 f.), which emphasizes his blamelessness from a Jewish point of view.

In 3:7 a minor new start is made.[72] It is marked by a loosely connective ἀλλά[73] and by a construction which is clearly instructive and thematic. The latter consists of the metapropositional base ἥγημαι, making it clear that Paul is now expressing an opinion or attitude. The proposition consists of the expression ἅτινα... ταῦτα, given emphasis by its position and construction, which refers to the qualifications just described and which can be regarded as an opening marker in its own right; the words διὰ τὸν Χριστόν, which state the reason for the assessment made; and the evaluative ζημίαν. This makes clear the nature of the opposition to what has gone before that is expressed by ἀλλά. In the preceding verses, Paul explained what he could invoke if he were to have confidence in the flesh. He does not do so, however; on the contrary, he regards these things as loss because of Christ.

In 3:8 the new beginning is repeated, with a statement correcting and elaborating on the opening construction. This beginning is marked by the particle collocation ἀλλὰ μενοῦνγε καί.[74] Thus even greater emphasis is given to the opening construction in 3:7 and the fresh start is more strongly marked. Additional emphasis is then created by a further repetition of the key elements, now expressed in even more drastic terms (δι' ὃν τὰ πάντα ἐζημιώθην, καὶ

---

[71] The text here is uncertain from both a text-critical and a linguistic point of view. The following interpretations are possible: (1) 'we who worship the Spirit of God'; (2) 'we who worship by the Spirit of God'; (3) 'we who worship God in (our) spirit'; (4) 'we who worship God by the Spirit'. All these interpretations can be reconciled with my understanding of the overall context.

[72] Here I proceed from the reading that has ἀλλά at the beginning of 3:7. This reading is uncertain, however. If we choose the reading without ἀλλά, which enjoys more or less as much support, we have to consider including the opening relative clause of v. 7 in the preceding text and reading the next section as beginning asyndetically with ταῦτα.

[73] Cf. p. 109, in particular note 59.

[74] According to LSJ (under μέν B.II.2), μενοῦνγε is above all used in replies, either to give strong confirmation to or to correct a preceding assertion. Here the first of these alternatives is probably applicable (cf. BDF § 450; Robertson 1934, pp. 1151 f.; Bauer 1979, under μενοῦνγε).

ἡγοῦμαι σκύβαλα). The lengthy reformulation of 3:7 is followed by a string of statements of purpose and consequences, continuing to v. 11 (v. 8 ... ἵνα...; v. 9 καὶ...; v. 10 τοῦ γνῶναι...; v. 11 εἴ πως...). The expressions in 3:8 f. refer back to the starting-point of the section, namely Paul's former gains (κέρδη in 3:7) and righteousness under the law (δικαιοσύνην τὴν ἐν νόμῳ in 3:6), while those in 3:9 f. lead up to a natural end-point — Paul's conformity (συμμορφιζ-όμενος) to the death of Christ and his hope of attaining the resurrection from the dead. This indicates that this part of the digression is being brought to an end.

The concluding statement about Paul's hope of attaining resurrection through conformity to Christ's death gives rise to a comment, in which Paul explains that he is not claiming already to have reached the goal, but that he is pressing on towards it. The beginning of this comment is marked by asyndeton, the metapropositional and metacommunicative οὐχ ὅτι, which indicates a clarification, and a proposition referring back to what has gone immediately before. In 3:13 the new beginning is then repeated as the opening statement is corrected and elaborated on (cf. the construction in 3:8). This restart is marked by the address ἀδελφοί in initial position, the emphatic statement of the grammatical subject ἐγὼ ἐμαυτόν, and the metapropositional οὐ λογίζομαι, which in terms of content is a recurrence of ἥγημαι/ἡγοῦμαι in 3:7 f. and confirms that the digression concerns Paul's attitude or thinking. The phrasing of the proposition that follows is very similar to that of the previous verse, with a repetition of the two verbs καταλαμβάνειν and διώκειν. The address, the heavy emphasis on the fact that this is Paul's thinking (ἐγὼ ἐμαυτόν), the highlighting of its unique significance (ἕν) and the fairly detailed statement of the ultimate goal which he is pressing on to make his own (εἰς τὸ βραβεῖον τῆς ἄνω κλήσεως τοῦ θεοῦ ἐν Χριστῷ Ἰησοῦ) together give the impression that this is the final formulation of Paul's attitude and hence the conclusion of this part of the text.

This is followed in 3:15 f. by a statement of the paraenetic consequences of the digression on Paul's attitude which began in 3:4b. This is indicated by the inferential particle οὖν, the anaphoric text-summarizing τοῦτο, the verb φρονῶμεν, which re-echoes the earlier verbs expressing attitudes or thinking, the change of mood from the indicative to the subjunctive, and the shift from the first person singular to the first and second person plural. The changes of both mood and person take us back to 3:2 ff. All of this confirms that the digression about Paul's attitude has now come to an end, while also indicating that the close of the longer section which began at 3:2 is at hand.

The exhortation at the beginning of 3:15, urging all who are perfect (τέλειοι) to be of *this* mind, i.e. the same mind as Paul, is followed by the comment that, if the Philippians think differently about anything, God will reveal this to them, too. This comment is interrupted by a construction beginning with πλήν which sets out the crucial final assessment and thus acts as a closing marker.[75] This construction presents significant problems of interpretation, above all attributable to the infinitive στοιχεῖν. The usual interpretation of it as 'imperatival' is not unproblematic, for example,[76] and it is

---

[75] In Koine Greek, the particle πλήν appears to have developed quite a wide range of uses. J. Blomqvist (1969, pp. 75–90) refers to 'exceptive', 'modifying', 'balancing', 'eliminative' and 'progressive' uses of the word. M. E. Thrall (1962, pp. 20–25) distinguishes between 'exceptive', 'balancing', 'progressive' and 'inferential' πλήν. Both note that the word occurs, *inter alia*, in connection with passages being brought to a close (Blomqvist 1969, p. 90; Thrall 1962, pp. 22 f.). Blomqvist (1969, p. 89) observes that πλήν is often used after a digression (cf. also Thrall 1962, p. 22). Since πλήν occurs in conjunction with endings, it can obviously serve as a closing marker. However, the exact shades of meaning of such occurrences of the word are open to discussion. In Philippians, a closing πλήν is found in 1:18, 3:16 and 4:14. Of these occurrences, the first differs syntactically from the other two in that it follows up the question τί γάρ; and is followed by a ὅτι-clause. As for the instances in 3:16 and 4:14, they clearly serve to break off what has gone before. In 4:14 it is clear that what is being interrupted is a side-issue (Paul's financial independence) and that with the word πλήν the discussion is returning to the main issue (Paul's joy at receiving the gift). In 3:16, too, it can be said that the consideration of a side-issue (the possibility that the Philippians might think differently) is being brought to an end and that πλήν returns the discussion to the main issue (the proper way of thinking). In both cases there is a contrast in content terms between the side-issue and the main issue, giving πλήν a modifying shade of meaning. I wonder whether it is not possible in both these cases to discern something of an 'exceptive' nuance: i.e. the final assessment that is expressed is distinguished from other possible assessments ('Nothing other than this, that...'). Such a sense is at any rate clear in the occurrence of πλήν in 1:18, which, although different in construction, exhibits quite a number of functional similarities with those in 3:16 and 4:14. In 1:18, too, it is a matter of leaving a side-issue (the motives of different groups who proclaim Christ) and returning to the main issue (the furtherance of the gospel as a result of Christ being proclaimed), and again there is a contrast in content between the side- and main issues. The three instances of πλήν in Philippians thus all appear to mark the beginning of a modified final appraisal and thus to serve a close-marking function.

[76] Imperatival infinitives are uncommon in Koine. In the papyri, they occur chiefly in official orders, but also occasionally in private letters in vulgar language (Mayser 1926 (II:1), p. 303). In the New Testament, BDF (§ 389) accepts without reservation only one case apart from Phil 3:16, namely Rom 12:15. On closer inspection, though, we find that in the latter case, too, it is unclear whether the infinitives really are imperatival. There, they are included in a paraenetic passage with a somewhat loose sentence structure, in which imperatives alternate with conjunctive participles, in addition to the two infinitives in v. 15. Possibly what we have in that case may simply be a couple of rather loosely attached infinitives of result. In Lk 9:3 at any rate, which is also mentioned in this context, the construction is surely an infinitive of result. BDF (§ 387:3) also draws a comparison with a corresponding imperatival use of ἵνα-clauses. However, the instances of this which are mentioned there (Eph 5:33; 1 Cor 7:29; 2 Cor 8:7) all differ from Phil 3:16 in that there is always a governing verb in the immediately prior context, to which the ἵνα-clause appears to be somewhat loosely linked (cf. Eph 5:32; 1 Cor 7:29; 2 Cor 8:6). It is doubtful, then, whether any other imperatival infinitives in fact occur in the New Testament, and if they do not there is also cause for doubt regarding στοιχεῖν in Phil 3:16. The problem is, however, that there are no really good alternatives. One possibility is of course to link the infinitive to πλήν and view the construction as an elliptical

not obvious whether the subject is 'we' or 'you'.[77] At all events, the expression probably describes a desired or expected consequence. If 'we' is chosen as the subject, the construction can be understood in relation e.g. to 1:27 f. and 4:1 (στήκετε); if 'you', it is a manifestation of the same pattern of thought as in 3:17 (καθὼς ἔχετε τύπον ἡμᾶς).

3:17–21

The occurrence of a close in 3:15 f. is confirmed by a distinct new beginning in 3:17, marked by asyndeton, a shift in mood to imperatives in the second person plural, and the attention-attracting address ἀδελφοί. The change of mood entails a return to directly exhortatory text after all the explanations and digressions in 3:3–16. In 3:17 the recipients are urged to become Paul's 'fellow imitators' (of Christ, I assume) and to observe those who walk thus (presumably as Paul's fellow imitators), in the same way as the Philippians have 'us' as their example. These exhortations are thus closely linked to the explanations and digressions of 3:3–16, in which Paul, in 3:9 ff., expounded on his wish to know Christ, to share his sufferings, to conform to his death and to attain his resurrection, and then, in 3:15 ff., made it clear that all of 'us' who are τέλειοι should be of this mind.[78] Now the Philippians are called upon to follow Paul and his 'fellow imitators' in this respect.

The exhortation in 3:17 is followed by a few explanatory comments (γάρ) in 3:18–21. Here, those who do not walk οὕτω (3:17), but as the enemies of the cross of Christ, those whose minds are set on earthly things (3:18 f.), are contrasted with 'us', whose citizenship is in heaven and who are expecting the Lord Jesus Christ as Saviour. The two relative clauses in 3:20 f. (ἐξ οὗ... ὅς...) elaborate on the consequences of 'our' citizenship being in heaven and thus apply an eschatological perspective, thereby indicating that this section is drawing to a close.

---

expression of the same type as in Phil 1:18. The meaning would then be: '(Nothing else will then be the case) other than that you are in line with the same as we have attained.' However, neither of these alternatives is entirely satisfactory.

[77] If the infinitive is understood in an indicative sense, the subject must be 'you', but if it is taken to be imperatival, either 'we' or 'you' is possible.

[78] The word τέλειος occurs quite frequently in the New Testament tradition, where it normally seems to be used to describe a person with the religious maturity which should be the object (τέλος) of everyone's striving. Cf. e.g. Mt 5:48; 19:21; 1 Cor 2:6; 14:20; Eph 4:13; Col 1:28; 4:12; Heb 5:14; Jas 1:4; 3:2. Cf. also the LXX, e.g. Gen 6:9; Deut 18:13; 2 Sam 22:26; 1 Kings 8:61.

4:1–9

Following the close in 3:20 f., there is a fairly clear new start in 4:1, marked by the lengthy address ἀδελφοί μου ἀγαπητοὶ καὶ ἐπιπόθητοι, χαρὰ καὶ στέφανός μου… ἀγαπητοί and the change of mood to a second person plural imperative. The switch to the imperative entails a return to direct exhortation after the long explanatory comments in 3:18–21. At the same time, the stressed ὥστε and the anaphoric text-summarizing οὕτως show that what is now beginning is a statement of consequences. Primarily, we may assume, it describes the paraenetic conclusion to be drawn from the contrast just described between 'them' and 'us', and οὕτως presumably refers first and foremost to the description of the latter group in 3:20 f. The question is, however, whether this statement of consequences does not encompass more than just the paraenetic implications of the two explanatory comments in 3:18–21. The following observations support such an interpretation:

1. The statement of consequences is very strongly stressed, partly as a result of the extended and emotionally charged address itself and partly because the inclusion of this address keeps the initial ὥστε 'on hold' for so long. This opening gives the distinct impression that what is to follow is more than just the conclusion to be drawn from a couple of explanatory comments.

2. The verb στήκετε does not immediately echo the wording of the preceding comments, but is quite general in character. This verb occurred in the first exhortation in the epistle and has been 'in the air' since then. Its emphatic repetition in 4:1 gives the impression that this is a recurrence of a central theme of the paraenetic sections of Philippians.

3. Similarly, the demonstrative οὕτως is not without its links beyond the immediate context. In 2:2 there was talk of being of *one* mind (τὸ ἕν) and in 2:5 of being of *this* mind (τοῦτο). In 3:13 ff., there was a new reference to *one* thing (ἕν), to 'our' being of *this* mind (τοῦτο), after which the Philippians were urged in 3:17 to observe those who walk *thus* (οὕτω). These 'imperatival' demonstratives have in other words occurred repeatedly in the paraenetic sections of Philippians. While their immediate definitions may vary somewhat from one instance to another, they appear to make an absolute claim (τὸ ἕν, ἕν) and to have a mutual connection that hinges on Christ (see e.g. 2:5; 3:10, 17 and 21). This occurrence of οὕτως in 4:1, then, also appears to link up with an overarching theme of the paraenetic passages of Philippians.

4. The earlier paraenetic section 1:27–2:18 exhibited a similar structure. There, too, an extensive closing section (2:12–18) began with a strongly

emphasized ὥστε and an emotionally charged address ἀγαπητοί μου. The listener would thus have this pattern at the back of his or her mind when confronted with ὥστε, ἀδελφοί μου ἀγαπητοί... in 4:1.

These observations suggest in my opinion that the section beginning in 4:1 rounds off the whole of the paraenetic section from 3:1 on.

The remainder of the section is heterogeneous and fairly loosely connected. In this respect it can be compared with the final paraenetic subsection of 1 Thessalonians (5:12–22). It consists mainly of short asyndetic exhortations, giving it considerable intensity and contributing to the impression that this is a critical phase, in this case the closing of a section.

The initial exhortation in 4:1 ends with an address placed in final position, which sets it apart as a fairly self-contained entity. It is followed by a few personal exhortations, departing from the overall pattern of entreaty to the Philippians in general. These exhortations also differ in formal terms, in that they consist not of imperatives, but of constructions with explicit meta-propositional and metacommunicative bases (4:2: ... παρακαλῶ καὶ... παρακαλῶ... ναὶ ἐρωτῶ...). The fresh start which they entail is marked by asyndeton, the personal references Εὐοδίαν, Συντύχην and σέ, γνήσιε σύζυγε, and the shift to the use of explicit metapropositional bases. The first two of the people mentioned are urged to be of the same mind in the Lord (τὸ αὐτὸ φρονεῖν ἐν κυρίῳ).[79] These exhortations end with a relative clause hinting at an eschatological perspective.

In 4:4–7 there is a new group of exhortations addressed to the Philippians in general. Its beginning is marked by a return to imperatives in the second person plural and an exhortation (χαίρετε ἐν κυρίῳ πάντοτε) that is strongly emphasized by a repetition (χαίρετε), which is in turn commented on metacommunicatively (πάλιν ἐρῶ). This heavily accentuated exhortation clearly echoes the opening of the paraenetic section at 3:1 and reinforces the impression that its conclusion is at hand. Using a number of imperative constructions joined by asyndeton, Paul then expresses his desire that the fitting conduct of the Philippians will become generally known and that they will not worry, but pray to God with thanksgiving. This group of exhortations is brought to an end with a statement of consequences beginning with καί, which sets out the beneficial consequence for the Philippians of heeding Paul's exhortations: their hearts and minds will be guarded in Christ Jesus. The statement of consequences looks back to the opening exhortation in 4:1, suggesting that this closing section will soon be coming to an end.

---

[79] Regarding the connection between 4:1 and 4:2 f., cf. the exhortation in 1:27 and the exposition of it in 2:2–5, where στήκετε was also linked to the unity motif and to the state of mind that was or is in Christ Jesus.

First, however, Paul adds a couple of general closing exhortations, beginning with τὸ λοιπόν and the address ἀδελφοί. If τὸ λοιπόν is ascribed inferential force here, which it is reasonable to do, these opening words alone suggest that the appeals that are to come are closing exhortations. This impression is then reinforced by the emphatic and summarizing constructions ὅσα... ὅσα... ταῦτα... and ἅ... καί... ταῦτα... The first of these refers back to the statement of consequences in 4:7 and concerns what the Philippians should think. The second holds up the gospel and Paul himself as a yardstick for the Philippians' actions and thus involves a recurrence of an overriding theme expressed in the very first exhortation in the letter (1:27) and since restated several times, e.g. in 3:17. These two general exhortations are followed by a statement of consequences re-echoing the one in 4:7, and with that the paraenetic section beginning at 3:1 is brought to a close.

To sum up, 3:1–4:9 can be said to be paraenetic in character and to be aimed at the Philippians in general ('you'). It can be divided into four parts: 3:1, 3:2–16, 3:17–21 and 4:1–9. The first (3:1) consists of a relatively self-contained exhortation to the Philippians to rejoice and a metacommunicative comment on the fact that Paul is repeating himself to a certain extent. The second part (3:2–16) begins with a threefold exhortation to the recipients to look at or pay attention to their opponents, followed by comments and digressions in which 'we' and Paul are contrasted with these opponents. The third section (3:17–21) then begins with an exhortation to the Philippians to become Paul's fellow imitators and to observe those who — as 'we' do — live thus, and this is followed by an explanatory comment contrasting the opponents with 'us'. The fourth and final part (4:1–9) is of a more diverse character. Apart from a couple of personal exhortations, it consists of a number of closing exhortations to the Philippians, urging them among other things to stand firm in the Lord, to rejoice, and to do what they have learned through tradition and seen in Paul.

4:10–18

That the paraenetic section has indeed come to an end in 4:8 f. is confirmed by a clear new beginning in 4:10, marked by the conjunction δέ and a construction containing new instructions to the recipients and stating a new theme. It begins with the metapropositional base ἐχάρην... ἐν κυρίῳ μεγάλως, indicating that Paul is now moving on from exhortation to make a statement and express a favourable assessment. As in 1:18, the latter is expressed by the verb χαίρειν, this time in the aorist (presumably ingressive). The proposition, the actual object of the favourable assessment, follows in a ὅτι-clause referring to the renewed flourishing of the Philippians' concern for Paul (τὸ ὑπὲρ ἐμοῦ φρονεῖν). Naturally, this represents an appreciable shift at the propositional level, too, even if the use of the verb φρονεῖν in 4:10 is not entirely unconnected with the expressions referring to thinking or the mind in 4:7 f. (cf. also 3:15 f. and 4:2, and earlier e.g. 2:2 ff., 5). What kind of concern Paul is referring to is not stated here, but it eventually turns out to be a matter of financial support (see 4:15–18).

The opening statement about Paul rejoicing at the Philippians' concern for him is followed by a clarifying digression, in which he modifies this assertion by explaining that he was not in need, since he is content with whatever he has. The beginning of this digression is marked by asyndeton, the meta-propositional and metacommunicative expression οὐχ ὅτι, which indicates a clarification, and a proposition consisting of a comment on the preceding statement. The assertion made in this opening construction — that Paul is not speaking from a situation of need — is then explained (γάρ) in three mutually asyndetic sentences (4:11b, 12, 13), in which Paul states that he has learned to be content with whatever he has.

In 4:14, πλήν interrupts the digression on Paul's financial independence and there is a return to the original theme of 'Paul's joy at the Philippians' concern'. Both πλήν and this recurrence give the impression that this is a final appraisal and thus suggest a close.

In 4:15 a fresh start is made, marked by the conjunction δέ, the address Φιλιππήσιοι and new instructions to the recipients and thematic statements. The new construction begins with the metapropositional base οἴδατε... καὶ ὑμεῖς, indicating that what follows is a reminder. The proposition is then set out in a ὅτι-clause, which is developed into quite a lengthy construction in 4:15 f. Here an account is given of how at one stage the Philippians were the only church to send Paul help. The verb ἐκοινώνησεν echoes the final assessment expressed in 4:14. Combined with the metapropositional base, this recurrence indicates that the new section is closely linked and subordinate to the preceding one. The reminder about past gifts is followed — like the reference to the recent one in 4:10 — by a clarificatory comment in which Paul explains that he is not seeking gifts from the Philippians. What he says he is seeking is the profit that accumulates to their account. Like the clarification in 4:11, this comment follows on asyndetically and begins with the metapropositional and metacommunicative expression οὐχ ὅτι.

Following this comment on his reminder in 4:15 f., Paul makes a new start in 4:18, marked by the conjunction δέ, and returns to the subject of the present gift and his favourable view of it (cf. 4:10, 14). This thematic recurrence confirms the subordinate character of 4:15–17 and hints at the closing of the section that began in 4:10. That impression is underlined by the succession of appositional phrases to express the beneficial character and results of the Philippians' support.

To sum up, in 4:10–18 Paul gives an account of his joy and his situation after receiving the Philippians' gift. The section can be divided into three subsections: 4:10–14, 4:15–17 and 4:18. In the first, Paul describes his joy at receiving the gift, in the second, he recalls earlier gifts from the Philippians, and in the third he describes his situation after receiving their latest gift.

4:19–20

The close in 4:18 is followed by a fresh start in 4:19, marked by the change of grammatical subject, the conjunction δέ and the shift in tense from past and present to future. The text that follows consists of two expressions of wishes or expectations.[80] The first is that God will fully satisfy every need of the Philippians, the second that to God will be the glory for ever and ever. This section clearly has the character of a closing passage. Closing markers include the wishes or expectations themselves, the eschatological perspective, and the final ἀμήν. The words used to express the first wish or expectation are very closely linked to those of the previous verse, so it would not be unreasonable to regard this concluding passage as part of the section beginning in 4:10. The reasons why I have nevertheless chosen to view it as a more independent section rounding off the letter as a whole are its general character (see e.g. πᾶσαν χρείαν ὑμῶν in 4:19) and the relatively clearly marked new beginning in 4:19 (cf. the expressed hopes in 4:7 and 4:9, both of which were introduced by καί).

4:21–23

Following the close of the body of the letter in 4:19–20, all that remains is the letter ending. In Philippians, this consists of four sentences, all of them juxtaposed asyndetically. The first begins with ἀσπάσασθε and urges the Philippians to greet every saint in Christ Jesus. The next two begin with

---

[80] The manuscript tradition vacillates here between the future indicative and the aorist optative. The future tense enjoys better external support. On the other hand, the future forms could be due to the influence of the corresponding forms in 4:7 and 9. Elsewhere in Paul's letters, similar closing formulae beginning ὁ δὲ θεός... often seem to be in the optative (cf. Rom 15:5, 13 and 33; 1 Thess 3:11–13; 5:23–24), although this fact can be interpreted in different ways and regarded as an argument for either one form or the other.

ἀσπάζονται and convey greetings from the brothers who are with Paul and from all the saints. The last one begins ἡ χάρις τοῦ κυρίου Ἰησοῦ Χριστοῦ and is a wish of grace.

That completes the basic analysis of Philippians. What remains to be done now is to summarize and analyse the observations that have been made. We shall begin with a tabular overview of the arrangement of the letter that has emerged from the basic analysis.

C. Arrangement of the text

For explanatory comments on the overview below, readers are referred to the corresponding section of the analysis of 1 Thessalonians.[81] A list of the abbreviations used to refer to the different types of transition marker will also be found there.

I. 1:1 Opening of the letter:

    1. 1:1 Particulars of senders and recipients

    2. 1:2 Wish of grace and peace

II. 1:3–4:20 Body of the letter: — <u>*Om:*</u> *Mp/Mc, H.* <u>*Cm:*</u> *W, Esch; Int, ἀμήν.*

    1. 1:3–2:30 Account of Paul's joy and thankfulness in persecution — <u>*Om:*</u> *See above.* <u>*Cm:*</u> *οὖν... οὖν... ἵνα, Re, Ex.*

        A. 1:3–11 Account of how Paul joyfully thanks God for the Philippians' sharing for the benefit of the gospel and prays for its completion — <u>*Om:*</u> *See above.* <u>*Cm:*</u> *(καί)... ἵνα, Re, Esch.*

            a. 1:3–8 Account of prayer of thanksgiving — <u>*Om:*</u> *See above.*

            b. 1:9–11 Account of prayer of intercession — <u>*Om:*</u> *(καί); Mp/Mc, H, Re.* <u>*Cm:*</u> *See above.*

        B. 1:12–2:18 Account of how Paul's persecution has resulted and will result in the furtherance of the gospel and in joy for him and the Philippians — <u>*Om:*</u> *δέ; Mp; Ad.* <u>*Cm:*</u> *ὥστε... ἵνα, Re, Esch; Ad, Int.*

            a. 1:12–18c Account of how Paul's imprisonment has resulted in the furtherance of the gospel throughout the praetorium and among the brothers, and of how he rejoices in this — <u>*Om:*</u> *See above.* <u>*Cm:*</u> *τί γάρ; πλὴν ὅτι, Re, Tsum, Ass.*

---

[81] See pp. 70 f.

α. 1:12–14 Opening statement concerning the furtherance of the gospel in the praetorium and among the brothers as a result of Paul's imprisonment — *Om: See above.*

β. 1:15–17 Digression commenting on the varying motives of those who proclaim Christ — *Om: Asyn.*

γ. 1:18a–c Concluding statement about the proclamation of Christ and Paul's rejoicing in it — *Om: (τί γάρ; πλὴν ὅτι), Re. Cm: See above.*

b. 1:18d–26 Account of Paul's knowledge concerning future joy, due to his persecution resulting in his salvation and the Philippians' furtherance and joy in faith. — *Om: ἀλλά; Mp(s), Top. Cm: Ass, Re, Tsum.*

α. 1:18d Opening statement about future joy— *Om: See above.*

β. 1:19–20 Explanatory comment: Paul knows that the present situation will result in his salvation and the exaltation of Christ, whether by life or by death — *Om: (γάρ); Mp(s).*

γ. 1:21–24 Explanatory exposition: Paul sees both dying and living in a favourable light, but the latter is more necessary for the Philippians' sake — *Om: (γάρ).*

δ. 1:25–26 Concluding statement of Paul's knowledge that he will remain for the sake of the Philippians' furtherance and joy in faith — *Om: (καί); Mp(s), Re. Cm: See above.*

c. 1:27–2:18 Exhortations setting out the prior conditions for future furtherance and joy — *Om: μόνον; Mp. Cm: See above.*

α. 1:27–30 Opening exhortation to live in a manner worthy of the gospel of Christ, to be one and to stand firm in persecution — *Om: See above.*

β. 2:1–11 More specific exhortations: — *Om: οὖν; Re; Int. Cm: διό... ἵνα, Esch.*

α'. 2:1–4 Exhortation to make Paul's joy complete by being 'of one mind' and humble — *Om: See above.*

β'. 2:5–11 Exhortation to be of the same mind as Christ Jesus — *Om: Asyn. Cm: See above.*

α". 2:5–8 The actual exhortation and a description of the attitude of Jesus — *Om: See above. Cm: Int.*

β". 2:9–11 Statement about God's response to Jesus's attitude — *Om: (διò καί); Top. Cm: See above.*

γ. 2:12–18 Concluding exhortations: — *Om: (ὥστε); Mp, H, Re; Ad. Cm: See above.*

α'. 2:12–13 Exhortation to the recipients to be obedient and to work out their salvation — *Om: See above.*

β'. 2:14–18 Exhortation to do all things without murmuring so that Paul can boast and so that he and the Philippians can rejoice — *Om: Asyn. Cm: See above.*

C. 2:19–30 Account of Paul's hope of sending Timothy soon and his decision to send Epaphroditus, so that Paul and the Philippians might rejoice — *Om: δέ; Mp; Top. Cm: See above.*

a. 2:19–24 Account of how Paul hopes in the Lord to send Timothy soon so that he may receive news of the Philippians and be cheered by it — *Om: See above. Cm: οὖν, Re, Tsum, Ass.*

α. 2:19 Opening statement concerning his hope — *Om: See above.*

β. 2:20–22 Explanatory comment describing Timothy's concern for the Philippians — *Om: (γάρ).*

γ. 2:23–24 Concluding statement concerning Paul's hope of sending Timothy soon and his conviction in the Lord that he himself will come soon — *Om: (οὖν); Re. Cm: See above.*

b. 2:25–30 Account of Paul's decision to send Epaphroditus so that he and the Philippians may rejoice — *Om: δέ; Mp(s), Top. Cm: See above.*

α. 2:25–26 Opening statement concerning his decision to send Epaphroditus because of the latter's longing and anxiety for the Philippians following his illness — *Om: See above.*

β. 2:27 Explanatory comment describing Epaphroditus's illness — *Om: (γάρ).*

γ. 2:28–30 Concluding statement concerning Paul's eagerness to send Epaphroditus and an exhortation to the Philippians to welcome him with joy — *Om: (οὖν); Re. Cm: See above.*

2. 3:1–4:9 Renewed exhortations to joy, *imitatio*, unity and firmness, in the light of the account in 1:3–2:30 — *Om:* τὸ λοιπόν; Mp, Mc; Ad. *Cm:* ὥστε... οὕτως... τὸ λοιπόν; Re, W; Ad, Int.

A. 3:1 Opening exhortation to the Philippians to rejoice in the Lord — *Om: See above.*

    a. 3:1a The actual exhortation — *Om: See above.*

    b. 3:1b–c Comment on the repetition — *Om: Asyn.*

B. 3:2–16 Exhortation to the Philippians to look at their opponents (τοὺς κύνας, τοὺς κακοὺς ἐργάτας, τὴν κατατομήν) — *Om: Asyn; Int. Cm:* οὖν... πλήν, Esch, Ex, Re, Tsum; Ad, Int.

    a. 3:2 The actual exhortation — *Om: See above.*

    b. 3:3–4a Explanatory comment contrasting 'us' with them: 'We' who worship the Spirit of God and have no confidence in the flesh are ἡ περιτομή — *Om: (γάρ); Top.*

    c. 3:4b–14 Digression concerning Paul's attitude: He if anyone could have confidence in the flesh, but he regards it as loss because of Christ — *Om: Asyn; H. Cm: Esch; Ad, Int.*

        α. 3:4b–6 Account of Paul's qualifications in the flesh — *Om: See above.*

        β. 3:7–11 Statement about his rejecting them for the sake of Christ — *Om:* ἀλλά; Mp, H; Int. *Cm:* ἵνα, Re.

        γ. 3:12–14 Digression explaining that he has not yet reached the goal but is pressing on towards it — *Om: Asyn; Mp/Mc; Int. Cm: See above.*

    d. 3:15–16 Closing expression of wish and assertion: 'We' should be of this mind and in line with it — *Om: (οὖν); Mp. Cm: See above.*

C. 3:17–21 Exhortation to become Paul's 'fellow imitators' and to observe those who are fellow imitators — *Om: Asyn; Mp; Ad. Cm:* ὅς, Esch.

    a. 3:17 The actual exhortation — *Om: See above.*

    b. 3:18–21 Explanatory comment contrasting the many who are enemies of the cross of Christ with 'us' — *Om: (γάρ). Cm: See above.*

D. 4:1–9 Concluding exhortations: — *Om: (ὥστε); Mp; Ad. Cm: See above.*

    a. 4:1 Exhortation to the Philippians to stand firm in the Lord — *Om: See above.*

b. 4:2–3 Personal exhortations: — *Om:* Asyn; Mp/Mc; Top. *Cm:* ὧν, Esch.

    α. 4:2 Exhortation to Euodia and Syntyche to be of the same mind in the Lord — *Om:* See above.

    β. 4:3 Exhortation to 'you', γνήσιε σύζυγε, to help them — *Om:* Asyn; Mp/Mc; Ad.

c. 4:4–7 Exhortations to the Philippians: — *Om:* Asyn; Mc, Re; Int. *Cm:* See above.

    α. 4:4 Twofold exhortation to rejoice in the Lord — *Om:* See above.

    β. 4:5 Expression of wish that the fitting conduct of the Philippians might be known to everyone — *Om:* Asyn.

    γ. 4:6–7 Exhortation not to worry, but to pray to God with thanksgiving — *Om:* Asyn. *Cm:* See above.

d. 4:8–9 Exhortations to think and act appropriately, in accordance with the gospel and Paul's example — *Om:* τὸ λοιπόν; H; Ad, Int. *Cm:* See above.

3. 4:10–18 Account of Paul's situation and joy after receiving the Philippians' gift — *Om:* δέ; Mp. *Cm:* Re; Int.

    A. 4:10–14 Account of Paul's joy at the Philippians' concern for him — *Om:* See above. *Cm:* πλήν, Re.

        a. 4:10 Opening statement concerning his joy at the Philippians' concern — *Om:* See above.

        b. 4:11–13 Digression explaining that Paul was not in need — *Om:* Asyn; Mp/Mc.

        c. 4:14 Concluding assertion that the Philippians have done right — *Om:* (πλήν); Re. *Cm:* See above.

    B. 4:15–17 Reminder of the Philippians' past gifts to Paul — *Om:* δέ; Mp(s); Ad.

        a. 4:15–16 Assertion about the Philippians' knowledge of past gifts — *Om:* See above.

        b. 4:17 Comment about Paul not seeking the gift, but rather the profit it brings to the Philippians — *Om:* Asyn; Mp/Mc.

    C. 4:18 Concluding statement about Paul having received the gift and now having more than enough — *Om:* δέ; Re. *Cm:* See above.

4. 4:19–20 Expressions of expectations or wishes: God will fully satisfy every need of the Philippians, and to him will be the glory for ever — *Om:* δέ; Top. *Cm:* See above (1:3–4:20).

III. 4:21–23 Closing of the letter:

    1. 4:21a Exhortation to the addressees to greet every saint

    2. 4:21b–22 Statement concerning greetings from the brothers with Paul and from all the saints

    3. 4:23 Wish of grace

D. Transition markers

For comments regarding the arrangement of this section, readers are referred to the introductory chapter and to the corresponding part of the analysis of 1 Thessalonians.[82]

Interaction

As in the section dealing with the transition markers in 1 Thessalonians, here too we can begin by noting that the various opening and closing markers constantly interact and are interdependent. An illustration of this was given in the analysis of 1 Thessalonians,[83] and further examples are therefore unnecessary.

It can also be observed that in Philippians, as in 1 Thessalonians, transitions are as a rule more strongly marked at higher levels of division of the text than at lower levels and that closings in particular are weakly marked at the lower levels. This is made clear by the following table of the average numbers of markers recorded per transition at the different levels of division:

	Transition markers	Opening markers	Closing markers
1st level	10	3.5	6.5
2nd level	6.1	2.7	3.4
3rd level	2.9	1.9	1
4th level	2.0	1.4	0.6
5th level	1	1	0
6th level	3	1	2

The comparatively large number of closing markers at the sixth level of division is due to the fact that the basic analysis only went down to this level in one instance, and that was in the case of an unusually strongly marked

---

[82] See pp. 33 f. and 74.
[83] See pp. 75.

close. The statistics for the sixth level are thus misleading. In every other respect, the pattern tallies closely with that found in 1 Thessalonians.[84] The reasons for this pattern are presumably the same here as in that context.

Instructive and thematic opening markers

In Philippians, too, we find that instructive and thematic markers look somewhat different at different levels. At the highest level of division we again find constructions expressing the sender's assessment of the addressees and what he wishes to see achieved in them, i.e. constructions giving prominence to the pragmatic dimension. This is seen most clearly in the opening passages of the two major sections at this level. At the beginning of 1:3–2:30, for instance, we find a metapropositional base expressing a favourable assessment (εὐχαριστῶ τῷ θεῷ μου ἐπὶ πάσῃ τῇ μνείᾳ ὑμῶν πάντοτε ἐν πάσῃ δεήσει μου... μετὰ χαρᾶς τὴν δέησιν ποιούμενος... πεποιθώς...) and propositions which not only concern what the addressees have done and are doing (ἐπὶ τῇ κοινωνίᾳ ὑμῶν εἰς τὸ εὐαγγέλιον ἀπὸ τῆς πρώτης ἡμέρας ἄχρι τοῦ νῦν), but also what they will do (ὅτι ὁ ἐναρξάμενος ἐν ὑμῖν ἔργον ἀγαθὸν ἐπιτελέσει ἄχρι ἡμέρας Χριστοῦ Ἰησοῦ). In addition, it may be noted that the statement of the metapropositional base is unusually long, which is in keeping with the pragmatic emphasis, and that the opening statement of the proposition has the character of an introductory orientation or heading.

At the beginning of the second major section at the first level (3:1–4:9), the opening exhortation χαίρετε ἐν κυρίῳ, whose imperative form entails an implicit statement of the metapropositional base, is followed by an extended metacommunicative comment stating what Paul is now doing (τὰ αὐτὰ γράφειν ὑμῖν) and why (ὑμῖν... ἀσφαλές).

The somewhat shorter section 4:10–18 begins with the metapropositional base ἐχάρην... ἐν κυρίῳ μεγάλως, where the aorist form may be assumed to be ingressive and the metapropositional base is in practice primary. The proposition that follows concerns the addressees' conduct (ὅτι ἤδη ποτὲ ἀνεθάλετε τὸ ὑπὲρ ἐμοῦ φρονεῖν). In the brief concluding section 4:19–20, the proposition is concerned with how God will act towards the addressees. The metapropositional base is not stated (unless we read πληρῶσαι here rather than πληρώσει), but it is safe to assume that the content of the proposition is not simply something which Paul believes or knows, but also something he hopes and wants.[85]

---

[84] For the corresponding figures for 1 Thessalonians, see p. 76.

[85] The future indicative is not necessarily volitionally neutral, but can for example be used in commands (see e.g. BDF §§ 362–3).

Opening-marking constructions which highlight the pragmatic aspect also occur at lower levels, but here they usually introduce either closing sections which refer back to an opening at the first level of division of the text (e.g. 1:9 τοῦτο προσεύχομαι ἵνα...) or subsections of the paraenetic sections.[86] In cases of the latter type, metapropositional instructions are given only by the use of the imperative.[87] At other lower-level transitions, we mainly find constructions consisting of metapropositional bases which are volitionally neutral (οὐχ ὅτι..., οἶδα)[88] or secondary (οἴδατε, χαρήσομαι, ἀναγκαῖον... ἡγησάμην),[89] and propositions which relate to the sender or to persons or concepts expressed in the third person.[90] One exception is γινώσκειν... ὑμᾶς βούλομαι... ὅτι..., which begins the major section 1:12–2:18 at the second level of division of the text. Here two metapropositional bases are combined: the first expresses the will of the sender (βούλομαι) and has a proposition relating to the addressees (γινώσκειν... ὑμᾶς), the second is secondary (γινώσκειν... ὑμᾶς) and has a proposition concerning the sender (ὅτι τὰ κατ᾽ ἐμέ...). Otherwise, metapropositional statements at these levels are often relatively brief. In one instance, the proposition is highlighted by a cataphoric text-summarizing τοῦτο (1:9). In a few cases we also find fronted subordinate clauses which function as headings (2:12; 3:7; 4:8).

At the lower levels there are also beginnings which only contain statements of the theme and lack metapropositional statements. This is the case in 3:3, for example, where the emphatic use of the explicit subject ἡμεῖς indicates something of a thematic shift, even though no metapropositional instructions are given.

Instructive and thematic closing markers

In 1 Thessalonians we observed that instructive and thematic closing markers showed the same kinds of variation between the different levels of division of the text as instructive and thematic opening markers, to which they of course correspond. This is the case in Philippians, too, although here the pattern is perhaps less clear.

---

[86] Second level: 3:17; 4:1. Third level: 1:27; 4:2, 4, 8. Fourth level: 2:12.

[87] One exception is 4:2, where the exhortations to individual members of the church begin with παρακαλῶ.

[88] οὐχ ὅτι: 3:12; 4:11, 17. οἶδα: 1:19, 25.

[89] οἴδατε: 4:15. χαρήσομαι: 1:18d. ἀναγκαῖον... ἡγησάμην: 3:25.

[90] There are two constructions at these levels in which the metapropositional base expresses an assessment or wish, but the proposition concerns the sender or is expressed in the third person. This is the case with ἐλπίζω... ἐν κυρίῳ ᾽Ιησοῦ Τιμόθεον ταχέως πέμψαι ὑμῖν in 2:19 and ... ταῦτα ἥγημαι διὰ τὸν Χριστὸν ζημίαν in 3:7.

At the two highest levels of division we find, in most cases at least, closings which express the sender's assessment of the addressees or what he wishes to see achieved in them, i.e. which highlight the pragmatic dimension. In the first major section at the first level (1:3–2:30), the first two subsections (1:3–11; 1:12–2:18) close with statements of consequences (1:9 f. καὶ τοῦτο…;[91] 2:12–18 ὥστε… ἵνα… εἰς… ὅτι…) which refer back relatively clearly to the favourable introductory assessment in 1:3–6 of the addressees' sharing for the benefit of the gospel. In the closing part of the third subsection (2:19–30), too, there are statements of consequences which to some extent echo the introductory assessment in 1:3–6, but here the link is not as clear as in the preceding subsections.[92] The second major section at the first level (3:1–4:9) is brought to a close with a statement of consequences (4:1–9 ὥστε… οὕτως… τὸ λοιπόν…) which clearly refers back both to the opening exhortation and to the metacommunicative comment in 3:1.[93] In the third section at the first level (4:10–18), the first subsection (4:10–14) ends with a statement of consequences (4:14 πλήν)[94] which looks back at both the metapropositional and the propositional level to the favourable assessment of the addressees' concern for Paul at the beginning of the section. At the end of the second subsection (4:15–18), too, essentially the same assessment is expressed, even if the mode of expression is somewhat different.[95]

With regard to 1 Thessalonians it was observed that the two sections at the first level of division of the text were both brought to a close with wishes concerning what God and the Lord would do with respect to the addressees (3:11 ff.; 5:23 f.). In Philippians we find similar constructions in 4:7 and 4:9, i.e. at the end of the second major section at the first level, and in 4:19 f., i.e. at the

---

[91] Regarding what this τοῦτο refers to, see p. 97.
[92] 1:3–6: εὐχαριστῶ τῷ θεῷ μου… ὑπὲρ πάντων, μετὰ χαρᾶς τὴν δέησιν ποιούμενος ἐπὶ τῇ κοινωνίᾳ ὑμῶν εἰς τὸ εὐαγγέλιον ἀπὸ τῆς πρώτης ἡμέρας ἄχρι τοῦ νῦν, πεποιθὼς αὐτὸ τοῦτο ὅτι ὁ ἐναρξάμενος ἐν ὑμῖν ἔργον ἀγαθὸν ἐπιτελέσει ἄχρι ἡμέρας Χριστοῦ Ἰησοῦ…
1:9 f.: καὶ τοῦτο προσεύχομαι, ἵνα ἡ ἀγάπη ὑμῶν ἔτι μᾶλλον… περισσεύῃ… ἵνα ἦτε εἰλικρινεῖς… εἰς ἡμέραν Χριστοῦ…
2:12–18: ὥστε… τὴν ἑαυτῶν σωτηρίαν κατεργάζεσθε… ἵνα γένησθε ἄμεμπτοι… λόγον ζωῆς ἐπέχοντες, εἰς καύχημα ἐμοὶ εἰς ἡμέραν Χριστοῦ, ὅτι… χαίρω καὶ συγχαίρω πᾶσιν ὑμῖν…
2:28 ff.: σπουδαιοτέρως οὖν ἔπεμψα αὐτόν, ἵνα… χαρῆτε κἀγὼ ἀλυπότερος ὦ. προσδέχεσθε οὖν αὐτόν… μετὰ χαρᾶς… ὅτι διὰ τὸ ἔργον Χριστοῦ μέχρι θανάτου ἤγγισεν… ἵνα ἀναπληρώσῃ τὸ ὑμῶν ὑστέρημα τῆς πρός με λειτουργίας.
[93] 3:1: χαίρετε ἐν κυρίῳ. τὰ αὐτὰ γράφειν ὑμῖν… ὑμῖν… ἀσφαλές.
4:1–6: ὥστε… οὕτως στήκετε ἐν κυρίῳ… χαίρετε ἐν κυρίῳ πάντοτε· πάλιν ἐρῶ, χαίρετε… μηδὲν μεριμνᾶτε…
[94] Concerning the close-marking function of this particle, see pp. 120, note 75.
[95] 4:10: ἐχάρην δὲ ἐν κυρίῳ μεγάλως ὅτι ἤδη ποτὲ ἀνεθάλετε τὸ ὑπὲρ ἐμοῦ φρονεῖν.
4:14: πλὴν καλῶς ἐποιήσατε συγκοινωνήσαντές μου τῇ θλίψει.
4:18: πεπλήρωμαι δεξάμενος… τὰ παρ' ὑμῶν, ὀσμὴν εὐωδίας, θυσίαν δεκτήν, εὐάρεστον τῷ θεῷ.

end of the letter body. These verses do not express wishes, but they do express what Paul believes and hopes God will do with regard to the addressees.[96] The fact that such expressions do not occur until the end of the second section at the first level of division may be assumed to be due to the close connection between the first two sections at this level.

At lower levels of division, closings more commonly contain volitionally more neutral or secondary metapropositional bases, and propositions which concern the sender or persons or concepts expressed in the third person. Sometimes the metapropositional base is not actually stated. At the third level we find consequence-indicating recurrences containing neutral or secondary metapropositional bases at the ends of the sections 1:12–18c (1:18 τί γάρ; πλὴν ὅτι... ἐν τούτῳ...),[97] 1:18d–26 (1:25 f. καὶ τοῦτο...),[98] 2:19–24 (2:23 f. τοῦτον μὲν οὖν...)[99] and 2:25–30 (2:28 ...οὖν...).[100] A close at this level in which the pragmatic dimension is clearly expressed is the ending of the comparatively long paraenetic section 1:27–2:18 (2:12–18 ὥστε... ἵνα...).[101] As we have seen, this close also brings to an end the second-level section 1:12–2:18 and, in addition to the recurrences of material from the opening of 1:27–2:18, includes references back to the opening of the letter body in 1:3–6. At the fourth level of division we can note a consequence-indicating recurrence in 3:7–11 (3:8 f. ἵνα...).[102]

As regards these statements of consequences, it may be observed that the concluding phrases at the end of the main body of the letter about what God will do with respect to the addressees are not introduced by any

---

[96] A striking similarity between the wishes in 1 Thessalonians and their counterparts in Philippians is the expression ὁ θεὸς τῆς εἰρήνης in 1 Thess 5:23 and Phil 4:9. Cf. also Phil 4:7.

[97] 1:12: ... τὰ κατ' ἐμὲ μᾶλλον εἰς προκοπὴν τοῦ εὐαγγελίου ἐλήλυθεν...
1:18: τί γάρ; πλὴν ὅτι... Χριστὸς καταγγέλλεται, καὶ ἐν τούτῳ χαίρω.

[98] 1:19: οἶδα γὰρ ὅτι τοῦτό μοι ἀποβήσεται... κατά... ἐλπίδα μου, ὅτι... μεγαλυνθήσεται Χριστὸς ἐν τῷ σώματί μου...
1:25: καὶ τοῦτο πεποιθὼς οἶδα ὅτι μενῶ... εἰς τὴν ὑμῶν προκοπὴν καὶ χαρὰν τῆς πίστεως.

[99] 2:19: ἐλπίζω δέ... Τιμόθεον ταχέως πέμψαι ὑμῖν...
2:23: τοῦτον μὲν οὖν ἐλπίζω πέμψαι ὡς ἂν ἀφίδω τὰ περὶ ἐμὲ ἐξαυτῆς.

[100] 2:25: ἀναγκαῖον δὲ ἡγησάμην Ἐπαφρόδιτον... πέμψαι πρὸς ὑμᾶς...
2:28: σπουδαιοτέρως οὖν ἔπεμψα αὐτόν...

[101] 1:27 f.: μόνον ἀξίως τοῦ εὐαγγελίου τοῦ Χριστοῦ πολιτεύεσθε, ἵνα εἴτε ἐλθὼν καὶ ἰδὼν ὑμᾶς εἴτε ἀπὼν ἀκούω... ὅτι στήκετε... ἥτις ἐστίν... ἔνδειξις... ὑμῶν... σωτηρίας...
2:12–16: ὥστε... καθὼς πάντοτε ὑπηκούσατε, μὴ ἐν τῇ παρουσίᾳ μου μόνον ἀλλὰ νῦν πολλῷ μᾶλλον ἐν τῇ ἀπουσίᾳ μου... τὴν ἑαυτῶν σωτηρίαν κατεργάζεσθε... λόγον ζωῆς ἐπέχοντες...

[102] 3:6 f.: ... κατὰ δικαιοσύνην τὴν ἐν νόμῳ γενόμενος ἄμεμπτος. ἀλλὰ ἅτινα ἦν μοι κέρδη, ταῦτα ἥγημαι διὰ τὸν Χριστὸν ζημίαν.
3:8 f.: ... ἵνα Χριστὸν κερδήσω... μὴ ἔχων ἐμὴν δικαιοσύνην τὴν ἐκ νόμου ἀλλὰ τὴν διὰ τῆς πίστεως Χριστοῦ...

consequence-indicating particles at all; that the other statements of consequences at the first to the third levels are introduced by coordinating consequence-indicating particles or contain anaphoric text-summarizing expressions; and that the only statement of consequences recorded at the fourth level consists of a subordinate construction (see above).

Finally, it should in addition be noted that in some closings the statements of consequences are pursued to a natural end-point by the indication of the ultimate, eschatological consequence. This is the case at the end of the opening section of the letter (1:3–11) and in the closing section, which expresses what God will do with respect to the addressees (4:19 f.). The same phenomenon occurs in certain subsections of the paraenetic sections (2:11, 16; 3:14, 21; 4:3).

Contrastive opening markers

As far as contrastive opening markers are concerned, we find that Philippians exhibits a similar pattern to 1 Thessalonians. Here, too, virtually all the transitions at the two highest levels of division of the text have markers of this kind. The only exception is the transition 3:21/4:1, where ὥστε begins the closing second-level section 4:1–9. Transitions at the lower levels far more commonly lack contrastive markers.

As regards the character of these markers, it may be noted that, at the first level, τὸ λοιπόν occurs at the beginning of the major paraenetic section 3:1–4:9 and the balancing adversative particle δέ at the beginning of the somewhat shorter sections 4:10–18 and 4:19 f. At the second level of division, δέ is the commonest marker of this type (1:12; 2:19; 4:15, 18), but two subsections (3:2–15; 3:17–21) of the major paraenetic section (3:1–4:9) begin with asyndeton. At the third and fourth levels, contrastive opening markers include, apart from δέ (2:25) and asyndeton,[103] ἀλλά (1:18d; 3:7), μόνον (1:27) and οὖν (2:1). The short concluding section 4:8 f. begins with τὸ λοιπόν, which presumably looks back to the opening of the major section concerned, at 3:1.

Attention-attracting and intensity-heightening transition markers

In Philippians, too, attention-attracting and intensity-heightening transition markers occur in particular at the highest levels of division of the text and in conjunction with the beginning and ending of major sections. Once again, the use of an address is the commonest type, although it is encountered less

---

[103] 1:15; 3:4b, 12; 4:2, 3, 11, 17.

137

frequently here (eight times) than in 1 Thessalonians (twelve). It occurs as an opening marker in almost half the sections at the two highest levels.[104] In one of these cases it introduces a concluding section (4:1–9) and there its primary function is perhaps that of a closing marker. At lower levels, opening-marking address forms are found in 4:8 f. and 2:12–18. In both these cases we are concerned with concluding sections, and here too the primary function may therefore be that of marking a close. A more unambiguous example of an address functioning as a closing marker is that in 3:13, which occurs within a closing section (3:12 ff.) and helps to maintain its intensity. Here both 3:4b–14 (third level) and 3:2–16 (second level) are being brought to a close.

Of the eight occurrences of an address in Philippians, half consist of the word ἀδελφοί alone.[105] At the beginning of the major paraenetic section 3:1–4:9, the pronoun μου is added, making the address more personal. An even more personal note is struck at the beginning of the closing subsection of the same section (4:1–9), where the address ἀδελφοί μου is enlarged upon by the addition of several emotionally charged and favourable attributes (ἀγαπητοὶ καὶ ἐπιπόθητοι, χαρὰ καὶ στέφανός μου... ἀγαπητοί). This increases the urgency and insistency of the exhortation. For the same reasons, but with less emphasis, 2:12–18, which rounds off the first, somewhat shorter paraenetic section (1:27–2:18), begins with ἀγαπητοί μου rather than ἀδελφοί. In 4:15 f. the address Φιλιππήσιοι is used, since here Paul is contrasting the Philippians with other churches.

As regards the position of the address, it can be noted that in 3:15, where it introduces an intensifying repetition, it is in initial position, and that in 4:1 there is a final ἀγαπητοί which further reinforces the urgency of this verse. Elsewhere, the address always occurs within the clause.

Three of the instances of an address serving as a closing marker occur together with other intensity-heightening phenomena. In the closing section 4:1–9, following the initial address in 4:1, the intensity is maintained by a construction consisting of short asyndetically juxtaposed sentences, the repetition in 4:4 with its associated metacommunicative comment, and the repetitive constructions in 4:8 f., involving fronted subordinate clauses which are then summed up in the demonstrative pronoun ταῦτα. In the closing section 2:12–18, the opening address is followed by an emphatic construction consisting of fronted comparative clauses, and in the closing section 3:12 ff. the fresh start and the emphatic ἕν in 3:13 combine with the address to add to the intensity. Other intensity-heightening closing markers observed in the basic analysis include the repetitive constructions in 2:8 (bringing to an end 2:5–8) and 4:18 (4:10–18), and ἀμήν in 4:20 (4:19 f. and the entire body of the

---

[104] First level: 3:1–4:9. Second level: 1:12–2:18; 3:17–21; 4:1–9; 4:15–17.
[105] 1:12; 3:13, 17; 4:8.

138

letter). Other opening markers of the intensity-heightening type are the repetitive constructions in 2:1 (2:1–11), 3:2 (3:2–16) and 3:7 (3:7–11). In the last-mentioned case, the intensity is also heightened by the use of a fronted relative clause which is subsequently summed up by a demonstrative pronoun.

E. Implications for the line of thought in the letter

Concerning the purpose and arrangement of the following section, readers are referred to the introductory chapter and the corresponding part of the analysis of 1 Thessalonians.[106]

Overall structure of the letter

The basic analysis undertaken shows that the Letter to the Philippians, like the First Letter to the Thessalonians, is more uniform than is generally assumed. Leaving aside the short concluding section with its expressions of expectations or wishes, in 4:19 f., the letter falls into three parts: 1:3–2:30, 3:1–4:9 and 4:10–18.

Of these, the first two, longer parts prove to be closely connected and fundamentally to serve one and the same purpose, namely — as in 1 Thessalonians — to strengthen and encourage the addressees in their persecution. Thus the first part begins with an instructive and thematic construction in 1:3–7 expressing Paul's favourable assessment of the way the Philippians have shared for the benefit of the gospel up to the present time and the future completion of this sharing which he is convinced God will achieve. That this is being written to the Philippians specifically in the context of their persecution is hinted at by the καθώς-clause in 1:7, which says that the addressees share in grace with Paul, who, in his bonds, is defending and confirming the gospel. The fact that it is a matter of the grace to suffer for Christ, and that sharing in it with Paul means that the Philippians are forced like him to strive for the gospel amid persecution, is only made clear later (see 1:27–30). It may also be noted that the prayer reported in 1:9 ff., which rounds off the opening section 1:3–11, also fits in well with this context. As in 1 Thessalonians, whose addressees were also persecuted, Paul prays here that the recipients' love will overflow

---

[106] See pp. 34 and 81.

more and more.[107] He qualifies this by adding 'with knowledge and full insight to help you to determine what is best', which is also appropriate in the face of persecution. The purpose of the favourable introductory assessment of the persecuted Philippians' sharing for the benefit of the gospel up to now and its expected completion is presumably to strengthen and encourage them in their persecution.

The instructive and thematic construction which begins the second subsection (1:12–2:18) of the first part (1:3–2:30) states that Paul now wishes to inform his addressees that his imprisonment has resulted in the furtherance of the gospel. Since nothing is said about why he wishes to do so, it is reasonable to assume that this information, too, is in some way intended to strengthen and encourage the persecuted Philippians. This is in fact confirmed by what follows: Paul begins by expressing joy at his situation (1:12–18c) and at the way he expects it to develop (1:18d–24), then explains that it will also result in his addressees' furtherance and joy in faith (1:25 f.), and then moves smoothly on (1:27 μόνον...) to exhortations which clearly relate to the preceding information (1:30 τὸν αὐτὸν ἀγῶνα ἔχοντες, οἷον... νῦν ἀκούετε ἐν ἐμοί) and which concern the addressees specifically in the context of their persecution (1:27 f. ... στήκετε... συναθλοῦντες τῇ πίστει τοῦ εὐαγγελίου καὶ μὴ πτυρόμενοι ἐν μηδενὶ ὑπὸ τῶν ἀντικειμένων...). It thus becomes clear that the information given from 1:12 on is not primarily intended to set the Philippians' minds at rest regarding the persecuted Paul or to serve some similar purpose, but to comfort and encourage them in their persecution.

The first part of the letter (1:3–2:30) concludes with a shorter section (2:19–30) concerning the contacts which Paul plans to arrange with the Philippians. First he mentions his hope of being able to send Timothy to them soon. The purpose of doing so is said in the opening construction (2:19) to be to find out how things are with his addressees. Sending Timothy is thus a manifestation of Paul's concern for them (cf. also 2:20). He then comments on his decision to send Epaphroditus. In the closing statement of consequences in 2:28, he says that his purpose in sending him is to enable the Philippians (and Paul himself) to rejoice. This section is thus also in line with the aim of strengthening and encouraging the persecuted Philippians. Hence the whole of the first part (1:3–2:30) appears to have this as its overriding object.

The second part of the letter (3:1–4:9) begins in 3:1 with a metacommunicative clause which explicitly states that Paul is now repeating himself. As was noted in the introduction to this chapter, there are many distinct links in terms of vocabulary and motifs between the section beginning in 3:1 and the text of the preceding part in general and its paraenetic subsection 1:27–2:18 in

---

[107] Cf. 1 Thess 3:12 f.; 4:1, 9 f.

particular.[108] This suggests that it is this text that is being repeated, and if this is the case the new section from 3:1 clearly also serves the purpose of strengthening and encouraging the persecuted addressees. What is more, this assumption is entirely compatible with the content of its exhortations: to rejoice in the Lord (3:1; 4:4; cf. 1:25 and 2:17 f.); to see what their opponents are like (3:2; cf. 1:28 and 2:15);[109] to become fellow imitators (3:17) alongside Paul, who shares in the sufferings of Christ and conforms to his death (3:10; cf. 1:30 and 2:5–11);[110] to stand firm in the Lord (4:1; cf. 1:27); to be of the same mind (4:2 f.; cf. 1:27 and 2:2 f.); not to worry, but rather to pray to God (4:6; cf. 1:28). These exhortations would appear to serve the purpose of strengthening and encouraging the addressees in their persecution. The majority of the epistle thus proves to exhibit a relatively high degree of uniformity in terms of both purpose and mode of expression.

The third and final part (4:10–18) deviates somewhat from the rest. It begins with an instructive and thematic opening marker indicating that Paul now wishes to express his joy at the Philippians' concern for him (4:10). In tangible terms, he is clearly talking about a gift which he has received from them through Epaphroditus (4:18). However, his favourable appraisal relates not to the gift as such, but to the concern which it manifests, a point which is made very emphatically (4:11, 17). At the end of the first subsection (4:10–14), Paul reiterates his favourable assessment, this time describing their concern in terms of their sharing with him in his distress (4:14; cf. 1:5, 7). Thus his assessment ultimately relates to the addressees' faith and their readiness to share its painful consequences. This interpretation is also borne out by the fact that Paul rounds off the entire section by describing the gift in terms of a sacrifice (4:18; cf. 2:17). Thus, this short section, too, is brought within the overall purpose of strengthening and encouraging the Philippians in their persecution.

Like 1 Thessalonians, then, the whole of Philippians seems ultimately to serve one and the same purpose, namely to strengthen and encourage the addressees in their persecution.

Key motifs

The arrangement of the text that emerged from my analysis of 1 Thessalonians resulted in the idea of *imitatio* assuming greater prominence in that epistle.[111]

---

[108] See pp. 94 f.

[109] Concerning who these opponents are, see p. 117, note 70.

[110] Regarding the connection between Phil 2:5–11 and 3:10 f., 17, see also Fowl 1990, pp. 98 ff.

[111] Concerning the use of the term *imitatio* here, see pp. 84 f., note 108.

The arrangement arrived at in the case of the Letter to the Philippians has a similar consequence. This time, however, it is not because this way of thinking becomes more accentuated in the opening section of the letter body (1:3–11). Certainly, in my view, it is present even there, in the concepts κοινωνία (1:5) and συγκοινωνός (1:7),[112] but this is of course not made any clearer by my arrangement of the text. However, the fact that the following section, 1:12–2:18, is kept together does help to give prominence to the idea of *imitatio* in that context, since it makes it clear that the description of Paul's situation in 1:12–16 serves a paraenetic purpose and constitutes the starting-point for the exhortations in 1:27–2:18. It also points up the affinity in content terms between the description in 1:12–26 and the exhortations in 1:27–2:18.

Briefly, what is described in 1:12–26 is as follows: Paul's imprisonment has resulted in the furtherance of the gospel (1:12). Because of his defence of the gospel, the reason for his imprisonment is now known to everyone and the brothers have been inspired with new confidence to proclaim Christ (1:13 f., 16). This causes him to rejoice (1:18c). But he will also have cause to rejoice in the future (18d), for he knows that this will turn out for his salvation, provided that he is not put to shame and Christ is exalted in his body, whether by life or by death (1:19 f.). For him, the life-determining principle is Christ, and death is therefore gain (1:21).

This can be compared with the following points in the exhortatory section 1:27–2:18. The Philippians are urged to live their lives in a manner worthy of the gospel, to stand firm and strive side by side for the faith of the gospel, in no way intimidated by their opponents (1:27 f.). This is evidence of their salvation (1:28). Their guiding principle is to be Christ Jesus, who was obedient to the point of death and was therefore exalted by God (2:5–11). The Philippians must therefore also be obedient and work out their salvation (2:12). If they hold fast to the word of life in the midst of a crooked and perverse generation (2:15 f.), they will have cause to rejoice with Paul and Paul with them, even if he is killed (2:17 f.).

There are in other words significant similarities between the way Paul is described in 1:12–26 and what the Philippians are urged to do in 1:27–2:18. Admittedly, it is not actually spelt out that the Philippians are to follow Paul's example, but in the opening part of the paraenetic section (1:30) it is at any rate clearly stated that they are having the same struggle which they now hear to be Paul's. This was also hinted at back in 1:7. If, then, Paul begins by saying that he and the Philippians are in the same situation, then describes how favourably his situation has developed and will continue to develop, and subsequently addresses exhortations to the Philippians that are closely linked to this description, at the same time as he once again stresses that they are in

---

[112] For the use and meaning of κοινωνία in Philippians, see Wick 1994, pp. 142–8.

the same situation as he is, one can hardly escape the impression that the account of Paul's situation is intended as a model for the Philippians in their situation. This impression is of course not made any less persuasive by the fact that, in both the description and the paraenetic section, we find expressions suggesting the idea of *imitatio Christi* (e.g. 1:21 and 2:5). If this interpretation is correct, it means that the strengthening and encouragement undertaken in the Letter to the Philippians — just as in 1 Thessalonians — are based on Paul and ultimately Christ being held up as standards for the addressees.

That the text of 1:12–2:18 really is determined by *imitatio* thinking is confirmed in the major paraenetic section 3:1–4:9. As we have already noted, this section is closely linked to the preceding text, and above all to the paraenesis of 1:27–2:18. An initial hint at the idea of *imitatio* is given in the very first exhortation, in 3:1, in which the Philippians are urged to rejoice in the Lord — as Paul does (see e.g. 1:18, 2:2 and 2:17 f.). This way of thinking is then made more explicit in the description of Paul's attitude (3:4b–14) which follows the next exhortation (3:2), in that this passage describes how Paul wants to be found in Christ (3:9), to share his sufferings and to conform to his death, in the hope of attaining the (presumably his) resurrection from the dead (3:11). What is said here corresponds to the expression used in 1:21. This description is followed in 3:17 by an express exhortation to the Philippians to become Paul's 'fellow imitators' (of Christ, presumably) and to observe those who live thus, i.e. as fellow imitators, in the same way as the Philippians have 'us' as their example. A clearer expression of the *imitatio* thinking which I suggest is present here is difficult to imagine. It should be observed in this context that the concluding καθώς-clause presupposes that the Philippians already have 'us' as their example, which supports the earlier interpretation of 1:12–2:18 as a coherent entity. It may also be noted that this exhortation is given extra emphasis by the address ἀδελφοί.

The exhortations which follow (4:1–6) — to stand firm in the Lord, to be of the same mind, to rejoice and not to worry but to pray to God — also correspond by and large to the description in 1:12–26 and the exhortations in 1:27–2:18. Final confirmation that the exhortations of the latter section really were governed by the standards of Paul and Christ is provided by the general closing exhortation in 4:9, in which the Philippians are called upon to do the things they have learned and received (concerning Christ) and heard and seen in Paul. It may be observed that the wording of the final part of this exhortation is strongly reminiscent of 1:30, which formed part of the first exhortation in the letter and which was in turn clearly linked to the description in 1:12–26.

All these things suggest that 1:12–2:18 and 3:1–4:9, in which a substantial proportion of the strengthening and encouragement to be found in

Philippians is undertaken, are fundamentally characterized by an idea of *imitatio* which focuses primarily on Paul and Christ — and in particular the persecuted Paul and Christ crucified — but which also refers to others who live up to these standards (see 3:17).[113] It is no coincidence, therefore, that the qualities in Timothy and Epaphroditus to which attention is drawn in 2:20 ff. and 2:29 f. correspond to those held up in Paul and Christ and to the conduct which the Philippians have been urged to embrace (compare these verses with e.g. 1:21, 23 f.; 2:4, 7).[114] That the Philippians are also examples in so far as they live up to these standards is shown by 2:15 and 4:5, for instance (cf. 1 Thess 1:7 f.; 4:1).

It is only when 1:12–2:18 is kept together as one section that it becomes clear just how fundamental a role this *imitatio* thinking plays in the strengthening and encouragement undertaken in the Letter to the Philippians. And it is only when we become aware of this role that we are able to discern the connections between the different parts of the text. An inability — and in certain cases perhaps an unwillingness — to appreciate the role played by the idea of *imitatio* is probably an important reason for the difficulties exegetes have experienced in discerning the internal coherence of this epistle, difficulties which have in general resulted in a fragmentation of the text and caused certain interpreters to feel obliged to propose compilation or interpolation theories.

---

[113] Concerning the paraenetic purpose of the account of the persecuted Paul, see also Willert 1995, pp. 139–242.

[114] See Bloomquist 1993, pp. 173–8.

4. The Letter to the Galatians

A. Introduction

As in the introductions to my analyses of the previous two letters, I shall begin here with a brief review of a number of modern proposals concerning the arrangement of the Letter to the Galatians and a consideration of the question of its unity.[1]

In this case, the unity issue can be dealt with quite briefly, since by and large scholars are agreed on the integrity of Galatians. Not even Schmithals, otherwise so deft with the scissors, contests it.[2] Relatively recently, it is true, Smit has argued that Galatians has a redactional history, but — quite rightly — he seems to have gained little support for his theory.[3]

---

[1] For my reasons for doing so, see p. 33.

[2] See Schmithals 1984, p. 87.

[3] Smit (1989) suggests that 5:13–6:10 is a coherent entity centred on the theme of σάρξ versus πνεῦμα and that it disrupts the sequence of thought in the letter. In his view, in Galatians Paul is following the rhetorical pattern of oratory of the deliberative type, but 5:13–6:10 does not fit this pattern. In addition, he argues that the ideas, perspective and tone of this passage are at odds with those of the rest of the epistle: the letter as a whole is concerned with the relationship between Jews and Gentiles in Christ, 5:13–6:10 with how Christians in general should behave towards one another; elsewhere in the letter, Christ and the law are mutually exclusive, while this passage talks about fulfilling the law of Christ; both before and after 5:13–6:10 the tone is aggressive, whereas here it is gentle and respectful. Smit's conclusion is that 5:13–6:10 is an addition, but one made by Paul himself to give the particular a more general relevance once the immediate occasion of the letter had passed.

As for Paul's relationship to ancient rhetoric, as expounded in Aristotle, Cicero and Quintilian for example, there are so many uncertainties that poorness of fit with particular rhetorical patterns can hardly form the basis for a redaction theory. What is more, Smit admits that other deviations from the pattern are to be found in Galatians: for example, he feels obliged to regard 6:11–18 as an *amplificatio* and to accept that there is no *divisio*. The other arguments which he puts forward do not convince me, either. The letter as a whole is concerned with whether or not the Galatians should submit to circumcision. To persuade them to refrain from doing so, Paul contrasts the way of freedom in Christ with the way of the law in slavery. That he goes on to define what the way of freedom entails in tangible, positive terms is not surprising, nor is it strange that he should choose in this context to use the word 'law' in a positive sense (cf. Rom 8:2; cf. also Barclay 1988, p. 144). Regarding Paul's tone, it is by no means unequivocally aggressive in the rest of the letter: for example, the address ἀδελφοί is used throughout; the tone in 4:10–20 must surely be described as quite gentle; and in 5:10 Paul has just expressed his conviction that the Galatians will think the same way as he does.

For my overview of the arrangements of the text proposed by other scholars, I have chosen to look more closely at 17 commentaries on Galatians, which I believe cover the most important proposals to be found in modern commentaries. In addition, I have studied the arrangements suggested in four monographs and three articles.[4]

Given the considerable measure of agreement on the unity of Galatians, it is somewhat surprising to note that views differ widely when it comes to its actual structure and the links between its constituent parts. Looking at the first, i.e. highest, level of division of the text, for example, it may be noted that the only sections on which more than half of the 24 sources examined are agreed are 1:1–5 (14 sources[5]) and 6:11–18 (20[6]). The situation is much the same at lower levels of division.

Turning our attention from sections to individual transitions in the text, we naturally find many transitions which have been noted by all the scholars reviewed. Often, however, there is considerable disagreement about the levels to which they should be assigned: for example, there are only three transitions which everyone has placed at one of the highest three levels (1:5/6; 2:21/3:1; 6:10/11). In several cases, moreover, views differ as to where the actual transitions occur.

All the sources consulted are agreed, then, that there is a major transition at 1:5/6. The majority also consider 1:1–5 to be a separate entity, a letter opening, but quite a few (eight) regard the following section as part of the opening, too.[7] As for the position of the next major transition, the beginning of the

Recently, V. Gregersen (1993, pp. 1–18), too, has advanced a compilation theory relating to Galatians. It is far too involved to be presented and discussed in detail here, and I must therefore confine myself to making the following general comment. The rearrangements and deletions of both more extensive and shorter sections of the text which Gregersen proposes often turn out to be a product of specific conceptions about Paul's personality, theology and mode of expression, and about the situation in Galatia and the early church in general. Methodologically this is highly questionable, given that the Letter to the Galatians is one of our principal sources of knowledge about such matters. It has to be asked, therefore, whether Gregersen is not in fact cutting the bough he is standing on when making such far-reaching incisions in Galatians. He should at least have given particulars of the other, more credible sources on which he bases his knowledge of Paul, the Galatians and the early church.

[4] *Commentaries:* Bonnard & Masson 1953, Cole 1965, Schlier 1971, Guthrie 1973, Mußner 1974, Arichea & Nida 1975, Becker 1976, Lührmann 1978, Betz 1979, Osiek 1980, Bruce 1982, Cousar 1982, Borse 1984, Krentz 1985, Fung 1988, Rodhe 1989 and Dunn 1993a. *Monographs:* Vielhauer 1978, Schmithals 1984, Jegher-Bucher 1991 and Pitta 1992. *Articles:* Hall 1987, Smit 1989 and Pelser *et al.* 1992.

[5] Schlier 1971, Guthrie 1973, Mußner 1974, Arichea & Nida 1975, Lührmann 1978, Vielhauer 1978, Betz 1979, Bruce 1982, Schmithals 1984, Hall 1987, Smit 1989, Jegher-Bucher 1991, Pitta 1992 and Pelser *et al.* 1992.

[6] All except Cole 1965, Cousar 1982, Schmithals 1984 and Pelser *et al.* 1992.

[7] Bonnard & Masson 1953, Becker 1976, Osiek 1980, Borse 1984, Krentz 1985, Fung 1988, Rodhe 1989 and Dunn 1993a.

extensive biographical section of the letter, opinions differ: 1:9/10, 1:10/11, 1:11/12 and 1:12/13 have all been suggested.[8] There is no agreement on where this biographical passage ends, either. The majority regard it as continuing as far as 2:21, but some sources (four) consider that it ends in 2:14 instead, while one suggests 2:10 and another 3:5.[9] At the next level of division, 1:24/2:1 and 2:10/11 are usually identified as transitions. In addition, quite a few of the works consulted see a transition at 2:14/15 (six) or at 2:16/17 (two).[10]

In the view of most scholars, the biographical section is followed by a lengthy section devoted to theological argument.[11] Just as opinions differ as to where this section begins, so too there is disagreement about where it ends. The commonest proposals are after 5:12 (12 sources) or 4:31 (six), but it has also been suggested that the section ends after 4:7 (two), 4:20 (two) or 5:1 (one).[12] The transitions most commonly recorded at the next level down are 3:5/6, 3:14/15, 3:29/4:1, 4:7/8, 4:20/21 and 4:31/5:1, but there are other suggestions, too.[13]

After this extensive section of theological reasoning, most of the sources consulted distinguish a major paraenetic section.[14] In this case there is greater agreement on where it ends than on where it begins: virtually everyone considers it to close at 6:10. Regarding the subdivisions of this section, the most commonly identified transitions are 5:15/16 and 5:26/6:1, but others have also been proposed.[15]

The arrangements proposed in the literature studied, then, vary widely, once again testifying to the difficulties exegetes have experienced in discerning the structure and coherence of the text.

With that, we can now move on to the actual analysis of Galatians.

---

[8] *1:9/10:* Cole 1965, Becker 1976, Osiek 1980, Hall 1987 and Pelser *et al.* 1992. *1:10/11:* Bonnard & Masson 1953, Schlier 1971, Guthrie 1973, Arichea & Nida 1975, Lührmann 1978, Vielhauer 1978, Bruce 1982, Cousar 1982, Borse 1984, Schmithals 1984, Krentz 1985, Fung 1988, Rodhe 1989, Pitta 1992 and Dunn 1993a. *1:11/12:* Betz 1979. *1:12/13:* Mußner 1974, Smit 1989 and Jegher-Bucher 1991.

[9] *2:14/15:* Betz 1979, Osiek 1980, Bruce 1982 and Fung 1988. *2:10/11:* Schmithals 1984. *3:5/6:* Jegher-Bucher 1991.

[10] *2:14/15:* Bonnard & Masson 1953, Borse 1984, Krentz 1985, Pitta 1992, Pelser *et al.* 1992 and Dunn 1993a. *2:16/17:* Cole 1965 and Jegher-Bucher 1991.

[11] At least three consider there to be two separate theological sections here: Betz 1979 (2:15–21; 3:1–4:31), Smit 1989 (3:1–4:11; 4:12–5:12) and Pitta 1992 (3:1–4:7; 4:8–5:12).

[12] *After 4:7:* Schmithals 1984 and Pelser *et al.* 1992. *After 4:20:* Borse 1984 and Jegher-Bucher 1991. *After 4:31:* Bonnard & Masson 1953, Guthrie 1973, Arichea & Nida 1975, Betz 1979, Osiek 1980 and Rodhe 1989. *After 5:1:* Cole 1965. *After 5:12:* Schlier 1971, Mußner 1974, Becker 1976, Lührmann 1978, Vielhauer 1978, Cousar 1980, Bruce 1982, Krentz 1985, Fung 1988, Smit 1989, Pitta 1992 and Dunn 1993a.

[13] E.g. 3:6/7, 3:9/10, 3:18/19; 3:22/23, 3:25/26, 5:1/2.

[14] Two consider there to be two paraenetic sections here: Osiek 1980 (5:1–24, 5:25–6:10) and Bruce 1982 (5:13–26; 6:1–10).

[15] E.g. 5:12/13, 5:18/19, 5:21/22, 5:24/25, 5:25/26, 6:6/7.

B. Basic analysis

Concerning the approach and method of the following analysis, readers are referred to chapter 1 and to the corresponding section of the analysis of 1 Thessalonians.[16]

1:1–5

Like the other Pauline epistles, Galatians begins with particulars of the senders and the recipients (1:1–2) and a wish of grace and peace (1:3–5). These elements are formulaic and are asyndetically juxtaposed. They are somewhat longer here than usual, owing to the addition of a number of attributes.[17] The conclusion of the extended wish of grace and peace is marked by a 'doxology' and the word ἀμήν in 1:5, which emphatically express a desired consequence.

1:6–10

Verse 1:6 marks the beginning of the actual body of the letter. In Galatians, too, the letter body can be described as an entity held together chiefly by conjunctions, although there is somewhat more asyndeton here than in 1 Thessalonians or Philippians. The more frequent occurrence of asyndeton in this letter is due primarily to its comparative abundance of rhetorical questions, the answers to which often follow on asyndetically.[18] Apart from in these instances, asyndeton occurs in particular in connection with digressions and exhortations, as in 1 Thessalonians and Philippians.

The start of a new section in 1:6 is marked by asyndeton and a construction that is clearly instructive and thematic. The latter begins with a statement of the metapropositional base, θαυμάζω, which informs the recipients that Paul regards the content of the proposition in an unfavourable light. The proposition then follows in the form of a ὅτι-clause, referring to the fact that

---

[16] See pp. 32 ff. and 48.

[17] Of Paul's letters, only Romans expands these elements to a greater extent than Galatians.

[18] See 1:10; 2:14 f., 17; 3:5 f., 19, 21.

the Galatians are so quickly deserting the one who called them in grace and turning to a different gospel. The opening of the letter body of Galatians is thus in fact fairly similar to the corresponding sections of 1 Thessalonians and Philippians (and most of Paul's other epistles).[19] In all these cases, the body of the letter begins with an assessment of the addressees' conduct. The only difference is that in Galatians this assessment is unfavourable (θαυμάζω), whereas in the other cases it is favourable (εὐχαριστῶ/οὖμεν).[20] Here, too, the assessment expressed presumably serves a paraenetic purpose, namely to put a stop to undesirable developments in Galatia.

The assertion that the Galatians are turning to *a different gospel* is then commented on and clarified in a relative clause, which explains that in fact there is no other gospel, other than in the sense that there are some who are confusing the Galatians and who want to pervert the gospel of Christ.[21] The

[19] A letter-body opening of a different kind is found in 2 Corinthians (and also in Ephesians and 1 Peter). There the body of the letter begins εὐλογητὸς ὁ θεός..., which expresses an assessment, not of the addressees' actions, but of how God has acted towards the senders. It thus differs from the corresponding sections of the other Pauline letters (including Galatians).

[20] It is not correct to claim, as many commentators do (e.g. Cole 1965, p. 38, and Rodhe 1989, p. 38), that this breaches every epistolary convention of the time. On the contrary, among the Hellenistic letters that have been preserved it is possible to find other examples of such openings, more specifically in letters in which the prevailing tone is one of indignation or dissatisfaction (White 1986, pp. 201 and 208).

[21] The linguistic construction here is somewhat unclear. The usual view is that in this case εἰ μή has the same meaning as ἀλλά, i.e. 'but (rather)' (e.g. BDF/BDR § 448:8). This assumption is not unproblematic, however, since there is little evidence of such a use of εἰ μή. What is quite clear is that ἀλλά is sometimes used instead of ἀλλ' ἤ or εἰ μή in the sense 'except' (see e.g. Mayser 1934, p. 116, and BDF/BDR § 448:8), but this does not necessarily mean that εἰ μή can assume all the senses of ἀλλά. It does seem, though, as if, in the New Testament at least, the fixed collocation εἰ μή following negation (usually = 'except') can approach the meaning of 'but (rather)' — cf. Mt 12:4; Lk 4:26 f.; Rom 14:14; Rev 21:27. This could perhaps be due to the influence of the Aramaic אלא. Another possibility is that this is a kind of contamination — cf. e.g. Lk 4:27 οὐδεὶς αὐτῶν ἐκαθαρίσθη εἰ μὴ Ναιμάν, which can be understood as a contamination between οὐδεὶς ἐκαθαρίσθη εἰ μὴ Ναιμάν and οὐκ αὐτοὶ ἐκαθαρίσθησαν ἀλλὰ Ναιμάν. However, all these cases involve the fixed form εἰ μή in the sense 'except'. When it comes to εἰ μή introducing a subordinate clause, there is no clear evidence of it being used to mean 'but (rather)'. The only example that tends to be adduced apart from Gal 1:7 is 1 Cor 7:17, but that instance is no clearer than Gal 1:7. In the 1 Corinthians example, εἰ μή may possibly be linked somewhat loosely to the preceding questions, the sense then being: '(What do you know), except that (or: if not)...?' My suggestion therefore is that the εἰ μή-clause in Gal 1:7 should be read as a conditional subordinate clause which — albeit somewhat clumsily — qualifies the assertion that there is no other gospel and specifies in what one sense it is possible to say, as Paul does in v. 6, that the Galatians are turning to a different gospel, namely if there are some who are confusing them and who want to pervert the gospel of Christ. The advantage of this reading is that it means that the εἰ μή-clause is subordinate to the preceding relative clause and thus does not compete with the ἀλλά-clause in v. 8. What is more, there is no need to assume a doubtful use of εἰ μή. It is necessary, though, to accept a linguistically clumsy construction, but that is the case even with the usual reading. If the conventional reading is preferred, one has to accept εἰ μή...

clarifying relative clause is followed by the pronouncement of an anathema upon anyone who proclaims as the gospel anything other than what 'we' proclaimed to the Galatians. This anathema corresponds to the negative clause 'which is not another one' and begins with ἀλλά.[22] It expresses a strongly unfavourable assessment of those who persuade the Galatians to turn to a different, perverted gospel and thus echoes the opening assessment in 1:6. As a result, it gives the impression of being a final appraisal and rounding off the clarificatory comment.

The text does not immediately move on from this final assessment, however; first, there is a comment on it in 1:9. The latter is added asyndetically and begins with a statement of the metapropositional base — ὡς προειρήκαμεν καὶ ἄρτι πάλιν λέγω — after which the anathema is repeated in an abbreviated and more general form. This indicates that it is not the proposition (the content of the anathema), but the metapropositional base (the actual pronouncement of it) that is being commented on. The point being made is that this anathema, which 'we' have expressed before,[23] is *also now* being pronounced by Paul.

This emphasis on Paul also pronouncing the anathema now is then explained (γάρ) in 1:10.[24] That this is what is being explained is indicated by

in v. 7 and ἀλλά... in v. 8 as two parallel but different answers to the negative assertion of the preceding relative clause. The semantic coherence of the text remains much the same with either alternative, however.

[22] Here, too, there is I believe cause to question the punctuation used in NTG. In my opinion, a full stop is too strong a separating mark after Χριστοῦ in v. 7 (cf. the comments on Phil 2:17 above, pp. 108–13).

[23] The verb προειρήκαμεν — like εὐηγγελισάμεθα in the preceding verse — probably refers to what Paul and his fellow missionaries have said in earlier contacts with the Galatians, rather than to what Paul has just written in v. 8 (contrary to the views of e.g. Cole (1965) and Schlier (1971)). Three arguments can be put forward in favour of the first alternative and against the second: (1) The use of ἄρτι, emphasized by καί and its position, highlights a *temporal* difference between the two statements. (2) Since εὐηγγελισάμεθα has just been used to describe the earlier missionary activities of Paul and presumably his fellow missionaries among the Galatians, it seems reasonable to assume that προειρήκαμεν, in the first person plural (perfect), also alludes to those activities. (3) Although Paul varies somewhat in his use of the first person singular and first person plural in his letters, I find it difficult to imagine him using, in one and the same sentence, the plural to refer to what he has just said and the singular to refer to what he is about to say.

[24] It is often questioned whether γάρ in fact has the function of a causal particle here. This is of course because, if it does have that function, a desired interpretation of the passage is ruled out. Doubts on this point are often raised with reference to Zahn (1922, p. 53), who, invoking Kühner-Gerth (1904, pp. 330 ff.), claims that γάρ is not a causal particle in this context, but a confirmative adverb (see e.g. Schlier 1971, p. 41, note 2; Rodhe 1989, p. 46, note 90). Proceeding from the generally held view that γάρ was the result of a fusion of γέ and ἄρα (see also Chantraine 1968, p. 210, and Frisk 1960, p. 289), Kühner-Gerth concluded that it originally served as an emphatic or inferential particle. This use of γάρ, he claimed, then lived on in parallel with its dominant use as a causal particle, at least in Homer and the classical authors. However, this position is

the strongly accentuated and instructive ἄρτι with which the explanation begins.[25] The explanation assumes the form of two rhetorical questions, concerning whether Paul is *now* trying (or should try)[26] to persuade people or God, and whether he is seeking (or should seek) to please people. They are followed by a conditional complex sentence stating the conclusion one would have been forced to draw if Paul had been pleasing people, namely that he would not then have been a servant of Christ. This brings to an end the comment in 1:9 f.

The line of thought here is not altogether clear. The only thing that is clear is that pleasing people is used in this context as a criterion of a person not being a servant of Christ, and that Paul believes that he surely cannot *now* be accused of this. But why? Because he pronounces the anathema? If that is the case, then 1:10 explains why Paul is now pronouncing it once again, despite the fact that it strikes at or threatens the Galatians. He is doing so because the task of a servant of Christ is not to please people. Thus Paul's pronouncement of an anathema is itself something which enhances his credibility. Or do the

---

contested. Denniston (1954, pp. 56 ff.), for example, accepts an 'asseverative' γάρ, but only in the collocations καὶ γάρ, καὶ γὰρ οὖν, καὶ γάρ τοι, τοιγάρ, τοιγαροῦν, τοιγάρτοι and perhaps ἀλλὰ γάρ; and he completely rejects an 'inferential' γάρ (see also Schwyzer & Debrunner 1950, p. 560). It is thus unclear whether a use of γάρ such as is proposed in Gal 1:10 actually occurs in Greek as we know it, and the suggestion is not made any more credible by the fact that Galatians is such a late text. I therefore consider it best to accept that γάρ is a causal particle here and to interpret the text accordingly. Cf. p. 58 f., note 70.

[25] Quite a number of exegetes consider the significant transition in the text to occur here, with v. 9 rounding off the general introduction and v. 10 introducing the argument that follows (e.g. Cole 1965, Becker 1976, Osiek 1980, Hall 1987, Pelser *et al.* 1992; see also NT-81). This view presumably stems partly from the fact that in Paul's letters rhetorical questions often seem to be used to introduce a new element in an argument (see e.g. Rom 3:1; 4:1; 6:1; 7:7; 9:14; 1 Cor 14:26; 15:35; Gal 2:17; 3:1–5, 19, 21). However, such a use of rhetorical questions differs from the one found in 1:10. The conjunction normally employed in such cases is not γάρ, but οὖν (see e.g. Rom 3:1; 4:1; 6:1; 7:7; 9:14; 1 Cor 15:35; Gal 3:19, 21). What is more, an immediate answer is usually given to the question, an answer which is then explained and reflected upon in the ensuing text. This is not what happens here. The questions are followed only by a conditional complex sentence, stating what conclusion would have had to be drawn if the answer had been the opposite to the obvious one, i.e. if Paul had still been pleasing people: in that case, it would have been necessary to conclude that he was not a δοῦλος of Christ. This suggests that the two questions function as statements rather than real questions, and the conclusion expressed in the conditional complex sentence points to the closing of the present section, rather than the beginning of a new one.

[26] The verb forms πείθω and ζητῶ can be understood as either indicatives or subjunctives. Below I shall treat them as indicatives, as this makes the text more open and allows a wider range of interpretations. If they are read as subjunctives, the sense must surely be that, after the anathema in 1:9, Paul is using the rhetorical questions to confront the Galatians with the choice facing them and then using the conditional complex sentence to express the consequences of choosing the opposite alternative to the one he himself has chosen in pronouncing the anathema.

rhetorical questions refer to some other circumstance in Paul's present situation? In the closing section of the letter, which may be expected to correspond to some extent to its opening section, the desire to please people is again used as a criterion to determine who is a true servant of Christ. There both Paul and his opponents are assessed: the latter are described as those who *want to make a good showing in the flesh* and who are trying to compel the Galatians to be circumcised *only to avoid being persecuted for the cross of Christ* (6:12), while Paul *wishes to boast only of the cross of Christ* (6:14) and *carries the marks of Jesus on his body* (6:17). In these closing verses, then, his opponents' desire to please people in order to avoid persecution is contrasted with his own willingness to take up the cross.[27] Is the same contrast perhaps relevant in 1:10, and is this verse then referring to a situation of persecution which Paul is 'now' enduring and which is well known to the Galatians?[28] If this is the case, the explanation in 1:10 relates to the actual highlighting of the fact that the anathema is being pronounced now, and is intended to enhance Paul's credibility. Whichever of these alternatives we choose, we can note that here, at the beginning of his letter, Paul is drawing attention to the desire to please people as a criterion of a person not being a servant of Christ, and using this criterion to strengthen his own credibility. Thus we have here an initial argument for his position.

---

[27] In 1 Thess 2:2 ff., too, a wish to please people is contrasted with Paul's persecution.

[28] As we shall see in the analysis below, the motif of persecution appears to play a crucial role in the rest of Galatians, too. Despite this, it has largely been neglected in modern commentaries. A specific study has been made of it, though, by E. Baasland in his article 'Persecution: A Neglected Feature in the Letter to the Galatians' (1984). Baasland observes that the persecution motif occurs both frequently and in important passages in Galatians, and then attempts to show that this is because, in his view, the 'Judaizers' in Galatia, in line with patterns of thought prevalent in the Old Testament and early Judaism, had claimed that Paul's weakness and persecution were a sign that he was under a curse as a result of having broken the law. This explanation leaves me unconvinced. I do not wish to go into the details of Baasland's analysis here, and will merely raise a few general objections: (1) His analysis is based on an arrangement of the text which in my opinion is incorrect. In particular, his conclusions are affected by his view that the *argumentatio* consists of 3:1–4:31, which I would question. (2) As I see it, his analysis greatly overemphasizes the curse or anathema motif. It appears only twice in Galatians (1:8 f.; 3:10–14), and nowhere in the epistle is it even hinted that it is linked to the motif of 'Paul's weakness and persecution' in the way Baasland claims. (3) I find it difficult to believe that it was possible in an early church whose founder had been persecuted and put to death a few decades earlier, and whose leaders and members had subsequently met with a similar fate, to claim that persecution was automatically a sign of sin and being under a curse.

1:11–2:21

1:11–12

After the added comment in 1:9 f. has been brought to an end, a clear new beginning follows in 1:11. It is marked by the address ἀδελφοί, a construction that is clearly instructive and thematic, and possibly the conjunction δέ.[29] The construction begins with the metapropositional and metacommunicative γνωρίζω... ὑμῖν, indicating a shift at the metapropositional level from assessment to information. The proposition then follows in the form of the proleptic τὸ εὐαγγέλιον τὸ εὐαγγελισθὲν ὑπ' ἐμοῦ and a ὅτι-clause stating that this gospel is not according to man. The heading-type prolepsis, which can be regarded as an opening marker in its own right, is not directly linked to 1:10, which seemed to allude to some circumstance in Paul's present situation which meant that he could not be accused of wanting to please people.[30] The following ὅτι-clause, on the other hand, does echo the criterion in 1:10 when it states that this gospel is not κατὰ ἄνθρωπον. Thus the prolepsis first announces a new theme, after which the ὅτι-clause indicates its connection with what has just been written. The precise nature of that connection can be discussed, but presumably the new section is intended to explain the criterion in the light of the nature of Paul's gospel. Ultimately, at any rate, the purpose of the information in this section is to provide support for Paul as he takes issue with his opponents in Galatia and seeks to win over the Galatians to himself and his gospel.

The opening statement about the character of Paul's gospel is followed by a comment in 1:12 explaining (γάρ) that, equally, this gospel is not something he received from a human being or was taught, but something that has come to him by revelation of Jesus Christ.

---

[29] 𝔓46, ℵ*.2, A, D1, Ψ, 𝔐 and the Syriac and Bohairic manuscripts have the reading δέ. ℵ1, B, D*, F, G, 33 p c and the Sahidic manuscripts read γάρ. The Latin manuscript tradition is divided. Both readings are thus well supported in the earliest manuscripts. Given the relatively modest difference in meaning between the two, it is not necessary here to find in favour of one or other of them. If the reading with γάρ is chosen, the new section is linked more closely to 1:10 and subordinate to it in terms of the line of thought. If this is the case, then this section is presumably intended to clarify or provide a further reason for the assertion that Paul is a δοῦλος of Christ. If we choose the reading with δέ, the transition is more strongly marked and the new section is semantically more independent of what has gone before.

[30] Nor does it appear to have a direct connection with 1:8, since the text now focuses expressly on *Paul's* gospel (ὑπ' ἐμοῦ).

1:13–2:21

1:13–24

Although there is no indication that the preceding text has been brought to a close, a fresh start is made in 1:13. The very fact that it comes unannounced suggests that it is a minor one, the beginning of a subsection. This is also indicated by the conjunction γάρ, which sets the new section within the ongoing argument. The new start is marked by a new instructive and thematic construction, beginning with the secondary metapropositional and meta-communicative ἠκούσατε,[31] which indicates that what follows is a reminder. The new section thus fits readily into the informative context indicated by γνωρίζω... ὑμῖν in 1:11.

The proposition then follows in the form of a cataphoric text-summarizing noun phrase — τὴν ἐμὴν ἀναστροφήν ποτε ἐν τῷ Ἰουδαϊσμῷ — and a ὅτι-clause. The noun phrase, which serves as a heading and can be seen as an opening marker in its own right, is linked in terms of content to 1:12 and hints that the reminder has to do with the way Paul has received his gospel. The long ὅτι-clause which follows, and which describes Paul's earlier life ἐν τῷ Ἰουδαϊσμῷ, focuses in particular on how he persecuted the church (1:13) and advanced beyond those of his own age ἐν τῷ Ἰουδαϊσμῷ (1:14). The change which receiving the gospel wrought in his life is thus shown to be a very far-reaching one, supporting his claim to divine intervention. The question is, though, whether the text is not also concerned here with the qualitative aspect of this change. In 1:10, Paul pointed out that he would not have been a servant of Christ if had *still* been pleasing people. This criterion of servant-hood then formed the starting-point for the opening statement of the new section beginning at 1:11, in which Paul asserted that his gospel was not according to man. When he now, in 1:13, recalls how he persecuted the church and advanced beyond those of his own age ἐν τῷ Ἰουδαϊσμῷ, he is clearly describing a man who was not a servant of Christ, but who pleased people. What is more, this introduction paves the way for seeing Paul's reception of the gospel and his calling as a servant of Christ in terms of his joining the persecuted (see 1:23), i.e. those who did not please people. This description of how he received the gospel thus fits in well with the criterion in 1:10. In addition, it may be noted that when, at the end of the letter, Paul applies the same criterion and accuses his opponents in Galatia of wanting to make a good showing in the flesh and trying to compel the Galatians to be circumcised so as to avoid persecution themselves — as we saw earlier — he is accusing them of pursuing the very opposite path to the one he himself

---

[31] The primary metapropositional base may be assumed to be 'I assert that...', 'I know that...' or some similar expression.

followed on receiving the gospel and becoming a servant of Christ, as described from 1:13 on. It is therefore justifiable to assume that the *nature* of the change in Paul's life, too, is of significance in this description and tells us something about his gospel. At all events, the new section beginning in 1:13 is closely linked to 1:11 f. at both the metapropositional and the propositional level, thus reinforcing the impression that it is subordinate to the one that began in 1:11.[32]

This is confirmed by the account which follows. Like narratives generally, it is organized along chronological lines. The first indication of time has already been given, by the heading-like noun phrase in 1:13: ποτὲ ἐν τῷ Ἰουδαϊσμῷ. Its indefinite character gives the impression that this is a background account.

The next time reference comes in the form of a long temporal clause in 1:15 f., which also describes a significant change in circumstances. The role of this clause as an opening marker is underlined by the conjunction δέ. It describes God's decision to reveal his Son to Paul so that he might proclaim him as the gospel among the Gentiles. This is a clear link with the verses (1:11 f.) which formed the starting-point for this section (see in particular the key words ἀποκαλύψαι and εὐαγγελίζωμαι), suggesting that we are now leaving the background account and moving on to the real subject-matter of the narrative. This is confirmed by the fact that the main clause then echoes the motif οὐδέ... παρὰ ἀνθρώπου from 1:12 by stressing that initially Paul did not confer with any human being.

In 1:18 we find another chronological statement: ἔπειτα μετὰ ἔτη τρία... The impression that this is the beginning of a new section is reinforced by the references to a place (εἰς Ἱεροσόλυμα) and a person (Κηφᾶν). This new section describes the very limited contact Paul had with the Jerusalem apostles after three years, and is presumably intended to lend further support to his claim in 1:12 that his gospel was οὐδέ... παρὰ ἀνθρώπου. It is brought to a close and given emphasis by the metacommunicative clause in 1:20: ἃ δὲ γράφω ὑμῖν, ἰδοὺ ἐνώπιον τοῦ θεοῦ ὅτι οὐ ψεύδομαι.

The narrative continues, however. The beginning of another new section in 1:21 is marked by the indication of time ἔπειτα, reinforced by the place reference εἰς τὰ κλίματα τῆς Συρίας καὶ τῆς Κιλικίας. In 1:22 there is yet another echo of the motif οὐδέ... παρὰ ἀνθρώπου from 1:12, further underlining the impression that this motif is crucial to the account up to this point. This is followed in 1:23 by a sentence summing up the change in Paul's life that has just been described. It contains clear recurrences of material from the background narrative in 1:13 f. — see e.g. διώκων, ποτέ (twice), ἐπόρθει — and from the long ὅτι-clause in 1:15 f. which introduced the essential part

---

[32] On this I differ from e.g. Mußner (1974), Smit (1989) and Jegher-Bucher (1991), all of whom regard 1:12/13 as a higher-order transition.

of the narrative — see e.g. εὐαγγελίζεται. These recurrences indicate to the audience that what is being brought to a close here is not just the subsection beginning at 1:21, but the whole of the narrative from 1:13 on. The rounding off of this narrative is completed by a statement of consequences in 1:24 about the Judaean churches glorifying God.

2:1–10

In 1:23 f., then, Paul brings to a close the story so far. But clearly he has more to tell his recipients. In 2:1 a fresh start is made and the narrative enters a new phase. The new beginning is marked by the time reference ἔπειτα διὰ δεκατεσσάρων ἐτῶν, the place reference εἰς ῾Ιεροσόλυμα and the personal reference μετὰ Βαρναβᾶ συμπαραλαβὼν καὶ Τίτον, which together set a completely new scene. Several features indicate that this new start is more important than the earlier ones in the narrative (1:15, 18, 21). First, we can observe that in 2:2 Paul once again builds on the two central concepts of the verses which formed the starting-point for the narrative section, i.e. 1:11 f.: ἀποκάλυψις and τὸ εὐαγγέλιον τὸ εὐαγγελισθὲν ὑπ᾽ ἐμοῦ. Secondly, such a long interval is said to have elapsed since Paul's conversion or calling that the purpose of this part of the narrative can hardly still be to describe the circumstances in which Paul received his gospel, a conclusion that is confirmed by the fact that the motif οὐδέ... παρὰ ἀνθρώπου plays a less significant role in the subsequent account. Thirdly, we can note a change in the actual mode of presentation from 2:1 on. In 1:13–24, Paul gave a broader view of a long sequence of events, summarizing briefly in four subsections the aspects of those events which were essential in the present context. In this new section, he reports in far greater detail on a single episode, dwelling in particular on its causes and results.

If from 2:1 on the narrative is no longer concerned with describing the circumstances of Paul's calling, what is its purpose? Some indication of the answer to this question is given in the first two verses, in which Paul says that, acting on God's initiative, he went up to Jerusalem and laid his gospel before those who were of repute there, to make sure that he was not running, or had not run, in vain. What Paul now wishes to relate, in other words, is the assessment which those of repute made of him and his gospel. The new section thus serves as a kind of comment on the account given in 1:13–24. The next three verses (2:3 ff.) pose a number of syntactic difficulties which need not be examined in detail in the present context. Suffice to say that these verses primarily seem to provide further information on the background to the assessment which is then reported in 2:6–10. The background is said to be a conflict between 'us' and a number of false brothers, a conflict which clearly had to do with an insistence on circumcision and thus appears to be related to the one in focus in the Letter to the Galatians. The background account culminates in the ἵνα-clause in 2:5, which makes it clear that the conflict ultimately centred on the truth of the gospel. What those of repute were being asked to reach a position on was thus Paul's claim, as presented in 1:11 f. and expounded in 1:13–24. This statement of purpose and consequences, with its element of recurrence, marks the conclusion of the background narrative.

In 2:6 a new start is made, marked by the accentuated change of agentive subject from 'I'/'we' to 'those who were of repute', and by the conjunction δέ. The comment about these people of repute which is inserted here, interrupting the construction embarked upon, and the restart which follows it reinforce the impression that this is the beginning of a new section. What is now being reported is how those of repute responded to Paul's request by confirming him and his gospel. This is done in a long construction which extends as far as 2:10. The main core of the construction (the grammatical subject and the predicates) describes how those who were of repute did not add anything, but gave 'us' the right hand of fellowship, that 'we' should go to the Gentiles and they to the circumcised. It thus speaks of a confirmation of both Paul's gospel and his calling. In the later part of the construction, the basis for this confirmation is indicated by two participial constructions. In the first it is said that those of repute saw that Paul had been entrusted with *the gospel for the Gentiles* and in the second that they understood (or recognized) the *grace of God* that had been given to him. Both these expressions clearly echo the central passage in 1:15 f. about God's decision with regard to Paul, showing that the confirmation given here relates to the matters reported on in 1:13–24. The explanation of the meaning of the handshake, given in the ἵνα-clause in 2:9, also looks back to 1:15 f. These recurrences and the very fact that the response of those of repute to Paul's request (cf. 2:2) is now being reported suggest that the section beginning at 2:1 has entered a decisive phase and is approaching its conclusion. Before it is finally brought to a close, however, there is a reference in 2:10 to the only (μόνον) addition or reservation made by those of repute, namely that 'we' should remember 'the poor', a point which is then commented on in a consequence-indicating relative clause. This clause, whose consequence-indicating function is given extra emphasis by the pleonastic and emphatic αὐτὸ τοῦτο, brings the section to an end.

2:11–21

Confirmation that the preceding section was indeed brought to a close in 2:10 is provided by the new beginning in 2:11, marked by the conjunction δέ and the ὅτε-clause, which indicates the time of the events to be related and also draws attention to a new constellation of individuals (Κηφᾶς) in a new location (εἰς 'Αντιόχειαν). The new section is similar in construction to the preceding one, in that it reports on a single episode and begins by outlining the background to it. The aim of the previous section was to comment on what was narrated in 1:13–24 by describing how it was confirmed by those of repute in Jerusalem. There is no reason to believe that the present section serves a completely different purpose.

In 2:11 it is made clear that the new section is concerned with how Paul confronted Cephas in Antioch. A brief account of the background (γάρ) is then given. This background narrative has a chronological structure (πρὸ τοῦ... ὅτε δέ...) and ends with a consecutive clause in 2:13. It describes how, after certain people came from James, Cephas and the other Jews in Antioch drew back from eating with the Gentiles, for fear of the circumcision faction. The problem here thus seems to be of the same kind as is described in the preceding section and as has arisen in Galatia.

In 2:14 a new start is made, with the loosely connective ἀλλά[33] and a time indication in the form of a ὅτε-clause which sums up the background account and once again places us in the situation described in 2:11. This clause makes it clear that, here too, we are ultimately concerned with the truth of the gospel (cf. 2:5), and the function of this section thus becomes evident. Once again, the claims made by Paul in 1:11 f. and 1:13–24 are being brought into focus for comment and assessment.[34] This time Paul himself provides the comment and the defence, by reporting what he said to Peter. This use of direct speech in a narrative is not unparalleled in ancient literature. On the contrary, the historians of antiquity commonly included speeches in their accounts, in order to comment and shed light on them. Such speeches were invented, but they were based on real ones and claimed to reflect their essential meaning.[35] In the New Testament, good examples of this mode of presentation can be found in Acts.[36]

---

[33] This ἀλλά is of the elliptical type. Before it, the words ἐγὼ δὲ οὐ (συναπήχθην) or some similar expression can be supplied. See pp. 108 ff.

[34] Cf. the commentary on 2:1–10 above.

[35] In Thucydides, at least. See Thucydides I.22.

[36] The understanding of the Antioch episode's role in the text which is presented here has certain consequences. It makes it clear, for example, that the address in 2:14c–21 should be understood not only in the light of the conflicts in Antioch and Galatia, but also in relation to Paul's narrative in 1:13–24. In addition, it means that there is no reason for further speculation about why Paul says nothing about the outcome of the dispute. A conclusion commonly drawn from his silence on the subject is that it was not in his favour, that he gained no support for his views and became embroiled in a continuing conflict with Peter and the others in Antioch and had to leave the town for good (see e.g. Haenchen 1959, p. 417; Stuhlmacher 1968, pp. 106 f.). With the interpretation proposed here, such speculation becomes both unnecessary and unfounded. Paul refrains from

The address to Peter is introduced by a secondary metapropositional and metacommunicative clause — εἶπον τῷ Κηφᾷ ἔμπροσθεν πάντων — and then follows in the form of a quotation.[37] As was noted earlier,[38] many exegetes consider that this quotation continues only as far as 2:14 and is then followed in 2:15–21 by a theological exposition addressed directly to the Galatians. Such a division of the text would rule out the proposed interpretation of the sequence of thought, but can and should be questioned quite regardless of that fact, for the following reasons:

1. There is nothing in the text to suggest that at this point Paul is abandoning the narrative level, turning to the Galatians and embarking on a theological discussion. In view of what we have seen up to now of the occurrence of opening markers in Paul's letters, we would have expected a fresh start of such a kind to contain, for example, an address, the conjunction δέ and a metapropositional or metacommunicative statement. The only indication that there is something of a new beginning here is the change of grammatical subject, accentuated by the use of ἡμεῖς, and possibly asyndeton. This would hardly be sufficient for a fresh beginning of the order that has been suggested, however.[39] As for the asyndeton, moreover, it may be noted that rhetorical questions are often followed by asyndetic constructions.[40]

2. The statement in 2:15 (f.) either does not contain an explicit finite verb, or withholds it until a late stage in the clause.[41] It would be strange to begin a new section in this way. An expression following up a rhetorical question, on

mentioning the outcome of the conflict for the simple reason that his interest here is in his speech in his own defence, not in the conflict at Antioch as such. This can be compared with the account in 2:1–10, where Paul was interested, not in the underlying conflict, but in the confirmation of himself and his gospel by those of repute. It should be noted that there, too, Paul says nothing about how this confirmation affected the conflict.

[37] The primary metapropositional base is presumably γνωρίζω ὑμῖν ὅτι... or the like.

[38] See p. 147.

[39] In my opinion the significance of this change of grammatical subject has been greatly exaggerated, e.g. by M. Bachmann (1992, pp. 28 f.)

[40] See e.g. 3:6, 19, 21.

[41] The linguistic construction in 2:15 f. is somewhat unclear, partly owing to a text-critical problem, namely whether or not εἰδότες in 2:16 is followed by δέ. The syntactic structure can be understood in two ways: (1) ἡμεῖς... ἁμαρτωλοί in 2:15 is an independent nominal clause, followed by a new main clause in 2:16; (2) 2:15 f. is a single clause, in which ἡμεῖς is the subject — καὶ ἡμεῖς is then a repetition of the subject — ἐπιστεύσαμεν the verb and Ἰουδαῖοι, ἁμαρτωλοί and εἰδότες predicative attributes (Ἰουδαῖοι and ἁμαρτωλοί possibly appositives). The difference in meaning between the two alternatives is not very great. In either case, attention is being drawn to the two basic preconditions for Peter and Paul: that they are Jews and that they have come to believe εἰς Χριστὸν Ἰησοῦν. If the first alternative is chosen, the first of these preconditions is given greater prominence and more clearly distinguished from the other. If, in addition, we choose the reading with δέ, a contrast between the two preconditions is suggested. For semantic reasons I am inclined to prefer this option, but the other alternative is also compatible with my understanding of the line of thought.

the other hand, could very well look like this. Such expressions are often abrupt, sometimes elliptical, or have an anomalous word order due to the influence of the preceding question.[42]

3. The ἡμεῖς which we encounter in 2:15–17 is probably best understood as a pronoun referring to Paul and Peter (and possibly also to the Jews who joined Peter in his hypocrisy), partly because these individuals have just been mentioned and no other referents are suggested in any way, and partly because what is said about this ἡμεῖς in 2:15–17 tallies so well with the preceding description of Peter's earlier conduct in Antioch — which was presumably the same as that of Paul — namely that he, though a Ἰουδαῖος, lived ἐθνικῶς καὶ οὐχὶ Ἰουδαϊκῶς (2:14) by eating with the Gentiles (2:12). The basis for the discussion in 2:15–21 is precisely the fact that ἡμεῖς, who are φύσει Ἰουδαῖοι καὶ οὐκ ἐξ ἐθνῶν ἁμαρτωλοί (2:15), εὑρέθημεν καὶ αὐτοὶ ἁμαρτωλοί (2:17), where ἁμαρτωλός may be assumed to stand for living ἐθνικῶς.[43] But if ἡμεῖς has this reference, it would have to have been made clear, had there been a change of addressee in 2:15 from Peter to the Galatians.

4. There is little to signal a close in 2:14, either. It could possibly be argued that the question is constructed as a conditional complex sentence, i.e. is based on a deduction,[44] but this is not very much, especially in view of the lack of clear opening markers in 2:15.[45] What is more, it may be observed that questions are normally used as opening rather than closing markers.[46]

5. In addition, it may be noted that the question in 2:14 would not only be a sudden, but also a remarkably lame and insubstantial ending to the narrative that begins in 2:11. The quotation evidently plays a key role in this account. The ground is prepared for it by a relatively detailed background description in 2:12 f. and an extended quotation formula in 2:14. This raises expectations in the listener — as, incidentally, does the very fact that a quotation is inserted into this otherwise very brief and succinct historical narrative, which up to now has not contained a single quotation, despite dealing with such crucial events as Paul's calling, his first meeting with Peter and the Council of Jerusalem. What is more, the quotation serves as the grand finale of the whole of the historical narrative. The brief and somewhat insubstantial question in

[42] E.g. Rom 3:1; 10:15; Gal 3:4, 6, 19.

[43] See note 51 below.

[44] Closing conditional complex sentences occur in 1:10 and 2:21, but it is also evident that sentences of this type are in addition used to make a new start in a text. Cf. e.g. Gal 2:17, Phil 2:1–4.

[45] A text may be cut short without warning, to achieve special rhetorical effect, but if it is, the fresh start after it has to be marked all the more clearly.

[46] See e.g. 2:17; 3:1–5, 19, 21. Note also how 'closing' questions, such as in 1:10 and Phil 1:18, are followed by statements. As for 1 Cor 4:21, I believe that — as Euthalius suggests — this question does not conclude the preceding section, but begins the following one.

2:14 falls well short of the expectations which all these factors have created. That is not the case, though, with the detailed and substantial address which results if 2:15–21 is included in the quotation.

6. The purpose of the whole of the historical narrative is to show (see γάρ in 1:13) that Paul's gospel is not according to man, but springs from a revelation of Jesus Christ (see 1:11 f.). The previous subsection (2:1–10) was clearly related to this overarching aim. In 2:5 it was made clear that the episode recounted there was concerned with Paul as the defender of the truth of the gospel, and then in 2:7 ff. it was explained how those who were of repute in Jerusalem saw that Paul had been entrusted with the gospel and how they recognized the grace given to him. The temporal clause in 2:14, which sums up the background account in 2:12 f. and establishes what Paul's address is an answer to, is once again related to the overall aim by its reference to the truth of the gospel. As a result, we expect Paul's answer to shed light on his gospel in some way. It does not do so, however, if we end the quotation in 2:14. If on the other hand it is seen as continuing up to 2:21, it will be found to touch on crucial aspects of his gospel and, moreover, to conclude in 2:21 with a direct reference to the grace of God (cf. 2:9).

7. In support of the view that there is a major discontinuity in the text at 2:14/15, it is commonly argued that the phrasing of 2:15–21 sometimes seems better suited to the situation in Galatia than to that in Antioch, and that its use of language more closely parallels what follows than what has gone before.[47] However, it is not really very surprising that the phrasing of 2:15–21 sometimes seems more appropriate to the situation in Galatia than to that in Antioch. 2:14b–21 is obviously not a verbatim report of what was actually said in Antioch, but rather a freer rendering of the main points of Paul's argument against those in Antioch who represented a Judaizing tendency. It goes almost without saying that, if the purpose of such a free rendering is to

---

[47] See e.g. Fung 1988, p. 112, Krentz 1985, pp. 104 f., note 21, and Bachmann 1992, p. 29. A common view among exegetes today is that 2:15–21 is, in *form*, a continuation of Paul's address to Peter, but, in *content*, an introduction to the theological exposition which follows. If those holding that view mean, as Fung at least appears to do, that the text has two distinct structures, a formal structure and a content structure, which need not be parallel but can look quite different, then it is a position which I must reject. As I see it, formal and content structure are intimately and indissolubly connected. On the other hand, I would agree without hesitation that the theological exposition which follows is — quite naturally — linked to the summary of Paul's main arguments against a Judaizing position which is provided by his account in 2:14b–21 of what he said to Peter. I can also agree that this account is coloured by the situation in Galatia. However, that does *not* mean that, *in the text*, 2:15–21 is anything other than a rendering of the address to Peter in Antioch. In other words, these observations provide no basis for asserting that in 2:15 Paul is suddenly abandoning his historical narrative and turning directly to the Galatians. It is necessary here to distinguish between the historical question of how accurately the address is reproduced and the question of the structure of the letter.

influence developments in Galatia, it will be coloured by the situation there.[48] This, incidentally, is true not only of the address in 2:14b–21, but of the whole of the historical account in 1:13–2:21. For the same reason, there is nothing strange about the language of 2:14b–21 exhibiting appreciable similarities to that of the following section. That the language of 2:15–21 does not more clearly echo the background account in 2:12 f. is not at all surprising in my view, since the latter is a text of an entirely different character, a narrative operating on an altogether different plane to the text of the address, which puts forward arguments and discusses principles. However, as we have already observed, there are also obvious links in terms of language — and content — between 2:15–21 and 2:14.[49]

8. Finally, there is the difference between the argumentation in 2:15–21 and that after 3:1. The former proceeds from 'our' common situation and 'our' common knowledge of the importance of faith in Christ, the latter from the Galatians' own experience and from scriptural quotations, in particular from the story of Abraham. The first of these starting-points is undoubtedly more suitable for an argument aimed at Peter, who is Paul's equal and who is knowledgeable but has acted hypocritically, than for one addressed to the misled and foolish Galatians. The second of them, however, is very apt in relation to the Galatians, who want to be circumcised and to be under the law. It should also be observed that the discussion in 2:15–21 is concerned with how it will be perceived if 'we', who are Jews and not Gentile sinners (2:15), are ourselves, in Christ, found to be sinners (2:17). This problem is relevant to Antioch rather than Galatia. The discussion after 3:1 however — which *inter alia* revolves around the fact that the promises were given to Abraham, who was 'free from the law', and applied to him and to the Gentiles, who are equally 'free from the law' — fits in very well indeed with the situation in Galatia.

For these reasons, then, I believe that 2:15–21 should be read as a continuation of the quotation of Paul's address to Peter in Antioch and that this address thus extends from 2:14c to 2:21 inclusive.

Regarding the structure of the actual address, we find that it can be divided into two main parts. The first begins with the rhetorical question in 2:14, which sets out the theme and purpose of the address. The question is why Peter is compelling the Gentiles to live like Jews, although he himself, a Jew, lives like a Gentile. It is thus indicated that the address is concerned with faith and the Jewish way of life and that its aim is to censure Peter for his conduct in Antioch. However, this topic also clearly echoes the account in 1:13–24, in

---

[48] See also Kieffer 1982, p. 15.
[49] See pp. 159 ff. above.

which Paul described how he once lived ἐν τῷ Ἰουδαϊσμῷ, but was then called through the grace of God and received a revelation of the Son of God and the commission to proclaim him as the gospel among the Gentiles. In the overall framework of the narrative section, therefore, this address serves as a comment on what has been recounted.

The opening question is then followed up in 2:15 f. with a description of what Peter and Paul have in common: they are Jews with a conviction that a person is justified by the faith of Christ and not by the works of the law.[50] The minor new beginning in 2:15 is marked by the change of grammatical subject, given emphasis by the use of ἡμεῖς.

The second part of the address begins in 2:17, and this is marked by another rhetorical question, introduced by a conditional clause, and by the conjunction δέ. This sentence is closely linked to what has gone before, however, as is indicated by the participial construction ζητοῦντες δικαιωθῆναι ἐν Χριστῷ, and presumably states what could be the problem for Peter and the other Jews in Antioch: if they ate with and thus behaved like Gentile sinners, was Christ then a servant of sin?[51] The rest of the address is then devoted to this problem. Here Paul changes from the first person plural to the first person singular. In the framework of the account given in 2:11–21, this shift can be understood as drawing attention to the point at which he and Peter were no longer in agreement.[52] In relation to the wider context, it means that there is now more of a focus on Paul's gospel, in line with the purpose of the historical narrative as a whole, as stated in 1:11 f. and re-echoed in 2:14. From both these points of view, the switch to the singular suggests to the listener that the narrative in 2:11–21 has reached a decisive stage.

The negative answer to the opening question in 2:17 is explained (γάρ) with reference to Paul having been crucified with Christ and having died to the law, so that he might live to God. It is now Christ who lives in him, and the life he now lives in the flesh he lives by the faith of the Son of God,[53] who loved him and gave himself for him. This exposition answers the opening question, but also sheds light on the account in 1:13–24 of Paul's journey from successful Jew and persecutor of the church (1:13 f.) to a persecuted proclaimer of the Son of God (1:16) and of the faith he himself had once tried

---

[50] Or 'by faith in Christ'. Concerning the question whether this genitive should be taken as a subjective or an objective genitive, see e.g. Hultgren 1980, Johnson 1982, Williams 1987 and Hooker 1989. See also Hays 1981.

[51] The word ἁμαρτωλοί is presumably used in the same way here as in 2:15, i.e. to designate the status of the Gentiles, who are 'free from the law'. Cf. Winninge 1995, p. 249 (especially note 50).

[52] As R. Kieffer (1982, p. 62) quite rightly points out, the text here is concerned not only with the conflict with Peter, but with more basic principles, and the 'I' in 2:18 and that in 2:19 thus represent two opposed theological positions.

[53] Or 'by faith in the Son of God'. See note 50 above.

to destroy (1:23). Another point to be noted is that this description of Paul's life in Christ clearly satisfies the criterion set out in 1:10: the fact that this life entails crucifixion with Christ must presumably mean that it does not please people, and it is also explicitly stated that it is a life for God (2:19).

This exposition is broken off and followed by a clause joined by asyndeton — οὐκ ἀθετῶ τὴν χάριν τοῦ θεοῦ — which signals a close, since it is at a different level in content terms to the preceding statements, involving an assessment of what has been claimed in them. It also corresponds closely to the two rhetorical questions in 2:14 and 2:17, which introduced the two parts of the address: eating with the Gentiles does not mean that Christ is a servant of sin (cf. 2:17); on the contrary, drawing back from doing so entails a nullification of the grace of God and, unlike Peter and the other Jews, Paul is not guilty of this (cf. 2:14). At the same time, by referring to God's grace, this clause is clearly linked to 1:15 f., the key passage of the narrative section 1:13–24 (cf. the corresponding link to 2:9 in the preceding section). The link with 1:15 f. is reinforced by the statement in the previous verse (2:20) about Paul living by the faith of the Son of God: in 1:15 f., Paul described how God decided to *call* him through *his grace* and to reveal *his Son* in him; in 2:20 f., he declares that he now lives by the faith of *the Son of God*[54] and does not nullify *the grace of God*. All these things signal that the section is drawing to a close. So too does the explanation which is then added, and which clearly has the character of a summary and conclusion (εἰ... ἄρα...), albeit in a negative form (cf. 1:10).

The closing markers in 2:20 f. primarily signal the end of the address in 2:14c–21 and of the narrative of 2:11–21. In addition, the recurrences of concepts from 1:15 f. suggest that this could also be the conclusion of the whole of the narrative section beginning in 1:13 and perhaps even of the whole of the section from 1:11 on. This possibility is also suggested by the long quotation in 2:14c–21 itself, since it is such a unique and emphatic element in this historical account. That what is being brought to a close here is indeed the whole of the historical narrative and the section beginning in 1:11 is confirmed in 3:1–5, where Paul returns to his unfavourable assessment of developments in Galatia, which formed the basis for the section beginning at 1:11. The return to this starting-point indicates that the argument embarked upon in 1:11 has now been concluded.

This completes the analysis of the first major section of Galatians (1:11–2:21). In summary, it may be said that its overarching aim appears to be to show that Paul's gospel is not according to man, but a revelation of Jesus Christ (1:11 f.), in order to support Paul as he takes issue with his opponents in Galatia (cf.

---

[54] Or 'by faith in *the Son of God*'. See note 50 above.

1:8 f.) and seeks to win over the Galatians to himself and his gospel (1:6 f.). This is achieved by means of a biographical account (1:13–2:21) consisting of three steps: first, in 1:13–24, Paul describes the circumstances surrounding his calling, a description which he then comments on by relating, in 2:1–10, how those who were of repute in Jerusalem confirmed him and his gospel and by describing, in 2:11–21, how in Antioch he defended himself and his gospel.

3:1–4:11

3:1–5

The close in 2:20 f. is followed by a distinct fresh start in 3:1, marked by asyndeton, which indicates a discontinuity in the text; a form of address strongly emphasized by its initial position and the use of ὦ, which shows that Paul is now leaving his account of what he said to Peter and turning directly to the Galatians; and a rhetorical question introducing a new theme. This question asks who has bewitched the Galatians. The following relative clause then contrasts the present confusion of this community with Paul's earlier preaching among them. This echoes the opening section of the letter body in 1:6–10, in which the Galatians' present situation was also considered in contrast to 'our' earlier preaching. The fact that the text thus now looks back to and proceeds from the starting-point and primary theme of the letter as a whole shows that the argument set out in the preceding section (1:11–2:21) has been concluded and that a new major section is beginning. It should also be observed, though, that the reference in 3:1 to Paul's earlier preaching among the Galatians represents a link with the description of the character of his gospel given in the previous section (1:11–2:21) and in particular in 2:18–21, where Paul's life in Christ was described in terms of his having been crucified with him and having died to the law.

The question asked in 3:1, then, is who has bewitched the Galatians. The relative clause that follows it presumably looks back to 2:18–21, where life in Christ was described in terms of crucifixion and dying to the law. The question itself is left unanswered, its chief function presumably being to express an unfavourable assessment of developments in Galatia and thus to try to put a stop to them.[55] It therefore involves a recurrence of 1:6–10 in functional terms, too. It is followed by a construction which is clearly instructive and thematic, and whose metapropositional bases — μόνον θέλω μαθεῖν ἀφ' ὑμῶν — state that Paul now wants to learn something from the Galatians. His reason for doing so is not ignorance, as is evident from the fact that the proposition consists of a clearly rhetorical question; rather, he wishes

---

[55] See also Hartman 1993, p. 132.

to remind the Galatians of and to get them to acknowledge a certain state of affairs. The proposition is anticipated by a cataphoric text-summarizing τοῦτο in initial position, which together with the following μόνον gives prominence to the proposition and can be ascribed an opening-marking function in its own right. The proposition itself, as has been noted, consists of a rhetorical question, which echoes 2:16 and asks whether the Galatians received the Spirit by the works of the law or by hearing with faith. The obvious answer is the latter alternative, as the questions which follow in 3:3 f. make clear. What the instructive and thematic construction in 3:2 appears to do then, after attention has been drawn in 3:1 to the purpose of the letter, is to introduce a new argument in support of Paul's cause, by reminding the Galatians that they did not receive the Spirit by the works of the law, but by hearing with faith. However, this new argument, with its appeal to the Galatians' own experience, is clearly linked to what has gone before, since it is evident from the question in 3:1 that what was heard with faith was Paul's gospel, as presented in 1:11–2:21.

As has been mentioned, the instructive and thematic construction is followed up with a number of questions in 3:3 f. They are linked to the initial question in 3:1, as their opening words, οὕτως ἀνόητοί ἐστε, make clear. Like the opening question, they serve to express an unfavourable appraisal of the current situation in Galatia.

There then follows a question introduced by οὖν, which clearly echoes the theme-indicating question in 3:2 and thus suggests that the section that began in 3:1 is now being brought to a close. This brief section consists almost exclusively of short asyndetically juxtaposed questions and is very intense. Consequently, it does not appear to be something complete in itself, but rather the beginning of a longer section.

3:6–4:7

3:6–14

The theme-indicating questions in 3:2 and 3:5 appeal to the Galatians' experience and thus require no answer from Paul. They are therefore followed, not by a direct reply, but by a comparison with what Scripture says about Abraham's faith and the law. This comparison indicates indirectly what the writer assumes will be the Galatians' answer to his questions and shows that answer to be in agreement with what was foreseen by Scripture, obviously lending added weight to the new argument introduced in 3:2–5.

The new subsection begins with a comparative clause, which is presumably linked to the assumed but unexpressed answer from the Galatians.[56] Its elliptical construction establishes a close connection with what has gone before and tones down the new beginning. That a new start is nevertheless being made here is indicated by the significant change of scene, marked by the reference to ᾿Αβραάμ in initial position.

The comparison begins in 3:6 with a parallel between the Galatians' experience of having received the Spirit by hearing with faith and a scriptural quotation concerning Abraham's faith and righteousness (Gen 15:6). The conclusion from this comparison which is of interest here — that those who are of faith are the sons of Abraham — is then drawn in 3:7, as is indicated by the particle ἄρα. The importance of this conclusion is underlined by the metapropositional γινώσκετε, which appears to echo the tone of rebuke in 3:1–5 and indicates that this is something the Galatians already know or ought to know. Verse 7 thus completes the first part of this section, and can also be said to state its theme.

The opening of the second part of the section is marked by the conjunction δέ and the secondary metapropositional and metacommunicative clause προϊδοῦσα... ἡ γραφή... προευηγγελίσατο τῷ ᾿Αβραάμ, which is an explicit announcement that this section will be centred on scriptural quotations. The key conclusion to be drawn from the new quotation (Gen 12:3; 18:8) — that those who are of faith are blessed with Abraham who had faith — is expressed in 3:9. This conclusion is introduced by ὥστε and clearly refers back to the one in 3:7, suggesting that this part of the section is coming to an end.

The beginning of the next part of the section is marked by the stressed change of grammatical subject, indicating that attention is turning to ὅσοι... ἐξ ἔργων νόμου εἰσίν. This new subsection is subordinate in content terms to the preceding one, as the opening γάρ indicates. The two preceding parts of the section dwelt on the positive alternative contained in the rhetorical questions in 3:2 and 3:5 (ἐξ ἀκοῆς πίστεως) and led up to a conclusion in 3:9 supporting that alternative. This is further underpinned now by a number of quotations which together show that all who are of the works of the law are under a curse, and which are thus arguments against the negative alternative in the rhetorical questions (ἐξ ἔργων νόμου).

The previous two subsections began with a quotation, from which a conclusion was drawn. The present one has the opposite construction: it begins with a statement, which is then supported (γάρ) by a combination of quotations. The beginning of this group of quotations is marked by the

---

[56] For a similar construction, see e.g. Rom 10:15.

secondary metapropositional and metacommunicative verb γέγραπται. The closing of this part is not indicated in any other way than by the fact that the opening assertion has been supported.

In 3:13 the chain of quotations linked by δέ is broken by asyndeton. What is more, the new sentence begins with an emphatic introduction of new persons with the words Χριστὸς ἡμᾶς.[57] This marks the opening of the fourth part of the present section, which is constructed in the same way as the preceding one: first a statement is made, then it is supported (ὅτι) with scriptural quotations, introduced by a secondary metapropositional and metacommunicative γέγραπται. In content terms, this subsection presumably serves the purpose of further underpinning the assertion in 3:10 that all who are of the works of the law are under a curse, and thus of further weakening the position of the negative alternatives in the rhetorical questions.[58]

---

[57] In 3:1–5 Paul spoke about 'I' and 'you' and in 3:6–12 about 'those who are of faith' and 'those who are of the works of the law'. When in 3:13 he suddenly starts to talk about 'us', it is not clear to whom he is referring: is it 'you and I', 'we Jewish Christians' or 'we Jews'? Most commentators believe the scope of 'we' here to be wide, including both Jews and Gentiles (e.g. Schlier 1971, pp. 136 f.; Rodhe 1989, p. 145), but some (e.g. Betz 1979, p. 145) take the view that the word refers only to the Jewish Christians. An examination of the use of pronouns in 3:1–4:11 as a whole reveals the following:

a) 'We' occurs in 3:13 f., 23 ff.; 4:3 ff., 6 and is used in statements describing the historical process of salvation: being under the law, being freed from it and receiving the Spirit.

b) In the opening and closing parts of the section (3:1–5 and 4:8–11), 'you' (plural) is used unequivocally to refer to the Galatians. In the comparative digression, 'you' occurs in 3:26–29 and 4:6 (and in the singular in 4:7) in statements mainly describing the status of Christians.

c) In 3:25 f. and 4:5 ff. Paul switches from 'we' to 'you' in the middle of his argument.

d) Towards the ends of his discussions, Paul tends to shift from a presentation in the third person plural to one using 'we' or 'you' (plural or singular).

The conclusions I draw from these observations are as follows:

a) 'You' refers to the Galatians, and Paul uses this pronoun in his statements about the status of Christians because his specific concern here is the situation of the Galatians. This is also why the various parts of his argument move towards and conclude with 'you' statements.

b) The reason why Paul does not use 'you' in his statements concerning the history of salvation is presumably that the Galatians were predominantly Gentile Christians and had therefore never in fact been under the law. Consequently it is scarcely possible for him to use 'you' in these statements, and he chooses to switch to an undefined 'we'.

c) This 'we' probably refers primarily to Paul and other Jewish Christians, but the way he then shifts to 'you' in his argument shows that these statements in the first person plural apply potentially to 'you' as well.

d) Paul's tendency to shift from the more general third person plural to the more personal 'we' and 'you' towards the ends of his discussions is natural, given that what is at issue is 'your' situation.

[58] The reasoning here would appear to be of the same type as in 2:21, i.e. it infers the problem from an awareness of its solution. According to E. P. Sanders (1977), this fits in with Paul's theological thinking in general (see e.g. pp. 442–7; on p. 443, for instance, he

The closing of the section is marked by the two purpose- or consequence-indicating ἵνα-clauses in 3:14, which involve evident recurrences. The first ἵνα-clause clearly echoes the 'positive' argument that opened the section (3:6–9), as is illustrated by the lexical links τὰ ἔθνη (3:8), ἡ εὐλογία (3:8 f.) and ὁ Ἀβραάμ (3:6–9); the second corresponds to the rhetorical questions in 3:2 and 3:5, as is indicated by the parallels τὸ πνεῦμα, λαμβάνειν and ἡ πίστις. These recurrences of concepts from the beginning of the section and the section from which it proceeded (3:1–5) suggest that not only the fourth part of the section, but the section as a whole is being brought to a close in 3:14.

With that, then, we reach the end of the section which began in 3:6 as a direct follow-up to the rhetorical questions in 3:2 and 3:5, and which had the character of a comparison. The characteristic feature of this section was its many scriptural quotations. Their role in the context is underlined by the fact that three of the four parts of the section contain metacommunicative expressions stating that what is being said originates in Scripture (3:8, 10, 13).

3:15–4:7

The somewhat more significant close in 3:14 is confirmed by a fairly significant fresh start in 3:15,[59] marked by asyndeton, the address ἀδελφοί in initial position, and a construction containing new thematic statements and instructions to the recipients. The new construction begins with the metapropositional and metacommunicative clause κατὰ ἄνθρωπον λέγω, which indicates that Paul now intends to say something in terms of human affairs. There is thus something of a shift here at the metapropositional level of

cites Gal 2:21 and 3:11 f. as evidence). To this, T. Engberg-Pedersen (1993, p. 198) objects that if 'the solution comes before the plight', it must presumably mean that 'seen in that way, there was no real *plight*' (my translation). If this really is what Sanders means, I would agree with the criticism. On the other hand, if Sanders is in fact suggesting that Paul's *awareness* of the solution preceded his *awareness* of the exact nature of the problem, I believe there is something in what he says. This at least appears to be the line of reasoning in both Gal 2:21 and 3:13.

[59] Hartman (1993) assigns the transition at 3:14/15 to the same level as the one at 3:7/8 (pp. 155 f.). I am doubtful about such an arrangement of the text, for the following reasons: (1) The address ἀδελφοί and the primary metapropositional base λέγω mean that the new beginning in 3:15 is more strongly marked than the one in 3:8. (2) From 3:15 on the character of the text changes, in that it no longer makes frequent references to Scripture. (3) The exposition beginning in 3:15 exhibits a striking parallelism with that of 3:6–14 (Abraham/the promise — the law — Christ — the Spirit). (4) The metapropositional λέγω frequently appears to have the sense 'I mean' and to introduce a clarification. Although in this case it is accompanied by an adverbial of manner (κατὰ ἄνθρωπον), in view of (2) and (3) above it is reasonable to perceive something of this sense here, too. Cf. τοῦτο δὲ λέγω in 3:17, which presumably provides a link with 3:15.

the text, since the previous section was characterized by metacommunicative expressions stating that what was being said originated in Scripture. At the same time, the construction, involving asyndeton, an address in initial position and the metacommunicative clause κατὰ ἄνθρωπον λέγω, gives the impression that, rather than something completely new, it is introducing an explanation of or comment on the preceding text. This impression is underscored by the fact that the ensuing proposition, concerning the inviolability of human wills or covenants once they have been ratified, is followed in 3:16 by the observation that the promises were made to Abraham; it thus turns out to refer back to 3:6–9. This new section thus proves to be a continuation of the comparative section beginning in 3:6.

The new section, then, begins with two assertions, one concerning the validity of human wills, the other concerning the giving of the promise to Abraham. Following a parenthetic comment in 3:16 stating that the offspring is Christ, a new start is made in 3:17, marked by the cataphoric text-summarizing τοῦτο, which gives prominence to the proposition that follows, the conjunction δέ, and the metapropositional and metacommunicative λέγω, which echoes the λέγω in 3:15. It is thus indicated that Paul now intends to explain the purpose of the two statements in 3:15 f. The proposition refers to the fact that the promise, i.e. a covenant ratified by God himself, cannot be annulled by the law, which came four hundred and thirty years later. That this proposition is a conclusion is indicated by the obvious lexical links with the two premisses in 3:15 f., namely διαθήκην προκεκυρωμένην (cf. 3:15) and τὴν ἐπαγγελίαν (cf. 3:16). This prepares the listener for a close, although it is not completed until after an explanatory comment (γάρ) in 3:18.

A fresh start is made in 3:19, marked by the conjunction οὖν and a theme-indicating question about the status of the law. This question is occasioned by (hence οὖν) the preceding discussion about the validity of the promise irrespective of the law, and looks back to the exposition in 3:10–12. There is therefore reason to regard the new section as a direct continuation of the explanatory or commentary section which began in 3:15. The thematic question in 3:19 gives rise to an exposition comprising three steps. In 3:19 f. the text offers an initial answer to the question by explaining why the law was added: τῶν παραβάσεων χάριν. The transition to the next step in the discussion is marked by the conjunction οὖν and a new theme-indicating question in 3:21, about whether the law is opposed to the promises, which is answered in the negative. The completion of this step in the exposition is hinted at by the ἵνα-clause in 3:22, which echoes the closing ἵνα-clauses in 3:14. As yet, however, Paul has not described the function of the law in positive terms. A new beginning in this discussion about the status of the law is therefore made in 3:23, marked by δέ and the indication of time πρὸ τοῦ...

ἐλθεῖν τὴν πίστιν, which highlights a new temporal context compared with the closing clause of the previous section. The purpose of the law is said to have been to guard 'us' and to be 'our' παιδαγωγός until faith and Christ came (3:23 f.).[60] The approach of a close is marked by ὥστε in 3:24 and a ἵνα-clause in the same verse, echoing the ἵνα-clauses of 3:14 and 3:22. Verse 24 corresponds to the question in 3:19 and can be regarded as the final answer to it. It is thus suggested that the subsection beginning in 3:19 is now coming to an end.

The beginning of the next subsection is marked by the time reference ἐλθούσης... τῆς πίστεως and the conjunction δέ. This opening corresponds to πρὸ τοῦ δὲ ἐλθεῖν τὴν πίστιν in 3:23, underlining the close connection with what has gone before. There are nevertheless grounds for regarding 3:25 as the beginning of a new subsection. In 3:24 there was a conclusion which clearly referred back to the thematic question in 3:19. In 3:25 we find a shift in content terms from the law and its function to the situation now that faith has come, which means that the law is no longer needed as a παιδαγωγός. This shift in content is subsequently reflected in, among other things, a change from 'we' to 'you' from 3:26 on, i.e. once the law is no longer in focus.[61] The shift to the situation following the coming of faith means that the commentary section which began in 3:15 now looks back to the discussion in 3:13–14. The approach of a close is marked by the conditional complex sentence and ἄρα in 3:29, which together indicate that a conclusion is being drawn and which refer back to the opening of the present section in 3:26. The wording of this verse also echoes 3:16 (τοῦ Ἀβραὰμ σπέρμα) and 3:18 (κατ᾽ ἐπαγγελίαν κληρονόμοι), i.e. the opening passage of the commentary section, thereby suggesting that the close of the whole of that section is approaching.

The commentary section beginning at 3:15 does not end yet, however. Instead, a new start is made in 4:1, marked by the conjunction δέ and the metapropositional and metacommunicative λέγω, which looks back to the corresponding metapropositional statements in 3:15 and 3:17 and indicates that Paul wishes to make a further explanatory or clarificatory comment. What follows is a section in which Paul uses a slightly modified imagery to sum up and clarify what he has said in the explanatory section. Once again he proceeds from the position regarding human wills (cf. 3:15), which he sets out in 4:1 f. By means of asyndeton and a summarizing οὕτως, he then moves on in 4:3 to apply it to 'us' and 'our' relationship to the elemental spirits of the world and to the law. He does so in three steps. First (in 4:3) he refers to 'our' former enslavement under the law, then (4:4 f.) to God sending his Son to redeem those who were under the law and adopt 'us' as sons, and finally (4:6)

---

[60] Concerning the use of this undefined 'we', see note 57 above.
[61] See note 57 above.

to God sending the Spirit of his Son into 'our' hearts. The transition to the second step is marked by the conjunction δέ and a time indication in the form of a temporal clause in 4:4, the transition to the third by the conjunction δέ. Towards the end of this exposition there is a clear link with the phrasing of the close of the section commented on (3:6–14), suggesting that the commentary section and presumably the whole of the digression from 3:6 on is coming to an end.[62] Particularly important is the reference to the Spirit in 4:6, which echoes not only the end of the section commented on (3:14), but also the rhetorical questions in 3:2 and 3:5 which formed its starting-point. The impression of a close is reinforced by the statement of consequences introduced by ὥστε in 4:7, which, with its use of δοῦλος and κληρονόμος, clearly looks back to the opening of this subsection in 4:1. This, then, brings to a close the whole of the comparative section beginning in 3:6, the purpose of which was to show that the obvious answer to the rhetorical questions in 3:2 and 3:5 was in agreement with what was foreseen by Scripture, and hence to give extra weight to the argument in 3:2–5.

4:8–11

The assumption that, in 4:7, Paul is drawing to a close the whole of the comparative section which began in 3:6 is confirmed by the section that follows it: here, he returns to the present unsatisfactory state of affairs in Galatia, which he last touched on in 3:1–5 and which formed the basis for the comparative section from 3:6 on. He does so with a critical question in 4:8 f., expressing an unfavourable assessment; this question is similar in content and function to the one in 3:1, which in turn referred back to the beginning of the letter body. It should be noted that, like the question in 3:1, the one in 4:8 f. is asked in the light of the Galatians' calling (τότε μὲν οὐκ εἰδότες θεόν..., νῦν δὲ γνόντες θεόν, μᾶλλον δὲ γνωσθέντες ὑπὸ θεοῦ; cf. 3:2–5). It may also be noted here that, with his use of the word εἰκῇ in 4:11, Paul is again taking up the 'in vain' motif from 3:4.

The beginning of a new section in 4:8 is marked by the opening, loosely connective ἀλλά[63] and the question that follows. Both, however, also express a link with the preceding text. The conjunction ἀλλά itself serves a connective function, even if the connection is sometimes relatively loose. As for the question, it is based on the contrast between past enslavement and present

---

[62] Compare ἵνα τοὺς ὑπὸ νόμον ἐξαγοράσῃ, ἵνα τὴν υἱοθεσίαν ἀπολάβωμεν... δέ... ἐξαπέστειλεν ὁ θεὸς τὸ πνεῦμα τοῦ υἱοῦ αὐτοῦ εἰς τὰς καρδίας ἡμῶν in 4:5 f. with ἡμᾶς ἐξηγόρασεν ἐκ τῆς κατάρας τοῦ νόμου... ἵνα τὴν ἐπαγγελίαν τοῦ πνεύματος λάβωμεν... in 3:13 f.

[63] Cf. Phil 1:18.

sonship that was expressed in the conclusion in 4:7 (see also 4:3–6), and it goes on to reiterate the reference in 4:3 to enslavement under the elemental spirits, among which Paul clearly includes, in addition to the law, the divine authorities which the Gentile Christians of Galatia had formerly revered. The new beginning in 4:8 should not therefore be regarded as the opening of a new major section, but as the beginning of a subsection which rounds off the major section preceding it (from 3:1 on).

With its clear echoes of 3:1–5, then, the section 4:8–11 serves a concluding function in itself.[64] The impression that this is a close is reinforced by the intensity-heightening asyndetic constructions in 4:10 f. and by the closing assessment in 4:11, which is a kind of conclusion or statement of consequences and which begins with the metacommunicative verb φοβοῦμαι, here expressing an unfavourable assessment. The concluding section beginning at 4:8 thus arrives at a natural end-point.

That completes the analysis of the second major section of Galatians (3:1–4:11). In summary, it can be said that in this section Paul pleads his own cause and that of his gospel by referring to the Galatians' own experience of having, at the time of their calling, received the Spirit as a result of hearing with faith and not — in line with his opponents' doctrine — as a result of the works of the law. This argument is first presented in 3:1–5 and taken up again in 4:8–11. Paul reinforces it in 3:6–4:7 by showing that the Galatians' experience in this regard is in agreement with what was foreseen by Scripture. This long section consists of two main subsections: one (3:6–14) quoting from Scripture for the purposes of comparison and the other (3:15–4:7) explaining and commenting on what was said in the first subsection.

4:12–5:10

4:12–20

The recurrences in 4:8–11 of material from the major new beginning in 3:1–5 and from the opening of the body of the letter in 1:6–10 gave the impression that these verses constituted a major close. This close reached a natural end-point in the concluding assessment in 4:11. The listener is therefore now prepared for a significant fresh start, which is in fact what follows in 4:12. It is marked by the address ἀδελφοί and by new thematic statements and other instructions to the recipients. The new section begins with an exhortation, the first in Galatians, followed by the metapropositional and metacommunicative clause δέομαι ὑμῶν, which reinforces and modifies the indication of the

---

[64] See also Hartman 1993, p. 134.

metapropositional base already provided by the imperative form. As a result, the shift at the metapropositional level which occurs at this point in the text is strongly marked, presumably because it is a crucial one. Like earlier passages relating directly to the Galatians' situation (1:6–10; 3:1–5), the preceding verses (4:8–11) expressed an unfavourable assessment. For the first time in the letter, Paul now switches to direct exhortation, and this proves to be an enduring change in the nature of the text. Although the appeal in 4:12 is not immediately followed by others, direct exhortations play such an important part in the ensuing text that it can be said to be fundamentally exhortatory. We thus get the impression that the letter is now entering a new phase, in which Paul draws practical conclusions from the arguments he has put forward in the preceding sections. It is this change in the character of the text which is marked by the stressed metapropositional statement in 4:12.

Turning next to the proposition, we find that the exhortation here is concerned with the Galatians becoming like Paul, since he has become like them. At the propositional level, too, there is thus a clear shift in relation to what has gone before. Paul's character is a subject that has not been dealt with specifically since 1:11–2:21 (cf. also 3:1).

The opening exhortation is followed by the assertion that the Galatians have previously done Paul no wrong. Their earlier attitude to him is thus held up as exemplary. What Paul is referring to here is the way they received him at the time of their calling, as is made clear by the following verses, 4:13 f. In this way the exhortation in 4:12 is also linked to the argument in 3:1–4:11, since that section, too, focused on the circumstances surrounding the Galatians' calling and their favourable conduct at that time (see e.g. 3:3 and 4:9).

In 4:13 a new start is made, marked by the conjunction δέ and a new instructive and thematic construction. The latter begins with the metapropositional base οἴδατε, which makes it clear that what follows is a reminder of something the Galatians already know. What they are being reminded of, the proposition, is then set out in a ὅτι-clause, which refers to the circumstances in which Paul previously announced the gospel to them and the way they welcomed him at that time. There is thus a clear link with the preceding assertion.

A striking feature of the proposition is its heavy emphasis on how weak and unattractive Paul was in the flesh when he previously preached among them (ὅτι δι' ἀσθένειαν τῆς σαρκὸς εὐηγγελισάμην... καὶ τὸν πειρασμὸν ὑμῶν ἐν τῇ σαρκί μου οὐκ ἐξουθενήσατε οὐδὲ ἐξεπτύσατε). This naturally brings out the Galatians' goodwill towards him. The question is, though, whether this is all there is to it. As we saw earlier, Paul wrote in the opening section of the letter body (1:6–10) that if he were still pleasing people he would not be a servant of Christ, and accordingly he went on to describe in 1:11–2:21 how he left his former, successful life ἐν τῷ 'Ιουδαϊσμῷ and began to proclaim the persecuted faith. It has to be asked whether the text here is not also following up the criterion set out at the beginning of the letter body in pointing out so emphatically that Paul was weak and unable to please people when he previously proclaimed the gospel to the Galatians, and that they received him as someone with precisely those characteristics. In the light of the exhortation in 4:12 and the assertion that follows it, the implication is presumably that the Galatians should continue to accept weakness and not seek to please people.[65]

Following the reminder in 4:13 f., a new start is made in 4:15, as Paul contrasts the present attitude of the Galatians with their earlier, exemplary attitude. The new beginning is marked by the theme-indicating question and οὖν, which indicates that the question is pursuing something already touched on and introducing a new element in the text. Following an explanatory comment (γάρ), the question is rephrased, the new version being introduced by ὥστε. These questions are related to the earlier ones which expressed an unfavourable assessment of the situation in Galatia (3:1–5; 4:8–10) and to the adverse assessment in the opening section of the letter body (1:6–10), and thus link the exhortation in 4:12 directly to the earlier parts of the letter.

The question in 4:15 f. is followed up in 4:17 ff. with statements about the present situation among the Galatians and what it ought to be like. Here the harmful zeal of Paul's opponents, with the aim of pleasing the Galatians, is contrasted with the desirable zeal shown when Paul visited them. The general reference in 4:18 to Paul's visit to the Galatians as something exemplary echoes the opening of the section in 4:12 ff. and thus suggests that a close is approaching. This impression is reinforced by the address which follows, τέκνα μου, which highlights the recurrence and paves the way for the imagery used in the following relative clause, and by that relative clause itself, which describes Paul's concern for the Galatians (οὓς πάλιν ὠδίνω) and its ultimate purpose (μέχρις οὗ μορφωθῇ Χριστὸς ἐν ὑμῖν). The use of ὠδίνω emphasizes the pain involved in Paul's concern, mirroring the emphasis on his weakness in 4:13 f. It may also be noted here that the purpose of his concern is expressed in terms of Christ being formed in the Galatians, which represents a link with 2:19 f., for example (cf. also 3:27 f. and 4:6). The close is completed in 4:20 by the expression of an unreal wish and a concluding assessment. This brings to an end the section that began in 4:12.

---

[65] Cf. Gal 6:12, in which Paul's opponents are accused of wanting to make a good showing in the flesh and trying to compel the Galatians to be circumcised, merely to avoid persecution for the cross of Christ. Cf. also 1 Cor 2:1–5, where Paul likewise stresses how he proclaimed the gospel in weakness and relates his preaching to the cross of Christ. There, too, weakness appears to serve something of a paraenetic function (see 4:10–13, 16). Cf. in addition 1 Thess 1:6; 2:1–8.

4:21–5:1

The close in 4:18 ff. is confirmed by a distinct new beginning in 4:21, marked by asyndeton, a construction that is clearly instructive and thematic, and the address οἱ ὑπὸ νόμου θέλοντες εἶναι, which not only attracts attention, but also serves to define and hence to instruct the recipients. The construction begins with the metapropositional bases expressed in λέγετέ μοι,[66] indicating that Paul wishes to be told something by the Galatians, namely the answer to the following question (the proposition). It turns out, though, that this question is rhetorical and in fact serves to justify and to introduce with a tone of rebuke the following exposition of Scripture — 'you' desire to be subject to the law, but clearly do not listen to what it says. The exposition that follows thus appears to consist of information from Paul. However, it emerges that this is not the whole truth, since the concluding exhortation in 5:1 shows the purpose of this information to be directly paraenetic. It thereby also becomes clear that this section does not depart from the fundamentally exhortatory character of the text from 4:12 on.[67] The new beginning in 4:21 does nevertheless entail an appreciable shift in the text, since the exhortation in the previous section (4:12–20) was issued against the backdrop of Paul's earlier visit to the Galatians, whereas the new section centres on the words of Scripture concerning Abraham and his two sons. If the preceding section looked back to the text of 3:1–5, 4:8–11 and to some extent 1:10 and 1:11–2:21, this one is linked to 3:6–4:7.

The opening question about whether the Galatians, who desire to be under the law, will not listen to what it says is followed by a statement of what it does say. The opening of this statement is marked by a new instructive and thematic construction, beginning with the secondary metapropositional and metacommunicative verb γέγραπται, which makes it clear that what follows is an account of what is written in the law. The proposition is that Abraham had two sons, one by a slave woman and the other by a free woman. The new section is thus primarily concerned with Abraham's two sons.[68] The statement of what the law actually says is rounded off by Paul's observation in the metacommunicative relative clause in 4:24 that this is an allegory.

There then follows an exposition of what the allegory means, introduced by γάρ. It begins with a general identification in 4:24b–27 of Abraham's two

---

[66] The imperative indicates both the primary metapropositional base 'I call upon you...' and the secondary base 'you must tell me...'.

[67] Examples of similar 'informative' sections in basically paraenetic passages are to be found in 1 Thess 4:13–18 and 5:1–11.

[68] In editions, translations and commentaries (e.g. NJB, Betz 1979, Fung 1988, Rodhe 1989), this section is usually given a heading along the lines of 'The allegory of Hagar and Sarah'. This choice of heading probably reflects a shift in interest from ethics to dogmatics.

women, the slave and the free woman, and their respective children. The women are said to be the Sinaitic covenant/the present Jerusalem and the Jerusalem above, and their children the inhabitants of the present Jerusalem and 'we', respectively. This general identification concludes in 4:27 with a supporting quotation (Isa 54:1), the opening of which is marked by the secondary metapropositional and metacommunicative γέγραπται.

A new start is then made in 4:28, marked by the change of grammatical subject, given emphasis by the use of ὑμεῖς[69] in initial position, the conjunction δέ and the address ἀδελφοί. It is thus suggested that Paul is now applying the testimony of Scripture directly to the Galatians' situation. He does so in three steps, separated by loosely connective ἀλλά. First (in 4:28), he observes that it is 'according to Isaac' that the Galatians are children of the promise.[70] So if they wish to be children of the promise, it is with him, the son of the free woman, that they should identify. Secondly (in 4:29), Paul points out that then, as now, he who was born according to the flesh persecuted the one who was born according to the Spirit. Once again, the criterion of 1:10 is brought into focus: as children of the promise, they do not please people, but must expect to be persecuted. Thirdly (in 4:30), Paul explains what Scripture commands in this situation, namely that the slave and her son be driven out, since her son will not share the inheritance with the son of the free woman. In other words, it is important that they do not yield to the slave woman's son, even it means being persecuted. The fact that there is a direct quotation here and that it is introduced by a question lends emphasis to this third step and suggests that the application of what Scripture says is now reaching its climax and presumably its conclusion. Once again there is a clear focus on Abraham's sons: it is from what is said about them that conclusions are drawn concerning the Galatians. It should also be noted that the third and final step consists of an exhortation, revealing that the application and hence the whole of the section beginning in 4:21 has an ethical perspective.

This assumption about the ethical emphasis of this section is confirmed by what follows. In 4:31 something of a new beginning is made, marked by the address ἀδελφοί and the change to the first person plural. The conjunction διό indicates that the section now beginning consists of the conclusions to be drawn from the application and thus probably brings to an end the section which began in 4:21. The first conclusion concerns 'us' and presumably refers

---

[69] ὑμεῖς... ἐστέ in 4:28 is an uncertain reading, the alternative being ἡμεῖς... ἐσμέν. Like NTG, however, I opt for the former. For the arguments for that reading, see Metzger 1975, p. 597.

[70] The word order gives prominence to κατὰ 'Ισαάκ rather than ἐπαγγελίας τέκνα. This clause is therefore probably not a general observation that the Galatians are children of the promise, but rather informs them that they only have or will have that status if they live 'according to Isaac'.

back to the quotation immediately preceding it. Since the son of the slave woman is to be driven out and not to share the inheritance with the son of the free woman, 'we' are sons of the free woman. This is followed asyndetically by an explanation which links this freedom to the work of Christ. The reference to 'us' then serves as the point of departure for the concluding exhortation to the Galatians in 5:1. Its concluding character is marked by the conjunction οὖν and the recurrences of prominent motifs found in the previous section. Among other things, it looks back to the opening exhortation in 4:12 by turning directly to the Galatians in their present situation and referring to their earlier, exemplary conduct (cf. 4:12 ff.). In addition, the detour via 'us' in the final exhortation in 4:31 f. corresponds to the exhortation in 4:12 to become like 'me'.[71] These recurrences reveal that both sections ultimately serve one and the same paraenetic purpose, namely to urge the Galatians to choose Paul and his gospel and consequently to reject his opponents and their 'gospel'.

5:2–10

The close in 4:31–5:1 is followed by a fresh start in 5:2, marked by asyndeton, the attention-attracting ἴδε and a construction that is clearly instructive and thematic. The latter begins with the metapropositional and metacommunicative clause ἐγὼ Παῦλος λέγω ὑμῖν, which gives considerable prominence to the author. The verb λέγω, on the other hand, is fairly neutral, merely stating that what follows is something which Paul is asserting; in addition, it may possibly indicate a clarification (cf. 3:15, 17; 4:1; 5:16). The combination of asyndeton, the attention-attracting ἴδε, the heavy emphasis on the subject ἐγὼ Παῦλος and the neutral verb does not give the impression that this is the beginning of a major new section, but seems rather to constitute the introduction to a closing proclamation.

The proposition is then set out in a ὅτι-clause, which says that if the Galatians let themselves be circumcised, Christ will be of no benefit to them at all. At the propositional level there is thus a shift in 5:2, in that Paul now — in contrast to the conclusions he draws in 4:31–5:1 — drops the imagery of the allegory altogether. At the same time, there are clear links between the new section and the preceding one. In 5:1 Paul urged the Galatians to stand firm and not to submit again to a yoke of slavery. Against the background of 4:27–30, the latter part of this exhortation was concerned with their not yielding to the children of the Sinaitic covenant. It is that possibility which

---

[71] Another reason for the switch to 'we' here could be the fact that the closing exhortation is related to Christ having brought freedom from the law. Cf. the use of the first person plural in 3:13 f., 23 ff.; 4:3 ff. See also note 57 above.

Paul now sums up in explicit terms in the conditional clause, and whose consequences he goes on to explain. This close link at the propositional level reinforces the impression that what is beginning in 5:2 is not something entirely new, but a concluding proclamation.

This impression is further underlined by the fact that in 5:3 Paul makes another (πάλιν), slightly modified proclamation. This time the meta-propositional and metacommunicative clause consists of the more emphatic verb μαρτύρομαι and the broader definition of the addressees, παντὶ ἀνθρώπῳ περιτεμνομένῳ. The proposition states that every such addressee is obliged to obey the entire law. This assertion is then explained and related to the proposition in 5:2 by a couple of brief comments added asyndetically and directed to 'you who are justified by the law'. The short asyndetic constructions and the address οἵτινες ἐν νόμῳ δικαιοῦσθε help to maintain the intensity of the section and reinforce the impression that the text has now reached a decisive stage. These comments are then pursued further in two explanatory γάρ-clauses about 'our' situation and life in Christ. These slightly longer, coordinated clauses somewhat reduce the intensity of the passage.

In 5:7–10 there is a return to the intense type of construction, made up of brief asyndetic clauses, suggesting that the text is now entering a new phase. The change in intensity is accompanied by a shift in the content. In 5:2–6 Paul described the consequences for the Galatians of failing to heed the exhortation in 5:1 and submitting to circumcision. In 5:7–10 he refers to the earlier, praiseworthy conduct of the Galatians, which is then contrasted with their present situation by the use of a question expressing an unfavourable assessment, followed by two brief asyndetic statements. This section thus clearly echoes 4:12–20, in terms of both content and construction. Lexical links such as καλῶς and ἀλήθεια (see 4:16 ff.) may also be noted. This indicates that what is now being brought to a close is the section that began in 4:12. The close is carried to completion by an extended construction expressing an assessment of what the future will hold for the Galatians and for Paul's opponents. Both the assessment itself, which is a conclusion with an eschatological perspective, and the long construction, which contrasts with the intense construction type made up of short asyndetic main clauses, can be regarded as closing markers. So, too, can the emphasis placed by the explicit use of ἐγώ in the metapropositional base on the subject making the assessment, since this can be regarded as echoing the opening of the final proclamation from 5:2 on (ἴδε ἐγὼ Παῦλος...).

The recurrences in 5:7–10, then, primarily look back to the opening passages of the sections that are being brought to a close here (5:2–10; 4:12–5:10). But it may be noted that there are also unusually clear links with words and motifs occurring in the opening section of the letter body (1:6–10), e.g. ἐκ τοῦ καλοῦντος ὑμᾶς (cf. 1:6), ὁ ταράσσων ὑμᾶς (cf. 1:7), and the statement about the judgment on 'the one who is confusing you' (cf. the anathema against such people in 1:8 f.). The fact that links with the opening of the letter are becoming stronger can be regarded as a sign that the end of the letter as a whole is approaching.

I thus consider the close of the section beginning in 4:12 to be completed in 5:10. However, I do so with considerable hesitation. It is possible that 5:11–13a should be included in the closing section that begins in 5:2. Such a breakdown of the text would be supported by the fact that the conditional complex sentence in 5:11, the following ἄρα-clause and the wish in 5:12 have the character of indications of consequences and could be regarded as closing markers. The forms of address used in 5:11 and 5:13, which in the discussion below will be viewed as opening markers, could also be interpreted as closing markers. In addition, the sudden focus on Paul in 5:11 could be regarded as looking back to the exhortation in 4:12, which began the major section now being brought to an end. The most important reasons for the arrangement I have nevertheless chosen are the fact that the conviction expressed in 5:10 about the future attitude of the Galatians and the ultimate destiny of Paul's opponents gives the clear impression of being a concluding assessment; that the shift in topic from 5:11 on is appreciable and comparatively strongly marked (see below); and that both the exhortations in 5:13b and the concluding section 6:11–13 are closely linked to 5:11–13a (see below). In my opinion, the arguments for the two alternatives are fairly evenly balanced. However, the choice between them is not crucial to my understanding of the overall line of thought in this part of Galatians.

I choose, then, to regard the third major section in Galatians (from 4:12 on) as ending in 5:10. To sum up, in this section Paul makes clear the practical conclusions to be drawn from the arguments he has put forward in the preceding sections (1:11–2:21; 3:1–4:11), by expressly urging the Galatians to decide in favour of himself and his gospel (4:12; 5:1). This exhortation is supported and elaborated on by means of a comparison with the former attitude of the Galatians (4:12–20), an allegorical interpretation of the scriptural narrative about Abraham (4:21–5:1) and an explicit statement of the consequences for the Galatians of choosing the alternative advocated by his opponents and letting themselves be circumcised (5:2–10).

5:11–6:13

5:11–13a

Following the close in 5:2–10, a new start is made in 5:11, marked by the conjunction δέ, the address ἀδελφοί and a construction introducing a new theme. The interpretation of this construction poses several difficulties. Here I shall merely state how I understand it; the arguments supporting that interpretation will be set out in the excursus on the interpretation of 5:11 below. The construction begins with a change of grammatical subject, accentuated by the use of the pronoun (ἐγώ) and its initial position, signalling that Paul is now once more in focus. The last time this was the case was in 4:12–20.[72] There, however, the topic was Paul's conduct among the Galatians; here, there is no direct link with that situation. The following conditional clause — 'if I am still preaching circumcision' — does admittedly take up the circumcision motif of 5:2–6 again, but puts it in a new context. 5:2–6 was concerned with the consequences for the Galatians of submitting to circumcision; here, the text refers to the purely hypothetical situation of Paul still preaching circumcision and makes it the basis for a conclusion. That conclusion then follows in the form of a rhetorical question, which in my opinion should be translated 'what further reason is there then that I should be persecuted?', 'is there then still any reason why I should be persecuted?' or in similar terms. The obvious answer to this question is that no such reason exists. The question is followed by a conclusion drawn from the obvious answer to it: 'In that case the offence of the cross has been made ineffective.' The underlying idea is presumably that the persecuted Paul manifests or embodies the cross of Christ (see e.g. 2:19 f.; 6:17) and that the offence of the cross therefore operates in Paul's persecution.

It is clear, then, that there is a shift in topic in 5:11, from the consequences for the Galatians of letting themselves be circumcised — they will fall away from grace — to what it would mean for Paul if he still preached circumcision — he would not be persecuted and he would thus render ineffective the offence of the cross. Once again the criterion of 1:10 appears to be brought into focus, and this time the listener has been prepared for it by the allusions to 1:6–10 in 5:7–10. The link with 1:10 is also suggested by certain similarities in construction between the two passages. In 1:10 it was said that if Paul were still pleasing people, he would not be a servant of Christ. Here we read that if Paul were still preaching circumcision, there would no longer be any reason why he should be persecuted. He would thus be pleasing people. But then he

---

[72] In Gal 4:31 and 5:5 there is also an undefined 'we'. The pronoun ἐγώ does admittedly occur in 5:2, 3 and 10, but there it serves as the subject of metacommunicative and metapropositional verbs.

would also be rendering ineffective the offence of the cross and hence he would not be a servant of Christ. As was noted above, exactly the same pattern of thought recurs in 6:11–17, where Paul accuses his opponents of wanting to make a good showing in the flesh and trying to compel the Galatians to be circumcised, merely to avoid being persecuted for the cross of Christ, whereas Paul only wishes to boast of that cross, by which he has been crucified to the world.

After his opening observation about what his opponents' preaching of circumcision would result in for his own part, Paul says in 5:12 what he considers those opponents should do — go all the way and castrate themselves. Obviously, this pronouncement represents an unfavourable assessment and a repudiation of those who seek to please people and preach circumcision. Perhaps it also incorporates the challenging idea that it would in fact be better for them to be despised as eunuchs than to be respected as circumcised men. At all events, Paul's pronouncement is followed by an explanatory comment (γάρ), which justifies this drastic repudiation of those opponents who unsettle the Galatians by referring to the fact that the Galatians were called to freedom.

Excursus (to p. 187): The interpretation of verse 5:11

The difficulties involved in the interpretation of 5:11 have to do with (1) the construction τί ἔτι, (2) the fact that the conditional complex sentence is constructed in a way which implies a 'real' (or 'objective') condition, and (3) the word ἄρα in the following clause. I propose the following reading: 'If I am still preaching circumcision, what further reason is there then that I should be persecuted? Then the offence of the cross has been made ineffective.' My reasons for this reading are as follows:

1. The rhetorical question in 5:11 can hardly be translated in the following, 'usual' way: 'If I am still preaching circumcision, why then am I still being persecuted?'[73] Such a translation would seem to presuppose that Paul had previously both preached circumcision and been persecuted, a combination which the same question indicates is incongruous at the time of writing. Bauer's lexicon solves the problem by noting that the adverb ἔτι can also be used to express degree and hence to indicate something additional;[74] in such cases it can be translated 'further, additionally'. According to Bauer, this is the sense we have in 5:11. I believe that there is something in what he says, but would like to make a few further comments.

An examination of the use of ἔτι in the New Testament[75] reveals that nine out of a total of over 90 instances of this particle, i.e. just under 10 per cent, occur in

---

[73] However, Guthrie (1973, p. 132), for example, proposes this interpretation.

[74] Cf. e.g. Schwyzer & Debrunner 1950, p. 564; Mayser 1934, pp. 136 f.; LSJ 1968; Bauer 1979.

[75] Here I shall base my conclusions solely on the language of the New Testament; the question is not so crucial to my thesis as to justify a more ambitious study. However, Professor Jerker Blomqvist, Lund, has kindly drawn my attention to the following 15

interrogative clauses, immediately after an introductory interrogative τί.[76] This suggests that we are concerned here with a more or less fixed and established expression. If we then look more closely at these nine cases of τί ἔτι in the New Testament, we find that in at least two of them the expression cannot easily be translated 'why... still...?' Rom 3:7, for example, reads εἰ δὲ ἡ ἀλήθεια τοῦ θεοῦ ἐν τῷ ἐμῷ ψεύσματι ἐπερίσσευσεν εἰς τὴν δόξαν αὐτοῦ, τί ἔτι κἀγὼ ὡς ἁμαρτωλὸς κρίνομαι. If τί ἔτι is translated 'why... still...?' in this context, it means that the 'I' of the text is already and has been subject to ongoing judgment by God, an idea which we would hardly expect to come across here (cf. e.g. Rom 2:3, 5, 12 f., 16, 26 f.; 3:3, 6, 20). The problem with τί ἔτι in Gal 5:11 has already been touched on. There is thus cause to ask whether τί ἔτι, which is evidently an established collocation, does not have some other sense than 'why... still...?'

The translation which I propose — 'what further reason is there then for...?' — is based on three observations. The first is the one just made, namely that τί ἔτι appears to be an established collocation, suggesting that the particles belong together and should be understood together. If ἔτι is accordingly associated with τί, rather than with the verb, the meaning is probably 'what further reason is there for...?' (if τί is understood adverbially) or 'what further... (what else...)?' (if τί is interpreted as an internal accusative).

The second observation is of an etymological nature. Unlike English *why*, which derives from an instrumental form (*hwi*) of Anglo-Saxon *hwæt* (*hwa*) and is thus fundamentally adverbial,[77] the Greek word τί has developed from an internal accusative. The question τί διώκομαι is thus related etymologically to the question τίνα διωγμὸν διώκομαι. How much of this etymological background is still perceptible in the fossilized form τί is of course difficult to say. It may be noted, however, that constructions with an internal accusative are still very common in Koine Greek and thus represent a living construction type. Consequently, it does not seem unreasonable to me to interpret the development of τί ἔτι, which is probably also a fossilized form, against the same etymological background. If we do so, a question like τί ἔτι διώκομαι could be related to the question τίνα ἔτι διωγμὸν διώκομαι, which literally means '(with) what further persecution am I persecuted?'[78] That question clearly differs in meaning, however, from 'why am I still being persecuted?', since the

occurrences of τί ἔτι in Epictetus, all of which are entirely in line with my observations in the New Testament: Epictetus 1.6.29; 1.7.30; 1.18.2, 8; 1.25.1, 1; 2.8.3; 2.17.26; 3.2.14; 3.24.56; 4.1.88, 88; 4.7.22, 28, 28.

[76] Mt 19:20; 26:65; Mk 5:35; 14:63; Lk 22:71; Rom 3:7; 9:19; Gal 5:11; Heb 11:32. In particular, it may be noted here that the parallel verses Mt 26:65, Mk 14:63 and Lk 22:71 all retain the collocation τί ἔτι, despite the fact that the word order varies in other respects.

[77] See e.g. Bosworth & Toller 1882; Weekley 1921.

[78] Cf. Heb 7:11: εἰ μὲν οὖν τελείωσις διὰ τῆς Λευιτικῆς ἱερωσύνης ἦν..., τίς ἔτι χρεία κατὰ τὴν τάξιν Μελχισέδεκ ἕτερον ἀνίστασθαι ἱερέα καὶ οὐ κατὰ τὴν τάξιν Ἀαρὼν λέγεσθαι. Both the context and the word order indicate that ἔτι should probably be read with τίς χρεία here, resulting in the sense 'what further need (is there) to...?' If in this case we chose to use a finite verb form and an internal accusative, rather than χρεία (ἐστίν), the construction would probably be τίνα ἔτι χρείαν χρῄζουσιν... or τί ἔτι χρῄζουσιν. Cf. also ποῖον ἔτι πρᾶγμα ἔχομαι in Epictetus 1.25.2.

latter concerns the reason for a persecution which is assumed to be taking place, while the former questions the actual occurrence of further persecution and corresponds most closely to the question 'what further reason is there for... ?'

The third observation is that such an interpretation of τί ἔτι gives a good sense to the two problematical questions discussed above (Rom 3:7; Gal 5:11), since in both of them the question is preceded by the elimination of an actual or conceivable reason for the action expressed by the verb in the question. That the question is a direct follow-up to this elimination of a reason is clear from the fact that in both cases the reason is eliminated in a conditional clause introducing the question itself. Regarding the remaining occurrences of τί ἔτι in the New Testament, it may be noted that here ἔτι can be interpreted as a temporal qualifier of the verb, but that it makes at least as much sense to understand it as going together with τί. For example, τί (οὖν) ἔτι μέμφεται in Rom 9:19 can be construed as 'why does he still blame us?' and taken to refer to God continuing to blame his people through the prophets, for instance; but it is equally possible, at least, to read it as 'what further reason is there for him to blame us?', especially as the question is both preceded and followed by expressions which appear to rule out any conceivable reason for the verbal action, namely the statements that God has mercy on whomever he chooses and hardens the heart of whomever he chooses (v. 18) and that no one can resist his will (v. 19). Similarly, τί ἔτι ὑστερῶ in Mt 19:20 can be taken to mean either 'what do I still lack?' or 'what further reason is there for my lacking anything?' (or 'what else do I lack?'). It may be noted, though, that the question is immediately preceded by a denial that, in certain possible respects, the young man does actually lack anything. In Mk 5:35, the question τί ἔτι σκύλλεις τὸν διδάσκαλον can be interpreted as 'why trouble the teacher any further?', but since the reason for troubling him has just been declared to be no longer valid, it is at least as natural to read it as 'what further reason is there for troubling the teacher?' In Mt 26:65, Mk 14:63 and Lk 22:71, the question τί ἔτι χρείαν ἔχομεν μαρτύρων (in Luke τί ἔτι ἔχομεν μαρτυρίας χρείαν) can be translated either 'why do we still need witnesses?' or 'what further reason is there for our needing witnesses?' (or 'what further need of witnesses do we have?'), but at all events its function in the context must surely be to question whether such a need still exists, since the reason for that need — the lack of evidence against Jesus — has just been eliminated by a confession by Jesus. The final occurrence of τί ἔτι in the New Testament is in Heb 11:32, where τί ἔτι λέγω can equally well be construed as 'what further reason is there for me to speak?' or 'why am I still speaking?'

To sum up: in the New Testament at least, there appears to be an established use of τί ἔτι in the sense 'what further reason is there for... ?' or 'what further... ?' and, if that is the case, then this is the meaning of the words in Gal 5:11.[79] For the subsequent discussion about the meaning of Gal 5:11, it should perhaps also be noted that, with the proposed interpretation of τί ἔτι, in all the cases discussed here the questions are concerned with potential rather than actual actions. In fact, they seem ultimately to be concerned with the possible factuality or realization of the actions described, e.g. with whether 'I' will in fact be judged (Rom 3:7), whether 'we' do need witnesses (Mt 26:65; Mk 14:63; Lk 22:71), whether 'I' do in fact lack anything (Mt 19:20), or whether 'you' should trouble the teacher (Mk 5:35).

---

[79] See pp. 182 f., note 75 above.

2. The second problem in Gal 5:11 concerns the significance of the fact that the conditional complex sentence is constructed in the manner used for a 'real' condition, rather than an 'unreal' one, despite the fact that the assertion in the subordinate clause at least is manifestly contrary to reality. Some argue that in the subordinate clause Paul is referring to a claim that has actually been made about him and is refuting it by drawing attention to the fact that he is being persecuted.[80] However, I consider this an unlikely interpretation. First of all, the Galatians, to whom Paul 'gave birth' (cf. 4:19) and who have since 'run well' (cf. 5:7), can hardly have been in any doubt as to whether or not Paul preached circumcision. Secondly, if they were, the argument in 5:11 would be an implausibly poor one. If the Galatians knew so little about Paul's teaching that they were unsure whether or not he preached circumcision, it would by no means be obvious to them that his persecution must be due to his not preaching circumcision; there must have been other possible reasons for it.

I would therefore suggest a different interpretation of Paul's use here of the 'real condition' type of conditional complex sentence. The term 'real condition' does *not* mean that the writer is claiming that what is said in the construction is in accordance with reality, but rather that he is not expressing any view as to whether it is or is not.[81] It is therefore also suitable for intellectual experiments and purely hypothetical reasoning. In my opinion, the most plausible interpretation is that the conditional complex sentence in 5:11 is precisely that, an intellectual experiment. What Paul is doing here, in other words, is leaving aside the real state of affairs and exploring what would be the result if he were to preach circumcision.[82] His conclusion is that, if he does so, there is no further reason why he should be persecuted. Like the subordinate clause, the main clause is describing an imaginary situation. The rhetorical question is thus concerned, not with what reasons there are *now*, i.e. at the time of writing, for him to be persecuted, but rather with what reasons there will be *then*, i.e. when he preaches circumcision. This interpretation fits in well with my earlier observation that the other rhetorical questions in the New Testament which begin τί ἔτι appear to relate to potential actions and are ultimately interested in the possible factuality or realization of those actions.

3. The third problem in Gal 5:11 concerns the meaning of ἄρα and the relationship between the clause which it introduces and the preceding conditional complex sentence. The usual interpretation is that this clause is a kind of answer to the rhetorical question, an answer which makes it clear that there is no reason for Paul to be persecuted if he preaches circumcision, since the offence of the cross has then been made ineffective.[83] The logic would then be: preaching of circumcision => no offence of the cross => no persecution. However, there are certain problems with this interpretation. If it is correct, then the ἄρα-clause serves as an explanation or clarification of the conditional complex sentence. Normally, however, ἄρα has an inferential sense in Koine Greek.[84]

---

[80] See e.g. Schlier 1971, p. 238; Guthrie 1973, p. 132; Howard 1990, p. 9.

[81] See e.g. Schwyzer & Debrunner 1950, p. 684; BDR §§ 371:1, note 1, 372:2b.

[82] Cf. 1 Cor 15:13.

[83] See e.g. Guthrie 1973, pp. 132 f.; Rodhe 1989, p. 223.

[84] Denniston argues that originally ἄρα was not a connective or inferential particle, but primarily expressed interest (roughly like *Siehe*). The dominant use in Attic, however, was not interest in general, but interest occasioned by information or disillusionment, and ἄρα was thus well on its way to becoming a logical connective particle, since information and disillusionment tend to result from what has just been said or done. In Aristotle, according

The natural particle to use for an explanation or clarification is not ἄρα, but γάρ. Furthermore, with this interpretation it is not quite clear what Paul is doing or wishes to do by observing that there is then no reason why he should be persecuted. Our expectation is of course that the preaching of circumcision will have some unfavourable result. But if the entire line of reasoning issues in the observation that Paul will in that case not be persecuted, he could do with explaining what is unfavourable about that fact, since it is hardly self-evident. Or does Paul actually want to show that the offence of the cross will be rendered ineffective if he preaches circumcision? But in that case, why do so in such a roundabout way, bringing in the intermediate step of persecution? The latter adds nothing, since it is understood that the offence of the cross will have been made ineffective before it is understood that Paul will not be persecuted.

For these reasons we should I believe consider the alternative possibility that ἄρα serves to indicate the conclusion to be drawn from the fact that Paul will not then be persecuted, and the unfavourable consequences of this. Now the logic is: preaching of circumcision => no persecution => no offence of the cross. The underlying idea is presumably that Paul's persecution is a manifestation of the cross of Christ[85] and that the offence of the cross is thus operative in this persecution of Paul. If he tries to avoid persecution, this manifestation of Christ will be lost. We have already come across similar ideas at several other points in Paul's letters. 1 Thess 1:6 f., for instance, describes how the Thessalonians received the word amid great affliction and thus became μιμηταί of 'us' and of the Lord and a τύπος for all the believers in Macedonia and Achaia, and 2:14 ff. describes how they became μιμηταί of the churches in Judaea when they suffered the same things at the hands of their own compatriots as the Judaean churches did at the hands of the Jews, who killed Jesus and persecuted 'us'. In Phil 1:13 a similar way of thinking is hinted at, when Paul's bonds are portrayed as something active and revelatory. The reference in Phil 1:20 to Christ being exalted in the body of the persecuted Paul and the parallel references in 4:9 to what the Philippians have learnt and received (presumably concerning Christ) and to what they have heard and seen in Paul (who is being persecuted) point our thoughts in the same direction. Apart from in the letters studied in this thesis, similar thinking can be found in 2 Cor 4:7–12, for example. This pattern of thought is thus well documented in Paul's writings.

Although both of these alternative interpretations are compatible with the context, I believe that the second of them makes for a clearer line of thought. Verses 5:11–13a correspond to 6:11–13. In the latter passage, 'those who are confusing you' are accused of wanting circumcision precisely to avoid persecution for the cross of Christ. Immediately after 6:11–13, in 6:14, Paul expresses the wish that he may not boast of anything except the cross of Christ, by which the world has been crucified to him and he to the world. In 6:16 he then wishes peace and mercy upon all those who are in line

to Denniston (1954, pp. 32–41), ἄρα no longer has a living meaning, having become a purely connective particle. Given this etymological background, it is reasonable to expect the ἄρα in Gal 5:11 to have an inferential sense. It could possibly be asserted that it has the emphatic meaning which Denniston ascribes to it in Attic, but, as has already been pointed out, in practice this use of ἄρα comes very close to the inferential sense.

[85] In this connection, Mußner, referring to E. Güttgemanns, speaks of the persecuted apostle as 'die Epiphanie des gekreuzigten Christus' (Mußner 1974, pp. 362 f.; Güttgemanns 1966, p. 134).

with this standard, after which, in 6:17, he points out that he carries the marks of Christ on his body.[86] These verses, following on from 6:11–13, suggest a pattern of thought like that of the second alternative, i.e. that Paul's persecution manifests or embodies the cross of Christ and that the offence of the cross thus operates in his persecution.

To sum up, then, I would propose the following understanding of 5:11: Paul is here stating what the unfavourable consequence will be if, like his opponents, he preaches circumcision, namely that he will then avoid persecution and thus render ineffective the offence of the cross. In other words, the line of thought in 5:11 is basically the same as in 6:12 f. In both passages, Paul contrasts his opponents and their preaching of circumcision, which favours the flesh, with himself and his persecution for the cross of Christ.

5:13b–6:10

In 5:13b, a new start is made, marked by the address ἀδελφοί in initial position,[87] μόνον and the change of mood from the indicative to the imperative. This does not give the impression that a major new section is beginning here. The address ἀδελφοί in initial position commonly seems to introduce digressions or subordinate sections of other types,[88] and μόνον is a modifying adversative particle and, as such, links the new section relatively closely to the previous one.[89] The change of mood does admittedly indicate a shift at the metapropositional level, from an adverse assessment of Paul's opponents and their preaching of circumcision (5:11–13a) to direct exhortations to the Galatians, but at the propositional level the text is clearly linked to what has gone before. This link is in fact already hinted at by the elliptical nature of the opening clause, but it is made explicit by τὴν ἐλευθερίαν, which directly echoes ἐπ' ἐλευθερίᾳ in 5:13a. In my opinion, all these factors suggest that the opening in 5:13b is less important than the one in 5:11 and introduces a subsection of the larger section that began in the latter verse.

The opening exhortation, in 5:13b-c, calls on the Galatians not to let their freedom provide an opportunity for the flesh, but rather to serve one another

[86] Cf. 2 Cor 4:10 ff.
[87] The address ἀδελφοί can be linked to either the preceding or the following text. However, it is unusual for such an address to be placed at the end of a clause, although there is one example of this in 6:18. In that instance, the address ἀδελφοί appears to me to have a special function at the end of the letter, that of making an appeal or striking a conciliatory note. This can hardly be its function in 5:13. A form of address is far more commonly used to introduce a digression or some other subordinate section, as exemplified by 3:15 and 6:1. For this reason, I am inclined to link this ἀδελφοί to what follows. Depending on which alternative we choose, the address can be said either to prepare for or directly introduce the digression and its direct exhortations in 5:13b–6:10.
[88] See note 87 above. If the address is assigned to the preceding text, the new start here is even more weakly marked.
[89] Cf. the comment on Phil 1:27, on p. 100.

in love. This is then justified (γάρ) with reference to the fact that the whole law is summed up in the commandment of love. If 5:11 is interpreted as proposed above, these exhortations can be seen as directly connected with that verse. Instead of submitting to circumcision and thus pleasing those persecutors who are 'according to the flesh' (see 4:29), they must not give the flesh a chance, but must serve one another in love. Instead of seeking a good showing in the flesh (cf. 6:12), then, they must choose *slavery* (δουλεύετε) in love. The explanation added in 5:14, at any rate, surely follows up the discussion about circumcision in 5:11 f. After this explanatory comment, there is another exhortation. It is introduced by a conditional clause and warns of the consequences of not heeding the twofold exhortation with which this section begins. Its consequence-indicating character means that to some extent it serves as a closing marker.

This is followed in 5:16 by a fresh start, marked by the conjunction δέ and a clearly instructive and thematic construction. The latter begins with the metapropositional and metacommunicative λέγω, which here — as in 3:15, 17 and 4:1 — probably indicates that the new beginning is a minor one and entails an explanation of or comment on what has gone before. This is confirmed by the proposition, which consists of a twin exhortation clearly linked to the one in 5:13, but differing from it in its emphasis on the Spirit as the principle and motive force of the positive alternative, as opposed to the flesh. These two opposite principles or motive forces are emphasized in the construction, suggesting that they are now the main concern of the text. The twofold exhortation in 5:17 is followed by a couple of comments explaining (γάρ) the opposition between them.

In 5:18 another minor new start is made, this time marked by δέ and the opening conditional clause. The text is now concerned with how the Spirit-led life to which Paul is exhorting his addressees relates to the law. This question, too, appears to follow up 5:13b–15, where the life Paul urged them to live was described on the one hand as freedom from the law (5:13) and on the other as its fulfilment (5:14).

The relationship of the Spirit-led life to the law is discussed in three steps. First, it is pointed out in 5:18 — developing on the reference to freedom from the law in 5:13 — that, if the Galatians are led by the Spirit, they are not subject to the law. This observation is then modified — developing on the reference to the fulfilment of the law in 5:14 — in the following steps (5:19–21, 22–23), which describe the works of the flesh and of the Spirit and point out that the former assuredly do not result in an inheritance in the kingdom of God, but that the latter are not in conflict with the law. Someone who heeds Paul's exhortation in 5:16 to walk in the Spirit and not to gratify the desires of the flesh is thus not subject to the law, but equally is not living in conflict with it. The idea presented in 5:14 is thus elaborated on in more detail.

The beginning of the second step in the discussion is marked by δέ in 5:19, its completion by the relative clause in 5:21, which is of a metacommunicative character and contains the anaphoric text-summarizing expression τὰ τοιαῦτα. The beginning of the third step is marked by the conjunction δέ and the change of grammatical subject (ὁ... καρπὸς τοῦ πνεύματος) in 5:22, and its conclusion by the anaphoric text-summarizing τῶν τοιούτων in 5:23 and the recurrence in the same verse of νόμος from 5:18.

Following the discussion in 5:18–23 about how the Spirit-led life relates to the law, a minor new start is made in 5:24, marked by the conjunction δέ and the change of subject (οἱ... τοῦ Χριστοῦ ['Ιησοῦ]). What follows is a description of the ethical starting-point of those who belong to Christ (5:24), namely that they have crucified the flesh with its passions and desires. This is closely linked to the preceding descriptions of the antithesis between the Spirit and the flesh and their respective works, and suggests that some sort of final formulation is now at hand. This impression is reinforced by the fact that the passage proceeds from the Christian's status as having been crucified with Christ, thus looking back to the question in 5:11 (as interpreted above), which formed the basis for the whole of the paraenetic section from 5:13 on.

This statement of the ethical starting-point is then followed up with two exhortations to 'us'.[90] The first begins with a conditional clause which is directly linked to the preceding statement, showing that the two exhortations are to be regarded as conclusions to be drawn from it. There have been no direct exhortations since the twofold exhortation at the beginning of the commentary section in 5:16. The fact that Paul is now returning to direct exhortations after all his comments and assertions therefore suggests in itself that this section is being brought to a close. That impression is underlined by the clear parallel in content terms between the exhortations in 5:25 f. and the twin exhortation in 5:16. Like the latter, the new exhortations consist of one expressed in positive and another expressed in negative terms. The positive exhortation (5:25) very closely echoes its counterpart in 5:16. The negative one (5:26) is more specific than the corresponding exhortation in 5:16 and touches in content terms on the warning in 5:15, which rounded off the introductory subsection of the paraenetic section 5:13b–6:10. These

---

[90] Previous exhortations have been expressed in the second person plural. The change to the first person here could be due to various factors. The most likely reason is perhaps that the generally worded statement in 5:24 (οἱ... τοῦ Χριστοῦ ['Ιησοῦ]) paved the way for a broadening of the subject of the exhortations. Another conceivable reason is that Paul is including himself in the subject as a conciliatory gesture.

recurrences of material from the opening of the commentary section (from 5:16 on) and from the close of the section on which it comments (5:13b–15) signal that what is being brought to a close here is the commentary section.

In 6:1 the paraenetic section gathers fresh momentum. The new beginning is marked by the address ἀδελφοί in initial position, an opening concessive clause introducing a new theme, and a return to imperatives in the second person plural. It is thus made clear that this opening is more significant than those in 5:18, 19, 22 and 24, although not so significant that the text that follows is not still part of the paraenetic section.

The preceding section, 5:16–26, focused on the two opposite principles of the Spirit and the flesh and was quite general in character. The exhortation that begins the new section from 6:1 refers directly to a tangible situation — someone falling[91] — and states what the Galatians should do in this situation: restore the person who has fallen in a spirit of gentleness and take care not to be tempted themselves. There is thus a clear shift in content in 6:1. However, there are also clear links with what has gone before. Up to this point, the core of the paraenetic section has consisted of three interrelated, twofold exhortations. The first (5:13) began the paraenetic section and called on the recipients not to give the flesh an opportunity, but rather to serve one another in love. The second (5:16) opened the commentary section and urged them to walk in the Spirit and not to gratify the desires of the flesh. The third (5:25 f.) rounded off the same section and was an appeal to be in line with (στοιχεῖν) the Spirit and not to seek vain glory or provoke or envy one another. The exhortation in 6:1 now looks back to these exhortations in several ways. Like them, it consists of two elements. It is addressed to 'you who are spiritual' (οἱ πνευματικοί) in a specific situation. In content terms, it primarily echoes the first exhortation in 5:13, but it is more specific. It thus stands out as an application of the earlier, more generally worded exhortations to a tangible problem in the Galatians' situation.[92]

The opening exhortation in 6:1 is followed in 6:2–6 by three more, which are coordinated by δέ and appear to belong together in terms of content. The

---

[91] According to Michaelis (1959, p. 172), παράπτωμα is not entirely synonymous with παράβασις, since the latter concept concerns the violation of a commandment, whereas the former refers more immediately to the disruption of a person's relationship with God. Hence. Paul is able to use παράπτωμα to refer for example to the Fall in Gen 3 (Rom 5:15. 17) or as a synonym of ἡ ἁμαρτία (Rom 5:20). There is therefore no reason to believe that the word is a milder or weaker term for sin, as is sometimes claimed (e.g. in Oepke 1973, p. 187; Rodhe 1989, pp. 258 f.). On the contrary, it evokes more serious associations, with something which entails a disturbed relationship to God or falling away, i.e. something of the kind that had arisen in Galatia (see Gal 1:6; 5:8).

[92] This impression is strengthened for example by the motivation set out in 6:2 (cf. 5:14) — οὕτως ἀναπληρώσετε τὸν νόμον τοῦ Χριστοῦ — and by the wording of 6:3, which presumably refers back to μὴ γινώμεθα κενόδοξοι in 5:26.

first two are each accompanied by an explanatory comment (γάρ). All three have to do with the responsibility of those who are spiritual for one another and themselves and appear to complement or modify each other (see e.g. the link and the tension between 6:2 and 6:5). They thus follow on from and expound the first part of the exhortation in 6:1 (καταρτίζετε τὸν τοιοῦτον ἐν πνεύματι πραΰτητος).

In 6:7, the pattern of coordinated exhortations is then broken by a further exhortation added asyndetically. If the exhortations in 6:2–6 took up the positive part of the opening exhortation in 6:1, the one in 6:7 (μὴ πλανᾶσθε) looks back to the warning in its second part (σκοπῶν σεαυτὸν μὴ καὶ σὺ πειρασθῇς). It is subsequently underpinned and justified by a statement in 6:7b and then by an explanatory comment in 6:7c–8, which makes it clear that the deception which Paul has in mind is sowing to the flesh instead of to the Spirit. Paul thus refers back to the core theme of the whole of the section 5:13b–6:10: Do not give the flesh an opportunity; walk in the Spirit (5:13b, 16, 25 f.).[93] The recurrence of these concepts suggests that that entire section is now drawing to a close.

In 6:9 there then follows an exhortation which is coordinated with the preceding one by the conjunction δέ and which has some semantic coherence with it. Like the previous exhortation, this one is expressed in negative terms, but it differs from it in that it focuses on Paul's positive alternative, rather than his opponents' negative one. As at the end of the commentary section (5:16–26), there is a sudden switch here from second to first person plural.[94]

The exhortations of 6:7–9 hinted that the whole of 5:13b–6:10 was coming to an end. This impression is now further reinforced by the general exhortation in 6:10, which is introduced by ἄρα οὖν and, with its call to 'us' to work for the good of all and especially for those of the family of faith, echoes the content of the opening exhortation in 5:13. This brings to an end the whole of the section 5:13b–6:10.

6:11–13

In 6:7–10, the section 5:13b–6:10 was brought to a close, and the listener is therefore now prepared for the beginning of a new section. A fresh start does indeed occur in 6:11, marked by asyndeton and the attention-attracting ἴδετε. If we subscribe to the common view that the large letters Paul refers to in the

---

[93] The centrality of this theme to other parts of Galatians, too, is indicated e.g. by 3:3, 4:21–5:1 and 6:12 f.
[94] Probably for the same reason as in that context: the generally worded statement in 6:7c–8 has presumably made it natural to broaden the grammatical subject, but Paul's inclusion of himself in the subject can also be understood as a conciliatory gesture.

same verse are intended to emphasize what is written, then they are intensity-heightening and can also be regarded as a transition marker.[95] Either way, the opening here is fairly weakly marked, suggesting that this is not the beginning of a major section. The new start is accompanied by a shift in the topic. The preceding section, being paraenetic in character, focused on the Galatians' future. This one focuses on Paul's opponents and their preaching of

---

[95] Paul calls on the Galatians in this verse to see with what large letters he is writing to them in his own hand, an exhortation on which many different interpretations have been placed. A common view is that at this point Paul takes over from an amanuensis and wishes to draw his audience's attention to this (e.g. Guthrie 1973, pp. 148 f.; Mußner 1974, pp. 409 f.; Rodhe 1989, p. 272.). Others are of the opinion that Paul wrote the whole of Galatians himself, and that this is what he wants to draw the recipients' attention to (e.g. Zahn 1922, p. 277; Foerster 1964, p. 136; also, according to Zahn (1922, p. 277, note 30), several of the Church Fathers, including Eusebius of Emesa, Ambrosiaster, Gaius Marius Victorinus, Augustine, Pelagius, John Chrysostomos and Theodoret). Regarding the comment about πηλίκοις... γράμμασιν, various interpretations have been suggested: that it is a reference to the length of the letter (e.g. Luther's translation of 1546 and the King James Version) and is intended to indicate how much effort it has cost Paul to write it; that it reflects the fact that Paul's handwriting differs from that of his amanuensis and is made to emphasize that Paul is now writing himself (so Deissmann 1895, p. 264; cf. also Deissmann 1923, pp. 132 f., note 6); that the large letters reflect Paul's desire to write legibly and bear witness to his care and love for the Galatians (Zahn 1922, p. 278); that the large letters are used to give emphasis to what is written — in roughly the same way as underlining, italics or bold-face in modern texts — and this is what Paul wishes to draw the Galatians' attention to (e.g. Schlier 1971, pp. 279 f.; Mußner 1974, pp. 409 f.; Rodhe 1989, pp. 271 f.). Of these suggestions, the last one in particular seems reasonable to me. Nevertheless, in my view, serious consideration should also be given to another possibility. Verses 6:11 f. and 5:11 f. seem to correspond: in both passages, Paul contrasts the desire of his opponents to please people with his own persecution and weakness. If this contrast is crucial here, as I believe it to be, it seems fairly reasonable to interpret the large letters as a manifestation of Paul's persecution or weakness 'in the flesh', since they could very well be a direct result of the ill-treatment he has repeatedly been subjected to (cf. 1 Cor 4:9–13; 2 Cor 11:23–29) or of the physical infirmity to which Paul refers in 4:13, immediately after his exhortation to the Galatians to become like him. Although many have, rightly, pointed out that the reference in 4:15 to the Galatians having been prepared to tear out their eyes and give them to Paul does not *necessarily* mean that this infirmity in fact affected his eyes, equally there is as far as I can understand no decisive reason why this should *not* be the case. On the contrary, certain details in the statement in 4:15 suggest that it was meant in a literal rather than a metaphorical sense (see Mußner 1974, p. 309). If Paul is indeed suffering from an eye condition which the Galatians know of, and it has already been given prominence as a key motif in the epistle, it is perfectly possible to regard the large letters as a reflection of this condition. Whichever of these two interpretations is chosen, the large letters demonstrate Paul's weakness in the flesh, and the exhortation in Gal 6:11 thus serves to draw the Galatians' attention to this weakness. Such an interpretation fits in well with the sequence of thought. In 6:7 f., Paul has just talked about the importance of sowing to the Spirit and not to the flesh, and in 6:12 the following sentence begins with the words ὅσοι θέλουσιν εὐπροσωπῆσαι ἐν σαρκί. If 6:11 is intended to illustrate Paul's weakness in the flesh, the contrast here between Paul and his opponents is pointed up even more clearly. For my own part, I am inclined to prefer such an interpretation, although my understanding of the overall line of thought in the text is also compatible with the alternative interpretations of 6:11.

circumcision, in contrast to Paul and his gospel. Formally, this change is reflected in a transition from a text dominated by imperatives to one with a preponderance of indicatives.[96]

With its focus on the contrast between Paul and his gospel, on the one hand, and his opponents and their preaching of circumcision, on the other, this new section involves recurrences of material from the short section (5:11–13a) which preceded and formed the basis for the paraenetic section 5:13b–6:10. These recurrences include περιτέμνεσθαι, τῷ σταυρῷ τοῦ Χριστοῦ and διώκωνται in 6:12 (f.), which represent lexical links with 5:11. Combined with the relatively weakly marked new beginning in 6:11, they suggest that in 6:11 Paul is not embarking on something completely new, but rather, after the paraenetic section, beginning to round off the section that commenced at 5:11 by once again drawing attention to the starting-point for the paraenetic section.

The opening exhortation in 6:11 is followed in 6:12 by an assertion about what Paul's opponents are trying to achieve by preaching circumcision. It follows on asyndetically and is introduced by a very strongly accentuated change of grammatical subject (ὅσοι θέλουσιν εὐπροσωπῆσαι ἐν σαρκί, οὗτοι...), which maintains the intensity of the section and contributes to the impression that the text has now entered a decisive phase. Paul's opponents are described here as those who want to make a good showing in the flesh, and their preaching of circumcision is said to be intended only (μόνον) to allow them to avoid persecution for the cross of Christ. Given the criterion set out in the opening of the letter body (1:10), they are thus revealing that — unlike Paul — they are not servants of Christ. To the assertion in 6:12, Paul then adds an explanatory comment (γάρ) in 6:13 which is closely linked to the preceding assertion and again highlights his opponents' desire to boast in the flesh. This brings to a close the section that began in 5:11.

To sum up, it can be said that in 5:11–6:13, the fourth and last major section of the Letter to the Galatians, Paul sets out how, in the light of his gospel, the Galatians should act in the present situation.[97] The section begins with a statement of the adverse consequences which the preaching of circumcision would have for Paul, and of what would be best for his opponents (5:11–13a). Against this background, there is then a lengthy paraenetic section (5:13b–

---

[96] The new section does admittedly begin with the imperative ἴδετε. However, this exhortation is definitely of a different kind to those that have preceded it. The latter were designed to persuade the Galatians to conduct themselves in a specific desirable way, whereas this one merely draws their attention to a tangible phenomenon.

[97] Regarding the question whether or not the exhortations in 5:13–6:10 relate to a specific situation in the Galatian churches, see Barclay 1988, pp. 217 f.

6:10), after which its starting-point is highlighted once again by a description of what Paul's opponents are seeking to achieve by preaching circumcision (6:11–13).

6:14–16

In 6:14, a fresh start is made, marked by the stressed change of person (ἐμοί), the conjunction δέ and the change of mood in the main clauses, from the indicative to the optative. The short new section, 6:14–16, is characterized by the expression of wishes and thus has a concluding character in itself. The question is how significant the new beginning in 6:14 is and to what level the concluding section 6:14–16 should be assigned. The wish in 6:14 is closely linked to 6:11–13,[98] which could be an argument for including this section in the one beginning at 5:11. Given the clear concluding character of 6:11–13 and the fact that in 6:15 f. the new section takes a partly new turn and becomes more general in character, however, I would nevertheless see 6:14–16 as a more independent section, rounding off the letter as a whole. I thus consider there to be relatively self-contained sections at both the beginning and the end of the letter, introducing and concluding the letter as a whole. The word 'relatively' is of course important here, and it does not necessarily make a great deal of difference if these sections are instead included in the following and the preceding sections, respectively.

Paul begins the section 6:14–16 with a wish concerning himself. It is linked very closely to 6:12 f. and expresses Paul's desire — in contrast to his opponents who want to make a good showing in the flesh and to avoid persecution for the cross of Christ — not to boast of anything except the cross of Christ, by which the world has been crucified to him and he to the world. Thus the cross of Christ is held up as a decisive standard for Paul's life (cf. 2:19; 3:1; 5:24). An explanatory comment (γάρ) is added in 6:15, echoing the wording of 5:6 and relating the wish in 6:14 to the problem in Galatia. The section concludes, in 6:16, with a wish of peace upon all those who are in line with this standard[99] and upon the Israel of God.

---

[98] See e.g. καυχᾶσθαι in 6:14 and 6:13 and ὁ σταυρός in 6:14 and 6:12.

[99] It is not entirely clear what is meant by ὁ κανὼν οὗτος in 6:16. The two most likely possibilities are that the words refer either to ὁ σταυρὸς τοῦ κυρίου ἡμῶν Ἰησοῦ Χριστοῦ in 6:14 (e.g. Guthrie 1973, p. 152) or to καινὴ κτίσις at the end of 6:15 (e.g. Barclay 1988, p. 99). The second alternative is supported by the fact that καινὴ κτίσις has just been mentioned and that in 5:25 Paul called upon 'us' to be in line with (στοιχεῖν) the Spirit, which is presumably a characteristic feature of this new creation. The arguments for the first alternative are the fact that in 6:14 Paul expressed a desire only to boast of the cross, a wish to which 6:16 probably refers after the comment inserted in 6:15; and the fact that the cross, persecution and weakness generally seem to play such an important role in Galatians. It is perhaps wrong in fact to oppose the two alternatives in this way,

6:17

In 6:17 another new start is made, marked by the emphatic τοῦ λοιποῦ, which follows on asyndetically, and by the change of mood to the imperative. Here, too, it is possible to discuss the importance of the new beginning and how this verse relates to what has gone before. I have chosen to regard the verse as relatively independent and loosely connected to the preceding text, a choice guided to some extent by the fact that it has the character of a summary and an ultimatum. It sums up the surprise and criticism that has repeatedly been expressed concerning the Galatians' conduct, by hinting that they have already afflicted the afflicted Paul, who carries the marks of the afflicted Jesus on his body, and it warns them not to do so again. It also gives the impression that this is Paul's final, impassioned word on the subject, and that it is now up to the Galatians to make their choice. The verse thus constitutes and marks the end of the entire body of the letter. The whole of the letter body, then, concludes with an expression which portrays Paul as someone in whom the crucified Christ is tangibly embodied. This is in line with the reasoning that has been pursued in the letter ever since the criterion in 1:10.

6:18

Unlike the other letters of Paul, Galatians does not include any greetings, and the letter ending is confined to a wish of grace in 6:18, aimed at the addressees. As usual, it follows on asyndetically, outside the context of the letter body. It echoes the opening of the letter and rounds off the epistle as a whole. Here, it is reinforced by the address ἀδελφοί and the word ἀμήν, giving it emphasis and the character of an appeal.

That completes my analysis of the structure of Galatians, on the basis of observations concerning transition markers and the overall line of thought in the letter.

since the crucified and the risen Christ are one and the same and have the same paraenetic significance. In the parallel to 6:15 which is found in 5:6, the expression corresponding to καινὴ κτίσις is πίστις δι᾽ ἀγάπης ἐνεργουμένη, i.e. the approach to life which is associated in 2:19 f. with Christ crucified and in 5:22 f. with the Spirit. I am inclined to regard ὁ κανὼν οὗτος as referring primarily to the cross, since the latter has played such a prominent role throughout Galatians and is highlighted again as a norm in 6:14 and 6:17, but at the same time it should be noted that the choice of interpretation here makes little difference to the overall progress of thought.

C. Arrangement of the text

For explanatory comments on the overview below, and a list of the abbreviations used for the different types of transition marker, readers are referred to the corresponding section of the analysis of 1 Thessalonians.[100]

I. 1:1–5 Opening of the letter:

>1. 1:1–2 Particulars of senders and recipients

>2. 1:3–5 Wish of grace and peace

II. 1:6–6:17 Body of the letter: — *Om:* Mp. *Cm:* W, Ex, Ass, Re; Int.

>1. 1:6–10 Statement of surprise at the Galatians falling away and pronouncement of an anathema upon anyone who proclaims a gospel other than the one 'we' proclaimed — *Om:* See above. *Cm:* Ass, Re; Int.

>>A. 1:6–8 Statement of surprise and pronouncement of anathema — *Om:* See above.

>>B. 1:9–10 Supporting comment: The anathema is being pronounced *now*, when Paul is evidently not seeking to please people, but is a servant of Christ — *Om:* Asyn, Mp/Mc. *Cm:* See above.

>2. 1:11–2:21 Argument for Paul and his gospel, proceeding from the comment in 1:10: His gospel is not according to man, but entails crucifixion with Christ and dying to the law in order to live to God — *Om:* (γάρ or δέ); Mp/Mc, H; Ad. *Cm:* ἄρα; Ass, Tsum, Re; Int.

>>A. 1:11–12 Statements about Paul's gospel: It is not according to man, nor has Paul received it from a human being, but by revelation of Jesus Christ — *Om:* See above.

>>B.1:13–2:21 Biographical account in support of these statements: — *Om:* (γάρ); Mp(s), H. *Cm:* See above.

>>>a. 1:13–24 Reminder of how Paul, with little contact with the apostles, abandoned his former life as a persecutor of the church and a Jew zealous for the law and began to proclaim the persecuted faith — *Om:* See above. *Cm:* Re.

>>>>α. 1:13–14 Paul's background as a persecutor of the church and a successful Jew, zealous for the law — *Om:* See above.

>>>>β. 1:15–17 Withdrawal into Arabia after receiving the commission to proclaim the Son of God among the Gentiles — *Om:* δέ; Chr, Top.

>>>>γ. 1:18–20 Brief meeting with Peter and James after three years — *Om:* Asyn; Chr, Top. *Cm:* Ass.

---

[100] See pp. 70 f.

δ. 1:21–24 Journey to Syria and Cilicia, with no contact with the Judaean churches — *Om: Asyn; Chr, Top. Cm: See above.*

b. 2:1–10 Confirmation of Paul and his gospel after 14 years by those who are of repute in Jerusalem — *Om: Asyn; Chr, Re, Top. Cm: (δέ)... ἵνα... ἵνα... ὅ, Re, Tsum.*

α. 2:1–5 Background: Paul seeks confirmation from those of repute in Jerusalem, after false brothers have insisted on circumcision — *Om: See above. Cm: ἵνα, Re.*

β. 2:6–10 Confirmation: Paul and his gospel are accepted without addition — *Om: δέ; Top; Int. Cm: See above.*

c. 2:11–21 Paul defends the truth of the gospel in an address to Peter in Antioch: Paul's gospel entails crucifixion with Christ and dying to the law in order to live to God — *Om: δέ; Chr, Top. Cm: See above.*

α. 2:11–13 Background: Peter and the other Jews in Antioch have drawn back from eating with the Gentiles for fear of the circumcised — *Om: See above.*

β. 2:14–21 Address — *Om: ἀλλά; Mp(s)/Mc, Chr, Re.*

α'. 2:14a–b Quotation formula — *Om: See above.*

β'. 2:14c–21 Quotation — *Om: Q. Cm: See above.*

α". 2:14c Critical question about Peter's conduct: Why is he trying to compel the Gentiles to live like Jews, if he does not do so himself? — *Om: See above.*

β". 2:15–16 What Paul and Peter have in common: They are both Jews who know that a person is justified by the faith of (or faith in) Christ, not by the works of the law — *Om: Asyn; Top.*

γ". 2:17–21 Paul's gospel means that he has been crucified with Christ and died to the law, in order to live to God, and he does not nullify this grace of God — *Om: δέ; Q. Cm: See above.*

3. 3:1–4:11 Argument for Paul and his gospel: The Galatians did not receive the Spirit by the works of the law, but by hearing Paul's gospel with faith — *Om: Asyn; Mp, Q, Re; Ad, Int. Cm: Ass, Re; Int.*

A. 3:1–5 Rhetorical questions appealing to the Galatians' own experience of receiving the Spirit as a result of faith on hearing the proclamation of Christ crucified — *Om: See above. Cm:* οὖν, *Re.*

B. 3:6–4:7 Comparison with what was foreseen by Scripture — *Om:* (καθώς); *Top. Cm:* ὥστε, *Re.*

   a. 3:6–14 Comparison with what Scripture says about Abraham's faith and the law: — *Om: See above. Cm:* ἵνα, *Re.*

      α. 3:6–7 Those who are of faith are the sons of Abraham — *Om: See above. Cm:* ἄρα, *Re.*

      β. 3:8–9 Those who are of faith are blessed with Abraham who had faith — *Om:* δέ; *Mp(s)/Mc. Cm:* ὥστε, *Re.*

      γ. 3:10–12 All who are of the works of the law are under a curse — *Om:* (γάρ); *Top.*

      δ. 3:13–14 Christ redeemed 'us' from the curse of the law, so that 'we' might receive the promised Spirit through faith — *Om: Asyn; Top. Cm: See above.*

   b. 3:15–4:7 Explanatory comment: — *Om: Asyn; Mp/Mc; Ad. Cm: See above.*

      α. 3:15–18 Discussion concerning the validity of the promise irrespective of the law — *Om: See above. Cm: Re.*

         α'. 3:15–16 Premisses: No one changes a human will once it has been ratified, and the promises were made to Abraham and his offspring — *Om: See above.*

         β'. 3:17–18 Conclusion: A covenant previously ratified by God cannot be annulled by the law — *Om:* δέ; *Mp/Mc, H. Cm: See above.*

      β. 3:19–24 Discussion on the status of the law: — *Om:* οὖν; *Q. Cm:* ὥστε... ἵνα, *Re.*

         α'. 3:19–20 The law was added because of transgressions — *Om: See above.*

         β'. 3:21–22 The law is not opposed to the promises, since it cannot impart life — *Om:* οὖν; *Q. Cm:* ἵνα, *Re.*

         γ'. 3:23–24 The law was 'our' παιδαγωγός until Christ came — *Om:* δέ; *Chr. Cm: See above.*

γ. 3:25–29 Discussion concerning the situation now that faith has come: In Christ, the Galatians are Abraham's offspring and heirs according to the promise — *Om:* δέ; *Chr.* *Cm:* ἄρα, Ass, Re.

δ. 4:1–7 Summary and clarification: — *Om:* δέ; Mp/Mc. *Cm:* See above.

α'. 4:1–2 Statement of the position regarding human wills: Heirs remain under guardians until a set date — *Om:* See above.

β'. 4:3–6 Application to 'us': — *Om:* Asyn, Top.

α". 4:3 'Our' situation as minors, enslaved to the elemental spirits of the world — *Om:* See above.

β". 4:4–5 God sent his Son to adopt 'us' as sons — *Om:* δέ; Chr.

γ". 4:6 God sent the Spirit of his Son into 'our' hearts — *Om:* δέ.

γ'. 4:7 Consequence for 'you' (singular): 'you' are a son and heir — *Om:* (ὥστε). *Cm:* See above.

C. 4:8–11 Concluding critical question, asked against the background of the Galatians' experience and the comparison with what was foreseen by Scripture: How can the Galatians, who have come to know and be known by God, turn back to the weak elemental spirits? — *Om:* ἀλλά; Q, Re. *Cm:* See above.

4. 4:12–5:10 Exhortations to the Galatians to decide in favour of Paul and his gospel and not let themselves be circumcised — *Om:* Asyn; Mp/Mc; Ad. *Cm:* Ass, Re, Esch; Ad, Int, ἴδε.

A. 4:12–20 Exhortation to the Galatians to become like Paul, in the light of their earlier attitude to him in his weakness — *Om:* See above. *Cm:* Ass, Re; Ad.

a. 4:12 The exhortation and a reference to their earlier attitude — *Om:* See above.

b. 4:13–14 Reminder of their earlier attitude: They received him in his weakness — *Om:* δέ; Mp(s).

c. 4:15–20 Critical discussion of their present attitude against that background — *Om:* οὖν; Q, Re. *Cm:* See above.

α. 4:15–16 Critical questions about their present attitude: What has become of their enthusiasm? — *Om:* See above. *Cm:* ὥστε, Re.

199

β. 4:17–20 Statements about what Paul's opponents want of the Galatians and what Paul wants — *Om:* Asyn. *Cm: See above.*

B. 4:21–5:1 Exhortation to the Galatians to stand firm, in the light of an allegorical exposition of Scripture — *Om: Asyn; Mp/Mc; Ad. Cm:* διό... οὖν, Ex, Re; Ad.

a. 4:21–24a Account of what Scripture says about Abraham's two sons: One is the son of the slave woman, born according to the flesh, the other the son of the free woman, born through the promise — *Om: See above. Cm:* ἅτινα, Ass.

b. 4:24b–27 General identification of the sons: The first represents the children of the Sinaitic covenant, the second the children of the Jerusalem above — *Om: (γάρ)*

c. 4:28–30 Application of this testimony of Scripture to the Galatians: It is 'according to' the persecuted Isaac that they are children of the promise — *Om:* δέ; *Top; Ad. Cm: Ass.*

d. 4:31–5:1 Conclusion about 'us' and exhortation to 'you': Stand firm in freedom, as 'we' do — *Om: (διό); Top; Ad. Cm: See above.*

C. 5:2–10 Concluding authoritative pronouncements — *Om: Asyn; Mp/Mc; Int. Cm: See above.*

a. 5:2–6 Statement of the consequences for the Galatians of letting themselves be circumcised: They will fall away from grace and have to obey the entire law — *Om: See above.*

b. 5:7–10 Concluding critical question in the light of the earlier, favourable attitude of the Galatians: Who prevented them from obeying the truth? — *Om: Asyn; Re; Int. Cm: See above.*

5. 5:11–6:13 Assessment of the conduct of Paul's opponents and exhortations to the Galatians in the light of his persecution and the cross of Christ — *Om:* δέ; Q, H, Re, Top; Ad. *Cm: Ass, Re; Int,* ἴδετε.

A. 5:11–13a Account of the adverse consequences which the preaching of circumcision would have for Paul: There would be no persecution and the offence of the cross would be made ineffective — *Om: See above.*

B. 5:13b–6:10 Exhortations to the Galatians in the light of the assessment in 5:11–13a: — *Om:* μόνον; *Mp; Ad. Cm:* ἄρα οὖν, *Re.*

a. 5:13b–15 Opening exhortations not to give the flesh an opportunity, but to serve one another in love — *Om: See above. Cm: Ass.*

b. 5:16–26 Clarification: — *Om:* δέ; *Mp/Mc. Cm:* Ass, Re.

α. 5:16–17 Opening exhortations: Walk in the Spirit and do not gratify the desires of the flesh — *Om: See above.*

β. 5:18–23 Discussion about how the Spirit-led life relates to the law: — *Om:* δέ; *H. Cm:* Tsum, Re.

α'. 5:18 Assertion that 'you' are not subject to the law if 'you' are led by the Spirit — *Om: See above.*

β'. 5:19–21 Listing of the works of the flesh, which do not result in an inheritance in the kingdom of God — *Om:* δέ. *Cm:* Ass, Tsum.

γ'. 5:22–23 Listing of the fruits of the Spirit, which are not in conflict with the law — *Om:* δέ; *Top. Cm: See above.*

γ. 5:24–26 Concluding exhortations in the light of 'our' belonging to Christ and 'our' crucifixion of the flesh: Let 'us' be in line with the Spirit and not seek vain glory — *Om:* δέ; *Top. Cm: See above.*

c. 6:1–9 Exhortations to the Galatians about what to do if someone falls: — *Om:* Asyn; H; Ad. *Cm:* Re.

α. 6:1 Opening exhortation: Restore the person who has fallen in a spirit of gentleness, but take care not to be tempted yourselves — *Om: See above.*

β. 6:2–6 Exhortations which develop on the first part of the opening exhortation: Bear one another's burdens, but test your own work — *Om:* Asyn.

γ. 6:7–9 Exhortations which develop on the second part: Do not be deceived; do what is right — *Om:* Asyn. *Cm: See above.*

d. 6:10 General concluding exhortation: Let 'us' work for the good of all, and especially for those of the family of faith — *Om:* (ἄρα οὖν); *H. Cm: See above.*

C. 6:11–13 Account of what Paul's opponents are trying to achieve by preaching circumcision: They want to make a good showing in the flesh and wish only to avoid persecution for the cross of Christ — *Om:* Asyn; *Int. Cm: See above.*

6. 6:14–16 Concluding wish concerning Paul and all who follow the same standard as he does: May he not boast of anything except the cross of Christ, and may peace and mercy be upon those who follow his example — *Om:* δέ; *Mp, Re, Top. Cm: See above (1:6–6:17).*

Markers and Meaning in Paul

7. 6:17 Concluding exhortation with the character of a summary and ultimatum: From now on, no one should make trouble for Paul, since he carries the marks of Jesus on his body — *Om:* Asyn; Mp, Chr, Re. *Cm:* See above (1:6–6:17).

III. 6:18 Closing of the letter: Wish of grace

D. Transition markers

For comments regarding the arrangement of this section, readers are referred to the introductory chapter and to the corresponding part of the analysis of 1 Thessalonians.[101]

Interaction

The transition markers in Galatians interact in largely the same way as in 1 Thessalonians and Philippians. In this letter, too, the various opening and closing markers clearly interact and are interdependent. There is no need to provide specific examples of this here, since it was illustrated in the analysis of 1 Thessalonians.[102] It can also be noted that in Galatians, as in the other epistles studied, transitions are generally more strongly marked at higher levels of division of the text than at lower levels, and that the differences between the levels are greater in the case of closing markers than when it comes to opening markers. This is shown by the following table of the average numbers of markers recorded per transition at the different levels of division:

	Transition markers	Opening markers	Closing markers
1st level	10.4	5	5.4
2nd level	4.8	2.6	2.2
3rd level	4.4	2.6	1.8
4th level	3.3	2.1	1.2
5th level	2.1	1.6	0.5
6th level	1.7	1.7	0

The reasons for these differences are naturally the same as in 1 Thessalonians.

[101] See pp. 33 f. and 74.
[102] See pp. 75.

202

Instructive and thematic opening markers

As far as instructive and thematic opening markers are concerned, Galatians differs in one respect from the other two letters examined. In 1 Thessalonians and Philippians, there were no rhetorical questions with this function; in Galatians, such questions make up over a third of the instructive and thematic opening markers recorded.[103] Their function in terms of providing instructions to the recipients is complex, since the metapropositional base indicated by the interrogative form *per se* — 'I ask' or some similar expression — is purely formal. The real function of these rhetorical questions emerges from the interaction between their propositions and various factors in their literary and historical context. Without wishing to delve into this too deeply, I would argue that the opening-marking questions found in Galatians are of two kinds: either they introduce the issue to be discussed in the new section[104] or they serve to rebuke or to express an unfavourable assessment.[105]

In other respects, we can discern the same tendencies as regards instructive and thematic opening markers in Galatians as in 1 Thessalonians and Philippians. Here, too, we find that at the highest levels of division of the text there is, within this category, a predominance of markers which indicate in one way or another what the sender wants to achieve with regard to the addressees and thus emphasize the pragmatic dimension of the communicative act. Thus in 1:6 the letter body as a whole begins with the metapropositional base θαυμάζω, which expresses an unfavourable assessment, and a proposition concerning the addressees' conduct (ὅτι... μετατίθεσθε...). The opening construction of 1:11–2:21 is not of this type, however, consisting instead of a metapropositional base indicating that what follows is to be regarded as information (γνωρίζω... ὑμῖν) and of a proposition relating to Paul's gospel. Nevertheless, this section is fairly closely linked to the assessments expressed in the previous section (especially if the reading with γάρ is chosen). The statement of the theme is reinforced by the proleptic construction (γνωρίζω... τὸ εὐαγγέλιον... ὅτι οὐκ ἔστιν...). The section 3:1–4:11 begins with a number of rhetorical questions, several of which primarily serve to express an adverse appraisal of the addressees' conduct. The key theme-indicating question is marked by an explicit statement of the metapropositional base and a cataphoric text-summarizing τοῦτο (3:2 τοῦτο μόνον θέλω μαθεῖν ἀφ' ὑμῶν). The next main section, 4:12–5:10, opens with a direct exhortation to the addressees, in which the metapropositional base is given extra emphasis by being made explicit after the exhortation itself (δέομαι ὑμῶν). In 5:11–6:13 we find an opening rhetorical question which

---

[103] 2:14c, 17; 3:1, 19, 21; 4:8 f., 15, 21; 5:11
[104] 2:17; 3:19, 21
[105] 2:14; 3:1; 4:8 f., 15 f., 21; 5:7

expresses an unfavourable view of the conduct of Paul's opponents, followed by a statement of what they ought to do. The following section, 6:14–16, does admittedly begin with a wish regarding the sender, but it is followed by a wish of peace upon all those who follow his example, among whom the sender naturally hopes to find his addressees. The concluding section, 6:17, opens with an exhortation aimed at the recipients of the letter.

Thus, all the sections at the highest level of division of the text, apart from 1:11–2:21, begin with constructions which in one way or another highlight the pragmatic aspect of the communicative act. In a couple of cases, in the opening verses of the major sections 3:1–4:11 and 4:12–5:10, we also noted that the metapropositional base was given particular emphasis by being made explicit, even though it had already been indicated by the construction of the proposition.

At lower levels, constructions which give prominence to the pragmatic dimension only occur at the beginning of the concluding section 4:8–11, which looks back to the opening of the first-level section 3:1–4:11; at the beginning of 4:15–20; and at the beginning of the paraenetic section 5:13b–6:10. In the first two of these cases, the constructions consist of rhetorical questions expressing unfavourable assessments, and in the third the metapropositional base is only indicated by the imperative forms. At other lower-level transitions, we primarily find opening-marking constructions consisting of metapropositional bases which are either volitionally neutral (λέγω[106] or rhetorical questions not expressing an assessment[107]) or secondary (ἠκούσατε,[108] εἶπον,[109] προευηγγελίσατο,[110] οἴδατε,[111] reported questions[112]); and of propositions which relate to the sender or to persons or concepts expressed in the third person. The second-level section 4:21–5:1 is introduced by a special kind of construction (λέγετέ μοι... τὸν νόμον οὐκ ἀκούετε...). It comprises metapropositional bases at three different levels ('I command you'; 'to tell me'; 'whether you listen to...'), the first of which expresses the will of the sender, but not the other two. The construction as a whole incorporates an element of assessment, but nevertheless chiefly serves to introduce the new theme of 'what the law says'.

At lower levels, there are also openings which contain thematic statements, but lack instructions at the metapropositional level. This is the case in 4:28 (third level), for example, where the change of grammatical subject emphasized

[106] 1:9; 3:15, 17; 4:1; 5:2, 16
[107] 3:19, 21
[108] 1:13
[109] 2:14
[110] 3:8
[111] 4:13
[112] 2:14c, 17

by the use of ὑμεῖς signals something of a shift in topic, but no metapropositional instructions are given. It should also be noted that references to times, places and people play a key role as thematic opening markers in narrative sections of the letter, chiefly in 1:13–2:21, but also in 3:23 ff. and 4:3 ff., for example.

Instructive and thematic closing markers

In 1 Thessalonians and Philippians we observed that instructive and thematic closing markers showed the same kinds of variation between the different levels of division of the text as instructive and thematic opening markers, to which they of course corresponded. This is the case in Galatians, too.

At the highest level we generally find closings in which the pragmatic dimension of the communicative act is highlighted. Thus the first section setting forth Paul's argument (1:6–10) closes with the pronouncement of an anathema in 1:8 ff., corresponding to the unfavourable opening appraisal of developments in Galatia (1:6). As for the second argument section (1:11–2:21), we noted above that, unlike the other sections at this level, it does not begin with a statement of what the sender wants of the addressees or of his assessment of their conduct or characteristics, but instead refers back to the appraisals expressed in the preceding section. The end of this section looks much the same: there is no such statement there, either. The following section (3:1–4:12), on the other hand, begins with a rhetorical question expressing an assessment, which clearly follows up the account given in the preceding section and echoes the assessment expressed in 1:6–10. This, the third and final argument section, then concludes in 4:8–11 with a rhetorical question (4:8 f.) and an assessment (4:11), which shed an unfavourable light on the addressees and their conduct and clearly look back to the assessments in 3:1–5 and 1:6–10. At the end of the first exhortatory section (4:12–5:10), we then find a similar rhetorical question (5:7) and assessment (5:10). The second exhortatory section (5:11–6:13) is rounded off with assertions about Paul's opponents and their aims (6:11–13). Naturally, these assertions indirectly express assessments and positions, but the metapropositional base, which is not stated explicitly, is probably volitionally neutral (λέγω or the like).[113] However, this section is followed by a short one containing wishes (6:14–16) and a closing exhortation (6:17) which more explicitly highlight the pragmatic dimension.[114]

---

[113] Cf. 5:2–6.
[114] 1:6: θαυμάζω ὅτι οὕτως ταχέως μετατίθεσθε ἀπὸ τοῦ καλέσαντος ὑμᾶς ἐν χάριτι [Χριστοῦ] εἰς ἕτερον εὐαγγέλιον,...

Markers and Meaning in Paul

In the exhortatory sections (4:12–5:10; 5:11–6:13), consequence-indicating recurrences which state what the sender wants of the addressees or how he assesses their conduct or attitudes also occur in closings at the second level of division of the text, and to a certain extent at the third and fourth levels, too. Expressions of this type conclude the following sections: 4:12–20,[115] 4:21–5:1 (5:1 οὖν)[116] and 5:13b–6:10 (6:10 ἄρα οὖν)[117] at the second level; 5:16–26 (5:25 f. εἰ..., ...)[118] at the third level; and 4:15 f. (4:16 ὥστε)[119] at the fourth level. At the fourth level, in the exhortatory sections too, we find a consequence-indicating recurrence which does not express the will or assessment of the sender concerning the addressees, namely at the end of 5:18–23 (5:23 κατὰ τῶν τοιούτων).[120]

In the argument sections (1:6–10; 1:11–2:21; 3:1–4:11), at other levels than the first, we only find consequence-indicating recurrences which do not express an assessment or the will of the sender. Such constructions occur in the closing passages of the following sections: 1:13–2:21,[121] 3:1–5 (3:1 οὖν)[122]

1:8 ff.: ἀλλὰ καὶ ἐὰν ἡμεῖς ἢ ἄγγελος ἐξ οὐρανοῦ εὐαγγελίζηται [ὑμῖν] παρ' ὃ εὐηγγελισάμεθα ὑμῖν, ἀνάθεμα ἔστω.
3:1–5: τίς ὑμᾶς ἐβάσκανεν, οἷς κατ' ὀφθαλμοὺς Ἰησοῦς Χριστὸς προεγράφη ἐσταυρωμένος;
4:8–11: ἀλλά... γνόντες θεόν, μᾶλλον δὲ γνωσθέντες ὑπὸ θεοῦ, πῶς ἐπιστρέφετε πάλιν ἐπὶ τὰ ἀσθενῆ καὶ πτωχὰ στοιχεῖα...; ... φοβοῦμαι ὑμᾶς μή πως εἰκῇ κεκοπίακα εἰς ὑμᾶς.
5:7–10: ... τίς ὑμᾶς ἐνέκοψεν [τῇ] ἀληθείᾳ μὴ πείθεσθαι; ... ἐγὼ πέποιθα εἰς ὑμᾶς ἐν κυρίῳ ὅτι οὐδὲν ἄλλο φρονήσετε· ὁ δὲ ταράσσων ὑμᾶς βαστάσει τὸ κρίμα, ὅστις ἐὰν ᾖ.
6:14 ff.: ἐμοὶ δὲ μὴ γένοιτο καυχᾶσθαι εἰ μὴ ἐν τῷ σταυρῷ τοῦ κυρίου ἡμῶν Ἰησοῦ Χριστοῦ... καὶ ὅσοι τῷ κανόνι τούτῳ στοιχήσουσιν, εἰρήνη ἐπ' αὐτοὺς...
[115] 4:12: γίνεσθε ὡς ἐγώ, ὅτι κἀγὼ ὡς ὑμεῖς... οὐδέν με ἠδικήσατε
4:18 ff.: καλὸν δὲ ζηλοῦσθαι ἐν καλῷ πάντοτε καὶ μὴ μόνον ἐν τῷ παρεῖναί με πρὸς ὑμᾶς...
[116] (4:12: γίνεσθε ὡς ἐγώ, ὅτι κἀγὼ ὡς ὑμεῖς... οὐδέν με ἠδικήσατε)
5:1: στήκετε οὖν...
[117] 5:13: ... διὰ τῆς ἀγάπης δουλεύετε ἀλλήλοις.
6:10: ἄρα οὖν... ἐργαζώμεθα τὸ ἀγαθὸν πρὸς πάντας, μάλιστα δὲ πρὸς τοὺς οἰκείους τῆς πίστεως.
[118] 5:16: πνεύματι περιπατεῖτε καὶ ἐπιθυμίαν σαρκὸς οὐ μὴ τελέσητε.
5:25 f.: εἰ ζῶμεν πνεύματι, πνεύματι καὶ στοιχῶμεν. μὴ γινώμεθα κενόδοξοι...
[119] 4:15: ποῦ οὖν ὁ μακαρισμὸς ὑμῶν;
4:16: ὥστε ἐχθρὸς ὑμῶν γέγονα ἀληθεύων ὑμῖν;
[120] 5:18: εἰ δὲ πνεύματι ἄγεσθε, οὐκ ἐστὲ ὑπὸ νόμον.
5:23: κατὰ τῶν τοιούτων οὐκ ἔστιν νόμος.
[121] 1:15 f.: ... εὐδόκησεν [ὁ θεὸς] ὁ... καλέσας διὰ τῆς χάριτος αὐτοῦ ἀποκαλύψαι τὸν υἱὸν αὐτοῦ ἐν ἐμοί...
2:20 f.: ... ἐν πίστει ζῶ τῇ τοῦ υἱοῦ τοῦ θεοῦ... οὐκ ἀθετῶ τὴν χάριν τοῦ θεοῦ.
[122] 3:2: ἐξ ἔργων νόμου τὸ πνεῦμα ἐλάβετε ἢ ἐξ ἀκοῆς πίστεως;
3:5: ὁ οὖν ἐπιχορηγῶν ὑμῖν τὸ πνεῦμα..., ἐξ ἔργων νόμου ἢ ἐξ ἀκοῆς πίστεως;

and 3:6–4:7 (4:7 ὥστε)[123] at the second level; 1:13–24,[124] 2:1–10[125] and 3:6–14 (3:14 ἵνα)[126] at the third level; and 2:14c–21,[127] 3:6–7 (3:7 ἄρα),[128] 3:8–9 (3:9 ὥστε),[129] 3:15–17,[130] 3:19–24 (3:24 ὥστε... ἵνα)[131] and 3:25–29 (3:29 εἰ..., ἄρα...)[132] at the fourth and fifth levels.

Concerning these statements of consequences, it may be noted that it is more common in Galatians than in 1 Thessalonians and Philippians for them not to be introduced by a consequence-indicating particle. This is not only true of the short wish section 6:14–16 and the closing exhortation in 6:17, which bring the entire letter body to a close; it applies to all the statements of consequences at the first level of text division and also some of those at the second and third levels.[133] Other statements of consequences at the second level are introduced by coordinating particles, and some of those at lower levels assume the form of subordinate constructions or contain anaphoric text-summarizing expressions.

In Galatians, Paul rarely applies an eschatological perspective in closing passages. He only does so at the end of the first exhortatory section (4:12–

---

[123] 3:6–14: ... οἱ ἐκ πίστεως... υἱοί εἰσιν 'Αβραάμ... Χριστὸς ἡμᾶς ἐξηγόρασεν... ἵνα ... ἡ εὐλογία τοῦ 'Αβραὰμ γένηται ἐν Χριστῷ 'Ιησοῦ, ἵνα τὴν ἐπαγγελίαν τοῦ πνεύματος λάβωμεν διὰ τῆς πίστεως.
4:4–7: ... ἐξαπέστειλεν ὁ θεὸς τὸν υἱὸν αὐτοῦ... ἵνα... ἐξαγοράσῃ, ἵνα τὴν υἱοθεσίαν ἀπολάβωμεν. ὅτι δέ ἐστε υἱοί, ἐξαπέστειλεν ὁ θεὸς τὸ πνεῦμα τοῦ υἱοῦ αὐτοῦ εἰς τὰς καρδίας ἡμῶν... ὥστε οὐκέτι εἶ δοῦλος ἀλλὰ υἱός.
[124] 1:13–16: ... ποτέ... ἐδίωκον τὴν ἐκκλησίαν τοῦ θεοῦ καὶ ἐπόρθουν αὐτήν... δὲ εὐδόκησεν [ὁ θεός]... ἀποκαλύψαι τὸν υἱὸν αὐτοῦ ἐν ἐμοί, ἵνα εὐαγγελίζωμαι αὐτόν...
1:23: μόνον δὲ ἀκούοντες ἦσαν ὅτι ὁ διώκων ἡμᾶς ποτε νῦν εὐαγγελίζεται τὴν πίστιν ἥν ποτε ἐπόρθει,...
[125] 2:2: καὶ ἀνεθέμην αὐτοῖς τὸ εὐαγγέλιον ὃ κηρύσσω ἐν τοῖς ἔθνεσιν,...
2:7 ff.: ... ἰδόντες ὅτι πεπίστευμαι τὸ εὐαγγέλιον τῆς ἀκροβυστίας... καὶ γνόντες τὴν χάριν τὴν δοθεῖσάν μοι,... δεξιὰς ἔδωκαν ἐμοί...
[126] 3:9: ... οἱ ἐκ πίστεως εὐλογοῦνται σὺν τῷ πιστῷ 'Αβραάμ.
3:14: ἵνα εἰς τὰ ἔθνη ἡ εὐλογία τοῦ 'Αβραὰμ γένηται ἐν Χριστῷ 'Ιησοῦ, ἵνα τὴν ἐπαγγελίαν τοῦ πνεύματος λάβωμεν διὰ τῆς πίστεως.
[127] 2:16: εἰδότες [δὲ] ὅτι οὐ δικαιοῦται ἄνθρωπος ἐξ ἔργων νόμου ἐὰν μὴ διὰ πίστεως 'Ιησοῦ Χριστοῦ, καὶ ἡμεῖς εἰς Χριστὸν 'Ιησοῦν ἐπιστεύσαμεν...
2:21: οὐκ ἀθετῶ τὴν χάριν τοῦ θεοῦ· εἰ γὰρ διὰ νόμου δικαιοσύνη, ἄρα Χριστὸς δωρεὰν ἀπέθανεν.
[128] 3:6: ... 'Αβραὰμ ἐπίστευσεν τῷ θεῷ...
3:7: γινώσκετε ἄρα ὅτι οἱ ἐκ πίστεως... υἱοί εἰσιν 'Αβραάμ.
[129] (3:7: γινώσκετε ἄρα ὅτι οἱ ἐκ πίστεως... υἱοί εἰσιν 'Αβραάμ)
3:9: ὥστε οἱ ἐκ πίστεως εὐλογοῦνται σὺν τῷ πιστῷ 'Αβραάμ.
[130] 3:15: ... κατὰ ἄνθρωπον λέγω·
3:17: τοῦτο δὲ λέγω·
[131] 3:19: τί οὖν ὁ νόμος;
3:24: ὥστε ὁ νόμος παιδαγωγὸς ἡμῶν γέγονεν...
[132] (3:16: τῷ δὲ 'Αβραὰμ ἐρρέθησαν αἱ ἐπαγγελίαι καὶ τῷ σπέρματι αὐτοῦ..., ὅς ἐστιν Χριστός)
3:29: εἰ δὲ ὑμεῖς Χριστοῦ, ἄρα τοῦ 'Αβραὰμ σπέρμα ἐστέ, κατ' ἐπαγγελίαν κληρονόμοι.
[133] *Second level:* 4:18 ff. (4:12–20). *Third level:* 1:23 f. (1:13–24); 2:6–10 (2:1–10).

5:10), where he expresses the conviction that his opponents will pay the penalty.[134]

Contrastive opening markers

Opening markers of this type occur more frequently in Galatians than in 1 Thessalonians or Philippians. In those letters, it was relatively common for lower-level transitions to lack contrastive markers; in Galatians, they generally occur at lower as well as higher levels of division of the text.

Concerning the character of these markers, it may be noted that asyndeton and the balancing adversative particle δέ are far and away the commonest types: they occur 18 and 20 times, respectively, and at more or less all the levels considered here.[135] Asyndeton is somewhat more frequent than δέ at the higher levels, and the converse is true at the lower levels.[136] In addition, οὖν occurs as a transition marker three times in all, at the third to the fifth levels — always in conjunction with rhetorical questions; ἀλλά twice, at the second and fourth levels; and μόνον once, at the second level of text division.[137]

Attention-attracting and intensity-heightening transition markers

In Galatians, as in the other letters studied, markers belonging to this category occur primarily at the highest levels of division of the text and in conjunction with the opening and closing of major sections. Here, too, the use of an address is the commonest type, occurring twelve times in the body of the letter. As an opening marker, it occurs in all the major sections at the first level,[138] at the beginning of two major sections at the second level[139] and at the beginning of two long and two short sections at the third level.[140] One of the short sections serves as a conclusion, and there the address perhaps functions primarily as a closing marker.[141] More unambiguous examples of

---

[134] It is interesting that Paul makes greater use of eschatological motifs in the 'positive' First Letter to the Thessalonians and Letter to the Philippians, than in the 'negative' Letter to the Galatians. Does this mean that he is more inclined to use such motifs to comfort and encourage than to threaten?

[135] The particle δέ is not found at the second level, but this is presumably a coincidence, since it occurs at every other level, including the first.

[136] *First level:* Asyndeton: 3:1; 4:12; 6:17; δέ: 5:11; 6:14 (possibly also 1:11). *Second level:* Asyndeton: 1:9; 4:21; 5:2; 6:11. *Fifth level:* Asyndeton: 4:3; δέ: 3:17, 23; 5:18, 22. *Sixth level:* Asyndeton: 2:15; δέ: 2:17; 4:4, 6.

[137] οὖν: 3:19, 21; 4:15; ἀλλά: 2:14; 4:8; μόνον: 5:13b.

[138] 1:11–2:21; 3:1–4:11; 4:12–5:10; 5:11–6:13.

[139] 4:21–5:1; 5:13b–6:10.

[140] Long sections: 3:15–4:7; 6:1–10. Short sections: 4:28–30; 4:31–5:1.

[141] 4:31–5:1, which brings to a close the second-level section 4:21–5:1.

address forms serving as closing markers are those in 4:19 and 5:4, which occur within 4:17–20 and 5:2–10, i.e. the sections which bring to a close 4:12–20 (second level) and 4:12–5:10 (first level).

Eight of the twelve cases of an address consist of the word ἀδελφοί alone. At the beginning of the major section 4:21–5:1, the address used is οἱ ὑπὸ νόμον θέλοντες εἶναι, which presumably also serves as a rebuke, since it is followed by the question τὸν νόμον οὐκ ἀκούετε. By contrast, the address οἵτινες ἐν νόμῳ δικαιοῦσθε in the concluding section 5:2–10 (5:4) probably has a classificatory function, while τέκνα μου at the end of 4:12–20 emphasizes the close relationship between Paul and the Galatians, as well as preparing for the imagery of the following relative clause.

In four instances, the address is in initial position. In 3:1, where it is emphatic, it breaks off the preceding account and returns the text to the present communication between Paul and the Galatians, but in the other three cases it introduces sections of a clearly subordinate character (3:15–4:7; 5:13b–6:10; 6:1–10). Elsewhere, the address occurs within a clause[142] or between clauses which are closely linked.[143]

One instance of an address serving as an opening marker and one serving as a closing marker occur together with other attention-attracting or intensity-heightening phenomena. They are the address in 3:1, which is given extra emphasis by the initial ὦ and is followed by a number of short, asyndetic rhetorical questions of a repetitive character; and the address in 5:4, which forms part of the section 5:2–10, where the intensity is also heightened by the attention-attracting ἴδε in 5:2, the intensified restart in 5:3 and a construction made up of many short, asyndetic sentences. In addition, we observed a heightening of intensity in the concluding section 6:11–13, resulting from the attention-attracting ἴδετε, the emphatic construction ὅσοι... οὗτοι and a certain amount of repetition. All three of these passages with heightened intensity are opening or closing passages of major sections at the first level of text division (3:1–4:11; 4:12–5:10; 5:11–6:13).

E. Implications for the line of thought in the letter

Concerning the purpose and arrangement of this section, readers are referred to chapter 1 and the corresponding part of the analysis of 1 Thessalonians.[144]

---

[142] 1:11; 4:28, 31; 5:11.
[143] 4:12, 19, 21; 5:4.
[144] See pp. 34 and 81.

Overall structure of the letter

Galatians is generally held to be concerned with one problem and to have one purpose. The problem, it is argued, is that someone, or a group of people, is trying to persuade the Galatians to let themselves be circumcised, and the purpose of the letter is to seek to prevent this and to persuade the Galatians to stand firm with Paul and his gospel.[145] The arrangement of the text that emerges from my basic analysis gives us no cause to question these views. It does, though, affect our understanding of the actual argument of the letter, showing it to be more uniform than is often assumed.

According to the basic analysis, the body of the Letter to the Galatians falls into seven parts: 1:6–10, 1:11–2:21, 3:1–4:11, 4:12–5:10, 5:11–6:13, 6:14–16 and 6:17. Of these, the first three consist of argumentation and are connected in such a way that they can be said to constitute one argument made up of three steps. The fourth and fifth sections are fundamentally exhortatory. There is a clear link between them, and they refer back to the argument of the first three sections. The sixth section is a short, closing passage containing wishes, while the seventh consists of a final exhortation.

Paul's line of reasoning begins in 1:6–10 with an unfavourable assessment of developments in Galatia, which are described in terms of the Galatians falling away from his gospel (1:6 ff.), and with an initial argument in favour of himself and his gospel: Paul is seeking to please God, not people, thus proving himself to be a servant of Christ (1:9 f.). The arrangement of the text that we have arrived at places this argument in the short, accentuated opening section of the letter body, giving it extra emphasis and hinting at its fundamental significance for the overall argument.

The second argument section (1:11–2:21) then begins with an instructive and thematic construction which makes it clear that this section is intended to show that Paul's gospel is not according to man. Its function is probably to explain why Paul would not have been a servant of Christ if he had pleased people.[146] This is confirmed by the concluding address in 2:14c–21, in which Paul explains that his gospel means that he has been 'co-crucified' with Christ (Χριστῷ συνεσταύρωμαι) and has died to the law, in order to live to God (2:19), and that he does not nullify this grace of God (2:21); both these choices of phrasing can be said to echo the opening statement in 1:11 and to explain the argument in 1:10. They also tie in closely with the opening section (1:13–24) of the biographical account (1:13–2:21), in which Paul describes how he was called through the grace of God, abandoned his former life as a successful Jew, zealous for the law, and a persecutor of the church and instead

---

[145] See e.g. Kümmel 1983, pp. 260–3; Guthrie 1973, pp. 11 f.; Dunn 1993a, pp. 11 f.

[146] The section probably serves this function whether we choose the reading with γάρ or the one with δέ in 1:11.

began to proclaim the persecuted faith (see in particular the opening and closing verses of the section, 1:13 ff. and 1:23 ff.). This shows that the expressions used in 2:19 ff. really are central to this second argument section, lending further support to the assumption that the ultimate purpose of 1:11–2:21 is to underpin and explain the argument in 1:10 by showing that Paul's gospel is not according to man, but entails 'co-crucifixion' with Christ and dying to the law, in order to live for God. In this connection, the reference to conformity with the crucified Christ can probably stand as an argument in its own right in favour of Paul and his gospel. However, it is also supported by other arguments in this section: in 1:12 and 1:13–24 it is pointed out that Paul has not received this gospel from a human being (see especially 1:16 f., 19, 22), but by revelation of Jesus Christ (see in particular 1:15 f.); and in 2:1–10 we are told how his gospel was confirmed without addition by those who were of repute in Jerusalem (see especially 2:6 f., 9).

The third argument section (3:1–4:11) then provides a further argument for this gospel of Paul's concerning the crucified Christ: the Galatians received the Spirit when they accepted it in faith (3:1–5). His gospel, in other words, has not only been confirmed by revelation of Christ and by those of repute in Jerusalem, but also by the giving of the Spirit to the Galatians when they received it in faith. That this argument is basic to the present section is indicated by the fact that — with our arrangement of the text — it is not only expressed in the rhetorical questions at the beginning of the section (3:1–5), but also essentially repeated at the end of the section, in the rhetorical question in 4:8 f., which criticizes the Galatians for turning back to the weak elemental spirits to which they were once enslaved, despite having come to know God, or rather to be known by God (presumably through the Spirit). The reference to the Galatians receiving the Spirit when they accepted Paul's gospel in faith is of course an argument in itself. However, it is also supported in this section by a long discussion (3:6–4:7) which is intended to show that this giving of the Spirit was in addition in accordance with what Scripture foresaw.

This completes the main body of the argument in the letter. The following sections (4:12–5:10; 5:11–6:13) are fundamentally exhortatory in character. They do, however, tie in closely with the preceding argument and, where necessary, draw attention to different aspects of it, thus demonstrating its practical emphasis and purpose.

The first exhortatory section (4:12–5:10) is ultimately concerned with the Galatians deciding in favour of Paul and his gospel. This is indicated by the fact that — as a result of our arrangement of the text — this section begins with an emphatic exhortation to the Galatians to become like Paul (4:12), and by the fact that its second and last major subsection (4:21–5:1) concludes with an exhortation to them to stand firm (5:1). The close connection between these exhortations and the preceding argument is made clear by the fact that the first of them is immediately followed by a reference to Paul's condition when the Galatians previously received him (4:13 f.; cf. 3:1–5) and that the second of them arises from the predictions in the scriptural narrative about Abraham (4:21–31; cf. 3:6–4:7, especially 3:6–9, 3:15–18 and 3:29). In addition, it may be noted that what is given particular prominence in 4:13 f. is that on his earlier visit to the Galatians Paul was in such a condition that he could not please anyone, and that in 4:29 it is specifically pointed out that Isaac, with whom the Galatians are called on to identify (4:28), was persecuted by his half-brother (representing the children of the Sinaitic covenant) and therefore was not a man who pleased people, either (cf. 1:10, 1:13–24 and 2:18–21).

The second exhortatory section (5:11–6:13) consists largely of more specific appeals to the recipients to conduct themselves in certain ways (5:13–6:10). With the arrangement we have arrived at, however, it both opens (5:11 f.) and closes (6:11 ff.) with short sections in which Paul's opponents and their conduct are unfavourably assessed in the light of Paul's persecution and the cross of Christ. What they are accused of in this context is preaching circumcision merely to 'make a good showing in the flesh' and to avoid persecution for the cross of Christ (5:10; 6:12 f.). This accusation provides an explanation for the heavy emphasis placed in the letter on Paul not pleasing people (1:10; 4:13 f.) and not giving in to those who require circumcision and observance of the law (1:13–24; 2:4 f., 14; 5:11), and on his gospel entailing crucifixion with Christ and dying to the law, in order to live to God (2:19; 3:1; cf. also 4:29).[147] It is against the immediate background of these assessments, then, that the exhortations of 5:13–6:10 are addressed to the Galatians. Thus

---

[147] Paul's final assessment of his opponents in 6:12 thus sheds light on the rest of the argument in Galatians and therefore deserves to be taken seriously. What is interesting is that his opponents are accused here of wanting circumcision *only* (μόνον) to avoid persecution. The following γάρ-clause in 6:13 explains this by pointing out that they themselves do not obey the law. In other words, they are accused of not being interested in the law itself, but merely using it as a means of making a good showing (6:12) and being able to boast (6:13) in the flesh, and of avoiding persecution (6:12). This raises questions as to the identity of these opponents. Such a charge does not in fact seem particularly applicable to anti-Pauline Jewish-Christian missionaries or to other Judaizing groups acting mainly on principle (despite Howard 1990, pp. 9 ff.). Rather, it would seem to be levelled at faint-hearted Galatians or some similar group. The present-tense form οὐ περιτεμνόμενοι in 6:13 (if that is the original reading) could also point in that direction (see e.g. Munck 1954, p. 81). Here I merely wish to raise the question. To answer it, a more extensive study would need to be carried out than would be reasonable in the framework of this thesis.

those exhortations, too, are directly linked to the earlier argument of the letter.[148]

The short section containing wishes (6:14–16) and the closing exhortation in 6:17 are fully in line with what has gone before. In sharp contrast to his opponents, who want to make a good showing in the flesh and to avoid persecution for Christ, Paul now declares his desire not to boast of anything except the cross of Christ, by which the world has been crucified to him and he to the world (6:14), after which he points out in his final exhortation that he carries the marks of Christ on his body (6:17).

The line of reasoning that emerges in Galatians as a result of the arrangement of the text arrived at in my basic analysis, then, is broadly as follows: Paul does not give in to those who insist on circumcision and observance of the law, and he is therefore persecuted. His opponents, on the other hand, want to make a good showing in the flesh and are trying to compel the Galatians to be circumcised, merely to avoid persecution. But someone who pleases people in this way is not a servant of Christ, for Paul's gospel entails crucifixion with Christ and dying to the law, in order to live to God. This gospel is something Paul has received, not from a human being, but by revelation of Christ, and it has been confirmed by those who are of repute in Jerusalem and by the fact that the Galatians received the Spirit when they accepted it in faith, entirely in keeping with what was foreseen by Scripture.

The whole of this coherent line of reasoning, as we have seen, serves the practical purpose of persuading the Galatians to stand firm with Paul and his gospel and not to be led astray by his opponents and their preaching of circumcision.

Key motifs

My analyses of 1 Thessalonians and Philippians both resulted in arrangements of the texts which gave greater prominence in those letters to the idea of *imitatio*,[149] with a particular focus on the crucified Christ and the persecuted Paul, than it is commonly assumed to have. The arrangement arrived at in the case of Galatians has similar consequences.

The first hint at this *imitatio* thinking is encountered in 1:10, where the basis for the whole of the subsequent argument is established in a statement of

---

[148] J. M. G. Barclay, too, notes that the exhortations in 5:13–6:10 are directly linked to the earlier argument of the letter and from this fact he concludes that 'these verses are not an independent or dispassionate account of Christian ethics tacked on to the end of an argumentative letter, but a continuation and completion of the argument' (1988, p. 143; see also M. Bachmann 1992, pp. 118–22). In my opinion, it also reveals the practical emphasis and purpose of this argument.

[149] Concerning the use of the term *imitatio* here, see pp. 84 f., note 108.

what Paul is like and what it would mean if he were different (that is, as we eventually see in 5:11 and 6:12 f., like his opponents). The text arrangement that emerges from my basic analysis places this first argument in the accentuated opening section of the letter body (1:6–10), giving it extra emphasis and suggesting that it will play a crucial role in the line of reasoning that follows (see above).

Turning to the next argument section (1:11–2:21), we can note that here the result of the text arrangement that has been established is that the address reported in 2:14c–21 serves to bring this section to a close, which affects our understanding of the section as a whole. What is of importance in this connection is that, in the core part of this address, we find expressions which clearly testify to *imitatio* thinking of the same kind as we found in both 1 Thessalonians and Philippians: they describe how Paul has been 'co-crucified' with Christ and died to the law, in order to live to God (2:19).[150] Now it is no longer he who lives, but Christ who lives in him, and the life he now lives in the flesh he lives by the faith of the Son of God, who loved him and gave himself for him (2:20).[151] Here, then, Christ, and above all Christ crucified, is held up as the principle determining the whole of Paul's life.[152] At the same time, it may be observed that the address to Peter is concerned with the gospel (see 2:14) and deals with basic principles.[153] This means that the 'I' of the address, i.e. Paul, serves as an example.

As has been noted, the fact that 1:11–2:21 is brought to a close in this way affects our understanding of the section as a whole. We observed earlier that the expressions used in the core part of the address tie in closely with the account in 1:13–24 of Paul's conversion, which shows that the nature of his conversion — from a Jew zealous for the law and a persecutor of the church to a man who proclaims the faith he once persecuted — is important in this context and illustrates the implications of Paul's gospel. Similarly, we have seen that the same expressions echo the argument in 1:10, reinforcing the suspicion that the fact that the argument proceeds from a statement about what Paul is like has to do with *imitatio* thinking. If this is the case, then the text of Galatians, too, takes as its starting-point the idea that Paul and ultimately Christ are the standard which the addressees are to follow. The argument is then largely concerned with making this standard credible and drawing attention to its character.

[150] Cf. Phil 3:8–11. Cf. also 1 Thess 1:6 and 2:14 ff.

[151] Cf. Phil 1:21 f.

[152] According to E. Larsson (1962, pp. 93 f.), the statements in Gal 2:19 f. are to be understood in the light of Paul's theology of baptism. They express the idea that Christ and the baptized have a common destiny, but they also have an ethical tendency, as the link with Gal 5:24 makes clear (p. 103).

[153] See p. 163, note 52.

Regarding the third argument section (3:1–4:11), it may be noted that it begins with a rhetorical question (3:1) which looks back to the wording of 2:19 and focuses on the *imitatio* thinking there. It is followed by another rhetorical question (3:2, 5), appealing to what the Galatians experienced as a result of their earlier favourable conduct. This argument, too, with its focus on personal experience, is in keeping with the idea of *imitatio* that is to the fore here.[154] With the demarcation of this section provided by our arrangement of the text, this argument is then also brought into focus at the end of the section. It thus becomes clearer that it is the basic argument of the section and that the comparisons in 3:6–4:7 with what was foreseen by Scripture serve to support it.[155] As regards the long exposition in 3:6–4:7, we can note that the story of Abraham is interpreted typologically (see e.g. 3:6–9) and that the passages describing the situation since the coming of faith (3:25–29; 4:5 ff.) bear clear traces of *imitatio Christi* thinking (see e.g. 3:27, the masculine form εἷς in 3:28, 3:29 in the light of 3:16, and 4:6).

As a result of the proposed arrangement of the text, the first exhortatory section in the letter (4:12–5:10) begins with the exhortation to 'become like me' (4:12). However we interpret the following ὅτι-clause, this exhortation holds Paul up as a standard in some respect. This beginning to the first exhortatory section of the letter corresponds to the starting-point for the preceding argument, i.e. the description in 1:10 (and then in 1:13–2:21) of what sort of a person Paul is. As we have already observed, the exhortation in 4:12 is followed by a reminder of what Paul was like when the Galatians previously received him, with a particular emphasis on his inability to please people. It may also be noted here that the subsection 4:12–20 is brought to a close with an expression in 4:19 which points to the idea of *imitatio*. There it is said that Paul's aim for the Galatians is that Christ should be formed in them (μορφωθῇ Χριστὸς ἐν ὑμῖν). The next subsection, 4:21–5:1, consists chiefly of a typological exposition of the story of Abraham, in which the addressees are encouraged to identify with Isaac (4:28).

Turning next to the second exhortatory section, 5:11–6:13, we find that the text arrangement established by my basic analysis results in the direct exhortations of 5:13b–6:10 being framed by short sections in which the conduct of Paul's opponents is assessed in the light of his persecution and the cross of Christ. Their behaviour is thus measured against the two standards set out in 1:10, 1:13–24 and 2:19, which are thereby brought into focus. The exhortations in 5:13b–6:10 are made to the addressees in express contrast to the conduct of Paul's opponents (5:13 ὑμεῖς γὰρ ἐπ᾽ ἐλευθερίᾳ ἐκλήθητε),

---

[154] Cf. e.g. 1 Thess 1:6 f., where the Thessalonians' *imitatio* of the sender and of Christ is said to result in their becoming examples themselves. Cf. also Phil 3:17, for example.
[155] See also the opening καθώς.

and consequently they, too, are based in the two standards. This link is then expressed in several ways. It comes across most clearly, I believe, in 5:24, which says that those who belong to Christ have crucified the flesh with its passions and desires (cf. 2:19),[156] but it can also be discerned in the repeated references to the law (5:14; 6:2), for example. Once again, then, the arrangement of the text arrived at here brings out more clearly the *imitatio* thinking in the letter.

Finally, it may be observed that Galatians closes with a fresh reminder to the addressees of the two standards laid down in the opening sections of the letter, the persecuted Paul and the crucified Christ. Thus in 6:14, Paul expresses his wish that — in contrast to his opponents (ἐμοὶ δέ...) — he will not boast of anything except the cross of Christ, by which the world has been crucified to him and he to the world, and in 6:17 he declares that he carries the marks of Christ on his body. A clearer expression of the idea of *imitatio* is surely difficult to imagine.

Consequently, in the Letter to the Galatians too, the arrangement of the text that has been identified results in the idea of *imitatio*, with a particular emphasis on the persecuted Paul and the crucified Christ, emerging as a crucial pattern of thought in the text.[157] Once again, therefore, there is reason to ask whether an inability — or perhaps an unwillingness — to recognize this pattern of thought has not been at least a contributory factor behind the difficulties which scholars have experienced in discerning the internal coherence of the epistle.

---

[156] T. Engberg-Pedersen (1993) also links Gal 2:19 and 5:24 and emphasizes the close connection between Paul's ethics and his view of the Christian as 'co-crucified' with Christ (pp. 193, 199 f.). He arrives at this conclusion by reading Galatians 'through Stoic spectacles' (p. 201, my translation).

[157] See also Dunn 1993b, p. 120.

5. Summary and conclusions

The point of departure for this study was a suspicion that inadequate understanding of or insufficient attention to Paul's use of language, combined with powerful and rigid theological expectations, may sometimes have resulted in the texts of the Pauline letters being divided in ways which fail to do justice to the linguistic evidence and which have prevented interpreters from recognizing important links within them. In the light of that suspicion, I defined the object of my study as being (1) to study the use of transition markers in 1 Thessalonians, Philippians and Galatians; (2) to examine what arrangements of the texts these markers result in; and (3) to explore the implications of these arrangements for our understanding of the line of thought in each of the letters. The intended analyses of the three epistles have now been completed and their results summarized and discussed in more detail at the end of each chapter. All that remains to be done now is to sum up and comment briefly on the overall results of these analyses.

Beginning with the first aspect of the study, we found considerable similarities between the three letters as regards the occurrence of transition markers. For example, in all of them, transitions and in particular endings of sections were more strongly marked at higher levels of division of the text than at lower levels. Instructive and thematic transition markers giving prominence to the pragmatic dimension of the communicative act were above all to be found at the highest level of division. Wishes serving as closing markers were also noted at the highest level, while consequence-indicating particles were more frequent at somewhat lower levels. Contrastive opening markers were generally common, but occurred most frequently at the higher levels: at the highest level, only δέ, asyndeton and (τοῦ) λοιποῦ were found, while at lower levels ἀλλά, μόνον and οὖν could also be noted. Attention-attracting and intensity-heightening transition markers mainly occurred at the highest levels of division of the text. Far and away the commonest type, especially as an opening marker, was the use of an address form.

The letters had much in common, then, when it came to the use of transition markers. But we also observed a number of differences. In particular, Galatians stood apart from the other two epistles. The most striking divergence was that over a third of the instructive and thematic opening markers in Galatians consisted of rhetorical questions, whereas such expressions did not occur at all as opening markers in the other letters. Other differences included the greater use in Galatians of contrastive opening markers and attention-attracting ἴδε and ἴδετε. These deviations can be understood and explained in the light of differences in the communicative situation. In 1 Thessalonians and Philippians, Paul is writing to addressees to whom he has a more unequivocally favourable attitude, and he writes to comfort and encourage them in a difficult situation, one of persecution. Such a text naturally tends to be relatively calm and coherent, with no unnecessary interruptions and outbursts. In Galatians, on the other hand, he is writing to rebuke and to try to put a stop to undesirable developments among his addressees. In such a situation, it is more natural for him to engage the attention of and challenge his recipients with rhetorical questions and to use attention-attracting words to underline important conclusions and assertions. It is also likely that such a text will make greater use of contrast. Given these differences in the communicative situation, the relatively significant similarities in the occurrence of transition markers in the three letters which can nevertheless be observed are even more worthy of note.

Concerning the second aspect of the study, the arrangements of the texts of the letters, the basic analyses carried out often revealed larger coherent textual entities than are usually discerned. We divided 1 Thessalonians into two main sections (1:2–3:13; 4:1–5:25), which were broken down into two (1:2–2:16; 2:17–3:10) and three parts (4:1–12; 4:13–5:11; 5:12–22), respectively, leaving aside the closing wishes (3:11 ff.; 5:23 f.) and the final exhortation (5:25). In the case of Philippians — again disregarding the closing wishes — the text was initially divided into three parts (1:3–2:30; 3:1–4:9; 4:10–18), the first two of which were so closely connected that they could conceivably be treated as a single entity at the first level of division of the text. In Galatians, finally, we discerned five sections at the first level of division (1:6–10; 1:11–2:21; 3:1–4:11; 4:12–5:10; 5:11–6:13), in addition to closing wishes and exhortations; of these five sections, the first three and the last two were so closely linked that an initial division of the letter into two parts could very well be considered. The arrangements of the texts emerging from my basic analyses thus showed the letters to be more uniform than is commonly assumed.

As for the third aspect of the study, the implications of these arrangements for our understanding of the line of thought in the letters, we noted that each of the letters ultimately served a single purpose. In 1 Thessalonians and Philippians, that purpose was to comfort and encourage the persecuted addressees; in Galatians, it was to try to persuade the recipients not to let themselves be circumcised and to hold fast to Paul and his gospel. In this regard, too, the text arrangements discerned thus showed the letters to be more uniform than they are usually believed to be. We also noted that in all three cases these arrangements resulted in the idea of *imitatio*, with a particular focus on the crucified Christ and the persecuted Paul, being given greater prominence and playing a more crucial role in the text.

The results of the analyses, then, were similar as regards both the use of transition markers and the implications of the arrangements discerned for our understanding of the line of thought in each letter. In addition, it emerged from them that the letters as such are more uniform than is generally assumed. These observations would seem to provide some confirmation of both the methods and the results of the analyses undertaken in this thesis.

The results of my analyses have consequences at the hermeneutic level. If each of the letters ultimately serves a practical purpose, it is quite clearly inappropriate to treat them as timeless theological treatises. And if conclusions about Paul's theological thinking are to be drawn from individual statements in any of them, those statements must surely first be related to the situation at hand and to the purpose of the letter concerned. The need to take account of the historical circumstances is lent additional urgency and a new dimension by the *imitatio* thinking that emerged from the text arrangements identified here, since according to this mode of thinking the person and actions not only of Christ, but also of Paul himself, become crucial aspects of the author's message. Paul is not just a man who *talks about* the gospel; he is also someone who *embodies* it. The gospel, in other words, is something which takes tangible shape in Paul's way of life. Consequently, the letters themselves are also to be seen as a manifestation of the gospel. To do full justice to the apostle's theological thinking, then, we must, to a greater extent than has generally been the case up to now, consider the person of Paul and regard his letters as an expression of the life of that person and as a proclamation of the gospel in precisely that capacity. It is thus absolutely essential to take the historical circumstances into consideration. This I believe is an approach which is unfamiliar to most of us who read Paul's letters today. After two thousand years of theological reflection, we are very strongly predisposed to read his letters as texts which contain and express abstract doctrines, rather than as manifestations, in their own right, of a lived and living gospel.

Abbreviations

BDF	See Blass, Debrunner & Funk 1961.
BDR	See Blass, Debrunner & Rehkopf 1976.
Bib	*Biblica*. Rome.
CathBibQuart	*Catholic Biblical Quarterly*. Washington, DC.
DDT	*Dansk Teologisk Tidsskrift*. Copenhagen.
EKK	Evangelisch-katolischer Kommentar zum Neuen Testament.
ETL	*Ephemerides Theologicae Lovanienses*. Leuven.
GNT	See *The Greek New Testament*.
HTR	*Harvard Theological Review*. Cambridge, MA.
Int	*Interpretation*. Richmond, VA.
JBL	*Journal of Biblical Literature*. Atlanta, GA.
JSNT	*Journal for the Study of the New Testament*. Sheffield, UK.
JSOT	*Journal for the Study of the Old Testament*. Sheffield, UK.
JTS	*Journal of Theological Studies*. Oxford.
LSJ	See Liddell, Scott & Jones 1968.
NEB	See *The New English Bible with the Apocrypha*.
NJB	See *New Jerusalem Bible*.
NovTes	*Novum Testamentum*. Leiden.
NT-81	See *Nya Testamentet*.
NTG	See *Novum Testamentum Graece*.
NTS	*New Testament Studies*. Cambridge, UK.
RevSciRel	*Revue des Sciences Religieuses*. Strasbourg.
SBL	Society of Biblical Literature.
StudTheol	*Studia Theologica*. Oslo.
ThWNT	Theologisches Wörterbuch zum Neuen Testament.
TOB	See *Traduction Œcuménique de la Bible*.
TynBul	*Tyndale Bulletin*. Cambridge, UK.
ZNTW	*Zeitschrift für die neutestamentliche Wissenschaft*. Berlin.
ZTK	*Zeitschrift für Theologie und Kirche*. Tübingen.

Bibliography

Editions and translations

Apostolic Fathers
(The Loeb Classical Library). Vol. 1. Ed. G. P. Goold. London: William Heinemann Ltd, 1976.

Biblia sacra, iuxta vulgatam versionem.
Eds B. Fischer OSB *et al.* Vol. II. Stuttgart: Württembergische Bibelanstalt, 1975.

Bibliorum ss. Graecorum, codex Vaticanus 1209 (Cod. B)
(Codices e Vaticanis selecti, phototypice expressi, ivssv, P II PP. X, consilio et opera, curatorum bybliothecae Vaticanae, vol. IV). Mediolani, 1904.

The Chester Beatty Biblical Papyri. Descriptions and Text ...
Fasciculus III Supplement Pauline Epistles. Ed. F. G. Kenyon. London: Emery Walker Ltd, 1937.

Codex Sinaiticus Petropolitanus... Reproduced in Fascimile from Photographs
Eds. H. and K. Lake. Oxford: Emery Walker Ltd, 1911.

The Codex Alexandrinus... in Reduced Photographic Facsimile...
Ed. British Museum. London 1909.

Dio Chrysostom
(The Loeb Classical Library). Vol. 5. Eds. T. E. Page *et al.* London: William Heinemann Ltd, 1951.

Epicteti Dissertationes ab Arriano Digestae
(Bibliotheca scriptorum Graecorum et Romanorum Teubneriana). Ed. H. Schenkl. Lipsiae: B. G. Teubneri, 1926.

The Greek New Testament (GNT)
Eds B. Aland *et al.* 4th ed. Stuttgart: Deutsche Bibelgesellschaft, 1994.

Holy Bible, Authorized King James Version.
New Scofield Reference Edition. Oxford 1967: Oxford University Press.

D. Martin Luthers Deutsche Bibel 1522–1546 (Luthers Druckterte)
(D. Martin Luthers Werke. Kritische Gesamtausgabe. 7.2). Weimar: Hermann Böhlaus Nachfolger, 1931.

The New English Bible with the Apocrypha (NEB)
2nd ed. Oxford: Oxford University Press, 1970.

New Jerusalem Bible (NJB)
Standard edition. London: Darton, Longman & Todd Ltd, 1985.

Novum Testamentum Graece (NTG)
Eds. B. Aland *et al.* 27th ed. Stuttgart: Deutsche Bibelgesellschaft, 1993.

Nya Testamentet. Bibelkommissionens utgåva 1981 (NT-81)
Stockholm: Skeab Förlag, 1981.

Pliny, Letters and Panegyricus
  (The Loeb Classical Library). Vol. 2. Ed. E. H. Warmington. London: William
  Heinemann Ltd, 1969.
Seneca, Ad Lucilium epistulae morales.
  (The Loeb Classical Library). Vol. 1–3. Eds T. E. Page *et al.* London: William
  Heinemann Ltd, 1917–25.
Thucydidis Historiae, post Carolum Hude
  (Bibliotheca scriptorum Graecorum et Romanorum Teubneriana). Ed. O. Luschnat.
  Lipsiae: B. G. Teubneri, 1960.
Traduction Œcuménique de la Bible (TOB)
  Comprenant l'Ancien et le Noveau Testament. Rev. ed. Paris: Alliance Biblique
  Universelle — Le Cerf, 1990.

Literature

Alexander, L.
  1989 'Hellenistic Letter-Forms and the Structure of Philippians'. *JSNT* 37,
        pp. 87–101.
Allwood, J.
  1976 *Linguistic communication as action and cooperation: A study in
        pragmatics.* (Gothenburg Monographs in Linguistics 2). Gothenburg:
        Göteborgs universitet.
Arichea, D. C. Jr., & E. A. Nida
  1975 *A Translator's Handbook on Paul's Letter to the Galatians.* (Helps for
        Translators 18). New York: United Bible Societies.
Baasland, E.
  1984 'Persecution: A Neglected Feature in the Letter to the Galatians'.
        StudTheol 38, pp. 135–50.
Bachmann, M.
  1992 *Sünder oder Übertreter. Studien zur Argumentation in Gal 2,15 ff.*
        (Wissenschaftliche Untersuchungen zum Neuen Testament 59). Tübingen:
        J. C. B. Mohr (Paul Siebeck).
Balogh, J.
  1927 'Voces Paginarum'. *Philologus* 82, pp. 84–109, 202–40.
Barclay, J. M. G.
  1988 *Obeying the Truth: A Study of Paul's Ethics in Galatians.* Edinburgh: T. &
        T. Clark Ltd.
Barth, K.
  1947 *Erklärung des Philipperbriefes.* 5th ed. Zürich: Evangelischer Verlag AG:
        Zollikon.
Bauer, W.
  1979 *A Greek-English Lexicon of the New Testament and Other Early Christian
        Literature.* Transl. and eds. W. F. Arndt, F. W. Gingrich & F. W. Danker.
        2nd ed. Chicago: The University of Chicago Press.

Beare, F. W.
1988   *A Commentary on the Epistle to the Philippians*. (Black's New Testament Commentaries). 3rd ed. London: Adam & Charles Black.
Beaugrande, R.-A., & W. U. Dressler
1983   *Introduction to Text Linguistics*. (Longman Linguistics Library 26). London: Longman.
Becker, J.
1976   'Der Brief an die Galater'. See Becker, Conzelmann & Friedrich (eds.) 1976, pp. 1–85.
Becker, J., H. Conzelmann & G. Friedrich
1976   *Der Briefe an die Galater, Epheser, Philipper, Kolosser, Thessalonicher und Philemon*. (Das Neue Testament Deutsch 8). 14th ed. Göttingen: Vandenhoeck & Ruprecht.
Best, E.
1972   *A Commentary on the First and Second Epistles to the Thessalonians*. (Black's New Testament Commentaries). London: Adam & Charles Black.
Betz, H. D.
1979   *Galatians. A Commentary on Paul's Letter to the Churches in Galatia*. (Hermeneia). Philadelphia: Fortress Press.
Black, M.
1981   *Romans*. (New Century Bible Commentary). New ed. Grand Rapids: William B. Eerdmans Publishing Company.
Blass, F., A. Debrunner & R. W. Funk (BDF)
1961   *A Greek Grammar of the New Testament and Other Early Christian Literature*. Chicago: The University of Chicago Press.
Blass, F., A. Debrunner & F. Rehkopf (BDR)
1976   *Grammatik des neutestamentlichen Griechisch*. 14th ed. Göttingen: Vandenhoeck & Ruprecht.
Blomqvist, J.
1969   *Greek Particles in Hellenistic Prose*. Lund: Berlingska Boktryckeriet.
1981   'On adversative coordination in ancient Greek and as a universal linguistic phenomenon'. In: L.-G. Larsson, *Three Baltic Loanwords in Fennic*. (Acta Universitatis Upsaliensis. Acta Societatis linguisticae Upsaliensis. Nova Series 3:2), pp. 57–70
Blomqvist, J., & P. O. Jastrup
1991   *Grekisk/Græsk grammatik*. Copenhagen: Akademisk Forlag.
Bloomquist, L. G.
1993   *The Function of Suffering in Philippians*. (JSNT. Supplement Series 78). Sheffield: Sheffield Academic Press.
Boers, H.
1975/76 'The Form-Critical Study of Paul's Letters: 1 Thessalonians as a Case Study'. *NTS* 22, pp. 140–58.
Bonnard, P., & Ch. Masson
1953   *L'épître de saint Paul aux Galates/ L'épître de saint Paul aux Éphésiens*. (Commentaire du Noveau Testament IX). Neuchâtel: Delachaux & Niestlé S.A.

Bornkamm, G.
1971   *Gesammelte Aufsätze Band IV: Geschichte und Glaube, Teil 2.* (Beiträge zur evangelischen Theologie. Theologische Abhandlungen 53) Munich: Chr. Kaiser Verlag.
Borse, U.
1984   *Der Brief an die Galater.* (Regensburger Neues Testament). Regensburg: Verlag Friedrich Pustet.
Bosworth, J., & T. N. Toller
1882   *An Anglo-Saxon Dictionary. Part II.* Oxford: The Clarendon Press.
Bruce, F. F.
1982   *The Epistle of Paul to the Galatians. A Commentary on the Greek Text.* (The New International Greek Testament Commentary 2) Exeter: Paternoster Press.
Caragounis, C. C.
1989   'Kingdom of God, Son of Man and Jesus' Self-Understanding (Part 1)'. *TynBul* 40, pp. 223–38.
Cavallin, A.
1941   '(τὸ) λοιπόν. Eine bedeutungsgeschichtliche Untersuchung.' *Eranos* 39, pp. 122–44.
Chantraine, P.
1968   *Dictionnaire étymologique de la langue Grecque. Histoire des mots. Tome I: A-Δ.* Paris: Éditions Klincksieck.
Clark, K. W.
1940   'Realised Eschatology'. *JBL* 59, pp. 367–83.
Cole, R. A.
1965   *The Epistle of Paul to the Galatians. An Introduction and Commentary.* (Tyndale New Testament Commentaries 9). London: Tyndale Press.
Collange, J.-F.
1973   *L'épître de saint Paul aux Philippiens.* (Commentaire du Noveau Testament Xa). Neuchâtel: Delachaux & Niestlé éditeurs.
Collins, R. F.
1979   'A propos the Integrity of 1 Thess'. *ETL* 55, pp. 67–106.
Cook, D.
1981   'Stephanus Le Moyne and the Dissection of Philippians'. *JTS* 2, pp. 138–42
Cousar, C. B.
1982   *Galatians.* (Interpretation). Atlanta: John Knox Press.
Cranfield, C. E. B.
1977   *A Critical and Exegetical Commentary on the Epistle to the Romans.* (The International Critical Commentary). Vol. 1. Edinburgh: T. & T. Clark.
Deichgräber, R.
1967   *Gotteshymnus und Christushymnus in der frühen Christenheit. Untersuchungen zu Form, Sprache und Stil der Früchristlichen Hymnen.* (Studien zur Umwelt des Neuen Testaments 5). Göttingen: Vandenhoeck & Ruprecht.

Deissmann, A.
1895   *Bibelstudien. Beiträge, zumeist aus den Papyri und Inschriften, zur Geschichte der Sprache, des Schrifttums und der Religion des hellenistischen Judentums und des Christentums.* Marburg: N.G. Elwert'sche Verlagsbuchhandlung.
1923   *Licht vom Osten. Das Neue Testament und die neuentdeckten Texte der hellenistisch-römischen Welt.* 4th ed. Tübingen: Verlag von J. C. B. Mohr (Paul Siebeck).
1925   *Paulus: Eine Kultur- und religiongeschichtliche Skizze.* 2nd ed. Tübingen: Verlag von J. C. B. Mohr (Paul Siebeck).
Demke, C.
1973   'Theologie und Literarkritik im 1. Thessalonicherbrief'. In: *Festschrift für Ernst Fuchs.* Eds G. Ebeling *et al.* Tübingen: J. C. B. Mohr (Paul Siebeck), pp. 103–24.
Denniston, J. D.
1952   *Greek Prose Style.* Oxford: Clarendon Press.
1954   *The Greek Particles.* 2nd ed. Oxford: The Clarendon Press.
Dibelius, M.
1937   *An die Thessalonicher: an die Philipper.* (Handbuch zum Neuen Testament 11). Tübingen: Verlag von J. C. B. Mohr (Paul Siebeck).
Dijk, T. van
1977   *Text and Context: Explanations in the Semantics and Pragmatics of Discourse.* (Longman Linguistics Library 21). London: Longman.
1985   *Handbook of Discourse Analysis.* 4 vols. New York: Academic Press.
Donfried, K. P.
1984   'Paul and Judaism. 1 Thessalonians 2:13–16 as a Test Case'. *Int* 38, pp. 242–53.
Doty, W. G.
1973   *Letters in Primitive Christianity.* (Guides to Biblical Scholarship. New Testament Series). Philadelphia: Fortress Press.
Dunn, J.D.G.
1993a   *The Epistle to the Galatians.* (Black's New Testament Commentaries). London: Adam & Charles Black.
1993b   *The Theology of Paul's Letter to the Galatians.* Cambridge: Cambridge University Press.
Eckart, K.-G.
1961   'Der zweite echte Brief des Apostels Paulus an die Thessalonicher'. *ZTK* 58, pp. 30–44.
Ellingworth, P., & E. A. Nida
1976   *A Translator's Handbook on Paul's Letters to the Thessalonians.* (Helps for Translators 17). Stuttgart: United Bible Societies.
Engberg-Pedersen, T.
1993   'Paulus som hellenist'. *DTT* 56:3, pp. 189–208.
Eriksson, L. O.
1982   *Filipperbrevet.* (Kommentar till Nya Testamentet 11). Stockholm: EFS-förlaget.

Fitzmyer, J.
  1988   'The Aramaic Background of Philippians 2,6–11'. *CathBibQuart* 50:3,
         pp. 470–83.
Foerster, W.
  1964   'Abfassungszeit und Ziel des Galaterbriefes'. In: *Apophoreta. Festschrift
         für E. Haenchen zum 70. Geb.* Berlin: Walter de Gruyter, pp. 135–41.
Fowl, S. E.
  1990   *The Story of Christ in the Ethics of Paul. An Analysis of the Function of
         the Hymnical Material in the Pauline Corpus.* (JSNT. Supplement Series
         36). Sheffield: Sheffield Academic Press.
Friedrich, G.
  1973   '1. Thessalonicher 5,1–11, der apologetische Einschub eines Späteren'.
         ZTK 70, pp. 288–315.
  1976a 'Der Brief an die Philipper'. See Becker, Conzelmann & Friedrich 1976,
         pp. 125–75.
  1976b 'Der erste Brief an die Thessalonicher'. See Becker, Conzelmann &
         Friedrich 1976, pp. 203–51.
Frisk, H.
  1960   *Griechisches etymologisches Wörterbuch. Band I: A-Ko.* Heidelberg: Carl
         Winter, Universitätsverlag.
Fung, R. V. K.
  1988   *The Epistle to the Galatians.* (New International Commentary on the New
         Testament). Grand Rapids: William B. Eerdmans Publishing Company.
Garland, D. E.
  1985   'The Composition and Unity of Philippians. Some Neglected Literary
         Factors.' *NovTest* 27:2, pp. 141–73.
Gnilka, J.
  1968   *Der Philipperbrief. Auslegung.* (Herders theologischer Kommentar zum
         Neuen Testament X:3). Freiburg: Herder.
Gregersen, V.
  1993   'Hedning og jøde. Litteraerkritiske undersøgelser til Galaterbrevet.' *DTT*
         56:1, pp. 1–18.
Grosse, E. U.
  1976   *Text und Kommunikation. Eine linguistische Einführung in die Funktion
         der Texte.* Stuttgart: Verlag W. Kohlhammer.
Gülich, E., & W. Raible
  1977   *Linguistische Textmodelle. Grundlagen und Möglichkeiten.* (Uni-
         Taschenbücher 130). Munich: Wihelm Fink Verlag.
  1979   *Linguistische Textanalyse. Überlegungen zur Gliederung von Texten*
         (Papiere zur Textlinguistik/ Papers in Text linguistics). 2nd ed. Hamburg:
         Helmut Buske Verlag.
Guthrie, D.
  1973   *Galatians.* (New Century Bible Commentary). London: Marshall, Morgan
         & Scott.
Guthrie, G. H.
  1995   'Cohesion Shifts and Stitches in Philippians'. See Porter & Carsson (eds.)
         1995, pp. 36–59.

Güttgemanns, E.
1966   *Der leidende Apostel und sein Herr. Studien zur paulinischen Christologie.*
       Göttingen: Vandenhoeck & Ruprecht.
Haenchen, E.
1959   *Die Apostelgeschichte.* (Kritisch-exegetischer Kommentar über das Neue
       Testament 3). 12th ed. Göttingen: Vandenhoeck & Ruprecht.
Hall, R. G.
1987   'The Rhetorical Outline for Galatians: A Reconsideration'. *JBL* 106:2,
       pp. 277–87.
Hartman, L.
1993   'Galatians 3:15–4:11 as Part of a Theological Argument on a Practical
       Issue'. In: *The Truth of the Gospel (Galatians 1:1–4:11).* Ed. J. Lambrecht
       (Monographic Series of «Benedictina». Biblical-Ecumenical Section 12).
       Rome: «Benedictina» Publishing, pp. 127–58.
Hays, R. B.
1981   *The Faith of Jesus Christ.* (SBL Dissertation Series 56). Chico: Scholars
       Press.
Hellholm, D.
1980   Das Visionenbuch des Hermas als Apokalypse. Formgeschichtliche und
       texttheoretische Studien zu einer literarischen Gattung. Vol. I. (Coniectanea
       Biblica. New Testament Series 13:1). Lund: Gleerup.
1993   'Amplificatio in the Macro-Structure of Romans'. See Porter & Olbricht
       (eds) 1993, pp. 123–51.
Hempfer, K. W.
1973   *Gattungstheorie. Information und Synthese.* (Uni-Taschenbücher 133).
       Munich: Wilhelm Fink Verlag.
Hirsch, E. D. Jr.
1967   *Validity in Interpretation.* New Haven: Yale University Press.
Hofius, O.
1976   *Der Christushymnus Philipper 2,6–11. Untersuchung zu Gestalt und
       Aussage eines urchristlichen Psalms.* (Wissenschafliche Untersuchungen
       zum Neuen Testament 17). 2nd ed. Tübingen: J. C. B. Mohr (Paul
       Siebeck).
Holtz, T.
1986   *Der erste Brief an die Thessalonicher.* (EKK 13). Zürich: Benziger Verlag.
Hooker, M. D.
1989   'ΠΙΣΤΙΣ ΧΡΙΣΤΟΥ'. *NTS* 35, pp. 321–42.
Howard, G.
1990   *Paul: Crisis in Galatian. A Study in Early Christian Theology.* (Society for
       New Testament Studies. Monograph Series 35). 2nd ed. Cambridge:
       Cambridge University Press.
Hübner, H.
1993   *Biblische Theologie des Neuen Testaments. Band 2: Die Theologie des
       Paulus und ihre neutestamentliche Wirkungsgeschichte.* Göttingen:
       Vandenhoeck & Ruprecht.
Hultgren, A. J.
1980   'The *Pistis Chistou* Formulation in Paul'. *NovTes* 22, pp. 248–63.

Jegher-Bucher, V.
1991   *Der Galaterbrief auf dem Hintergrund antiker Epistolographie und Rhetorik. Ein anderes Paulusbild.* (Abhandlungen zur Theologie des Alten und Neuen Testaments 78). Zürich: Theologischer Verlag.

Jewett, R.
1986   *The Thessalonian Correspondence. Pauline Rhetoric and Millenarian Piety.* (Foundations and Facets: New Testament). Philadelphia: Fortress Press.

Johanson, B. C.
1987   *To All the Brethren. A Text-Linguistic and Rhetorical Approach to 1 Thessalonians.* (Coniectanea Biblica. New Testament Series 16). Stockholm: Almqvist & Wiksell International.

Johnson, L. T.
1982   'Rom 3:21–26 and the Faith of Jesus'. *CathBibQuart* 44, pp. 77–90.

Johnston, G.
1967   *Ephesians, Philippians, Colossians and Philemon.* (The Century Bible). London: Nelson.

Juel, D. H.
1985   '1 Thessalonians'. See Krentz, Koenig & Juel 1985, pp. 211–51.

Käsemann, E.
1980   *Commentary on Romans.* London: SCM Press.

Kennedy, G. A.
1984   *New Testament Interpretation through Rhetorical Criticism.* (Studies in Religion) Chapel Hill: The University of North Carolina Press.

Kieffer, R.
1982   *Foi et Justification a Antioche. Interprétation d'un Conflit (Gal 2,14–21).* (Lectio Divina 111). Paris: Les Éditions du Cerf.

Kilpatrick, G. D.
1968   'ΒΛΕΠΕΤΕ, Philippians 3:2'. In: *In Memoriam Paul Kahle.* Eds. M. Black & G. Fohrer. (Zeitschrift für die altestamentliche Wissenschaft. Beihefte 103). Berlin: A. Töpelmann, pp. 146–48.

Knox, B. M. W.
1968   'Silent Reading in Antiquity'. *Greek, Roman and Byzantine Studies* 9, pp. 421–35.

Koenig, J.
1985   'Philippians'. Se Krentz, Koenig & Juel 1985, pp. 119–82.

Koperski, V.
1993   'The Early History of the Dissection of Philippians'. *JTS* 44:2, pp. 599–603.

Köster, H.
1979   '1 Thessalonians. Experiment in Christian Writing'. In: *Continuity and Discontinuity in Church History. FS. for G. H. Williams.* Eds. F. F. Church & T. George. (Studies in the History of Christian Thought 19). Leiden: E. J. Brill, pp. 33–44.

Krentz, E.
1985   'Galatians'. See Krentz, Koenig & Juel 1985, pp. 9–118.

Bibliography

Krentz, E., J. Koenig & D. H. Juel
1985   Galatians, Philippians, Philemon, 1 Thessalonians. (Augsburg Commentary on the New Testament). Minneapolis: Augsburg Publishing House.
Kühner, R., & B. Gerth
1904   Ausführliche Grammatik der griechischen Sprache. Teil 2: Satzlehre. Vol. 2. 3rd ed. Hannover: Hahnsche Buchhandlung.
Kümmel, W. G.
1962   'Das literarische und geschichtliche Problem des ersten Thessalonicherbriefes'. In: Neotestamentica et Patristica. Freundesgabe O. Cullmann. (NovTest Suppl. 6). Leiden: E. J. Brill, pp. 213–27.
1983   Einleitung in das Neue Testament. 21th ed. Heidelberg: Quelle & Meyer.
Kurzova, H.
1985   'Zum Typus des Allgriechischen'. Listy filologické 108, pp. 3–13.
Larsson, E.
1962   Christus als Vorbild. Eine Untersuchung zu den Paulinischen Tauf- und Eikontexten. (Acta seminarii neotestamentici Upsaliensis XXIII-1962). Uppsala: Almqvist & Wiksells Boktryckeri Aktiebolag.
Larsson, K.
1978   Modeller och metoder i textlingvistiken. (Ord och stil, Språksamfundets skrifter 10). Lund: Studentlitteratur.
Le Moyne, S.
1685   Notae et Observationes, Varia Sacra II. Leiden: Daniel à Graesbeeck.
Liddell, H. G., R. Scott & H. S. Jones (LSJ)
1968   A Greek-English Lexicon. 9th ed. Oxford: The Clarendon Press.
Lietzmann, H.
1926   Messe und Herrenmahl. Eine Studie zur Geschichte der Liturgie. (Arbeiten zur Kirchengeschichte 8). Bonn: A. Marcus und E. Weber's Verlag.
Loh, I.-J., & E. A. Nida
1977   A Translator's Handbook on Paul's Letter to the Philippians. (Helps for Translators XIX). Stuttgart: United Bible Societies.
Lohmeyer, E.
1928   Kyrios Jesus. Eine Untersuchung zu Phil 2,5–11. (Sitzungsberichte der Heidelberger Akademie der Wissenschaften. Philosophisch-historische Klasse. Jahrgang 1927/28. 4. Abt.). Heidelberg: Carl Winters Universitätsbuchhandlung
1953   Die Brief an die Philipper, an die Kolosser und an Philemon. (Kritisch-exegetischer Kommentar über das Neue Testament 9). 9th ed. Göttingen: Vandenhoeck & Ruprecht.
Lührmann, D.
1978   Der Brief an die Galater. (Züricher Bibelkommentare: Neues Testament 7). Zürich: Theologischer Verlag.
Lyons, G.
1985   Pauline Autobiography. Toward a New Understanding. (SBL. Dissertation Series 73). Atlanta: Scholars Press.
Mackay, B. S.
1960/61 'Further Thoughts on Philippians'. NTS 7, pp. 161–70.

229

Malherbe, A. J.
1983   'Exhortation in First Thessalonians'. *NovTes* 25, pp. 238–56.
Maly, E. H.
1979   *Romans*. (New Testament Message 9). Wilmington: Michael Glazier, Inc.
Marshall, I. H.
1983   *1 and 2 Thessalonians*. (The New Century Bible Commentary). Grand Rapids: William B. Eerdmans Publishing Company.
Martin, R. P.
1959   *The Epistle of Paul to the Philippians. An Introduction and Commentary*. (The Tyndale New Testament Commentaries). London: The Tyndale Press.
Mayser, E.
1926   *Grammatik der griechischen Papyri aus der Ptolemäerzeit. Mit Einschluss der gleichzeitigen Ostraka und der in Ägypten verfassten Inschriften. Band II:1: Satzlehre*. Berlin: Walter de Gruyter & CO.
1934   *Grammatik der griechischen Papyri aus der Ptolemäerzeit. Mit Einschluss der gleichzeitigen Ostraka und der in Ägypten verfassten Inschriften. Band II:3: Satzlehre*. Berlin: Walter de Gruyter & CO.
Metzger, B. M.
1975   *A Textual Commentary on the Greek New Testament. A Companion Volume to the United Bible Societies' Greek New Testament (Third Edition)*. London: United Bible Societies.
Michaelis, W.
1959   'πίπτω, πτῶμα...'. In: *ThWNT*. Ed. G. Friedrich. Vol. 6. Stuttgart: W. Kohlhammer, pp. 161–92.
Morris, Ch. W.
1938   *Foundations of the Theory of Signs*. Chicago: University of Chicago Press.
Morris, L.
1984   *The Epistles of Paul to the Thessalonians. An Introduction and Commentary*. 2nd ed. (The Tyndale New Testament Commentaries 13). Leicester: Inter-Varsity Press.
1988   *The Epistle to the Romans*. Grand Rapids: Inter-Varsity Press.
Müller, U. B.
1988   'Der Christushymnus Phil 2:6–11'. *ZNTW* 79:1–2, pp. 17–44.
Munck, J.
1954   *Paulus und die Heilsgeschichte*. (Acta Jutlandica. Teologisk serie 6). Aarhus: Universitetsforlag i Aarhus.
Murro, W.
1983   *Authority in Peter and Paul: The Identification of a Pastoral Stratum in the Pauline Corpus and 1 Peter*. (Society for New Testament Studies. Monograph Series). Cambridge: Cambridge University Press.
Mußner, F.
1974   *Der Galaterbrief. Auslegung*. (Herders theologischer Kommentar zum Neuen Testament IX). Freiburg: Herder.
Nida, E. A., & C. R. Faber
1974   *The Theory and Practice of Translation*. (Helps for Translators 8). Leiden: E. J. Brill.

Nygren, A.
    1944   *Pauli brev till romarna. Tolkning.* (Tolkning av Nya Testamentet 6).
            Stockholm: Svenska Kyrkans Diakonistyrelses Bokförlag.
O'Brien, P. T.
    1991   *The Epistle to the Philippians. A Commentary on the Greek Text.* (New
            International Greek Testament Commentary). Grand Rapids: William B.
            Eerdmans Publishing Company.
Oepke, A.
    1973   *Der Brief des Paulus an die Galater.* (Theologischer Handkommentar zum
            Neuen Testament 9). 3rd ed. Berlin: Evangelische Verlagsanstalt GmbH.
Okeke, G. E.
    1980/81 '1 Thess II, 13–16. The Fate of the Unbelieving Jews'. *NTS* 27, pp. 127–
            36.
Olsson, B.
    1974   *Structure and Meaning in the Fourth Gospel. A Text-linguistic Analysis of
            John 2:1–11 and 4:1–42.* (Coniectanea Biblica. New Testament Series 6).
            Lund: CWK Gleerup.
Osiek, C.
    1980   *Galatians.* (New Testament Message 12). Wilmington: Michael Glazier,
            Inc.
Pearson, B. A.
    1971   '1 Thessalonians 2:13–16: A Deutero-Pauline Interpolation'. *HTR* 64,
            pp. 79–94.
Pelser, G. M. M., *et al.*
    1992   'Discourse analysis of Galatians'. *Neotestamentica* 26:2 (Addendum).
Pitta, A.
    1992   *Disposizione e messagio della lettera ai Galati. Analisi retorico-letteraria.*
            (Analecta Biblica 131). Rome: Editrice Pontificio Istituto Biblica.
Plett, H. F.
    1975   *Textwissenschaft und Textanalyse. Semiotik, Linguistik, Rhetorik.* (Uni-
            Taschenbücher 328). 2nd ed. Heidelberg: Quelle & Meyer.
    1989   *Einführung in die rhetorische Textanalyse.* 7th ed. Hamburg: Helmut
            Buske Verlag.
Plevnik, J.
    1979   '1 Thess 5,1–11: Its Authenticity, Intention and Message'. *Bib* 60, pp. 71–
            90.
Pollard, T. E.
    1966/67 'The Integrity of Philippians'. *NTS* 13, pp. 57–66.
Portefaix, L.
    1988   *Sisters Rejoice. Paul's Letter to the Philippians and Luke-Acts as Received
            by First-Century Philippian Women.* (Coniectanea Biblica. New Testament
            Series 20). Stockholm: Almqvist & Wiksell International.
Porter, S. E., & D. A. Carson (eds.)
    1995   *Discourse Analysis and Other Topics in Biblical Greek.* (JSNT Supplement
            Series 113). Sheffield: Academic Press.

Porter, S. E., & T. H. Olbricht (eds.)
1993   *Rhetoric and the New Testament. Essays from the 1992 Heidelberg Conference.* (JSNT Supplement Series 90). Sheffield: JSOT Press.

Rahjten, B. D.
1959/60 'The Three Letters of Paul to the Philippians'. *NTS* 6, pp. 167–73.

Reed, J. T.
1993   'Using Ancient Rhetorical Categories to Interpret Paul's Letters: A Question of Genre'. See Porter & Olbricht (eds.) 1993, pp. 292–324.

Riesenfeld, H.
1983   'Unpoetische Hymnen im Neuen Testament? Zu Phil 2,1–11'. In: *Glaube und Gerechtigkeit. In Memoriam Rafael Gyllenberg (18.6.1893–29.7.1982).* Eds. J. Kiilunen & V. Riekkinen & H. Räisänen. (Schriften der Finnischen Exegetischen Gesellschaft 38). Helsinki: Exchange Centre for Scientific Literature, pp. 155–68.

Rigaux, B.
1956   *Saint Paul: Les Épîtres aux Thessaloniciens.* (Études Bibliques). Paris: Libraire Lecoffre J. Gabalda et Cⁱᵉ.
1974/75 'Tradition et redaction dans 1 Th V.1–10'. *NTS* 21, pp. 318–40.

Robertson, A. T.
1934   *A Grammar of the Greek New Testament in the Light of Historical Research.* Nashville: Broadman Press.

Rodhe, J.
1989   *Der Brief des Paulus an die Galater.* (Theologischer Handkommentar zum Neuen Testament IX). Berlin: Evangelische Verlagsanstalt.

Rolland, P.
1990   'La structure litteraire et l'unité de l'Épître aux Philippiens'. *RevSciRel* 64:3–4, pp. 213–16.

Sanders, E. P.
1977   *Paul and Palestinian Judaism: A Comparison of Patterns of Religion.* London: SCM Press.

Sanders, J. T.
1962   'The Transition from Opening Epistolary Thanksgiving to Body in the Letters of the Pauline Corpus'. *JBL* 81, pp. 348–62.

Schenk, W.
1984   *Die Philipperbriefe des Paulus. Kommentar.* Stuttgart: Verlag W. Kohlhammer.

Schenke, H.-M., & K. M. Fischer
1978   *Einleitung in die Schriften des Neuen Testaments. I: Die Briefe des Paulus und Schriften des Paulinismus.* Gütersloh: Gütersloher Verlagshaus Gerd Mohn.

Schlier, H.
1971   *Der Brief an die Galater.* (Kritisch-exegetischer Kommentar über das Neue Testament 7). 14th ed. Göttingen: Vandenhoeck & Ruprecht.

Schmidt, D.
1983   '1 Thess 2:13–16: Linguistic Evidence for an Interpolation'. *JBL* 102, pp. 269–79.

Schmithals, W.
1957   'Die Irrlehrer des Philipperbriefes'. *ZTK* 54, pp. 297–341.
1964   'Die Thessalonicherbriefe als Briefkomposition'. In: *Zeit und Geschichte.*
        Dankesgabe an Rudolf Bultmann. Ed. E. Dinkler. Tübingen: J. C. B. Mohr
        (Paul Siebeck), pp. 295–315.
1984   *Die Briefe des Paulus in ihrer ursprünglichen Form.* (Zürcher Werk-
        kommentare zur Bibel). Zürich: Theologischer Verlag.
Schnider, F., & W. Stenger
1987   *Studien zum neutestamentlichen Briefformular.* (New Testament Tools and
        Studies 11). Leiden: E. J. Brill.
Schoon-Janssen, J.
1991   *Umstrittene „Apologien" in den Paulusbriefen. Studien zur rhetorischen
        Situation des 1. Thessalonicherbriefes, des Galaterbriefes und des
        Philipperbriefes.* (Theologische Arbeiten 45). Göttingen: Vandenhoeck &
        Ruprecht.
Schrader, C.
1836   *Der Apostel Paulus. V.* Leipzig: Christian Ernst Kollmann.
Schubert, P.
1939   *Form and Function of the Pauline Thanksgivings.* (Beihefte zur Zeitschrift
        für die neutestamentliche Wissenschaft und die Kunde der älteren Kirche
        20). Berlin: Walter de Gruyter & CO.
Schweitzer, A.
1930   *Die Mystik der Apostels Paulus.* Tübingen: Verlag von J. C. B. Mohr (Paul
        Siebeck).
Schweitzer, E.
1962   *Erniedrung und Erhöhung bei Jesu und seinen Nachfolgern.* (Abhand-
        lungen zur Theologie des Alten und Neuen Testaments 28). 2nd ed. Zürich:
        Zwingli.
Schwyzer, E., & A. Debrunner
1950   *Griechische Grammatik, auf der Grundlage von Karl Brugmanns
        griechische Grammatik. 2. Band: Syntax und syntaktische Stilistik.*
        (Handbuch der Altertumswissenschaft II:1:2). Munich: C. H. Beck'sche
        Verlagsbuchhandlung.
Siegert, F.
1985   *Argumentation bei Paulus, gezeigt an Röm 9–11.* (Wissenschaftliche
        Untersuchungen zum Neuen Testament 34). Tübingen: J. C. B. Mohr
        (Paul Siebeck).
Smit, J.
1989   'The Letter of Paul to the Galatians: A Deliberative Speech'. *NTS* 35:1,
        pp. 1–26.
1993   'Argument and Genre of 1 Corinthians 12–14'. See Porter & Olbricht
        (eds.) 1993, pp. 211–30.
Starr, R. J.
1991   'Reading Aloud: Lectores and Roman Reading'. *Classical Journal* 86,
        pp. 337–43.

Stendahl, K.
  1976   *Paul Among Jews and Gentiles, and Other Essays*. Philadelphia: Fortress
          Press.
Stuhlmacher, P.
  1968   *Das Paulinische Evangelium. I. Vorgeschichte*. (Forschungen zur Religion
          und Literatur des Alten und Neuen Testaments 95). Göttingen:
          Vandenhoeck & Ruprecht.
Thiselton, A. C.
  1979   'Semantics and New Testament Interpretation'. *New Testament Interpreta-
          tion*. Ed. I. H. Marshall. Exeter: Paternoster Press, pp. 75–104.
Thrall, M. E.
  1962   *Greek Particles in the New Testament. Linguistic and Exegetical Studies*.
          (New Testament Tools and Studies, vol. III). Leiden: E. J. Brill.
Traugott, E. C., & M. L. Pratt
  1980   *Linguistics for Students of Literature*. New York: Harcourt Brace Jova-
          novich.
Vielhauer, Ph.
  1978   *Geschichte der urchristlichen Literatur. Einleitung in das Neue Testament,
          die Apokryphen und die Apostolischen Väter*. Berlin: Walter de Gruyter.
Vincent, M. R.
  1897   *A Critical and Exegetical Commentary on the Epistles to the Philippians and
          to Philemon*. (The International Critical Commentary). Edinburgh: T. & T.
          Clark.
Wanamaker, C. A.
  1990   *The Epistles to the Thessalonians. A Commentary on the Greek Text*. (New
          International Greek Testament Commentary). Grand Rapids: William B.
          Eerdmans Publishing Company.
Watson, D. F.
  1988   'A Rhetorical Analysis of Philippians and its Implication for the Unity
          Question'. *NovTest* 30:1, pp. 57–88.
Weatherly, J. A.
  1991   'The Authenticity of 1 Thessalonians 2:13–16: Additional Evidence'. *JSNT*
          42, pp. 79–98.
Weekley, E.
  1921   *An Etymological Dictionary of Modern English*. London: John Murray.
Weima, J. A. D.
  1994   *Neglected Endings. The Significance of the Pauline Letter Closings*. (JSNT
          Supplement Series 101). Sheffield: JSOT Press.
Weiss, J.
  1897   *Beiträge zur paulinischen Rhetorik*. Göttingen: Vandenhoeck & Ruprecht.
White, J. L.
  1972   *The Form and Function of the Body of the Greek Letter. A Study of the
          Letter-Body in the Non-Literary Papyri and in Paul the Apostle*. (SBL
          Dissertation Series 2). Missoula: Printing Department, University of
          Montana.
  1986   *Light from Ancient Letters*. Philadelphia: Fortress Press.

Wick, P.
1994   *Der Philipperbrief. Der formale Aufbau des Briefes als Schlüssel zum Verständnis seines Inhalts.* (Beiträge zur Wissenschaft vom Alten und Neuen Testament 135). Stuttgart: Verlag W. Kohlhammer.

Wienold, G.
1983   'Narrative Texts and Models of Hierarchical and Sequential Structure'. In: *Allgemeine Sprachwissenschaft, Sprachtypologie und Textlinguistik. FS. P. Hartmann.* Ed. M. Faust. Tübingen: Narr, pp. 417–30.

Wiklander, B.
1984   *Prophecy as Literature. A Text-Linguistic and Rhetorical Approach to Isaiah 2–4.* (Coniectanea Biblica. Old Testament Series 22). Rev. ed. Malmö: Liber/Gleerup.

Wiles, G. P.
1974   *Paul's Intercessory Prayers. The Significance of the Intercessory Prayer Passages in the Letters of St. Paul.* (Society for New Testament Studies. Monograph Series). Cambridge: Cambridge University Press.

Willert, N.
1995   'The Catalogues of Hardships in the Pauline Correspondence: Background and Function'. In: *The New Testament and Hellenistic Judaism.* Ed. P. Borgen & S. Giversen. Aarhus: Aarhus University Press, pp. 217–43.

Williams, S. K.
1987   'Again *Pistis Christou*'. *CathBibQuart* 49, pp. 431–37.

Winninge, M.
1995   *Sinners and the Righteous. A Comparative Study of the Psalms of Solomon and Paul's Letters.* (Coniectanea Biblica. New Testament Series 26). Stockholm: Almqvist & Wiksell International.

Zahn, Th.
1922   *Der Brief des Paulus an die Galater. Ausgelegt.* (Kommentar zum Neuen Testament 9). 3rd ed. Leipzig: A. Deichert'sche Verlagsbuchhandlung.

Index of authors

Alexander, L. 35, 88, 89, 90, 92, 101
Allwood, J. 16
Arichea, D. C. Jr. 146, 147
Baasland, E. 152
Bachmann, M. 32, 159, 161, 213
Balogh, J. 20
Barclay, J. M. G. 15, 145, 193, 194, 213
Barth, K. 116
Bauer, W. 54, 118, 182
Beare, F. W. 88, 89, 101, 103
Beaugrande, R.-A. 18, 21, 22, 36
Becker, J. 146, 147, 151
Best, E. 38, 39, 40, 41
Betz, H. D. 13, 36, 146, 147, 168, 176
Black, M. 14
Blass, F. (BDF) 21, 118, 120, 133, 149
Blomqvist, J. 30, 61, 100, 120
Bloomquist, L. G. 144
Boers, H. 35, 40, 41, 42
Bonnard, P. 146, 147
Bornkamm, G. 90, 91, 93
Borse, U. 13, 146, 147
Bosworth, J. 183
Bruce, F. F. 13, 146, 147
Caragounis, C. C. 44
Cavallin, A. 61
Chantraine, P. 150
Clark, K. W. 44
Cole, R. A. 146, 147, 149, 150, 151
Collange, J.-F. 88, 89, 101
Collins, R. F. 40
Cook, D. 90
Cousar, C. B. 146, 147
Cranfield, C. E. B. 14
Debrunner, A. (BDF, BDR) 21, 31, 118, 120, 133, 149, 151, 182, 185
Deichgräber, R. 105

Deissmann, A. 105, 192
Demke, C. 40, 41
Denniston, J. D. 30, 31, 58, 109, 151, 185, 186
Dibelius, M. 105, 116
Dijk, T. van 36
Donfried, K. P. 40, 43, 44
Doty, W. G. 35, 38, 39
Dressler, W. U. 18, 21, 22, 36
Dunn, J.D.G. 146, 147, 210, 216
Eckart, K.-G. 40
Ellingworth, P. 38, 39
Engberg-Pedersen, T. 169, 216
Eriksson, L. O. 116
Faber, C. R. 20, 22
Fischer, K. M. 40
Fitzmyer, J. 105
Foerster, W. 192
Fowl, S. E. 105, 117, 141
Friedrich, G. 38, 39, 40, 46, 88, 89, 101, 103
Frisk, H. 150
Fung, R. V. K. 13, 146, 147, 161, 176
Funk, R. W. (BDF) 21, 118, 120, 133, 149
Garland, D. E. 95
Gerth, B. 150
Gnilka, J. 88, 89, 101, 103, 116
Gregersen, V. 146
Grosse, E. U. 16, 25, 26
Gülich, E. 16, 22, 25, 26, 27, 36
Guthrie, D. 13, 146, 147, 182, 185, 192, 194, 210
Guthrie, G. H. 36
Güttgemanns, E. 186
Haenchen, E. 158
Hall, R. G. 146, 147, 151
Hartman, L. 165, 169, 173
Hays, R. B. 163

Hellholm, D. 25, 26, 27, 36
Hempfer, K. W. 25
Hirsch, E. D. Jr. 17
Hofius, O. 105
Holtz, T. 15, 38, 39, 41, 42, 62
Hooker, M. D. 163
Howard, G. 185, 212
Hübner, H. 15, 103
Hultgren, A. J. 163
Jastrup, P. O. 30
Jegher-Bucher, V. 146, 147, 155
Jewett, R. 35, 38, 39, 50
Johanson, B. C. 25, 26, 27, 28, 35, 36, 38, 39, 58, 59
Johnson, L. T. 163
Johnston, G. 88, 89, 101
Jones, H. S. (LSJ) 118, 182
Juel, D. H. 38, 39
Käsemann, E. 14
Kennedy, G. A. 35, 38, 39
Kieffer, R. 162, 163
Kilpatrick, G. D. 117
Knox, B. M. W. 20
Koenig, J. 88, 90, 101, 103
Koperski, V. 90
Köster, H. 35
Krentz, E. 146, 147, 161
Kühner, R. 150
Kümmel, W. G. 40, 41, 210
Kurzova, H. 46
Larsson, E. 84, 214
Larsson, K. 25
Le Moyne, S. 90
Liddell, H. G. (LSJ) 118, 182
Lietzmann, H. 105
Loh, I.-J. 88, 89, 90
Lohmeyer, E. 88, 89, 90, 105, 116
Lührmann, D. 146, 147
Lyons, G. 41
Mackay, B. S. 95
Malherbe, A. J. 84, 85
Maly, E. H. 14
Marshall, I. H. 15, 38, 39
Martin, R. P. 88, 89, 90, 101
Masson, Ch. 146, 147
Mayser, E. 120, 149, 182
Metzger, B. M. 177

Michaelis, W. 190
Morris, Ch. W. 16
Morris, L. 14, 38, 39, 49
Müller, U. B. 105
Munck, J. 212
Murro, W. 40
Mußner, F. 146, 147, 155, 186, 192
Nida, E. A. 20, 22, 38, 39, 88, 89, 90, 146, 147
Nygren, A. 14
O'Brien, P. T. 88, 89, 90, 101
Oepke, A. 190
Okeke, G. E. 40, 43
Olsson, B. 27
Osiek, C. 146, 147, 151
Pearson, B. A. 40, 42
Pelser, G. M. M. 36, 146, 147, 151
Pitta, A. 146, 147
Plett, H. F. 16, 36
Plevnik, J. 40, 47
Pollard, T. E. 95
Portefaix, L. 117
Pratt, M. L. 20, 21
Rahjten, B. D. 90, 91, 93, 94
Raible, W. 16, 22, 25, 26, 27, 36
Reed, J. T. 35, 36
Rehkopf, F. (BDR) 149, 185
Riesenfeld, H. 105, 106
Rigaux, B. 40, 58, 59
Robertson, A. T. 118
Rodhe, J. 13, 146, 147, 149, 150, 168, 176, 185, 190, 192
Rolland, P. 88, 89, 90, 94
Sanders, E. P. 168, 169
Sanders, J. T. 35, 40
Schenk, W. 36, 88, 89, 101, 103
Schlier, H. 146, 147, 150, 168, 185, 192
Schenke, H.-M. 40
Schmidt, D. 40, 42, 43, 44, 45
Schmithals, W. 40, 41, 91, 93, 145, 146, 147
Schnider, F. 35
Schoon-Janssen, J. 41, 117
Schrader, C. 90
Schubert, P. 35, 41
Schweitzer, A. 14

Schweitzer, E. 106
Schwyzer, E. 31, 151, 182, 185
Scott, R. (LSJ) 118, 182
Siegert, F. 32
Smit, J. 35, 145, 146, 147, 155
Starr, R. J. 20
Stendahl, K. 14
Stenger, W. 35
Stuhlmacher, P. 158
Thiselton, A. C. 22
Thrall, M. E. 120
Toller, T. N. 183
Traugott, E. C. 20, 21
Vielhauer, Ph. 13, 14, 15, 38, 39, 88,
    89, 90, 91, 93, 146, 147
Vincent, M. R. 116

Wanamaker, C. A. 38, 39
Watson, D. F. 35, 88, 89, 90, 101
Weatherly, J. A. 40, 44, 45
Weekley, E. 183
Weima, J. A. D. 35
Weiss, J. 105
White, J. L. 35, 149
Wick, P. 142
Wienold, G. 28
Wiklander, B. 17
Wiles, G. P. 35, 58
Willert, N. 87, 143
Williams, S. K. 163
Winninge, M. 163
Zahn, Th. 150, 192

Index of Greek words (selected)

ἀγαπητοί 138
ἀδελφοί 75, 81, 138, 187, 209
ἀλλά 30, 99, *108–113*, 137, 149 f.,
  208
ἁμαρτωλός 163
ἀμήν 29, 81, 138
ἄρα *185 f.*, 207
ἄρα οὖν 206
ἁρπαγμός 106
ἄρτι 58, 150 f.
βλέπετε 92, 117
γάρ 58 f., 150 f.
δέ *30*, 75, 80, 111, 137, 208
διὰ τοῦτο 45, 55, 78 f., 81
διό 78
εἰ μή 149 f.
εἷς 215
εἰς ἡμέραν Χριστοῦ 112
ἐν 103 ff.
ἕν 102, 138
ἐν Χριστῷ ('Ιησοῦ) 103 ff.
ἐπίγειος 95
εὐλογητὸς ὁ θεός 149
εὐχαριστῶ 41, 48 f., 76, 96, 133,
  149
ἡγεῖσθαι 95
θαυμάζω 148 f., 203
ἴδε 31, 209
ἴδετε 191 ff., 209
ἰδού 31, 155
ἴσος 106
καὶ διὰ τοῦτο καί 42, 45, 54 f.
καταχθόνιος 106
καύχημα 100, 112
κέρδος 94
κερδαίνειν 94
κοινωνεῖν 125
κοινωνία 142
λέγω 77, 169, 204, 205
λοιπόν 61, 92, 117, 135, 137

λοιπὸν οὖν 61, 80
μέν... δέ 30
μενοῦνγε 118
μέντοι 30
μιμητής 84 f.
μόνον *30*, 100, 137, 187, 208
μορφή 106
μορφοῦσθαι 215
οἴδατε 52 f., 77, 134, 204
ὅσος... οὗτος 124, 209
ὅστις (ὅς)... οὗτος 124, 138
οὖν 30, 136, 137, 206 f., 208
οὕτως 75, 79, 135
παράπτωμα 190
πίστις 163
πλήν 30, 98, *75*, 125, 135 f.
πνεῦμα 118, 194 f.
πολιτεία 94
πολιτεύεσθαι 94
συγκοινωνός 142
συμμιμητής 121, 143
συμμορφίζεσθαι 95
σύμμορφος 95, 106
συναθλεῖν 95
σχῆμα 95, 106
σχηματίζειν 95
ταπεινοῦν 95
ταπεινοφροσύνη 95
ταπείνωσις 95
τέλειος 121
τί γάρ; 98, 136
τί ἔτι 182 ff.
τοιγαροῦν 79, 151
τοῦτο 77, 102, 134, 135 f., 203
ὑπερυψοῦν 106
ὑπήκοος 106
χαίρω 99, 133
ὥστε 75, 79, 135 f., 137, 206 f.

Index of passages (selected)

Old Testament

Genesis
3   190
6:9   121
12:3   167
15:6   167
18:8   167

Deuteronomy
18:13   121

2 Samuel
22:26   121

1 Kings
8:61   121

Isaiah
54:1   177

New Testament

Matthew
5:48   121
9:4   104
12:4   149
19:20   183 f.
19:21   121
26:65   183 f.

Mark
5:35   183 f.
14:63   183 f.

Luke
4:26   149
9:3   120
22:71   183 f.

Acts
4:1–22   117
5:17–40   117

7:58   44
8:1–3   117
8:3   44
9:23   44
12:1–19   117
13:50   44, 117
14:2   44, 117
14:5   44
14:9   117
14:19   44, 117
17:5   44, 117
17:13   117
18:12   117
20:3   117
20:19   117
21:27 f.   117
23:12   117

Romans
1:8–15   14
1:13   14
1:16–17   14
2:3   183
2:5   112, 183
2:8   42
2:12 f.   183
2:16   112, 183
2:20   106
2:26 f.   183
3:1   151, 160
3:3   183
3:6   183
3:7   183
3:20   183
4:1   151
5:15   190
5:17   190
5:20   190
6:1   151
7:7   151

8:2	145
8:29	106
9:14	151
9:19	183 f.
9:27 ff.	43
10:1	69
10:6 f.	106
10:15	160, 167
10:21	43
11–14	46
11:1	42
11:25 ff.	42, 43
12:15	120
13:6	45
14:14	149
15:5 f.	41, 126
15:13	41, 112, 126
15:33	112

1 Corinthians

1:8	112
1:9	40 f.
1:14	41
2:1–5	175
2:6	121
3:2	109
4:4	109
4:9–13	192
4:10–13	175
4:14–21	41
4:16	175
4:17–20	92
4:21	160
5:3	112
6:12	109
7:17	149
7:29	120
9:12	94
12:24	110
14:18	41
14:20	69, 121
14:26	151
15:9	44
15:27 f.	106
15:30 ff.	83
15:35	151
16:19–24	70
16:21	31

2 Corinthians

1:3	149
1:14	112
4:7–12	186
4:10 ff.	187
7:4	112
8:6 f.	120
11:7–11	94
11:7	106
11:23–29	192
11:23 ff.	117
11:24 f.	44
13:11	92
13:12 f.	70

Galatians

1:1–5	*148*
1:6–10	*148–52*, 165, 173–5, 179 f., 181, 190, 210, 213 f.
1:10	160, 176, 193, 195
1:11–2:21	174 f., 176, 180, 2:10 f., 2:14
1:11 f.	*153*, 160
1:12	36
1:13–24	*154 ff.*, 158, 162 ff.
1:13 f.	44
1:14	42
1:23	44
2:1–10	*156 f.*
2:2 f.	110
2:11–21	*157–65*
2:15–21	13 f.
2:15	36, 42
2:17	151, 160
2:19 f.	174, 181, 195, 214, 216
2:21	168 f.
3:1–4:11	211, 215
3:1–5	151, 160, *165 f.*, 168, 169, 172 ff., 176
3:3	174, 191
3:4	160
3:6–4:7	176
3:6–14	*166–9*
3:6	160

241

3:13 f.	178	6:17	69, 84, 152, 181,
3:15–4:7	*169–72*		187, *195*, 213, 216
3:15	69,178, 187, 188	6:18	187, *195*
3:17	178, 188		
3:19	151, 160	**Ephesians**	
3:21	151, 160	1:3	149
3:23 ff.	168, 178	4:13	121
3:27 f.	174	5:32 f.	120
4:1	178, 188		
4:3 ff.	168, 178	**Philippians**	
4:5 ff.	168	1:1–2	*96*
4:6	84	1:3–11	41, *96 ff.*, 101,
4:8–11	*172 f.*, 175		139 f., 142
4:12–20	*173 ff.*, 179 f., 181,	1:4	110
	211 f., 215	1:5	114
4:13	192	1:9	41, 45
4:15	192	1:10	112
4:17	83	1:11	40 f.
4:19	84, 106, 185	1:12–26	94
4:21–5:1	*176*, 191, 2:11 f.,	1:12–18c	*98*, 101, 104, 107 f.,
	215		111, 140, 142 f.
4:29	188	1:12	100, 114
4:31	181	1:13	186
5:1	36	1:18	58, 110, 120, 121,
5:2–10	*178 ff.*		124, 160, 172
5:6	194	1:18d–26	*99 f.*, 101, 104,
5:7	185		107 f., 111 f., 140,
5:8	190		142 f.
5:11–6:13	215 f.	1:20	186
5:11–13a	*181–7*, 193, 212	1:21 f.	214
5:11 f.	192	1:25 f.	116
5:13	100	1:25	45, 110
5:13b–6:10	145, *187–91*, 193,	1:27–30	91, *100 ff.*, 104,
	212 f.		107 f., 111, 140,
5:16	178		142 f.
5:22 f.	195	1:27 f.	121
5:24	214, 216	1:27	114, 116, 123 f.
6:1	69	1:28	117
6:11–18	145	2:1–11	*102–6*, 142 f.
6:11–17	182	2:1–4	160
6:11–13	180, 186, *191–4*,	2:2–5	123, 125
	212	2:2	110, 116, 122
6:12	152, 175, 188	2:5	122
6:14–16	59, 69, *194*, 213	2:12–18	*106–13*, 122, 142 f.
6:14	152, 186, 216	2:17 f.	116
6:16	112, 187 f.	2:17	58
		2:19–30	41
		2:19–24	*113 f.*, 140, 144

2:19	112	2:1–12	14 f., *52 ff.*, 55, 59, 82, 85 f.
2:25–30	93, 94, *114 f.*, 140, 144	2:1–8	175
2:27	109	2:2 ff.	152
2:28	110	2:2	69
2:30	93	2:9	63, 69, 94
3:1–4:9	90 ff., 93	2:13–16	42–6, *54 ff.*, 61, 82, 86
3:1	110, *115 ff.*, 123, 140, 143	2:13	40 f., 50 f., 67, 69
3:2–16	*117–21*, 141, 143	2:14 ff.	65, 117, 186, 214
3:5 f.	42	2:16	69
3:6	44	2:17–3:10	40 f., *56–59*, 82, 92
3:8–11	214	2:17–20	40 ff.
3:10 f.	104	3:1–5	40 ff.
3:10	84, 106, 122	3:4	69
3:13 ff.	122	3:6–10	40 ff.
3:13	69	3:6	60, 82
3:17–21	*121*, 141, 143 f.	3:7	69
3:17	105, 215	3:9 f.	67, 69
3:21	84, 106	3:11–13	40 f., *60*, 68, 69, 82, 126
4:1–9	*122 ff.*, 141, 143	3:11	92
4:1	110, 121	3:12 f.	140
4:4	110	4:1–12	*61 ff.*, 66, 69, 82 f., 86
4:7	112, 136	4:1	66, 82, 92, 140
4:9	112, 136, 186	4:9 f.	140
4:10–20	93 f.	4:13–18	46 f., *63 f.*, 64 ff., 69, 83, 176
4:10–18	*124 ff.*, 141	5:1–11	46 f., *64 ff.*, 69, 83, 176
4:10	110		
4:14	120		
4:19–20	*126*		
4:21–23	70, *126 f.*	5:12–22	*66 ff.*, 69, 83 f., 87, 123
Colossians		5:23–24	40 f., *68*, 69, 84, 112, 126
1:28	121	5:23	136
4:12	121	5:25	40 f., *68 f.*, 84
		5:26–28	40 f., *69 f.*
1 Thessalonians			
1:2–10	*48–52*, 54, 82, 84 ff.	*2 Thessalonians*	
1:2–7	59, 82	2:16	92
1:2	40 f., 67, 69	3:1	92
1:3	60, 61		
1:5 ff.	52 f., 55, 61	*Philemon*	
1:6 f.	186, 215	23 ff.	70
1:6	36, 42 f., 54 f., 65, 69, 175, 214		
1:9 f.	52 f., 55, 82		
1:10	40 f.		

Hebrews
5:14   121
7:11   183
11:32   183 f.

James
1:4   121
3:2   121

1 Peter
1:3   149

Revelation
14:14   149

Apostolic Fathers

Polycarp
3:2   90

Greek and Roman writings

Dio Chrysostom, Disc.
70.6   87

Epictetus, Epp.
1.6.29   183
1.7.30   183
1.18.2   183
1.18.8   183
1.25.1   183
2.8.3   183
2.17.26   183
3.2.14   183
3.24.56   183
4.1.88   183
4.7.22   183
4.7.28   183
1.25.2   183

Pliny, Epp.
8.13   87

Seneca, Epp.
6.5 f.   87
11.9 f.   87
100.12   87